NIGEL GRAY

TOO FAR EAST?

東すぎます?か

My Gray ancestors make a 300-year round trip across
5 continents, steered by life-changing world events

First published in Great Britain in 2021
Copyright © Nigel Gray

Design, typesetting and publishing by
UK Book Publishing
www.ukbookpublishing.com
ISBN: 978-1-914195-30-3

CONTENTS

FOREWORD

I have wanted to learn more about my ancestry since I was quite young. As a teenager growing up in a London suburb during the '60s, announcing your place of birth as Calcutta to your mates was a risk, with a broad range of possible responses. Some of these were not particularly pleasant, so having a plausible explanation was essential. However, answering the "Are you Indian then?" question by saying my father was born in Yokohama never really helped. If I then responded to the usual follow-up statement "So you're Japanese then" by explaining my grandfather was also born in Japan, things usually got very complicated! This is because there is no short answer. It has taken me this book, to explain "briefly" just the last seven generations of my Gray pedigree! And I have loved every one of the discoveries I have made along the way. I had the motivation to learn more about my Gray ancestors, because these two births in Japan and the fact that several members of my immediate family were imprisoned by the Japanese was about all I knew of my family history. I needed to know more.

William Gray
(1720-1795)   >   *John Gray*
                          (1770-1830)   >   *James Gray*
                                                    (1813-1880)   >   *Jesse William Gray*
                                                                              (1855-1894)   >

I am totally fascinated by the "journey" I have tracked so far and felt I had to tell someone, hence this book. Briefly, it tells the story of how one family, through 5 generations, travelled from rural Leicestershire to Japan, onwards through China and India, back to southern England before returning to the same county some 150 years later. It explores the world events that shared these timelines with my family, and shows how such happenings steered my ancestors along their incredible paths. It relates stories of how the early pioneers prospered as part of the Meiji Restoration but also how "My Magnificent 7"–seven members of my immediate family–suffered hardships as prisoners-of-war in Shanghai and Hong Kong. Finally, it closes the family's circular journey, describing how I have emulated my 4xgreat grandfather by settling in Leicestershire to pursue a career path. I have posed a question in the title, and have tried to present the evidence for you readers to answer that question yourselves. You will arrive at your conclusion after sharing their fascinating story.

Key historical events featured through the book that have had major impacts on the family's "journey" include:

- The drift from country to town, allied to the Industrial Revolution in England
- Emigration from Britain in search of "a better life"
- The Meiji Restoration–the transformation of Japan from feudalism to industrial superpower
- The Great Kanto Earthquake of 1923
- The emergence of Shanghai as a megacity

- WWII in the Far East; the attack on Pearl Harbour and the dropping of the atomic weapons to achieve peace in the Pacific

- The formation of the People's Republic of China

- The drift back to England of 3rd generation "colonialists" as Britain's influence waned across the world

This book tries to appeal to a range of potential readers on different levels:

- To family historians–I have tried to explain some of the techniques required to build a family tree from the basic facts of birth, marriages and deaths through more advanced searches like shipping records, wills, special interest archives like freemasonry or military records, immigration documents, etc., all to flesh out the story

- To WWII history 'buffs'–by sharing one family's experiences of significant events in the Pacific theatre particularly;

- To anyone who likes "human interest" stories–around how my extended family members faired in other countries with differing cultures, and specifically how they endured years of captivity under the Japanese.

For these latter sections, I have actually enlisted the help of four members of my close family (all now deceased), who tell of their own personal experiences as Japanese POWs in their own words. For example, my mother kept a daily diary for the whole of 1942 when she was in Stanley Internment Camp, Hong Kong. I have reproduced many of their letters, diaries and/or memoirs never before given an audience outside the family. As I was writing these sections of the book, about the impact of the war in the Far East, the world was holding numerous celebrations in 2020 for the 75th anniversary of VJ Day, the ending of the war with Japan. I realised how appropriate it was that I should be telling, in this small way, some of the story of the "Forgotten War" as it has become known, because the story of the many thousands of unsung heroes from that conflict should be told.

The whole book is such a fascinating story of how life changed for my ancestors across 7 generations; a story that not many people had yet heard–so I wanted to tell it! I hope you will enjoy reading it as much as I have enjoyed writing it.

ACKNOWLEDGEMENTS

I wasn't sure how to do this bit, where I say a big Thank You to all the many people who have helped me with this book, but I just knew it was essential that I added it in. But where to start? I think it has to be with the person who actually turned me into a genealogist. One day way back (I can't actually believe it was probably nearly 10 years ago) I received a letter that basically asked "Are you THE Nigel Gray?". Not a bad way to capture the recipient's attention, don't you agree. It contained enough basic biographical details to mean that it was definitely intended for me. It had been sent by a 2nd cousin once removed on my maternal line called Hilary Graves and she was inviting me to a reunion of all the living descendants of my maternal great grandparents–Thomas Evans and Ellen Louise Salter. My wife Jenny and I actually went, together with my only sibling Ian, and it was a marvellous day out when we met many of our extended maternal line relations. I have been in contact with Hilary ever since and her initial approach set me thinking that I actually knew very little about my wider family, especially on my paternal side. You could say it's all Hilary's

| William Gray (1720-1795) | > | John Gray (1770-1830) | > | James Gray (1813-1880) | > | Jesse William Gray (1855-1894) | > |

fault but there is no doubt I am eternally grateful to have received her letter, as I have discovered that researching my family history is now my favourite hobby!

Before committing "pen to paper" to write this book, I have had to research so much of the story from a wide range of resources and indeed sources. These include family memorabilia, online genealogy records and general historical information, actual physical records in a number of archives and some background reading of my own. The whole process has been a wonderful experience for me, in terms of bringing so many of my ancestors to life. Due to my parents' divorce when I was a child and my father's death when I was eighteen, much of my paternal ancestral line was an unknown quantity to me, hence my desire to explore it. I think the fact that the discovery trail started with just the first generation back (wanting to expand my knowledge of my own father and his siblings) gave the project an extra level of motivation. It also gave it an extra level of complexity, since the traditional family historian's tactic of interviewing elderly relatives was not open to me. For instance, my wife can remember her great grandfather being part of her childhood, whereas my paternal grandfather died some four years before I was born.

All that was to explain that I could not have written this book without the invaluable assistance of a network of family, friends and "colleagues" from the wider world of genealogy. I consider it as an additional bonus, to obtaining the research material for the book, that I have assembled a network of friends who can now enhance my life beyond supplying fascinating insights into my

>   *Jesse Esdale Gray*   >   *Cecil Jesse Austen*   >   *Peter Nigel Austen Gray*
          (1885-1946)   *Gray (1908-1968)*   *(1950-present)*

extended family. I have either reunited with long lost cousins or found brand new ones around the globe. The latter is a direct result of the travel gene that seems to run deep through so many of my ancestors. This has meant I now have a revised travel itinerary for my own global meanderings, since so many places that were pencilled in on my "places to visit" wish list now have a family history component.

Simply because of the sheer quantity of information it revealed about my ancestors' lives in Japan, I have to award pride of place in my resources' league table to the Meiji Portraits. This amazing piece of research work carried out by Bernd Lepach enabled me to learn so much about the extended Gray family in Japan. He has assisted me by sharing his knowledge gathered from his precious set of Japan Trade Directories, which are virtually a "Who's Who" of the early days of Yokohama. I shall always be indebted to him.

Then I have to thank the various staff members at my two local archives—The Leicestershire Records Office and the Nottinghamshire Archives—whose staff have always been helpful in guiding me through their catalogues. Armed with confirmation of the accuracy of my internet findings, I have been able to contact a wide network of fellow genealogists, who have provided further information from their searches. The joy that comes from discovering the back stories of shared ancestors and adding foliage to the bare branches of one's own tree is very satisfying. It really does assist in fleshing out the skeleton of a story that mere data first reveals. And the beauty of this particular hobby is that there is no perceived end-point to one's search.

So, I am now going to "name names" in terms of my valued research assistants, albeit with the caveat used by certain reality shows—"in no particular order"! I went for alphabetical, how conventional! If you happen to be reading this and feel your name has been omitted from the list, I can only apologise in advance, with only the frailty of a senior's memory in my defence. I offer sincere thanks to the contributions of the following:

Andrea V; Andrew R; Angeline; Anita W; Ann B; Avril W; Bernd L; Bruce R; Carrie de C-B; Coreen G; David T; Dawn; Gay F; Graham R; Hilary G; Jeremy H; Jill P; Jo S; Keith W; Mark C; Nancy; Pam; Ross E; Sean H; Sharon E; Sharon G; Stuart R; Tom; Tony; Wendy P;

Finally, I have to thank the one person who has not simply put up with what she called my obsession but actually joined in whole-heartedly. My wife Jenny has been there every step of the way with me through the journey of this book, in a wide variety of roles. These include researcher, secretary, typist, travel agent, sounding-board, travelling partner, motivator, proof-reader, designer, planner, financial controller, archivist and problem-solver. I guess this could be summed up as my manager! I don't know how she managed it but I do know I never could have managed "it" without her!

I AM BRITISH- MY DAD PROVED IT

I don't remember exactly when it was first said but I have always been instructed not to lose my birth certificate. It was probably when I needed to send it off to some official government department as proof of my DOB. Oops–jargon already. For non-genealogists, DOB is date of birth. It may have been to accompany my first application for a passport renewal in my own name. I have been a holder of a British passport from a very early age but this was me taking responsibility for this very special birth certificate myself. I shall deal with what makes it special a bit later but essentially it is because the Registrar made some alterations to the original.

As she handed it over to me, my mother said "Please don't lose it, dear. Your father went through a lot of work to get it changed. It is probably the only way you can prove you're British!". Whatever did she mean? What did Dad have to change? Had she just let some dark family secret out of the bag? Her remarks certainly prompted some questions from me and there followed quite a revealing conversation that probably explains why I am now officially

---

William Gray > *John Gray* > *James Gray* > *Jesse William Gray* >
(1720-1795)   *(1770-1830)*   *(1813-1880)*   *(1855-1894)*

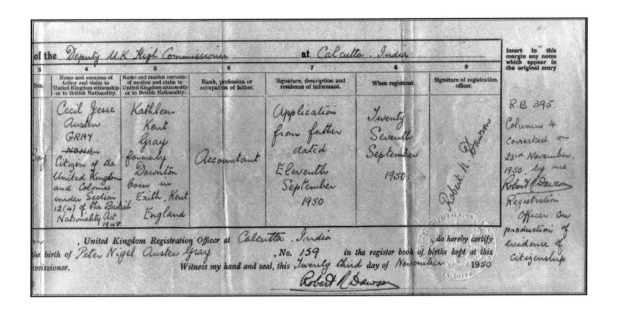

a family history geek.

She explained that I was the third generation on the Gray parental line to have been born overseas. The details go something like this:

Peter Nigel Austen Gray (yours truly) born Calcutta, India; 1950

Cecil Jesse Austen Gray (my father) born Yokohama, Japan; 1908

Jesse Esdale Gray (my grandfather) born Yokohama, Japan; 1885

Jesse William Gray (my great grandfather) born Camberwell, England (hoorah!): 1855

She said my great grandfather was the last Gray direct parental line ancestor to be born on English soil. She showed me the alteration in the last column of the certificate where the Registrar General had hand-written a few words to grant my father British nationality under legislation passed in 1948. As this made him British, I was indeed British by birth. That's a relief then. I knew very little about these Japanese roots of the family tree as it was never

---

>   *Jesse Esdale Gray*   >   *Cecil Jesse Austen*   >   *Peter Nigel Austen Gray*
>   *(1885-1946)*   *Gray (1908-1968)*   *(1950-present)*

spoken of whilst I was growing up. I never met my grandfather (Jesse Esdale Gray) as he died 4 years before I was born and, with my parents divorcing when I was aged seven, the topic never cropped up at any time. But, by doing all the work required to "make me British", my father had actually left me a paper trail through birth and marriage certificates, that effectively did my first 150 years of research for me. Any novice family historian has to prove an indisputable line of descent, by collecting the appropriate evidence such as birth certificates and marriage certificates covering the past generations. Normally, the strategy is to interview all one's elderly relatives, to 'pencil in' a family tree as far back as their living memories can reach. Then, it all has to be verified by the researcher through cross-referencing against actual archived records, before they 'ink it in' on their growing family tree. Whereas I regret never having had the opportunity to pick the brains of either my father or grandfather on family history matters, my father had actually done much of the initial work for me. This was the genealogical 'bequest' he left me, actual documented evidence of the bare bones of the family history. It made me want to put the flesh on those bones!

The necessity of "keeping my birth certificate safe" was proved when I did have to renew my passport some years later for a trip to Poland as part of my mining studies. I had a college classmate who needed to renew his at the same time. His application form went off under the name Bronislav Richard Olezkiewicz (son of a Polish immigrant but born in Derby) and mine under the name Peter Nigel Austen Gray (son of an Englishman but born in Calcutta).

| William Gray (1720-1795) | > | John Gray (1770-1830) | > | James Gray (1813-1880) | > | Jesse William Gray (1855-1894) | > |

His came back by return of post, duly renewed, but mine prompted a letter asking me to provide proof of being English. It's not all in the name, obviously. Posting my certificate to them eventually resulted in a new 10-year passport being issued to me.

The veracity of her warning about "keeping it safe" was also confirmed several years later when my then wife was expecting our third child Helen. Whereas our two older girls had been born in England, we were actually planning a holiday abroad when Val was pregnant the third time. When I was chatting about this to the doctor and explaining the line of overseas births, he recommended us being in England for the actual birth if we wished Helen to be officially British!

This was how I became aware of a family connection with Japan. I also knew of another link to the Japanese which was brought starkly into focus by a piece of schoolwork my eldest daughter Ann was doing some years after I took ownership of the birth certificate. There was to be a debate at her school concerning the pros and cons of nuclear weapons. The teacher had introduced the topic to her pupils and encouraged them to ask questions of anyone they wanted, by way of preparing for the debate. When Ann talked to me about it, I said "Why don't you go and talk to Grandma Katie about it? I'm sure she'll tell you something interesting." Grandma Katie is what the girls called my mother. Ann duly went to speak to her and asked her if she thought the dropping of the bombs in WWII was a good or bad thing. Grandma replied "Well they saved my life, so I thank God they did drop them!". Not a bad "sound bite" for Ann to collect in her research was it? My mother went on to explain that she had been taken prisoner by the Japanese in Hong Kong when their armies captured it. She spent nearly 4 years in the Stanley Internment Camp and was only freed after the surrender, brought about by the dropping of the bombs.

Ann certainly got quite a personal insight into her Grandma's views on nuclear weapons. She was probably quite unsure of the reception she would get when she fed back into her school debate. I have always thought that her teacher probably introduced the subject from quite a strong anti-nuclear weapons slant. After all, the CND (Campaign for Nuclear Disarmament) tended to unite the opinions of many individuals from the 1960s onwards against nuclear weapons. The teacher was probably expecting the majority of views gathered by the children to be reinforcing a "nuclear arms are bad" stance. I wish I could have been a fly on the wall, listening to the following imagined conversation:

Miss X: "Well let's continue to hear your feedback on whether the use of nuclear weapons is a good thing or bad. Ann, did you manage to speak to anyone about it?"

Ann: "Yes Miss. My Dad said I should speak to my Grandma."

Miss X: "And did you speak to her?"

Ann: "Yes Miss."

Miss X: "Well what did your Grandma say?"

Ann: "She said it saved her life."

Miss X: "What! I mean, how? Why? Whatever did she mean?"

| *William Gray* | | *John Gray* | | *James Gray* | | *Jesse William Gray* | |
| *(1720-1795)* | > | *(1770-1830)* | > | *(1813-1880)* | > | *(1855-1894)* | > |

Ann: "She said she was being held prisoner by the Japanese, and that she was really, really hungry because she hardly got anything to eat, and that she sometimes ate fried banana leaves when there was nothing else."

Miss X: "Oh my Go…Goodness! She said all that! Wow that must have been a surprise for you."

Ann: "Yes it was. She said lots more and I could tell she was getting quite upset, so we stopped talking about it."

Miss X: "Well what can I say! That's certainly a very personal story to share with us today. Ooh your poor Grandma. Er…um…well I shall have to try and explain to you what Ann's Grandma meant. It has certainly given us another opinion on this topic and a lot to think about…"

I cannot actually imagine how the rest of the debate went that day but I am willing to bet that her teacher was not expecting anything like Ann's feedback. In one simple statement the topic had been turned upside down and Miss X was faced with introducing a case for possible benefits from using nuclear weapons. One imagines she probably wished she had never asked Ann for her input!

It was many years later that I actually caught the genealogy bug and began a hobby that has now become a keen favourite of mine. It is because I knew so little about my roots and my ancestors that I have such an incentive for doing family history research. I am literally like a sponge, keen to soak up as much as I can discover. I was very fortunate in being able to pick up from my Dad's work on the Gray parental line to give me a tremendous head start. As I

>	*Jesse Esdale Gray (1885-1946)*	>	*Cecil Jesse Austen Gray (1908-1968)*	>	*Peter Nigel Austen Gray (1950-present)*

said previously, in amongst the paperwork inherited when my mother passed away was a lot of documentation needed in support of Dad's application. There was a fully traceable line through my father and grandfather (the ones inconveniently born abroad) back to my great grandfather born in the UK. It even included a copy of his birth certificate showing that he, Jesse William Gray, was born in Camberwell in 1855, and naming his parents.

There I was, effectively fast-tracked back through 3 generations and in possession of facts and figures that usually take the novice family historian many hours of work to verify. It got me safely around the obstacle of not having quizzed two key ancestors. These were my aforementioned father, who died when I was aged 18yrs, and my aforementioned grandfather, who died when I was aged minus 4yrs!

Armed with this genealogical windfall, I set about trying to understand how the Grays came to be in Japan in the first place. Some of the answers surely had to come from knowing more about the young Master Jesse William. After all, I had proof he was born in London but married in Yokohama. Now conventional family history research techniques would have you looking at BMD records (sorry, another bit of jargon–Births, Marriages and Deaths!) for the neighbouring parishes to where he was born. I daresay it would have taken me roughly half of the intervening century and a half since his birth to work outwards from Camberwell all the way to Japan. Now you will begin to see the value of the paperwork Dad left me.

From Jesse William's birth certificate, I knew his father was James Gray

| *William Gray* (1720-1795) | > | *John Gray* (1770-1830) | > | *James Gray* (1813-1880) | > | *Jesse William Gray* (1855-1894) | > |

and his mother Mary Elizabeth Gray (nee Keetley). A quick search for their marriage and any reference to them in any censuses delivered the first of many shocks I have had along my genealogical path so far. It is probably one of the more thought-provoking coincidences as well. It was a major factor in making me want to write this story. For I discovered that my 2xgreat grandfather James Gray was born in the parish of St Martins in Leicester. Now I can almost hear you all thinking–"so what", "big deal", "I don't think so". I shall try to explain. When I moved to Leicestershire in 1975 as part of my career path, I thought I was the only member of my family to have ever lived in the county that has been my home ever since, over 40 years now. We are southerners you see; I lived in Kent from the age of 7 after returning from India. The family home was in the Greater London Borough of Bexley. I accept I can hardly be called a cockney; my hearing would have been pretty amazing to catch the sound of Bow bells from the Elgin Nursing Home, Calcutta. I was totally convinced that no other member of the family had ever lived in Leicestershire, but now I learnt that I had actually led the return of the Grays to said county. I needed to know more.

This then explains what this book will try to do. I want to share some of my understanding of how one family, through 5 generations, travelled from a county in the East Midlands to the Land of the Rising Sun, onwards through the Orient via China and India, back to southern England before returning to the very same county some 150 years later. I shall explore the world events that dominated this shared timeline and speculate as to how they steered my

> *Jesse Esdale Gray*   >   *Cecil Jesse Austen*   >   *Peter Nigel Austen Gray*
> *(1885-1946)*   *Gray (1908-1968)*   *(1950-present)*

ancestors along their incredible paths. I shall attempt to "close the circle" of

circumstances that saw the earlier pioneers prosper alongside their Japanese

hosts but also subsequent generations endure terrible suffering from the same

hands. Then I shall trace the resilience of this later generation, attempting

to achieve a recovery of sorts "back from the brink". Finally, I shall make

some conclusions to the amazing round trip that saw my mother and myself

undertake the final legs of the journey. So, hold onto to your hats–as we speed

back to rural Leicestershire at the start of the 18th century.

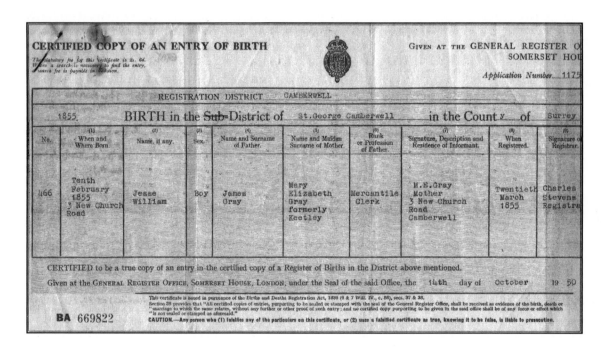

THE NEWTOWN
LINFORD GRAYS

You may recall that my 2xgreat grandfather James Gray was born in Leicester. He was christened at St Martin's Church on 12th July 1813. This "discovery" of mine led me to questioning whether he was the first paternal line ancestor to have lived in Leicestershire. I started to focus my research on him and soon discovered that he was actually the grandson of the first "Leicestershire" Gray.

William Gray (1720-1795; 4xgreat grandfather)

That particular honour falls upon a certain William Gray, James's grandfather, which makes him my 4xgreat grandfather. I am going to make this slight leap backwards, through two generations, because I want to then lead you down my parental line in chronological order through the remainder of this book. This is because we are following the round trip from Leicestershire to the Far East and back to Leicestershire and William is the starting point.

William was actually born in the small village of Colwick, Nottinghamshire

---

on 14th October 1720–nearly a century before the birth of his grandson James. He was the 2nd eldest son of William (my 5xgreat grandfather) and Hannah Higham. William Jnr was a basket maker, just like his father. Colwick at that time was a small hamlet near to the town of Nottingham. In the early 18th century there were only 30 families living there, including the Grays. There is still a Colwick Hall in existence, currently as a hotel, but when William Jnr lived there, it was at the heart of an estate centred on Colwick Park. It was a country seat of the Musters family and I can only assume that many of the villagers were their tenants. There appears to have been a thriving basket making business at this time in the village, because there were at least 2 other basket makers besides the father-and-son combination of William Grays! On a visit I made to the village some years ago there was still plenty of evidence of the reed beds which presumably supplied the raw materials necessary for these craftsmen.

William was one of 8 children born to William and Hannah whilst they were living in Colwick. The others were Mary born 1715; Joseph born 1717; Elizabeth born 1725; John born 1728 who died in infancy and was replaced by another John born 1731; Richard born 1733; Priscilla born 1735. The eldest son Joseph was named after his grandfather and illustrates a pattern for choosing family names that is often repeated through the generations. Parents in that day often named their offspring after their own parents and/or their siblings.

William's elder sister Mary married Mundy Musters (1712–1770), a case of "village girl marries the Lord of the Manor". The Musters family seat was

Descendant Chart for
William Gray(Colwick)

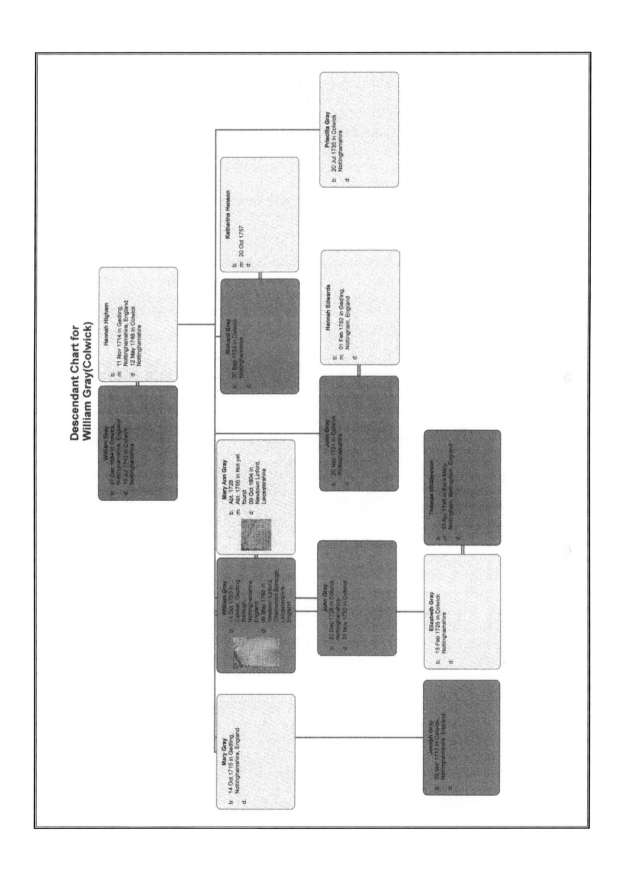

> Jesse Esdale Gray
(1885-1946)

> Cecil Jesse Austen
Gray (1908-1968)

> Peter Nigel Austen Gray
(1950-present)

Colwick Hall, and Mundy Musters inherited the estate in 1750 and was made Sheriff of Nottingham in 1753. The couple had a son John and a daughter Mary. John Musters inherited the estate on the death of his father in 1770 and in 1775 he had the old Colwick Hall pulled down and the present one built in 1776, presumably for his wedding in the same year. His son, also John Musters, married a Mary Ann Chaworth, who was the childhood sweetheart of the poet Lord Byron.

When it comes to identifying William Jnr's wife, I have to admit that it is one of the twigs on my tree about which I am missing some concrete evidence. Basically, I am unable to find their marriage details from which to state definitely William's spouse's maiden name. I have my best guess based on some reasonable assumptions. I know she was a Mary. My searches for a possible bride for William include a Mary Wombell. If you remember I stated earlier that there were only a few families living in Colwick around the time of William and Mary's likely wedding date. The fact that there was a Wombell family living there gives me a strong possibility of the bride being Mary Wombell. Everything else in terms of their ages, when they started their own family, weddings usually taking place in the bride's parish, etc. support my assumption. However, I shall continue to search for the definitive clinching "piece of the jigsaw". This is what genealogy research is all about anyway.

William and Mary started their family in Colwick with the birth of "their" William in 1753, followed by Mary in 1755 and Elizabeth in 1757. By the time Thomas was born in 1760 the family had moved to Newtown Linford in

Leicestershire. It is a small village that formed part of the estate of Bradgate owned by the Grey family, the Earls of Stamford. Now this is where I would get very, very excited if I was researching my family tree from "over the pond". Without wishing to over-generalise, it is probably fair to say your average family historian in America is absolutely desperate to link their ancestry to the British monarchy. And here I was–within touching distance of the branch of "that" particular family tree that provided Lady Jane Grey, the "Queen for Nine Days" of Tudor England. I shall divulge a little later how I believe my ancestors may or may not link to royalty but for now I shall remain with what brought this young couple to Newtown Linford.

I am speculating slightly here but I think the reason behind my 4xgreat grandfather's move to Newtown Linford was a need to provide for a growing family. As yet another basket maker in Colwick and a second generation one at that after his father William, he probably decided he needed to move away and increase his prospects in pastures new. I am aware of some kind of family link between Colwick and Newtown Linford already existing at the time and this probably assisted William Jnr. to make his mind up and settle on the latter as the family's new home. Thus, I always call this ancestor "William of Newtown Linford" and consider him to be the head of the Leicestershire Grays.

After Thomas was born in 1760 there followed the births of 5 more children at regular intervals over the next sixteen years. They were Hannah 1762, Ann 1765, Joseph 1770, John 1773 (my 3xgreat grandfather) and finally Sarah 1776. With the growing family William had the issue of housing them adequately

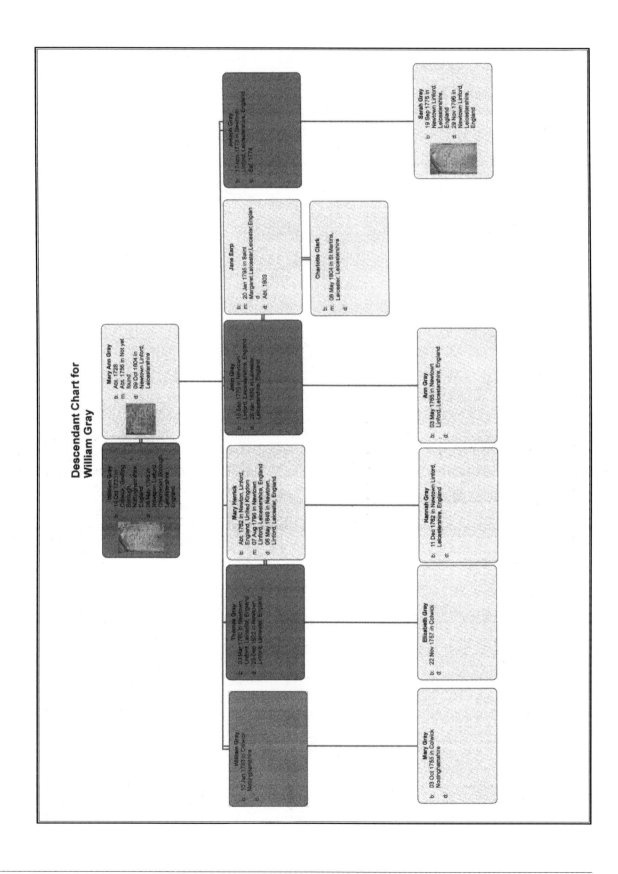

Descendant Chart for
William Gray

and I was amazed to gather such detailed information from one of my visits to the Leicester Records Office. I actually got to study the land tax records for property in Newtown Linford which revealed so much about where the Grays were living.

The table below are extracts from the family's land tax history. The tax was collected at the rate of 4 shillings in the £. In an attempt to put these monetary values into some sort of perspective I researched monetary values in the early 1800s. The key facts were:

1. **The value of £1 would be well over £100 today; remember there were 20 shillings(s) in a £ and 12 pence(d) in a shilling pre-decimalisation**

2. **Around 1800 the average weekly labour's wage was 6-10 shillings**

There is quite a lot of information buried in this table when you start "reading between the lines". For example, the tax doubled over the decade 1780 to 1790 but then it doubled again between 1790 and 1795! As William and Mary's family was complete in terms of no more children after Sarah was born in 1776, the increase has to reflect inflation only. The only inflation I can think of is that the children were getting bigger but it is doubtful all of them survived into adulthood or stayed at home. The fact that Thomas emerges as head of the family after William's death in 1795 means his elder brother William is not around. One can also easily imagine romance blossoming between Thomas and a local girl called Mary Herrick as they must have grown up together in the village. He obviously took some time to decide she was "the one" because they didn't marry until he was 35 years old and she was about 33. The fact that they moved in next door to her father when they were married says a lot, I guess!

Year	Property	Occupants	Amount (£.s.d)
Pre 1780	Message Cottage/Town End Close	William, Mary + children (William's son Thomas seems to be the eldest boy)	£0 2s 9d
1780	Message Cottage	William, Mary + children	£0 3s.0d
1789	Message Cottage	William, Mary + children	£0 7s.4d
1790	Message Cottage	William, Mary + children	£0 7s 4d
1794	Message Cottage	William, Mary + children	£0 14s.8d
1795	Message Cottage	William passed away in 1795 and his son Thomas became the tenant	£0 14s.8d
1796	Message Cottage	Thomas marries Mary Herrick	£0 14s.8d
1800	Message Cottage	The combined families (widowed Mary with her family) and Thomas & Mary with 2 children	£0 14s.8d
1801	Message Cottage	Widowed Mary, with her brood, remains in her original home	£0 14s 8d
1801	Heabyland (a new bigger property next door to Thomas's father-in-law Richard Herrick)	Thomas, his wife Mary and their children (Sarah 4yrs, William 2yrs and new baby Thomas born 1801)	£3 17s 4d
1803	Message Cottage	Widow Mary and family	£0 14s 8d
1803	Heabyland	Thomas and his family	£2 15s 1d
1803	Late "Taft"–a third Gray property	Possibly Thomas' siblings who have outgrown "living at home with Mother"!	£1 16s 0d
1812	(not clear how many properties are being rented by Grays)	Record shows "Thomas Gray and Richard Herrick"; are they possibly joint tenants? Thomas's mother Mary died in 1804 and her son John (my 3xgreat grandfather) had moved to Leicester before her death; other Grays still lived in these properties covered by the "combined" land tax being paid	£8 9s 6d
1820	*The Old Vicarage		£4 0s 6d
1820	Message Cottage	Assumed to be the same old cottage from the land tax amount	£0 15s 9d
1822		Thomas Gray (my 4th great uncle and head of the family in Newtown Linford) died in 1822, leaving his widow Mary (nee Herrick) and 6 children–Sarah (25), William (23), Thomas (21) Joseph (19), John (17) and Mary (15)	£3 18s 4d
1822			£0 15s 4d

In the table I have made reference to the Old Vicarage. This is the name on a wall plaque adorning this property now in Newtown Linford but I don't know for sure when it changed from the farmhouse of the early 19th century to become the vicarage. It was certainly where Thomas and family lived "back in the day" and I find it very exciting that I can stand and look at it today, whilst imagining my ancestors there over 200 years ago. It overlooks the current cricket ground near the heart of the village, a short walk along from the church. I can also feel very close to this particular family when strolling in the graveyard, for there are a number of ancestral gravestones in front of the church to the right of the path leading up to the door.

There are 5 gravestones that feature Gray ancestors. Quite rightly the heads of the Newtown Linford branch of the tree (William Gray and his wife Mary) are buried here, along with their youngest daughter Sarah who never married. Their first boy born in Newtown Linford, Thomas Gray, shares a grave nearby with his wife Mary (nee Herrick) and their youngest daughter Mary who died a spinster aged 60. One imagines it was quite common in those days for the youngest daughter of a large brood of children to "end up an old maid" as the saying goes. So, it was for this Mary, just like her great aunt Sarah in the neighbouring grave. Joseph Gray, the 3rd son of the afore-mentioned Thomas and

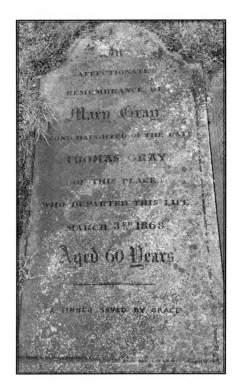

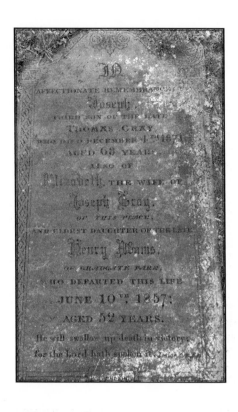

Mary, is buried in the next grave, together with his wife Elizabeth. I shall tell more about this couple a bit further on.

My direct family line doesn't come down through Thomas but through his younger brother John who was born in 1770 when Thomas was 10 years old. More of John later, as he was the ancestor who moved the family from the countryside into Leicester itself. That part of my story will be covered in the next chapter.

Joseph Gray (1803-1871; 1st cousin 4xremoved)

The next main character in the family history played out in Newtown Linford was Thomas's son Joseph, who's grave I mentioned earlier. Joseph was born in 1803, the third son of Thomas and Mary, after William (named after his grandfather) in 1799 and Thomas (named after his father) in 1801. These particular parents had to look a bit further afield for a third boys' name, settling for the child's uncle Joseph. It was a family name coming as it did from the lad's 2xgreat grandfather born back in Colwick.

Joseph became the head of the household aged only 19, when his father Thomas died in 1822. He became the farmer of the Newtown Linford Grays, taking over the farmhouse which would eventually become home to his own family. His marriage was something special in terms of his status, because in Elizabeth Adams he had made quite a catch. She was the daughter of Henry Adams, the head gamekeeper to the Earl of Stamford at Bradgate Park. The couple themselves certainly wanted to mark the union of the families because they added the name Adams to all their children. These were Hannah Adams Gray born 1829, Elizabeth Adams Gray born 1831, William Adams Gray born 1832, and (I'm not making this up) Fanny Adams Gray born 1834. Never did I think, when I encountered the saying "sweet FA" earlier in my life, that I would find one in the family!

Joseph certainly featured at the centre of events in Newtown Linford because he eventually held an important position in village life. He was appointed as Overseer of the Poor by the parish church. The role involves acting as the supervisor of all persons classified as "poor" by the parish and in need of support and guidance through their daily lives. I guess you would call him a social worker of his day. I don't know all the details of what the Overseer did but I have found at least one newspaper item featuring Joseph Gray in his role. It was in the Leicester Journal of Friday August 31st, 1855 as follows:

"…James Shaw was charged by the Newtown overseers for non-payment of the poor rate. Mr Gray, Overseer for Newtown Linford, produced the poor rate made on the 12th May. The defendant was rated for house and land £14 5s 0d; his rate amounted to 8s 0d which he refused to pay; Mr Gray also produced the rate made on 15th July, he was rated for the same property to the amount of 5s 11d which he had also refused to pay; ordered to pay…"

> *Jesse Esdale Gray (1885-1946)*   >   *Cecil Jesse Austen Gray (1908-1968)*   >   *Peter Nigel Austen Gray (1950-present)*

Now I am prepared to accept that doesn't sound too much like a social worker but things were different back then! I have another article that shows Joseph off in a different light altogether. It is from the Leicestershire Mercury for Saturday March 30th, 1839 as follows:

"a boy of 14 or 15, charged by Mr Joseph Gray, farmer, of Newtown Linford, with behaving in a most disorderly manner, was dismissed from his service and ordered to pay the costs. The boy had threatened Mr Gray with his knife and his only excuse was intoxication! Had Mr Gray been desirous of retaining him in his service (where he had been but a fortnight) the Magistrates would have punished the boy severely..."

Presumably my 1st cousin 4xremoved Joseph was not too bothered about employing a knife-wielding teenager any longer than he had done already! Not all youngsters whom he encountered were as violent. There is one rather tragic story concerning Joseph and a pauper whom he found wandering in the village during a particularly harsh winter. He took pity on the young lad and gave him shelter in his house, providing him with some nourishment. He had to send him on his way, probably as the house was already pretty full. A day or so later the body of a young boy was discovered huddled up under a hedgerow and Joseph was actually the person able to identify him, since it was the very same lad he had helped by his kindness. I can't help thinking that Joseph would have been terribly distressed that he could not have actually done more for the boy which might have avoided the tragedy.

The most bizarre incident I unearthed involving Joseph is what I like to call the "Chicken Identity" case. This is how it was reported in the Leicester Journal of Friday July 16th, 1858:

"SHAW V. GRAY–This was an action for slander, brought by Mr Shaw of Charley, against Mr Gray of Newtown Linford. Mr McCaulay, Q.C. and Mr Bell appeared for the plaintiff and Mr Mellor for the defendant. Mr McCaulay, having presented the case to the jury, called the plaintiff, who said he had lived as a tenant farmer under Lord Stamford at Newtown Linford. Two years ago, he purchased a farm at Charley and repaired there partly in 1856. His time at Newtown expired last Lady-Day when he made a request for improvements to his farm, and a valuation was made; after which all the persons employed repaired to the Bradgate Arms, kept by Mr Beck at Newtown Linford, where they had their dinner, feeding off a couple of fowls which had been supplied by the plaintiff.–Anne Wesley said she lived at Newtown Linford where she occasionally acted as cook at Mr Beck's. She said she remembered Mr Gray coming to her and asking her if she had not cooked a couple of fowls and she replied in the affirmative. He had said he believed they were his, because Shaw's daughter had been to his house talking about their fowls, saying if they were not locked up, she would have a couple of them before she went. The heads of the fowls were thrown into the yard, one of which Mr Gray believed was his.–William Taylor said he attended the valuation of the farm in company of others and had dinner with them at Beck's. Dined off a couple of fowls. On the following morning he heard a conversation about the fowls, when Mr Shaw's name was mentioned. One of the parties named Bosworth said he did not like

newly-killed fowls. Mr Shaw said they were killed on the Saturday. At this point in the evidence his lordship ordered a nonsuit."

His lordship in question was actually Mr Justice Wightman and it seems pretty obvious that he had heard quite enough of this particular nonsense! I don't know whether Joseph's chicken had any particularly distinguishing features to help him identify her but the case says something about the relative value of a chicken in those days. Whether the two parties were able to afford such a case is questionable, although Joseph presumably had little say in the matter. Thank heavens his lordship drew the matter to a close, before it escalated into the biggest poultry-related crime of the century! And remember they did not have the advantage of DNA testing back then. If the case had actually gone before the assizes in Leicester there may well have been a conflict of interests, as Joseph often did jury service on the Grand Jury, representing Newtown Linford! It does leave you pondering that solicitors haven't changed all that much–as Messrs McCaulay, Bell and Mellor were obviously quite happy to take the case on behalf of their respective clients, at the fee rates prevailing at the time!

The fact that the aforementioned fowls were served up for dinner at the Bradgate Arms is another mind-blowing link to my life today. For my wife and I went to our yoga class on Tuesday evenings in the Newtown Linford village hall, immediately next door to the very same Bradgate Arms, for over six years! And many of the Yoga class Christmas meals have been held there. Apart from us "going about our business" in the same village as our ancestors

---

did over two centuries earlier, what if we have actually eaten chicken descended from "a fowl" that I have nicknamed Henrietta ever since hearing of Joseph's loss in 1858!

John Gray (1770–1830; 3xgreat grandfather)

As I mentioned earlier the direct male ancestral line does not come down through Joseph and his father Thomas but through Thomas's younger brother John. John was one of the first Gray boys to be apprenticed into a trade and for this he had to thank the influence of his grandfather William (of Colwick). Just as John's father had to leave Colwick for Newtown Linford to further his career as a basket maker, so John's uncle Richard needed to learn a trade to get a job. This Richard Gray was apprenticed on 26 September 1747 to a Richard Place of Mountsorrel, to learn to become a carpenter and wheelwright. So, when my 3xgreat grandfather John had reached the age of starting work, he too was apprenticed. It was 1785 and, at the age of 14, he was apprenticed to Abraham Sapcote, a baker in Leicester. He would have served his time as an apprentice for about 7 years and he obviously dedicated himself to his chosen trade, because on 5th December 1794 he was made a Freeman of the City of Leicester with the profession of baker. In fact, he spent all his working life as a baker, right up to his death in 1830. His shop was in Cank Street, quite near to the site of the present market. I have enjoyed the fact that I have walked along this street quite often over the years and it means something special to think I am walking past the site of my 3xgreat grandfather's bakery!

Discovering John Gray had been a baker in Leicester was another fascinating coincidence when linked to my own working life. It is also another reason why I call this story a "circular journey" through my Gray ancestors. Because I finished my working life as a Quality Assurance technician working at Walker & Son's bakery in Beaumont Leys, a suburb of Leicester! Can pastry handling genes actually pass through 5 generations, from the 1820s to the 21st century? My wife would probably say my inherited baking skills manage to keep themselves well hidden! It is extraordinary that my career stages should have meandered through trainee army officer, mining engineer, human resources manager, property developer and seen me ending up as a QA

WORLD HISTORICAL EVENTS		GRAY FAMILY HISTORY EVENTS	
1720	The last major bubonic plague in Europe arrives in the port of Marseilles, France	1720	**William Gray (2xgreat grandfather)** born in Colwick, Nottinghamshire
1728	The Mughal Empire in India is fragmenting, after defeat by the Hindu Marathas at battle of Palkhed	1728	**Mary (2xgreat grandmother)** born Nottinghamshire (?)
1753	Scottish physician James Lind publishes that citrus fruit is the only effective cure for scurvy	1753	1st son William born in Colwick, Nottinghamshire
1756	Seven Year War begins in Europe	1755	1st daughter Mary born in Colwick
		1757	2nd daughter Elizabeth born in Colwick
1760	Britain wins control over France in America	1760	2nd son Thomas born in Newtown Linford, Leicestershire
		1762	3rd daughter Hannah born in N.Linford
1763	The Seven Years War ends in Europe		
1764	A French trading company establishes St. Louis on the Mississippi River	1765	4th daughter Ann born in N.Linford
1770	Captain Cook arrives in New Zealand, unaware of French explorer de Surville being anchored there; Cook claims the area for King George III and sails to Australia	1770	**3rd son John (3xgreat grandfather)** born in Newtown Linford
1773	Tea selling businessmen are upset because British East India Company given right to sell direct to colonists; they threw 342 chests of tea into Boston Harbour - to be known as the Boston Tea Party	1773	4th son Josesh born in Newtown Linford
1774	King George III closes Boston Harbour, and expands Governor's powers in Massachusetts; Colonists hold "First Continental Congress" and send their grievances in a letter to King George		
1776	A Second Continental Congress meets and on 4th July declares independence	1776	5th daughter Sarah born in Newtown Linford, the last child born to William and Mary

William Gray (1720-1795) >	*John Gray (1770-1830)* >	*James Gray (1813-1880)* >	*Jesse William Gray (1855-1894)* >

technician in a Leicestershire bakery. If that's not some kind of spooky kismet in action then I don't know what is. By becoming a master baker John Gray equipped himself with the skills to start a new chapter in the Grays history, as his was the generation that moved from the country into the town at the end of the 18th century.

I have been trying to devise some interesting ways of presenting all these facts and figures to anyone who dips into my story. I have settled on some timeline diagrams and charts which hopefully captures the wealth of detail in a reader-friendly way. I shall finish each chapter with timeline charts placing Gray family events in the context of general worldwide historical events.

WORLD HISTORICAL EVENTS		GRAY FAMILY HISTORY EVENTS	
1788	Britain sends its' first 732 convicts to a place in Australia named after Lord Sydney, Secretary of State for Britain's colonies	1785	John Gray (3xgreat grandfather) begins apprenticeship with Abraham Sapcote (Master Baker), so moves to Leicester
1789	Commoners created a new National Assembly in France; Parisians storm the Bastille; Louis XVI agrees to become a constitutional monarch		
1790	Rhode Island becomes the 13th and last state to ratify the US Constitution		
1793	Louis XVI is executed;France is procaimed a republic; Britain,Holland and Spain decare war on France	1794	John Gray (3xgreat grandfather) becomes Freeman of Leicester as a baker under Abraham Sapcote
1795	The first graphite pencils are introduced	1795	William Gray (4xgreat grandfather) died in Newtown Linford
		1795	John Gray (3xgreat grandfather) married Jane Earp in St. Margaret, Leicester
1796	Edward Jenner tested innoculation during a smallpox epidemic in London	1795	John's 1st son William born 18th November in Leicester
1799	George Washington (1st US President) died	1799	John's 1st daughter Mary born in Leicester
1800	England's population reached approx.9 million, with London the world's 5th most populous city at 865,000		
1801	Britain makes Ireland part of single British kingdom	1801	John's 2nd son John Earp born in Leicester
		1803	John's 3rd son Thomas born in Leicester
1804	The Royal College of Surgeons founded in London; Japan refuses trade with arriving ships	1804	John Gray (3xgreat grandfather) married Charlotte Clark in St. Martins, Leicester
1805	Britain's Navy is victorious at the Battle of Trafalgar, frustrating Napoleon's invasion plans	1805	John's 4th son Richard Henry born in St Margaret, Leicester
		1808	John's 5th son Joseph born in St Margaret, Leicester
		1811	John's 2nd daughter Eliza Jane born in St Margaret, Leicester
1812	Workers called "Luddites" destroy mill machinery across England in protest against mechanisation; some are executed		

THE LEICESTER GRAYS

It is mainly my assumption that John Gray had to move into the town of Leicester to find work. As the 3rd eldest of William and Mary's four sons, he probably struggled to find any suitable employment in his home village of Newtown Linford, which is why his father sent him to Leicester as an apprentice baker. After his 7-year apprenticeship under his master Abraham Sapcote, he became a Freeman of Leicester in 1794 and started his own bakery in Cank Street.

In trying to discover some details of his life in Leicester I learned a very valuable genealogical lesson, namely persistence and attention to detail. I found a marriage for him in 1804 to a Charlotte Clark at St Martins, Leicester. Then I found a number of children born to the couple. These were Richard Henry born 1805, Joseph born 1808, Eliza Jane born 1811, James born 1813, Frederic born 1816. This all seemed straight forward until I made a chance discovery in the Leicester Records Office that made me doubt my own research. Since starting out on my family history journey I have always tried to adopt the best practice of verifying all internet discoveries by cross checking with actual records in archives. Thus "a nice day out" for my wife has very often been a visit to the Leicester Records Office; no one can say I don't know how to treat a lady! On this particular occasion I discovered a wonderful book that was a register of all apprentices and freemen of Leicester from the mid-18th century into the early 20th century. It was a mine of information regarding my Gray ancestors and I summarise all these little genealogical gems in the following table. However, this information source also gave me lots of headaches regarding the sons of John Gray.

Traditionally an entry in the register for an apprentice gives the date he was indentured, name of apprentice, profession, father's name, father's profession, name of Master, master's profession. Similar data is given for all freemen. This is very helpful for supporting father-son relationships discovered from births/ baptisms records. When looking for sons of John Gray who were apprenticed, I found the following:

William Gray–eldest son of John Gray

John Gray–2nd son of John Gray

Thomas Gray–3rd son of John Gray

Joseph Gray–5th son of John Gray

James Gray (my 2x great grandfather)–6th son of John Gray

What was all this about? It didn't stack up at all; I had a Richard Henry as the eldest son, Joseph as the 2nd, James as the 3rd. And I only had a total of 4 boys born to John & Charlotte so suddenly I was panicking that I had an error in my parental line, doubting if John even was the father of James. How was I to resolve this quandary? How could there be three boys born between Richard Henry's birth in 1805 and the parents' marriage in May 1804? Then you have one of those "Eureka" moments as I call them, when a thought pops into your head. John must have had another wife! I began searching for an earlier marriage and discovered that John Gray married a Jane Earp on 10th January 1795 in Leicester and guess what, they had a William born 1795, a Mary born 1799, a John Earp (how considerate they were when they chose names!) born in 1801 and a Thomas in 1803. Bingo! The numbering of the sons now fits exactly including 2xgreat grandfather James as the 6th son. I was now one happy and relieved little genealogist; strange how the things that excite you change over time. I have to admit that I have not actually found a death for this first wife Jane Earp, so maybe my 3xgreat grandfather was a bigamist; I prefer my own alternative theory, whereby Jane died in childbirth having Thomas. It was quite a common occurrence back in those days.

John was obviously a firm believer in the apprenticeship system of the day, since he both acted as master to young lads he took in as apprentices and also sent almost all his own sons into apprenticeships. It has to be understood that apprenticeships were an excellent way of being able to afford a large family, as well as a valuable source of labour if you were running your own business. In the table you can see that, between 1796 and 1830 (when he died), John was Master to 5 apprentices. The last of them was his own son Richard Henry who was indentured in 1822 aged 17. Of his own sons William was an apprentice

LIST OF GRAY FAMILY MEMBERS AS APPRENTICES AND/OR MASTERS (in red; direct parental line members bold & red)

Col	Year	Date	Surname	First Name	[F]or (A	Birth	Profession	Father	Father's professi	Master	Profession2
1	1747	26-Sep	Gray	Richard	A	1733		William Gray (late of Colwick)	Basketmaker	Richard Place of Mountsorre	Carpenter & wheelwright
2	1785		Gray	John	A	1770	Baker	William Gray (of Newtown Linford)		Abraham Sapcote	Baker
3	1794	05-Dec	Gray	John	F	1770	Baker	William Gray		Abraham Sapcote	Baker
4	1796	12-May	Bates	Benjamin	A			John Bates	Scourer	John Gray	Baker
5	1803	13-May	Hughes	George (the elde	A			William Hughes	Farmer (in Newt	John Gray	Baker
6	1809	14-Apr	Gray	William	A			John Gray	Baker	Jos,Wheatley(Snr)&Jos.Whe	Worsted-makers
7	1810	20-Feb	Bown	Garrett	A			Thomas Bown	Maltster	John Gray	Baker
8	1813	14-Dec	Hughes	George						John Gray	Baker
9	1813	14-Dec	Gray	John	A			John Gray (eld.s.of)	Baker	Richard Lee	Baker
10	1821	18-May	Gray	William	F			John Gray	Baker		
11	1822	01-Oct	Gray	Richard Henry	A	1805		John Gray	Baker	John Gray	Baker
12	1822		Hammersley	James	A			John Hammersley	Hosier	Thos.Wood/William Gray	Woolstaplers & co-partners
13	1823	24-Jun	Gray	Joseph	A			John Gray	Baker	Robert Boot	Cooper
14	1823	28-Oct	Bates	George	A		Hosier	Thomas Bates	Warehouseman	Thos.Wood/William Gray	Hosiery Manufacturers
15	1826	09-Jun	Gray	Thomas	F	1803	Tailor	John Gray (3rd.s.of)	Baker		
16	1826	16-Jun	Gray	John	F	1801	Baker	John Gray (2nd.s.of)	Baker		
17	1827	28-Sep	Gray	James	A	1813	*aged 14 yr	John Gray	Baker	Henry Dalby	Gent.
18	1829	27-Mar	Adams	Francis Haygarth	A		Hosier	John Johnson	Victualler	Thos.Wood/William Gray	Hosiery Manufacturers
19	1830	30-Mar	Gray	Henry	A			William Gray	Lacemaker	Jonathan Mallet	Tin plate worker
20	1831	22-Feb	Hammersley	James	A					William Gray[8] (of Wood&	Hosiers
21	1832	20-Jan	Gray	Joseph	F	1808		John Gray (5th.s.of)	Baker		
22	1832	20-Jan	Langley	George William	A		"an infant o	William Elgood -guardian?	Bookkeeper	Joseph Gray	Cooper
23	1833	19-Jul	Bates	George	A					William Gray[8] (of Wood&	Hosiers
24	1833	15-Oct	Withers	William	A		Hosier	William Withers (yr.s.of)	Butcher	Thos.Wood/William Gray	Hosiery Manufacturers
25	1835	10-Apr	Gray	James	F	1813		John Gray (6th.s.of)			
26	1838	08-Oct	Dalby	John Jarvis (aged	A		Hosier	Thomas Dalby	Dyer	Thos.Wood/William Gray	Hosiery Manufacturers
27	1856	21-Apr	Gray	Charles William	F	1834	Woolsorter	William Gray (1st s of)[;WG was 1st.of John)			
28	1859	04-Jul	Gray	John	F		Tailor	Thomas Gray (1st s.of); [TG was 3rd s.of John)			

> *Jesse Esdale Gray (1885-1946)* > *Cecil Jesse Austen Gray (1908-1968)* > *Peter Nigel Austen Gray (1950-present)*

worsted maker (involved in the manufacture of worsted cloth), John an apprentice baker, Thomas an apprentice tailor and Joseph an apprentice cooper. The strangest direction any of the boys went off in has to be my 2xgreat grandfather James. In the register he is listed as being indentured in 1827 to Henry Dalby who has as a profession "Gent". The definition of "Gentleman" in the 19th century was "a member of the gentry, a descendant from an aristocratic family whose income came from the rental of his land". It is not clear if James was actually an apprentice gentleman but his apprenticeship was very likely cut short when his father died in January 1830. He appears to have taken over the family bakery after John's death, even though it was his elder brothers (John Gray Jnr and Richard Henry Gray) who were apprentice bakers.

In the 1841 census James is shown as aged 27, Baker, living at Cank Street. He would have been too old at the time of his fathers' death to begin another apprenticeship so he was probably self-taught from assisting one or other of his brothers in the business between 1830 and 1841. He became a Freeman of Leicester in 1835 presumably in the profession of baker. How successful he was at it is not clear, because I found the following article in the Leicester Journal and Midland Counties Advertiser dated 17th April 1840:

"The following parties were summoned by the Churchwardens of St. Martin's for non-payment of church rates and allowed judgement to go by default:–James Gray, baker, Cank Street; ………….;–Warrants of distress were granted against the following for non-payment of church-rates:–Messrs ……..,
…………, James Gray, ……, …………., ………."

| William Gray | > | John Gray | > | James Gray | > | Jesse William Gray | > |
| *(1720-1795)* | | *(1770-1830)* | | *(1813-1880)* | | *(1855-1894)* | |

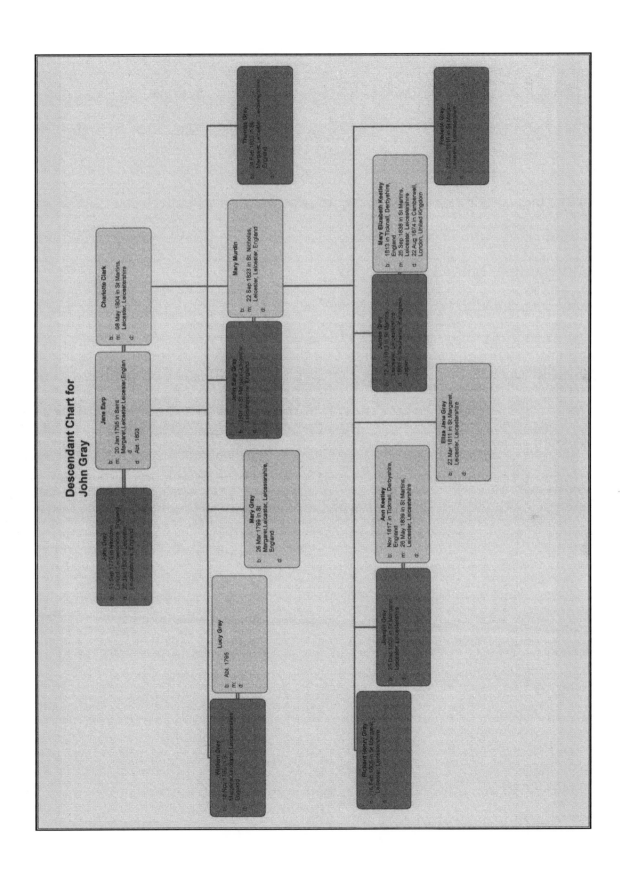

Descendant Chart for
John Gray

In researching what these various legal terms meant, I discovered it meant that James would probably not have appeared to answer the summons and the Magistrates had passed judgement that the summons should stand. In addition, they had issued the distress warrant against James, meaning bailiffs or the like could seize goods to pay the "debts" i.e. the Church rates. In those days making a financial contribution to your parish church meant more than putting some coins on the collection plate!

He eventually put the bakery business up for sale later in that year 1840, presumably to settle these church rates. It seems quite ironic that James basically lost his livelihood (in the form of the family bakery he inherited from his father) just when the government of the day were trying to push through sweeping changes to the laws around ecclesiastical finances! This included the abolishment of compulsory church rates in 1865? I am speculating here but I think these must have been very difficult times for smaller independent traders generally and bakers in particular. It was about the time that larger bakery firms were setting up to service the needs of a wider range of customers.

Alongside his 7 sons John Gray had two daughters, one each by his two wives. Mary was born 1799 to Jane Earp and Eliza Jane was born 1811 to Charlotte Clark. Although he had the 9 children over a 21-year period, they would not have all been living at home, as the apprenticed boys would go to live with their respective masters aged about 13 or 14 years old. Even so it would have been quite crowded in the premises in Cank Street.

Some of John Gray's boys obviously felt they had benefitted from being apprentices, as they in turn either sent their sons off to masters in a range of trades or indentured apprentices to themselves as masters, as the attached spreadsheet shows. His eldest son William is a particular good example of this pattern of behaviour. He became a Freeman of Leicester in 1821 and the following year indentured a James Hammersley (the son of a John Hammersley, hosier) into his hosiery business with his co-partner Thomas Wood. Subsequently they jointly indentured the following apprentices into their business–George Bates 1823 and Francis Adams 1829. Another son Joseph Gray, having been apprenticed as a cooper to Robert Boot in 1823, indentured George William Langley in 1832, the same year that he, Joseph, became a Freeman of Leicester.

James's career path after the closure of the bakery follows a number of jobs– in 1851 census "warehouseman", 1861 "clerk in Newsagents", 1871 "booksellers' clerk". Having observed this drift from manual labour towards becoming a pen-pusher (or should that more accurately be called a quill-pusher!), I can see the beginnings of employment in commerce that follows through some of his sons and culminates with his grandson and great grandson both being accountants.

James Gray (1813–1880; 2xgreat grandfather)

It is James that I shall focus upon now, since he is my 2xgreat grandfather and follows on from John Gray. I shall explain a little about James's family life. I think of him as the wanderer as his travels can be traced through the first 4 national censuses. He married Mary Elizabeth Keetley on 25 September 1838 in St Martins, Leicester–the same church in which he was baptised. This was the parish church for this part of the town and is now Leicester Cathedral. It was chosen after Leicester achieved city status which meant there needed to be a cathedral. There is an interesting side story to the wedding. Their witnesses were Joseph Gray, the groom James's older brother and Ann Keetley, the bride Mary Elizabeth's younger sister! Some 4 years later there is a second wedding, Joseph Gray marries Ann Keetley and the witnesses are Mr and Mrs Gray aka James and Mary Elizabeth. So, a double marriage connection–2 Gray brothers marrying 2 Keetley sisters. The 2 families lived close to each other: James in Cank Street and Joseph around the corner in Market Place, according to the 1841 census.

James and Mary Elizabeth's first 2 children were born in Leicester and baptised in their parish church St Martin's–John in 1840 and Charlotte Anne in 1841. Their second son Thomas was born in 1844 in Clerkenwell, Middlesex. It is hard to say what was happening with the family's fortunes at this time. James had sold up the bakery and may have been away looking for work; it is possible Mary was visiting a relative in Clerkenwell (with the 2 little children) for her confinement. The next two boys–James Joseph born in 1846 and Walter born in 1847–were both baptised at St Mary, Nottingham. This indicates a further move for the family, probably governed by James's work.

In order to help explain why it took this particular direction, I need to update my story in terms of where James's elder brother Joseph and sister-

---

in-law Ann were living. By the 1851 census they were living in the parish of St Mary, Nottingham, at 8 Smithy Row. Joseph, now in his 40s, had changed his profession. No longer a cooper in which he served his apprenticeship, he was then working as a Master Cheesemonger. Three more children had been added to Mary, the only child born to this couple when they were close neighbours to James and Mary Elizabeth in Leicester at the time of the 1841 census. The first addition to Joseph and Ann's family was a daughter Ann, who was actually born in Birmingham in 1842. She was followed by a son Joseph b.1844 and another daughter Elizabeth b.1847, both born in Nottingham. It seems likely that Joseph, the elder of these two Gray brothers, moved to Nottingham shortly before 1844 when his son Joseph was born. The younger brother followed on quite quickly thereafter, because James's two boys James Joseph and Walter were also born in Nottingham as mentioned earlier. James and Mary Elizabeth's next child Mary Eliza was also born in Nottinghamshire and baptised at St Mary's Nottingham in 1849.

By the 1851 census the family of the younger Gray brother is living in the parish of St Thomas, Birmingham; father, mother, 4 sons and 2 daughters.

I don't know why James had moved to Birmingham but it is clear from the census that he had changed professions. The only reference to Birmingham that I can find prior to this move of James's family is the birth of his brother Joseph's daughter Ann in Birmingham in 1842. This is 8 years before the earliest James could have moved there from Nottingham, following Mary Eliza's birth in 1849. The census states James is working as a warehouseman but it is fairly short lived because, by 1855, the family is living in Minerva Cottage,3 New Church Road in the parish of Camberwell St George in the borough of Lambeth. This is evidenced by my great grandfather's birth certificate which shows Jesse William Gray (the youngest of James and Mary's seven children)

Descendant Chart for James Gray

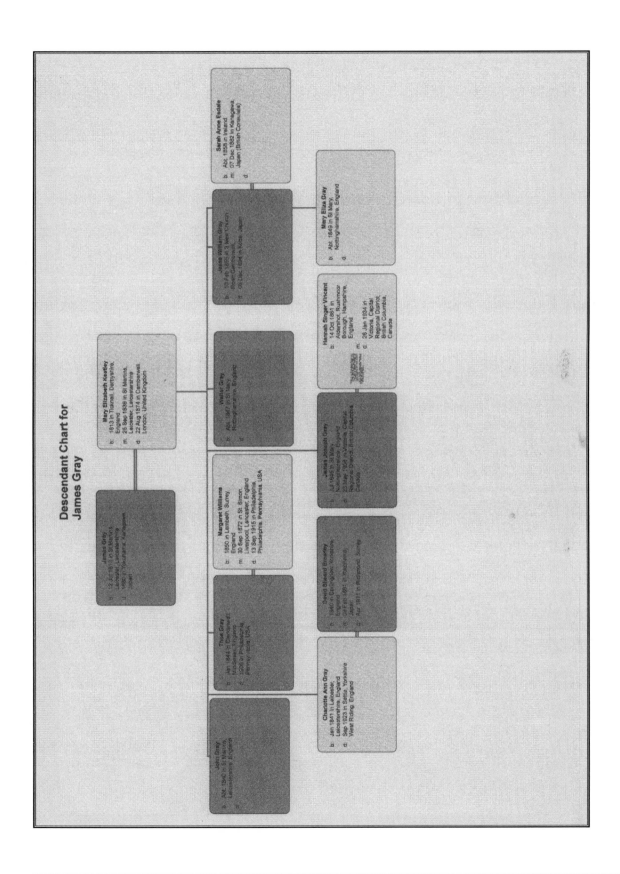

born there on 10th February 1855. James's profession on the birth certificate is shown as clerk, confirmed in the 1861 census as "Clerk, Newsagents". I have wondered what might have led James to the London area. Was it connected to his apprenticeship with "Henry Dalby, Gent"?

By the time of this census there are only 5 children living at home. The addition of my great grandfather Jesse William has been offset by the departure of two of my great uncles, John (aged 21) and James Joseph (aged 15). I obviously wanted to know where these 2 young men had gone and this formed the next part of my family research. I shall move onto this in the next chapter.

Whereas Jesse William's birth completed my great, great grandfather's family, his brother Joseph was still to add one more child to the family as recorded in the 1851 census. His last daughter Sophia was born in Birmingham in 1852. Joseph and his family were still living in St Mary's, Nottingham in 1851 but at the time of Sophia's birth, they are in Birmingham. Now we come to the ultimate "work related" move by either of these two families. In May 1853 Joseph Gray, his wife Ann and their 5 children travelled on a ship called Asia from Liverpool to Victoria, Australia. The passenger list recording this event is entitled "Assisted and Unassisted Passenger List". I am speculating here but my bet is that this Gray family was taking advantage of the assisted passages scheme–to start a new life on the other side of the world. The age range of their children was from Mary aged 12 to the new baby Sophia aged under 1! This was emigration for sure. They probably had the plan in place before Sophia's birth and maybe went to stay with James in Birmingham for the birth, before continuing on to Liverpool to embark on "the voyage".

This pattern of moving about to find work gives me a big clue that many of James's children were probably influenced by both their uncle Joseph's emigration and their father's belief that you have to be prepared to "go where the work is". It goes a long way to explaining the extraordinary events that covered the next five generations of my family. It is a fact that 5 of James and Mary's children set out to destinations around the world in search of jobs and their descendants have continued the Gray exodus to North America, Asia, Australasia and Africa. Less than half of James Gray's grandchildren were born in England! For this reason, I have labelled his children as the "Pioneer Generation".

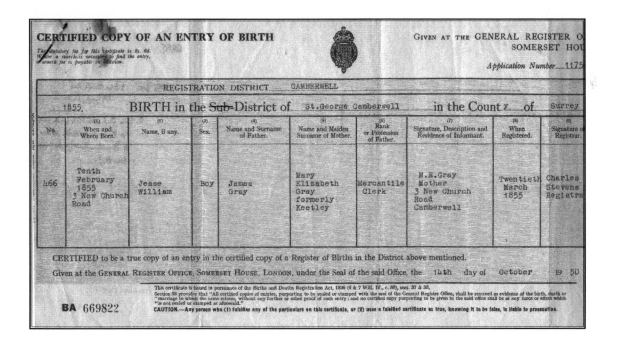

Timeline for Two Gray Brothers' Parallel Lives

	Joseph Gray	James Gray (2xgreat grandfather)
1808	born 25th December–Leicester	
1813		born 12th July–Leicester
1823	became apprentice cooper to Robert Boot–Leicester	
1827		Became apprentice to Henry Dalby–Gent in London
1832	Became Freeman (20th January) as Cooper–Leicester	
1835		Became Freeman (10th April)–Leicester
1838		married Mary Elizabeth Keetley at St. Martins, Leicester on 25th September
1839	married Ann Keetley at St. Martins, Leicester on 26th May	
1840	daughter Mary born Leicester	son John born Leicester
1841	**Census:** living at Market Place, Leicester Joseph (30)–Cooper Ann (20) Mary (9 mths)	daughter Charlotte Ann born Leicester, January **Census:** living at Cank Street, Leicester James (27)–Baker Mary (27) John (1½) Charlotte Ann (3 mths)
1842	daughter Ann born Birmingham	
1844	Son Joseph Edward born Nottingham, Nottinghamshire in October	son Thomas born Clerkenwell, Middlesex in January
1845		son James Joseph born St Mary, Nottingham in July
1847	daughter Elizabeth born Nottingham	son Walter born St Mary, Nottingham
1849		daughter Mary Eliza born St Mary, Nottingham
1851	**Census:** living at 8 Smithy Row, St. Mary, Nottingham Joseph (42)–Master Cheesemonger Ann (34) Mary (16) Ann (9) Joseph Edward (7) Elizabeth (4) Mary Griffin (24)–house servant	**Census:** living at Wynn Street, Birmingham James (37)–Warehouseman Mary Elizabeth (37) John (11) Charlotte Ann (10) Thomas (7) James Joseph (5) Walter (3) Mary Eliza (2)
1852	Daughter Sophia born	
1853	Joseph (profession–Cooper), Ann + 5 children travel to Australia on assisted passage scheme	
1855		son Jesse William (great grandfather) born at 3 New Church Road, Camberwell

William Gray	>	John Gray	>	James Gray	>	Jesse William Gray	>
(1720-1795)		(1770-1830)		(1813-1880)		(1855-1894)	

	Joseph Gray	James Gray (2xgreat grandfather)
1861		**Census:** living at Minerva Cottage, New Church Road, Camberwell James (47)–Clerk, Newsagents Mary Elizabeth (47) Charlotte Ann (20) Thomas (17) Walter (14) Mary Eliza (12) Jesse William (6)

WORLD HISTORICAL EVENTS		GRAY FAMILY HISTORY EVENTS	
		1813	6th son **James Gray (2xgreat grandfather)** born in St Martins, Leicester
1815	Wellington defeats Napoleon at Waterloo on June 18th	1816	John's 7th son Frederic born in St Martins, Leicester
1820	The Third Anglo-Maratha War ends, with Britain in control of most of India		
1820	George IV becomes King, succeeding his father George III		
1822	The accordion is invented in Vienna		
1824	The RSPCA is founded in Britain		
1830	The Mormon Church is formed in US; in Britain, the lawn mower is invented	1830	**John Gray (3xgreat grandfather)** died 26th January in Leicester
1837	Victoria becomes Queen in Britain		
1838	Charles Darwin develops a theory of evolutionary selection and specialisation	1838	**James Gray (2xgreat grandfather)** married **Mary Elizabeth Keetley** in St. Martin's, Leicester
		1839	Joseph Gray (James's brother) married Ann Keetley in St. Martin's, Leicester
1840	China's government seizes 20,000 cases of British opium, starting the 1st Anglo-Chinese War	1840	James's 1st son John born in St Martins, Leicester
		1841	James's 1st daughter Charlotte Anne born in St Martins, Leicester
1843	Charles Thurber invents a typewriter in US	1844	James's 2nd son Thomas born in Clerkenwell, Middlesex
1845	Mold on potatoes survives the faster shipment times from US, causing potato crop failures across Europe and famine in Ireland	1845	James's 3rd son James Joseph born in St. Mary, Nottingham
		1847	James's 4th son Walter born in St. Mary, Nottingham
1848	Karl Marx, with Friedrich Engels, writes a theory of political development, siding with the proletariat against the capitalists; his book is The Communist Manifesto	1849	James's 2nd daughter Mary Eliza born in St. Mary, Nottingham
1854	Construction of Big Ben clock tower completed		
1855	Much of Edo(Tokyo) destroyed by earthquake	1855	**Jesse William Gray (great grandfather)** born in Camberwell
		1858	**Sarah Anne Esdale (great grandmother)** born in Ireland
1859	Charles Darwin finally publishes "Origin of the Species"		

THE JAPANESE CONNECTION EXPLAINED

As I indicated in the introduction to this book, I have always known from when I was a child that both my father and grandfather were born in Yokohama, Japan. In the same way that I had accepted the fact that I was born in India, I somehow just filed these extra vital pieces of genealogical data away into my memory for a later date. Maybe to be used to impress a school mate who was boasting about his parents or even how well travelled he was. I never really gave it much thought until I started researching my own parental line in my newly adopted role as family historian.

Even with my fairly limited knowledge of genealogy at the time, I quickly concluded that, if my grandfather was born in Japan, there was a fair chance that his mother had visited Japan! At the risk of making an unsubstantiated connection, I then pondered the fact that her husband (my great grandfather Jesse William Gray) might also have been in Japan! At least to take part in the conceptual part of this notion. What I am trying to say is that, à la Brooklyn Beckham, my great grandfather might just as easily have been christened

William Gray
(1720-1795)   >   *John Gray*
(1770-1830)   >   *James Gray*
(1813-1880)   >   *Jesse William Gray*
(1855-1894)   >

Yokohama Gray! As the youngest of James Gray's children, was it possible that he was the link from a suburb of Leicester to Yokohama, a suburb of Tokyo (or Edo as it was called then)?

A green light suddenly turned on for my research plan. I needed to prove how the son of a one-time baker from Leicester might possibly connect to the most influential of the emerging trading ports of the Far East. How exciting was that! Compared to the more traditional challenge of proving that a bride from parish A actually married a groom from parish Z rather than from her neighbouring parishes of B, C or even D. But it was going to be challenging. No way that I could pop down to the Yokohama Records Office, even if such a place existed. Thankfully I was doing my research in the time of the modern genealogist's greatest resource–the Internet.

I was rewarded fairly quickly in my search with several solid pieces of evidence, with one in particular being the gateway to a veritable Aladdin's Cave of detailed information that has assisted me greatly in writing this section of my story.

When I searched for a death record for my 2xgreat grandfather James Gray, I found many collaborating items. From online BMD registers I learned that he died in Yokohama in 1880. Fantastic news, they didn't say Edo or Nagasaki or Kyoto; no–they actually named Yokohama. As I had not been able to continue tracking James beyond the 1871 census, the date of 1880 for a death was a positive. I then searched for a grave for him and amazingly discovered that he was actually buried in the YFC (Yokohama Foreigners Cemetery). Sometime later I found the following newspaper article:

"GRAY–On the 19th Oct., at Yokohama, James Gray, of Leicester, aged 67" Leicester Chronicle–Saturday 18 December 1880"

These basic details are repeated in other Leicestershire newspapers. I had to believe that I had proved that James Gray born 1813 in St Martins, Leicester had actually died in Yokohama, Japan. Now I needed to work out how and why he was in Japan in 1880. This brings me to the biggest "accidental" discovery of all my research findings, when I stumbled upon something called the Meiji Restoration.

After a lot of fruitless surfing concerning Grays and Japan, I googled "Jesse Esdale Gray" with no great optimism for success, other than it is quite an unusual combination of names. Surely anything that popped up would relate to my Jesse Esdale. I still cannot quite believe just what did pop up. The link was to something called the Meiji Portraits and related to a project whereby an individual interested in photographic portraits has carried out an amazing piece of research work. His name is Bernd Lepach and I shall explain how his fascinating documents have assisted my own research later in this chapter.

Firstly, I need to explain a little of Japanese history from the mid-19th century into the early 20th century. For some 250 years before the 1850s, Japan had completely closed itself from the outside world in the belief that it should remain true to its' traditional national, cultural and economic values and beliefs. The situation across the country in the 1850s however was one of stagnation in terms of growth and prosperity, with a feeling of falling well behind the rest

| *William Gray* *(1720-1795)* | > | *John Gray* *(1770-1830)* | > | *James Gray* *(1813-1880)* | > | *Jesse William Gray* *(1855-1894)* | > |

of the world. Global trade was on the increase between the developed West (chiefly America, Britain, France, Germany, Holland, Portugal, etc.) and the East (like India and China). There was a desire for change from the old feudal systems along with removal of the Samurai-based Shogun power structures. It came into sharp focus with the beginning of the reign of a new imperial leader, the Emperor Meiji in 1867. Meiji's accession to the throne coincided with the end of the Tokugawa shogunate and the restoration to the emperor of supreme executive authority in the country. Unlike his father Kōmei, he supported the growing popular consensus on the need for modernization of Japan along Western lines, that had developed as a result of the country's resumption of contact with other nations after a 250-year period of cultural and economic isolation. In 1868 Meiji took the "Charter Oath of Five Principles," which launched Japan on the course of westernisation.

The methodology used for accessing the skills and knowledge base of the "advanced countries of the West" was a two-pronged strategy. On one hand the higher echelons of Japanese society–the would-be leaders, entrepreneurs, industrialists, etc.–went to the West to be educated and developed. Secondly the country accelerated its' programme of inviting entrepreneurs to start up new businesses in Japan. This was a deliberate policy of importing the latest technologies from around the world, to fast-track themselves through the early phases of an industrial revolution that countries like America and Britain had already surpassed. In a way it was like someone starting a new football team to go straight into the English Premier League without bothering with climbing up the league structure from grass roots level. Japan wanted to short circuit the long, slow "learning curve" undertaken by the industrialised countries of the West. They did this by "importing" the best practices of the world; cherry-picking the successful businesses to come and set up in Japan as "the finished article". Then the aspiring Japanese business moguls could learn "on the job" from the best and begin to compete with the West within a greatly accelerated timescale.

This approach produced a kind of industrial "Klondike" in the second half of the 19th century, as westerners flocked to the new trading ports in Japan, seeking to make their fortunes. Not from gold as such but from being the first at whatever business venture they chose to launch. The profit potential was substantial due to the initial monopoly status of these businesses. There was actually a mini gold rush in Yokohama for a short period, caused by an abnormal exchange rate/gold pricing differential between the economies of India, China and Japan. At its' height Britain was shipping as much silver as it could daily from China just to buy Japanese gold. It was fairly short lived but provided the foundation for much of the wealth of many British companies founded at that time.

It was this dream of instant prosperity that lured so many westerners to Japan. Yokohama emerged as probably the most influential of the Japanese ports and it underwent a population explosion between 1865 and 1910. New businesses sprang up everywhere, covering a broad spectrum of industrial sectors. These included large scale infrastructure projects in transport, civil engineering, manufacturing and shipping. These were government awarded contracts and were the building blocks for a host of smaller scale capital ventures. These even went down to small traders starting up individual enterprises built on their personal skill sets as tailors, chemists, photographers and the like. Soon there was at least one business to provide anything and everything the Japanese might need, even before they realised that they needed it! There were even printers–because one of the publications that was printed each year was a trade directory! This was the Yellow Pages of the day; a list of all the businesses operating in the area with contact details, addresses, etc. I am guessing maybe not telephone numbers! It was how the businesses advertised their services to potential clients and detailed the proprietors etc. I have researched similar documents in England; indeed, my 3xgreat grandfather John Gray is listed as "Baker, Cank Street" in one of the Leicester directories.

Bernd Lepach (the compiler of the Meiji Portraits project) has a complete set of the Japan Directories that cover most of the reign of Emperor Meiji. It is this resource that has provided me with so much information about some of my Gray ancestors. In particular it clearly shows that at least two of James Gray's sons could not resist the lure of the "get-rich-quick" environment prevailing in Yokohama at the latter end of the 19th century.

THE PIONEER GENERATION

In trying to understand why some of my ancestors took the extraordinary step of seeking their fortune on the other side of the world, I started to question what their prospects were like in England and how did they hear about what was going on in Japan. I have already speculated about job opportunities not being that good for James Gray in the mid-19th century. This had caused him to move his family at least four times between 1841 and 1871, as he changed jobs. One imagines it was equally difficult for his sons as they grew to an age when they needed to find suitable employment. It was a time of large families, a drift from country into the towns, continuing industrialisation and increased mechanisation. Their father could not afford to indenture them as apprentices anywhere. They were probably very conscious of having to leave home when they reached working age; this is borne out by the fact that the two oldest boys (John and James Joseph) were not living at home at the time of the 1861 census. John would have been 21 years old then and James Joseph only 15.

Regarding how they might have got to know about the employment

Klondike in Japan, I have a theory in the absence of any better hard evidence. James Gray's profession in the 1861 census was given as "clerk, Newsagents". What if he got to take some of his work home? By that, I mean he had access to newspapers that may have informed him of the exciting changes happening in Japan. Maybe he fuelled his sons' imagination with stories of ambitious, determined young men not happy with their lot at home and courageous enough to take their chances in the Land of the Rising Bank Balance!

I lost track of both of them after the 1851 census at this stage of my family history research. It was before I had discovered the Meiji Portraits website but I managed to pick James Joseph up again for certain in 1871. This is by way of another chance discovery. As I was aware of some involvement with freemasonry by later generations of Grays, I made a speculative Google search for "James Joseph Gray freemason". Hoorah–another positive result appeared complete with a surprise twist. James Joseph had indeed been involved with the masons. He was only initiated into the Yokohama lodge of the Freemasons on 1st February 1871! His profession was given as steward. Result! There was even this likely explanation as to how he got there, because the profession "steward" relates to a ship's steward rather than a youth at Wembley in a high viz jacket!

So, there it was–a Gray had gone to Japan, to the very place where I knew my ancestors had been born, lived, worked, had families, etc. I was so excited with the discovery and it was relatively soon afterwards that the Meiji Portraits fell into my genealogical lap! I was on a family history high and have since

---

> *Jesse Esdale Gray*   >   *Cecil Jesse Austen*   >   *Peter Nigel Austen Gray*
(1885-1946)   *Gray (1908-1968)*   *(1950-present)*

thoroughly enjoyed my ongoing interaction with Bernd in Leipzig, as we continue to piece together the lives of the Grays in Japan.

The depth of detail contained in the trade directories that form the basis of Bernd's project is staggering. When I started out on my family history journey, I only knew that my father and grandfather were born in Yokohama. Now I can trace 3 generations of Grays from the late 1860s to at least 1918 when my grandfather moved his wife and 4 children to Shanghai, China. Naturally we'll get around to what happened there much later in my story but I shall continue now with which Grays were in Yokohama, where they worked and even where they lived.

In terms of my direct male parental line, I knew that my great grandfather Jesse William G. must have been in Japan, as that's where his son Jesse Esdale G. was born. From the Meiji Portraits data, I now know Jesse William married his wife Sarah Anne Esdale there, they had 4 children (3 boys and I girl) there, Jesse William died there, his second eldest Jesse Esdale married my grandmother Winifred Leila Austen there, they in turn had 4 children there including Cecil Jesse Austen G. my father! (Don't worry if you are getting my Jesses, Esdales, Austens and even Grays a bit mixed up, I have included an expanded family tree into my story at this point to help explain it.) I also know where and when these main players worked and lived which I found very exciting to learn about after all these years. I never actually met my grandfather Jesse Esdale as he died four years before I was born. With my own father dying when I was aged 18, doing this family history research has brought them very much alive

| William Gray | > | John Gray | > | James Gray | > | Jesse William Gray | > |
| (1720-1795) | | (1770-1830) | | (1813-1880) | | (1855-1894) | |

Descendant Chart for
James Gray

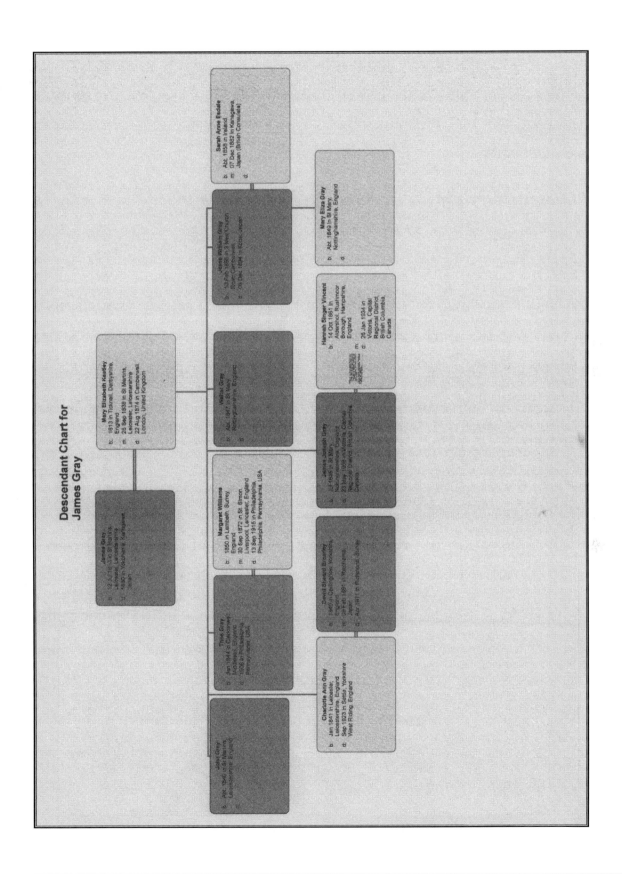

> *Jesse Esdale Gray*
(1885-1946)

> *Cecil Jesse Austen*
Gray (1908-1968)

> *Peter Nigel Austen Gray*
(1950-present)

for me, together with the extended family in Japan. I have loved discovering as much as possible about them all, and continue to do so as I discover more and more.

James Joseph Gray (1846–1908; 2nd great uncle)

From my research to date I believe my 2nd great uncle James Joseph was the first Gray to arrive in Japan. From the directories in the Meiji Portraits database I have tracked the following employment career. He came to Japan in 1869 and was employed as a barman at The Japan Hotel. After receiving a favourable job offer, he left the hotel and signed a contract with the Japanese government, Ministry of Public Works, Lighthouse Department. The contract ran from June 3, 1870 to May 13, 1871; at first, he served as Chief Steward on the Lighthouse Tender SS *Thabor*. His contract was repeatedly extended until his discharge on February 26, 1874.

It was very early on in his life in Japan that James Joseph became a mason. From my research into the history of freemasonry in Japan, I learned that the O.Tentosama Lodge in Yokohama was in its' infancy in 1871 when James Joseph was initiated on 1st February. He was listed as a steward and there was a broad range of professions among his colleagues, including merchant, auctioneer, clerk, mariner, storekeeper, engineer and machinist. In my opinion the Lodge was really a business people's club whereby they could all look out for each other's interests. It was not the preserve of the rich or gentry as those types were not really present yet in these early days of Yokohama. I feel it was

---

| *William Gray* | > | *John Gray* | > | *James Gray* | > | *Jesse William Gray* | > |
| *(1720-1795)* | | *(1770-1830)* | | *(1813-1880)* | | *(1855-1894)* | |

more a case of all the early settlers grouping themselves together in a mutually beneficial partnership arrangement. The original "you scratch my back and I'll scratch yours" organisation for collective success. One of the interesting observations I made when examining the United Grand Lodge of England Freemason Membership Registers record was that the name above James Joseph's was a certain Henry James Vincent. He was the father of Hannah Singer Vincent, who became the wife of James Joseph Gray! They married in 1881 about ten years after the two men became masons together. It doesn't really take Hercule Poirot to work out that maybe Henry introduced his daughter to my 2nd great uncle.

Around 1874 he became a partner of A. Hearne & Co., General Storekeepers, Yokohama # 70 (this numbering system relates to the entry in the Japan Directories). I believe it also has a geographical significance, possibly relating to business units or plots in the commercial area of the newly emerging port of Yokohama. This partnership did not last for long; in 1876 they separated their business into A. Hearne & Co. Storekeeper, located at Yokohama # 51 and J. J. Gray & Co., remaining at the former site at Yokohama # 70. From 1874, when he "came ashore" from off the lighthouse tender, he lived at No. 46 Bluff. The Bluff was the name of the residential area built by the westerners in Yokohama; I am guessing the numbering system was 1 for the first built and going up as new settlers came to town and built properties. One year after moving in he had some company, because my great grandfather Jesse William arrived in Japan and moved into 46 Bluff with his brother. Almost immediately after his arrival Jesse William was initiated into the Yokohama Lodge on December 1st,1875 with the profession of clerk.

In 1877 James Joseph got another offer to work temporarily as Chief Steward on the Lighthouse Tender *Meiji-maru*, stationed at Yokohama Benten. After completing three years at this contract, in 1880 he revived his firm J. J. Gray & Co. and established the Yokohama Coal Depot, Yokohama # 117; in 1882 he transferred the company to Yokohama # 158 + 159. Two years later in 1884 he started to work for Whitfield & Co., Yokohama Iron Works, Yokohama # 69 but ceased in the following year again. He leased out his coal business Gray & Co. to H. MacArthur, located at # 70 and # 117.

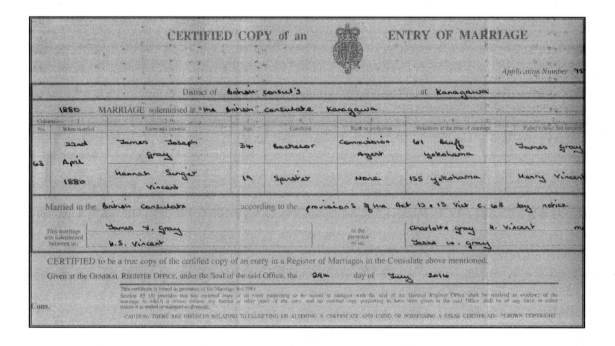

I need to take you back a few years to tell you a little about James Joseph's personal life. The year is 1880 and it is a significant date in my Gray ancestral

timeline because on 19th October James Gray (my 2xgreat grandfather) died–
in Yokohama! The question of how he came to be there has been quite pivotal
to this whole story.

The bare facts are quite straight forward. James appears in the 1871 census
as Head of the household, aged 57, residing at 13 Wellington Road, Lambeth,
Surrey. With him are Mary Elizabeth (57, wife), Charlotte Ann (30, daughter),
Walter (24, son), Mary Eliza (22, daughter) and my great grandfather Jesse
William (16, son). His wife Mary Elizabeth died on 22nd August 1874 in
Camberwell; her death was registered by her son Walter. I asked myself why it
wasn't her husband James reporting the death and can only presume the only
son still at home or local to his parents wanted to spare his father the task at
this difficult time. I cannot really find concrete evidence of what happens next
with James but feel able to speculate on what I do know. At this time his three
eldest boys–John, Thomas, and James Joseph–have left home and within the
next year, his youngest son Jesse William (my great grandfather) has also left.
In his case it was for Japan to be with his brother. What if James now thought
"What's stopping me taking a trip somewhere now? I always thought I might
like to meet up with one of the boys. Maybe Thomas up in Lancashire? Or
what about Japan! After all it's been me feeding them with all these ideas of
"the world is your oyster, grab your opportunity now"! Maybe I should go and
see for myself". This is speculation of course but the next fact is that he did
travel to Japan, which would prove to be his last trip and his proverbial "last
resting place". He is buried in the Yokohama Foreigners Cemetery, the first of

---

> *Jesse Esdale Gray*
(1885-1946)

> *Cecil Jesse Austen*
Gray (1908-1968)

> *Peter Nigel Austen Gray*
(1950-present)

several Gray ancestors to be interred there.

I cannot really comprehend how the family kept in touch in those days. We have grown up through the progression of airmail, telegram and telephone through to email and the now almost instant "live" communication of video messaging apps and social media via the Internet. At the time I am talking about, "breaking news" was probably 5 or 6 weeks old depending on which ship brought the letter through whatever kind of weather! My point is that the news about life in Japan must have been quite positive; it was certainly favourable enough to convince James's daughter Charlotte she should go out there. When exactly she went is unclear; I can only pinpoint it to between the 1871 census and her wedding on 5th February in 1881. Given that she was still a single woman aged 30 at home in 1871, maybe she had decided to remain at home while her mother was still alive. I am suggesting the death of her mother in 1874 freed her to make the move away. One also assumes it could have taken a few years for her to meet and fall in love with her future husband David Sheard Brearley. He arrived in Yokohama in 1878 and established his own company, operating under the name DS Brearley and Co., Merchants at Yokohama #28-A. The firm was relocated to #4B in 1884 and he operated the company successfully until 1891. His private residence from his arrival in 1878 was #87 -B Bluff and he was joined there by the Rev. William Thomas Austen. The latter came to Japan in 1873 and ended up as a missionary of the Seaman's Mission of the English Church. The Yokohama Seamen's Mission was permanently located at #82-B Yokohama and Rev. Austen acted as its' chaplain. In 1880 he married Leila Ada Shapcott at Newton Abbott in Devon and they set up home in Yokohama at #60 Bluff, in time for the birth of their first child, Albert William S. Austen later that same year.

If I appear to have gone off on a tangent with the Rev. Austen I apologise and will attempt to explain why. He is the reason why I have Austen as my third forename (Peter Nigel Austen Gray). His second child, born 1882, was Winifred Leila who would eventually marry my grandfather Jesse Esdale Gray. Thus, Austen became a family name and my grandfather wanted it to continue down the line. His first born was called Cecil Jesse Austen Gray, my father! Not to be out done, my Dad thought it only right that Austen should find its' way into my moniker!

Returning to my story and trying to keep things in some kind of chronological order, I should complete my account of the romance between my 2nd great aunt Charlotte Anne Gray and David Sheard Brearley. She must have travelled to Yokohama towards the end of the 1870s and it is not clear if she was accompanied by her father James or not. Maybe James Joseph or Jesse William or even both of them invited Charlotte to join them, a little while after the death of their mother Mary Elizabeth (1874). She probably arrived more or less at the same time as her future husband, around 1878. Maybe later, when her feelings towards David Brearley had led to accepting his proposal, she wanted her father at her wedding to walk her down the aisle. The basic fact is that James Gray eventually did make the journey to Yokohama, only to die before the wedding.

The blossoming romance culminated in their wedding on 5th February, 1881, and this was one of three Gray family weddings in a couple of years involving children of James Gray. Her older brother James Joseph married Hannah Singer Vincent in 1881, followed by her youngest brother Jesse William (my great grandfather) the next year. It is strange what jumps into one's head when you discover a name like Hannah Singer Vincent. Had my 2nd great uncle married a sewing machine heiress? Apparently not–as Hannah was the daughter of Henry James and Eliza Ann Vincent, a couple who resided at Yokohama # 61 Bluff. Incidentally James Joseph's mother-in-law Eliza Ann Vincent was a successful businesswoman in Yokohama by the time her daughter married James Joseph. She had founded a millinery and drapery business ten years earlier, in 1871. Maybe her business was full of a certain brand of sewing machine after all, hence her daughter's middle name!

After their marriage James Joseph and Hannah moved into #61 Bluff, leaving Jesse William as a bachelor in #46 Bluff. James Joseph and Hannah had three children in Japan–Ethel Penelope b.1882, Vincent Keetley b.1884 and Harold Leicester b.1888. When it comes to naming their children, this particular couple win my "Most Helpful Names for Offspring" award! Their first son was actually called by his mother's maiden name and his grandmother's maiden name. It helps that Vincent is a recognised boy's name but Keetley isn't really. Maybe this is where the family tradition of using surnames as forenames actually began. I hadn't thought of it before but it could explain why my father, my cousin and myself all have Austen as our 3rd forename,

| *William Gray* | > | *John Gray* | > | *James Gray* | > | *Jesse William Gray* | > |
| *(1720-1795)* | | *(1770-1830)* | | *(1813-1880)* | | *(1855-1894)* | |

and why my grandfather and another cousin have Esdale in their names. So it goes on–my brother has Downton as his third name, which is our mother's maiden name; another cousin even has Gray in his collection. James Joseph and Hannah could not have pioneered the Beckham's idea of using the name of the place where the child was conceived, because that was Yokohama for young Harold not Leicester! James Joseph may have been confused; it was his father who was born in Leicester, but it certainly helped me as a family historian coming along over a century later.

John Gray (1840–unknown; 2nd great uncle)

After many discussions with my invaluable genealogical data supplier Bernd, we have jointly concluded that quite a lot of his information concerning a John Gray relates to James Joseph's brother. He was the eldest son of James Gray, my 2xgreat grandfather from Leicester and named after my 3xgreat grandfather. If you have been following the story so far, this John Gray made the move into the town of Leicester to start his bakery in Cank Street.

John Jnr was listed on the 1851 census with the family in Birmingham aged 11 but, by the 1861 census aged 21, he had already left the family home in Nottingham. I could not find any mention of this John being apprenticed which would have happened when he was aged about 14, roughly midway between the censuses. Given the reason that James had to move home at least three times through the period 1841–1861 was job hunting, it is highly likely that his first-born also had to leave home to find employment. There is an element of guesswork about where he was and what he was doing, after my last definitive placement of him i.e. at home as a scholar in Birmingham in 1851. I cannot find any census information for him after this date in England nor a death, and the fact that Bernd has evidence for a John Gray in Yokohama covering my "blank" period, leads me to believe my John Gray did follow his brother to Japan. My theory is that he was probably persuaded by positive feedback from James Joseph, who I believe was the first to actually start work in Yokohama. I know that there was communication between the first Gray emigrants to Japan and home, because my great aunt Charlotte Anne Gray definitely travelled out to join her brothers there. And these siblings' father James Gray (my 2x great grandfather) eventually journeyed out at an advanced age, probably for Charlotte's wedding. Unfortunately, it proved to be his last trip, as he passed away in 1880 just before her wedding.

Back to the eldest sibling John Gray. He gained a Japanese government contract within the Railroad Department of the Ministry of Public Works. He was in charge of train transportation and car structure. This first contract ran from 18th June 1873 to 17th June 1876 but it was continuously extended, until his final contract expired in 1884. At first, he worked in the locomotive department in Kobe but was shifted to Yokohama in 1874, working for the Tokyo-Yokohama line. In 1880 he was responsible for the Yokohama assembly department. At the termination of his contract in 1884, Bernd Lepach loses track of a John Gray and suggests he left Japan for England. I am unable to verify this at present.

| William Gray (1720-1795) | > | John Gray (1770-1830) | > | James Gray (1813-1880) | > | Jesse William Gray (1855-1894) | > |

Jesse William Gray (1855-1894; great grandfather)

Having shared quite a lot about my 2nd great uncle's career in Yokohama, it is high time I updated you in terms of my great grandfather's career history. Jesse William began his working life with A Hearne & Co., General Storekeepers at #Yokohama 70 in 1875. In that same year, on 1st December he was initiated as a Freemason into the O Tentosama Lodge of Yokohama, joining elder brother James Joseph who had been a member since 1871. It is interesting that he became a Freemason just as he started work. In a way this supports my earlier theory that these newly formed lodges (O Tentosama was only started in 1870) were more like Chambers of Commerce or trade bodies than the exclusive, secretive and hence often maligned masonic groups of later years. It was probably a requirement for any foreigner trying to progress in late 19th century Japan that they joined what was effectively a trade association. In modern times it would be called a network, and would be internet-based! I am prepared to accept it would have no place within the modern concepts of diversity and equality, but it was probably necessary to keep the wheels of the Yokohama business and economic society turning. My great grandfather obviously considered it beneficial for him, as he transferred to the Rising Sun Lodge in Kobe on 26th November 1890 as his career path took him there.

Two years later he started a career in insurance, joining Findlay, Richardson & Co., Insurance Agency Yokohama #6. He remained with them for nearly a decade before joining another insurance agency Butterfield & Swire in 1886. His commute to work would not have changed much, as this new firm were

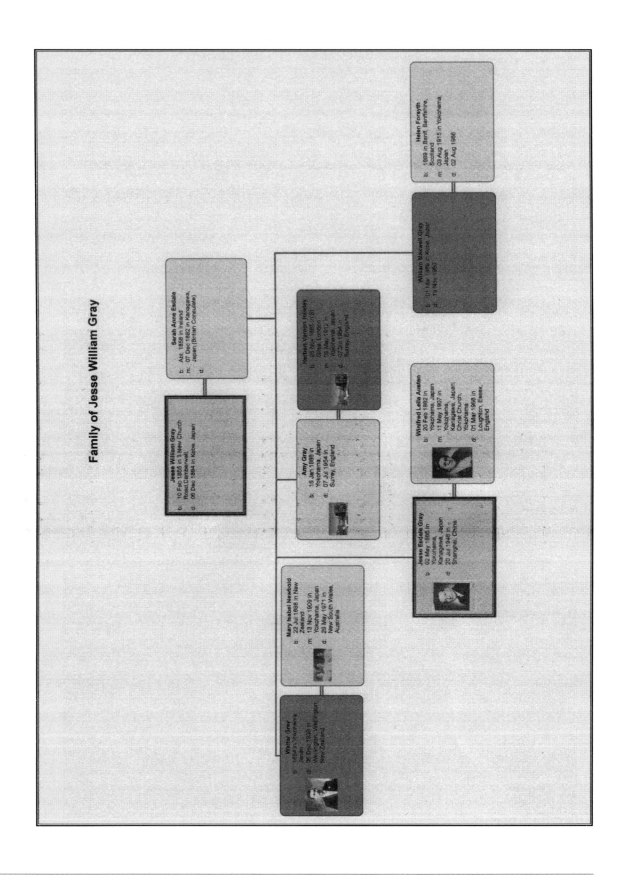

Family of Jesse William Gray

based at Yokohama #7! In 1888 he actually moved to Kobe to work for WM Strachan & Co., Insurance Agency in their Kobe branch. His next move was to Nickel & Co., also in their Kobe branch.

I like to think that there must have been some kind of career progression going on through these changes of employer, with promotions and a higher status in each subsequent opportunity. This is only based on an assumption that he would have wanted the economic stability to support a growing family. After marrying Sarah Anne Esdale in 1882 (witnessed by his sister Charlotte Anne), he steadily grew his family over the next few years. Their first child was a boy, Walter born 1883 in Yokohama. Next came another boy, my grandfather Jesse Esdale, born on 2nd May 1885, also in Yokohama. Their only daughter Amy was born in 1888 possibly in Kobe.

I remember reading somewhere that having a new baby and moving house are two of the most stressful events in any couple's life. Admittedly it was probably talking about the 1980s rather than the 1880s but Jesse William and Sarah certainly experienced both in that year. The family was completed by the arrival of William in 1889, definitely born in Kobe.

The move to Kobe was a mixed experience for this family. Whereas Jesse William was moving away from his siblings (James Joseph and Charlotte Ann), his wife Sarah would be reuniting with some of her Esdale family. Her older brother Charles Esdale had moved to Kobe briefly in 1873, then had a number of jobs back in Yokohama and Tokyo before settling back in Kobe in 1880. His wife Anna bore him 4 children between 1881 and 1885 but unfortunately

Charles died in 1886 aged only 32. So maybe Sarah was wanting to help support her widowed sister-in-law bringing up these 4 young children, as they were of a similar age and she had two young boys herself.

If my great grandfather Jesse William had been filling in a census form in 1891 in the style of those back in England, it would have read something like this:

Name	Relationship to head	Gender	Age	Where born	Profession
Gray, Jesse William	Head	M	36	England, Camberwell	Clerk, Insurance
Gray, Sarah Anne	Wife	F	33	Ireland	
Gray, Walter	Son	M	8	Japan, Yokohama	Scholar
Gray, Jesse Esdale	Son	M	6	Japan, Yokohama	
Gray, Amy	Daughter	F	3	Japan, Yokohama or Kobe	
Gray, William	Son	M	2	Japan, Kobe	

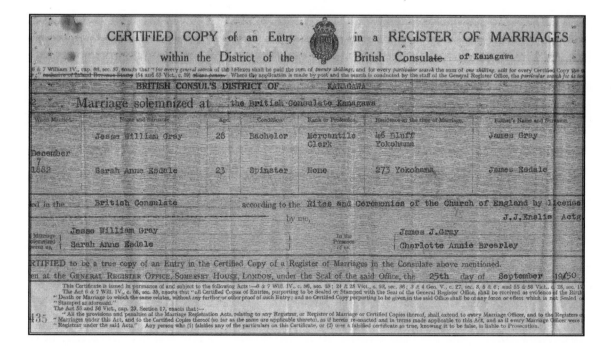

Tragedy struck the family in 1894 when Jesse William died suddenly, aged only 39. He was buried in the Yokohama Foreigners Cemetery, alongside his

No.	When and Where Born	Name	Sex	Name and Surname of Father	Name and Maiden Surname of Mother	Rank or Profession of Father	Signature, Description, and Residence of Informant	When Registered
234	Yokohama 119 Bluff May 2 1885	Jesse Esdale Gray	Male	Jesse William Gray	Sarah Anne Esdale	Merchants Clerk	Sd. Jesse W.Gray Merchants Clerk 119 Bluff	September 10th 1885

CERTIFIED to be a true Copy of an Entry in the Certified Copy of a Register of Births in the District above mentioned.
Given at the GENERAL REGISTER OFFICE, SOMERSET HOUSE, LONDON, under the Seal of the said Office, the 9th day of June

Cons. B 9339

father James. I imagine my great grandmother Sarah could hardly believe that lightning would strike twice within the family. First her brother Charles and now her husband had died in their thirties, leaving widows with very young children.

The effect on Sarah must have been traumatic. Not only was she a 36-year old widow with 4 young children but she was now also "alone" on the other side of the world. This is because her brother-in-law (my 2nd great uncle James Joseph) had left Japan with his family for a new life in Canada in 1890. Then, in 1892, her sister-in-law (my 2nd great aunt Charlotte Anne) had returned to England as Mrs Brearley. Sarah had no doubt been disappointed over these previous years, as the support network of her extended family gradually departed for pastures new. It would have been bearable to have been a mother trying to bring up a young family while Jesse William was still alive but now

> *Jesse Esdale Gray (1885-1946)* > *Cecil Jesse Austen Gray (1908-1968)* > *Peter Nigel Austen Gray (1950-present)*

it was just her in terms of Gray relatives. She continued to live in Kobe until 1896, when she moved back to Yokohama, moving her young family in with her parents at #179 Bluff. Her parents were both in their late 70s. Her father James died in July 1902 aged 84 followed by his wife Hester only 8 days later! She was aged 85. They were both buried in the YFC, together with their eldest son who had died years earlier aged only 22!

The deaths of her parents in 1902 meant that this now 44-year old widow was effectively the head of the Gray family still left living in Yokohama. Her eldest son Walter was just 19, working for the China & Japan Trading Company at Yokohama #89. Her second son Jesse Esdale (my grandfather) was 17 and working for Helm Brothers (Stevedores, Landing and Forwarding Agents) at Yokohama Drayage Co., Yokohama #44. He had moved there a year earlier from the Yokohama Steam Laundry at Yokohama #125 to be with his elder brother Walter, who had started work with Helm Bros. in 1900 aged 16 yrs.

The family (mother Sarah with 3 sons and a daughter) were then living at #179 Bluff, her parents' house. Apart from Walter and Jesse Esdale already working, there were youngest son William and only daughter Amy at home as scholars. This seems a good point to move on to the next chapter of my tale, as we follow these four siblings of my grandfather's generation through their early working lives and starting their own families.

WORLD HISTORICAL EVENTS	GRAY FAMILY HISTORY EVENTS
1867 Crown Prince Mutsuhito (aged 14) ascends the throne as Emperor Meiji in Japan	1869 James Joseph Gray arrives in Yokohama
1869 The Suez Canal opened	
	1874 **Mary Elizabeth Gray (2xgreat grandmother)** died Camberwell
1876 Alexander Graham Bell invents the telephone	1875 **Jesse William Gray** arrives in Yokohama
1877 Thomas Edison develops the gramophone and phonograph	
	1880 **James Gray (2xgreat grandfather)** died in Yokohama
1881 1st Boer War ends in S.Africa when Gladstone returns self-rule to the Boer Republic	1881 Charlotte Gray married David Brearley in Yokohama
	1881 James Joseph Gray married Hannah Vincent in Yokohama
	1882 **Jesse William Gray** married **Sarah Anne Esdale**
1883 German physician Robert Koch discovers the bacterium that causes tuberculosis; the following year he discovers the bacterium that causes cholera	1884 Jesse William's 1st son Walter born in Yokohama
	1885 2nd son **Jesse Esdale Gray (grandfather)** born in Yokohama
	1886 Jesse William's only daughter Amy born in Yokohama; family moves from Yokohama to Kobe
1888 In London, the murder of 5 prostitutes is attributed to Jack the Ripper	
1889 Washington becomes a state of the US; Adolf Hitler born in Austria	1889 3rd son William Maxwell born in Kobe
1890 Vincent Van Gogh commits suicide	

> *Jesse Esdale Gray*   > *Cecil Jesse Austen*   > *Peter Nigel Austen Gray*
> *(1885-1946)*   > *Gray (1908-1968)*   > *(1950-present)*

GRANDFATHER JESSE ESDALE'S GENERATION IN JAPAN

We shall reunite with my great grandmother Sarah some three years later in 1905; the family have now moved to Bluff # 87-B. Presumably this was a larger property, more suited to a widow and her 4 adult children.

It was also the year that my great uncle William, the youngest of the three sons, started work. This was with the International Banking Corporation at Yokohama #75. This position was short lived however, as the following year sees him joining Healing and Co., Electrical and Mechanical Engineers, at Yokohama #22. Now that all three of her sons are working Sarah must have had more optimism about the future for the family. Life was settling into a more regular pattern and the next phase would be Sarah's children all finding themselves spouses over the next 10 years. I have no idea if there would have been wedding bells ringing out over the city but it was obtaining copies of these marriage certificates that provided me with concrete proof of Walter, Amy and William being members of my extended family.

Hopefully you will recall that I had my grandfather Jesse Esdale's marriage

| William Gray (1720-1795) | > | John Gray (1770-1830) | > | James Gray (1813-1880) | > | Jesse William Gray (1855-1894) | > |

certificate as part of Dad's research documentation to make me British! That meant that it was easy for me to make the link with all the biographical data Bernd Lepach had provided me from his Japan Trade directories with regard to my grandfather. However, there was a mountain of other information from Bernd that appeared to show my grandfather had siblings–two brothers and a sister. This included where they lived in the Bluff residential area–addresses that he called "Gray houses" because we could link them to either the "pioneer" Grays from earlier years or to Austens and/or Esdales through the various marriages I was sure about. My challenge was to obtain proof that Jesse William Gray (my great grandfather) was named as "Groom's father" in the case of Walter and William and "Bride's Father" in Amy's case. Even though Jesse William had died over 12 years before the first of these weddings, the name of the father of the bride/groom still has to be entered onto the marriage certificate. On my grandfather's marriage certificate, it states as father of the groom "Jesse William Gray (deceased)". It is one of the fundamental building blocks for compiling any family tree, as it immediately confirms a father/child connection, just like a birth record will do it for a mother/child connection (with hopefully the father named as well!)

Now the above process is quite straight forward normally. Just pop into your local records office and start searching the marriage registers under the names you are interested in. But that is overlooking one small tiny fact. These marriages must all have taken place in Yokohama! That's if they all actually did get married in the first place! Maybe not so straight forward after all. It started

---

> *Jesse Esdale Gray*   >   *Cecil Jesse Austen*   >   *Peter Nigel Austen Gray*
(1885-1946)   *Gray (1908-1968)*   *(1950-present)*

a piece of research that fell very much under the title "a shot in the dark".

I started by examining the one piece of evidence I had, namely Jesse Esdale's certificate mentioned above. It is called a consular certificate and was a copy issued from the General Registry Office (GRO) to my father. Knowing you can apply for copy certificates for any birth, marriage or death record since civil registration began in 1837, I visited the GRO website to see what the score was for all overseas BMDs. Fortunately, I found a collection called Consular Records which was in turn sub-divided into births, marriages and deaths. Here we go I thought, with renewed optimism that at least I would be searching in the right place. If any of Walter, Amy or William had married in a consular wedding in Japan this was the place to find it. I entered the name Gray into the Consular marriages database with an approximate date range that would cover any possible weddings and hit the Search button. Hey presto! Out popped a list with about 20 weddings involving Grays but not all in Japan. However, the list did have weddings for a Walter Gray, an Amy Gray and a William Gray with dates that could well fit. This was very encouraging and I lost no time in applying for copies of the actual certificates.

For those of you who are not aware, entries in the GRO registers only give the names of bride and groom, place, date and the quarter of the year of the marriage. For instance, my grandfather's certificate would be "Gray–Austen; Japan; 1905; Q2". To gather the full data contained on the certificate, it is necessary to order a copy from GRO; roughly £9.50 per certificate.

It was a nervous three weeks or so waiting for them to arrive but it was

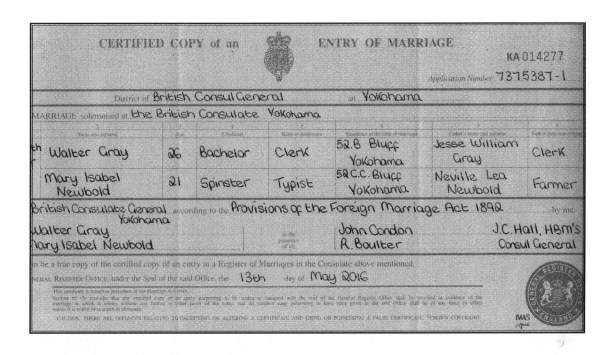

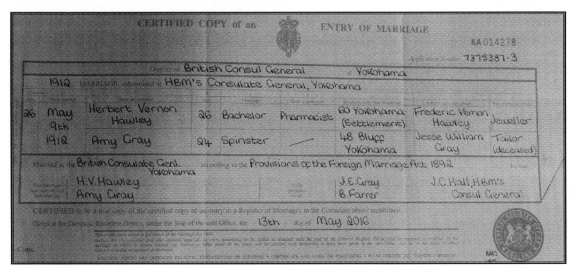

well worth it in the end. Sure enough, the name of the father of the two Gray grooms and one Gray bride was none other than Jesse William Gray, my great grandfather! What joy I felt on reading these documents! Here was the proof I needed to assimilate immediately all the biographical details contained in the trade directories Bernd had in his collection relating to Jesse William's

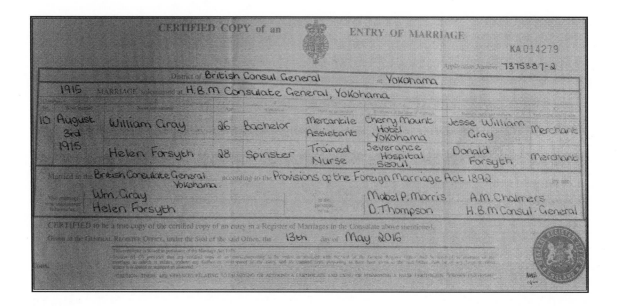

four children–Walter, my grandfather Jesse Esdale, Amy and finally William. I think it was when she saw my reaction to these documents that my wife Jenny commented "it's strange what gets you excited the most these days!".

Fitting these vital pieces of my Gray parental line together has essentially allowed me to fill this book with much of its' detail. In particular, this chapter would have been about a couple of pages long if I had not demonstrated that my grandfather had these siblings. In reality I now feel so much closer to my grandfather, whom I never met, and his extended family.

Walter Gray (1883-1930; great uncle)

So now I shall tell you a little about each of these 4 family members, starting with the eldest boy Walter, my great uncle. Firstly, he was probably named after his uncle, Jesse William's 4th eldest brother. This Walter stayed in England whilst nearly all his siblings travelled to far off places like Japan and America.

This Walter also registered the death of his mother Mary Elizabeth (nee Keetley) who was Walter Jnr's grandmother. Walter Jnr, my great uncle, was actually the second of these siblings to marry. On 13th November 1909 he married Mary Isabel Newbold at Yokohama. Walter was 26 and Mary Isabel was 21. At first glance it appears that none of  the bride's or groom's family members acted as the witnesses to their marriage. These were a John Condon and a R. Boulter together with JC Hall, HBM's Consul General. I discovered what HBM stood for from some later research and I have to admit that it got me quite excited. It stands for "His Britannic Majesty's" and it evokes a real sense of the Empire and colonial system active at this time. Having said that, Yokohama was never a colony or part of the Empire but this link straight back to the British monarchy helps place the event in its' historical context. It was over a century ago and yes, there was a King on the throne–Edward VII. One imagines that the presence of the Consul General was required to make it all legal.

Having explained the presence of Mr JC Hall, I wanted to know who John Condon was, because he was a witness. I finally discovered the truth of his story from a "cousin" located through Ancestry and, on hearing it, I was quite amazed. It would not be out of place in an episode of "Long Lost Family" and actually explains how Walter and Mary Isabel met. So it earns its' place in my narrative and I shall try to explain it as simply as I can. Mary Isabel Newbold

> *Jesse Esdale Gray*
(1885-1946)

> *Cecil Jesse Austen*
Gray (1908-1968)

> *Peter Nigel Austen Gray*
(1950-present)

was known as Isy (pronounced Eye-see) in the family. She was the third child and eldest daughter of Neville Lea Newbold and Agnes Jane (nee Teasdale). Neville and Agnes had numerous children. Agnes' younger sister Ann, who married the afore-mentioned John Condon, was unable to have children. So Isy (Mary Isabel) was unofficially adopted and brought up by the Condons, and was known by that surname. However, at age 14, Isy was sat down and told about her actual parentage. It must have come as a shock to her that her aunt Agnes and uncle Neville were really her parents and that her cousins were actually her siblings.

The Condons were Salvation Army devotees–Ann Teasdale met John Condon through the SA activities. John and Ann left New Zealand, taking Isy with them, in February 1905. A newspaper article stated that John was taking charge of a house for British and American sailors in Yokohama. Bingo! There the future couple (Walter and Mary Isabel) were–in the same place (Yokohama) at the same time (the first decade of the 20th century). So, Mary did have a relative at her wedding–her uncle John who had been her Dad until she was 14 years old!

On the marriage certificate the groom's address is given as 52 B, The Bluff, Yokohama and the bride's as 52 CC, The Bluff, Yokohama. This may have been a building with a number of apartments in it or "infill" properties built after the initial numbering, but it still means they were next door neighbours when they wed. Walter's profession was given as "clerk" the same as his late father Jesse William. Mary was listed as a "typist", with her father Neville Lea

| William Gray (1720-1795) | > | John Gray (1770-1830) | > | James Gray (1813-1880) | > | Jesse William Gray (1855-1894) | > |

Newbold down as a "farmer".

He must have had a reasonable standard of education at school, to be able to obtain a clerical job. This initial academic grounding was achieved at the College of the French Fathers in Tokyo. As the eldest of Jesse William's 4 children, Walter was the first child of the 2nd generation Grays to be educated in Japan. Again, I am offering my best guess as to what the financial circumstances were for this family in the late 19th century but I believe a school in Japan was all my great grandfather Jesse William could afford for his sons. As mentioned previously, his profession was given as "clerk" on his son Walter's wedding certificate. The next generation e.g. my grandfather Jesse Esdale were educated either locally or by being sent back home. By the time this story gets to his grandsons' generation, it is more the norm for the boys to be sent home to England for their education. In the case of my father and his brother, they were sent to Blundell's School.

In terms of Walter's working life, he started work aged 16 in 1898 when he joined Bruhl Bros., Agents of Manufacturers, Yokohama # 61. A year later he moved to Helm Bros., Stevedores, Landing and Forwarding Agents, Yokohama Drayage Co., Yokohama # 42. Both of these positions were very likely clerical jobs although Helm Bros. were a freight handling company working in the Yokohama docks. No doubt they employed a lot of manual labourers but Walter was descended from a family of pen pushers! His father Jesse William was an insurance broker and his grandfather James finished his working life as a newsagents' clerk. By the time he was listed in Electoral Rolls in Australia,

> Jesse Esdale Gray
(1885-1946)
> Cecil Jesse Austen
Gray (1908-1968)
> Peter Nigel Austen Gray
(1950-present)

Walter's profession was given as "Accountant" so my guess is that these jobs were junior clerical roles within the accounts departments. If so, Walter may well have the honour of being the first of my many Gray male ancestors to become an accountant!

From 1900 on he worked for the China and Japan Trading Co., Import, Export and Commission Merchants, Yokohama # 89. I think he must have made reasonable progress as an accountant, because he did become both an Associate of the Institute of Accountants and a Fellow of the Royal Economic Society, London. This information comes from a short obituary in the Sydney Morning Herald of 7th January 1931 and it provides a fine example of how a modern family historian can use the internet to find pieces of their particular genealogical jigsaw! You will hopefully recall the Meiji Portraits of Bernd Lepach as my primary source of information concerning my Gray ancestors in Japan. His collection of trade directories only extends as far as 1908 so I needed to explore other research leads to follow the lives of these Gray families beyond that date. All the key biographical data given on their copy wedding certificates (date, names, ages, professions, fathers' names and professions, witnesses, etc.) makes searching the various online databases relatively easy. It allows you to build up a network of internet contacts including actual cousins. Granted, it does become complicated to work out exactly how you are related but some of the commercial sites actually do it for you. So up pop "1st cousin, twice removed" or "2nd cousin" and, if they are active within the online family history community, it is quite easy to contact them.

| *William Gray* | > | *John Gray* | > | *James Gray* | > | *Jesse William Gray* | > |
| *(1720-1795)* | | *(1770-1830)* | | *(1813-1880)* | | *(1855-1894)* | |

It has to be said that, with regards to my extended Gray family, the expression "distant cousins" could not be more apt! They are literally spread around the globe, including Australia, Canada and America. There are even some in England! However, even many of these England-based cousins share my experience of being born overseas and only gravitating to these shores due their parents' particular circumstances. But it is really exciting tracking them down and it goes a long way to explain my own love of travel. I have definitely inherited this shared "travel bug" gene.

Back to great uncle Walter, as a young business man finding his way in the fast-growing finance and commerce sectors of Yokohama life. On 7th November 1911 he was initiated as a Freemason into the O Tentosama Lodge in Yokohama. In this regard he followed his father Jesse William but he may not have actually been aware of his parent ever having been a Freemason. This is because Walter was only 10 years old when his father died. Maybe his mother advised him it would be a good move for the young Walter starting up his career ladder. She maybe said something like "Well, it never did your father any harm", before proceeding to advise him about the pros and cons of freemasonry as she understood it. Despite his father being deceased, there were plenty of other males within his circle of extended family and friends who were masons, as it seems men from a whole range of jobs and/or professions were joining the Lodge.

Walter's membership of the O Tentosama Lodge was short lived, as his stay in Japan was soon to come to end. The next location where I can positively place

---

> *Jesse Esdale Gray*
(1885-1946)

> *Cecil Jesse Austen*
Gray (1908-1968)

> *Peter Nigel Austen Gray*
(1950-present)

him and his relatively new wife is Australia! In the Electoral Rolls for both 1913 and 1914, their address is given as 40 Stirling Street, Kew, Kooyong District, Victoria. And the good news is that now his profession is given as Accountant, so he is moving up in the world professionally, even though he has moved down geographically! As I am writing this, my wife has Googled property prices in Stirling Street, Kew and there are some in excess of £1million. I have no idea what Walter might have paid for a home in 1913 and am guessing the properties from then are long gone–but it might indicate he had moved to "an up-and-coming area" in estate agent speak!

The timing for this emigration from the land of his birth probably needs some explanation and setting in context. If you remember from an earlier chapter, I hinted at my family's Japanese adventure coinciding with the Meiji period in the history of the country. This period represents the first half of the so called "Empire of Japan", the historical nation-state and great power that existed from the Meiji Restoration in 1868 to the enactment of the 1947 constitution of modern Japan. The Meiji period was when Japanese society moved from being an isolated feudal society to a westernised form. Fundamental changes affected its social structure, internal politics, economy, military and foreign relations. In terms of dates, the period corresponded exactly with the reign of Emperor Meiji–October 23, 1868 to July 30, 1912.

I shall now recap that my 2nd great uncle James Joseph was probably the first Gray parental line individual to arrive in Japan–and the date was 1869. Yes, just a year after Emperor Meiji's reign began. And, as stated above, my great uncle Walter emigrated from Japan in… sometime between 1911 and 1913! That sounds quite like 1912 to me, when Emperor Meiji's reign ended.

By 1912 much of the rationale of the Meiji transformation had been achieved and I believe that it boils down to no more than the vast array of opportunities and entrepreneurial openings beginning to dry up and run out. Putting it quite bluntly, the Japanese were "doing it for themselves"–to quote the Annie Lennox' vocal. Therefore, they no longer needed Westerners as they had done. They had almost used and abused them to achieve their objectives and 2nd generation Westerners were beginning to think they needed to look outside of Japan for their opportunities. Walter's emigration was probably one of the earliest of this post-Meiji exodus, but James Joseph (the first one in) had already moved on. By 1891 he was resident in British Columbia, Canada and I imagine the move to be a wish to repeat much of the pioneering experience he had been through in Yokohama but in a brand new "frontier-type" development area.

So great uncle Walter was now working in Australia as an accountant. It is difficult to be sure of the correct sequence of events but this stay in Australia didn't last very long. My source for confirming this was again the United Grand Lodge of England Freemason Membership Registers. I discovered that Walter was transferred from the O'Tentasama Lodge, Yokohama (1263) into the Royal Sussex Lodge in Shanghai (501) on 28th October 1916, with his profession given as "Accountant". I find it significant that he does not appear to have joined any masonic lodge whilst in Australia, whereas in Yokohama and

---

> *Jesse Esdale Gray* (1885-1946)   >   *Cecil Jesse Austen Gray (1908-1968)*   >   *Peter Nigel Austen Gray (1950-present)*

subsequently in China, he seems to consider being a Freemason as essential for his employment prospects to succeed. Alternatively, the masonic network may not have been so well established in Australia.

By way of confirming that Walter's stay in China was more than a few years, I found records that suggest it lasted for at least 9 years. On 25th June 1925 Walter arrived in London on board the SS *Narkunda*. His last country of permanent residence is given as China. However, he states that his "future intended country of permanent residence" is England. If Walter was planning to settle in the UK, he appears not to have actually achieved it. Because at the time of his death in 1930 his residence was given as Sydney. Thus, he moved from Shanghai back to Australia at some point between 1925 and 1930.

All this travelling around makes it very difficult to gather the basic facts concerning Walter's family life. This is particularly true concerning the birth of Walter and Mary Isabel's only child. Much of the information any family historian gathers together is a mixture of persistent detective work and sheer good luck. Within my network of "extended family" historians, I have a distant cousin on the Austen side of the family living in Sydney. He was able to talk with his great aunt Marjorie. She said that Kenneth Walter Gray (Walter and Isy's son) was her cousin and that he was about the same age as her sister Edna, which makes his birth date around 1916. This is a good example of how I have been piecing together my family history jigsaw. It also reinforces one of the golden rules for anybody attempting to put some "meat on the bones" of basic facts and figures discovered on Internet-based research. Namely you must talk to all the possible living members of your extended family sooner rather than later–before it's too late. Speaking from personal experience, you do run the risk of being accused by your spouse of living more in the past than the present, but such is the cross any self-appointed family historian has to bear.

MR. WALTER GRAY.

Mr. Walter Gray, 47, who lost his life in Wellington (New Zealand), while trying to rescue an elderly woman from a burning boarding-house, was a resident of Brighton-le-Sands. Born at Yokohama, of Scottish parents, he was educated at the College of the French Fathers, Tokio. He was an associate of the Institute of Accountants and a fellow of the Royal Economic Society, London. He is survived by a widow and one son. The remains were cremated.

Mr. Walter Gray, who was seriously injured when he jumped from an upstairs window in a blazing house in Oriental Bay on Wednesday night, died at the Hospital at 10.30 a.m. to-day.

It is thought that Mr. Gray, who was an accountant, of Sydney, returned to his room, after the alarm had been given, to secure some papers, and was shut off from the stairs by the fire, and that he rushed to the bathroom and jumped to the yard, suffering head injuries as well as burns and shock. He was taken to the Hospital unconscious, but made generally satisfactory progress till this morning, when he collapsed and died.

Having started this section of my book with a "Long Lost Family" style introduction to Walter's wife Isy, I shall draw it to a conclusion with an account of Walter's death that could easily belong in a television drama. In December 1930 he was on a business trip to Wellington, New Zealand staying at a boarding house on Hay Street, Oriental Bay. There was a fire in the building during the night of 4th December, in which an elderly lady became trapped. My great uncle attempted to rescue her from the building but was unsuccessful. He only escaped from the building by jumping from a bathroom on the top storey. Despite being taken to the hospital and making some recovery after treatment for head injuries, burns and shock, Walter collapsed and died at 10.30 am on 6th December. There was an inquest on 18th December when the Coroner concluded there were

> *Jesse Esdale Gray (1885-1946)* > *Cecil Jesse Austen Gray (1908-1968)* > *Peter Nigel Austen Gray (1950-present)*

two victims of the fire; Mrs Watson who died at the boarding house from asphyxiation and scalding, and Mr Gray who died at the hospital from the injuries he sustained jumping from the top storey window. An obituary in the Sydney Morning Herald of 7th January 1931 states that *"...his remains were cremated and he is survived by a widow and one son."*

Jesse Esdale Gray (1885–1946; grandfather)

My grandfather Jesse Esdale was actually the first of Jesse Williams' children to marry. He married Winifred Leila Austen on 11th May 1907 at the British Consulate General, Yokohama. The witnesses were the bride's father, Rev. William Thomas Austen and the groom's mother Sarah Anne (Annie) Gray, together with A E Wileman, the Acting British Consul General. The groom's father Jesse William was already deceased. I have obviously known more about this marriage than those of his siblings, since he is on my direct parental line and I found a copy of his wedding certificate among my Dad's "How do I make Nigel British" papers.

Only after I began my quest to learn as much as possible about my ancestors in Japan did I get a sight of a second "wedding certificate" for the happy couple. And what a charming piece of family memorabilia it turns out to be. It really brings my grandparents' special day to life for me, as if I was a guest meeting so many people whom I had only previously "met" as a collection of data. I shall explain by telling you that my grandparents had 2 wedding ceremonies on the day. The first one at the British Consulate General, witnessed by the Acting British Consul General, was the equivalent of a civil ceremony nowadays but particularly necessary for British subjects wanting to be married "according to the provisions of the Foreign Marriages Act 1892". This is the actual wording used on the first copy wedding certificate. However, the best was yet to come.

For the couple were married again–"in Christ Church, Yokohama according to the rites and ceremonies of the Church of England, by me" this certificate read. It was signed by none other than the Rev. William T Austen, the bride's father. The witnesses were the bride's mother Leila Ada Austen, her brother Albert Austen, her two sisters Mabel Austen and Dorothy Austen, the groom's mother Annie (Sarah Anne) Gray, his brother William Gray and his sister Amy Gray. Now that's what I call a family affair! There were two other witnesses–Edwin Wheeler and Jennie J Scott–whom I have still to research. I can imagine that my grandparents only felt truly married after this church service, although it was the ceremony at the British Consulate that counted legally.

But my interest in this couple stems from two other reasons. Firstly, Granny Gray, as I called her, was the ancestor furthest back up my family tree that I actually met. Although her husband Jesse Esdale died in 1946, 4 years before I was born, my paternal grandmother lived until 1968. So, she was then a real live person, whom we visited and talked to and had tea with in her flat in Loughton, Essex. She is not just a name on the tree with dates and places

| > | *Jesse Esdale Gray (1885-1946)* | > | *Cecil Jesse Austen Gray (1908-1968)* | > | *Peter Nigel Austen Gray (1950-present)* |

attached. The second reason relates to something I have already shared with you readers–namely that her maiden name was Austen! Yes folks–her marriage to my grandfather Jesse Esdale Gray is the reason I have Austen as my third forename.

Now it really isn't so bad as far as forenames go, unless of course someone mispronounces it at an inappropriate moment. Wind the clock forward some thirty odd years and picture this scene. I was just about to marry my second wife Jenny, so we went for a rehearsal at the chapel on the Thursday before the Saturday wedding. Four of our five shared daughters were bridesmaids, standing just behind us at the front of the imaginary "congregation". They were all well within earshot of the lady vicar. When she got to the vows, she said quite loudly "Do you, Peter Nigel OARSTEN Gray take…" Well actually she hardly got past this peculiar-sounding first syllable that sounded like something you might use to row a boat, when all four girls howled with laughter and were soon joined in a range of chuckles, giggles and smirks from everybody else! Remember that this was a wedding rehearsal, so by definition the "everybody else" were my nearest and dearest, my supposed loved ones, my friend. To say it was chaos is an understatement. It took quite a long time for calm to be restored and the rehearsal could continue. The only saving grace was that it actually was the rehearsal and a few minutes of tuition with the vicar in a more acceptable pronunciation managed to avoid a potentially worse repetition on the actual day. That's because the other guests were either extended family and/ or friends who had probably never before heard this middle name of mine.

| *William Gray* | > | *John Gray* | > | *James Gray* | > | *Jesse William Gray* | > |
| *(1720-1795)* | | *(1770-1830)* | | *(1813-1880)* | | *(1855-1894)* | |

I need to introduce my grandmother to you properly. She was christened Winifred Leila Austen, born 20th April 1882 in Yokohama. She was the eldest daughter of the Rev. William Thomas Austen and his wife Ada Leila (nee Shapcott). Rev. Austen came to Yokohama in 1877 as a Christian missionary, working in the Seamen's Mission, Yokohama #82. He married Ada Shapcott in 1880  at Newton Abbot in Devon, presumably in the bride's parish which was the tradition those days. Their daughter Winifred was the second of 6 children, with a brother before and after her, then three younger sisters. Sadly, the youngest girl died as an infant. I definitely met my great aunt Mabel Beatrice Austen and think I met the youngest surviving girl Dorothy Elizabeth Austen. These latter two ladies both outlived my grandmother; Mabel remained a spinster all her life but Dorothy married and had a family. We shall meet her again a bit later in the story. Some of my first cousins tell me they definitely used to meet these two ladies, whom they knew as Maimie and Dodo.

Now you are familiar with my grandmother Winifred Leila, I should return to concentrate on my Grandpa. After his basic education, he started work at just 14 years old. You will recall that his father had died when he was just nine years of age, leaving his mother Sarah Anne a widow with 4 young children. I am guessing there was a need for all her 3 boys to start bringing in a wage as quickly as possible. And maybe all that was on offer to young Jesse Esdale was

---

> *Jesse Esdale Gray (1885-1946)*   >   *Cecil Jesse Austen Gray (1908-1968)*   >   *Peter Nigel Austen Gray (1950-present)*

basic manual work. He actually started work at the Yokohama Steam Laundry, Yokohama #125. After a year he moved to Helm Bros., Stevedores, Landing and Forwarding Agents, Yokohama Drayage Co., at Yokohama #42, to join his elder brother Walter. I have no real way of knowing what type of job it was at Helm Bros. but I am offering a feasible scenario that might explain the move. Walter actually moved on from Helm Bros. in the same year that Jesse Esdale joined. I am suggesting that maybe Walter wished to move on in his own career and was able to persuade his employers that he knew of a very capable young man whom he felt sure could fill his shoes, namely his brother. This could all be a wild fantasy of mine but stranger things have happened. Walter would know better than anyone if the young Jesse Esdale was capable of undertaking the duties that he was carrying out and could confidently recommend his brother, maybe with a promise to train him during a short handover period of on-the-job tuition. It may go some way to explaining how Jesse Esdale was able to "move on" two years later into a definite commercial role as below. This move saw him joining Winckler & Co., Export and Import Merchants at Yokohama #256.

I don't really know in what capacity he worked for them but this was perhaps his first position dealing fully with imports and exports. It was something clerical, because his profession on his marriage certificate in 1907 is shown as "clerk". My assumption is that it may have been as an accounts clerk, because he worked as an accountant at the time of the family's move to Shanghai, China in 1917. The remainder of his working life was spent in the accounts departments of various businesses; initially in Japan and then until his death in 1946 in China. This is another discovery that has helped bring him alive for me, as it was obviously this influence that led my father to be an accountant all his life. I also have a little chuckle to myself that some of his accountancy genes (if there are such things) have been inherited by my youngest daughter Helen. She currently works as a management accountant for a business in the extractive industries sector. Since finding out my grandfather worked in the import/export business, I have also elevated his general street credibility to somewhere near that of a certain James Bond. One has to dream anyway.

Jesse Esdale was just 17 when he stepped onto his "import/export" career ladder in 1902. By 1904 he had moved to G. Blundell, Import and Export Merchants, at Yokohama #41. He remained there for 3 years until the year of his marriage, when he joined Lane, Crawford & Co., General Storekeepers, House Furnishers, Dress Makers, Tailors and Outfitters, at Yokohama #59. I like to think he was progressing up through the ranks of finance positions with each of these moves; certainly, I imagine the move to Lane, Crawford & Co. was timed to coincide with his engagement and subsequent marriage to Granny Gray. It must have been important in pressing his suit of an Anglican missionary's eldest daughter to be able to demonstrate good prospects.

I cannot really imagine how a young man in his early 20s would go about courting a missionary's daughter in a rapidly westernising Japanese port in the first decade of the 20th century. The one thing I did notice, in sifting through all the interconnecting pieces of genealogical evidence I possessed, was that

---

>   *Jesse Esdale Gray*
(1885-1946)   >   *Cecil Jesse Austen*
Gray (1908-1968)   >   *Peter Nigel Austen Gray*
(1950-present)

Jesse Esdale's aunt (Charlotte Anne Brearley nee Gray) lived at no.61 The Bluff, next door to the Austens at no 60. Admittedly the future newly-weds were only toddlers then. Maybe enough of a spark was lit between the pair when Jesse Esdale visited his aunt that, when he returned to Yokohama from Kobe after the death of his father, he made contact again with the Austens as the latter were Gray family friends. He would have been 11 years old then but my grandmother was three years older; she would have been very much a young woman of 14. Whatever technique he adopted seems to have worked, because the couple were married at the Christ Church in Yokohama on May 11th 1907.

From their wedding certificate I am able to say where my grandparents were living at the time of their marriage. The bride, Winifred Leila, was living at the Austen family home–no. 60 The Bluff and the groom, Jesse Esdale, was at no. 24 The Bluff. Granny Gray joined Grandpa at no. 24 and it wasn't long before the "patter of tiny feet" was heard in their home. Long enough to move house though, because their first child was actually born at no. 64B, The Bluff. This was my father–Cecil Jesse Austen Gray, born 9th July 1908. I'm guessing that no. 24 was only ever going to be a first home for the newly-weds, because Jesse Esdale had only moved into it just before the wedding. Before then he lived with his siblings and his widowed mother at no. 87 the Bluff.

It is the vast amount of detail in Bernd's collection of trade directories that allows me to track just where my Gray ancestors were living in the growing port of Yokohama. I have attempted to capture this information in Appendix 1 at the back of this book and all the various wedding and birth certificates help

| William Gray (1720-1795) | > | John Gray (1770-1830) | > | James Gray (1813-1880) | > | Jesse William Gray (1855-1894) | > |

me to cross-reference addresses for the various Gray-related households.

Making the simple statement that my father Cecil was born at no. 64 made me realise that a home birth would have been the only option at that time. I suppose I should have known this anyway, as I have recently been enjoying a television series called "Call the Midwife". This drama relates the work of a team of midwives in Poplar, London during the 1960s. And it shows the gradual change from home births being the norm towards purpose-built maternity units in hospitals. Wind the clock back another half century, to a fast- developing Japanese city, and it was probably a bonus to have even a midwife attending at the home to assist with the new arrival.

The circumstances surrounding the birth of Jesse and Winifred's second child make quite a story. It requires some guess work as to what the sequence of events was and also when the true scenario unfolded. So, I shall stick to the facts as I discovered them and then you, the reader, can come up with your own interpretation. In 1910, Grandpa and Grandma and their 20-month old son Cecil boarded a ship in Yokohama bound for London. This ship, the SS *Asia*, had departed from Hong Kong on 2nd April and picked up passengers at Shanghai and Kobe before arriving in Yokohama. Also boarding the SS *Asia* in Yokohama is Granny Gray's father, the Rev. William Austen, travelling to London. The ship departs Yokohama on 13th April and departs Honolulu, Hawaii on 23rd April, bound for San Francisco. It arrives in San Francisco on 30th April. I find it fascinating that this initial stage of the journey takes four weeks; presumably they didn't make London until sometime in June. This is

>	*Jesse Esdale Gray* (1885-1946)	>	*Cecil Jesse Austen Gray* (1908-1968)	>	*Peter Nigel Austen Gray* (1950-present)

because the trip predates the opening of the Panama Canal in 1914 and so would necessitate going down the west coast of South America, around Cape Horn and back up north before eventually crossing the Atlantic Ocean on route to London. I have no way of knowing when the SS *Asia* made port in London so I shall leap forward to the next known date–6th September 1910. On this day Winifred Leila gave birth to Horace Austen Esdale Gray! To stop you wondering, I shall inform you that the birth was at the home of Granny Gray's grandparents (Henry and Mary Shapcott) in Devon. Hooray! The SS *Asia* did eventually make port in London, in time for the journey down to Devon. But there cannot have been too long between Granny Gray's arrival and that of her second son Horace!

Now for some of the possible explanations as to why she made the entire journey from Japan to England whilst pregnant. Maybe the proud parents wanted to show off my father Cecil, who was only 2years old, to his great grandparents. They may have booked their passage on the ship before knowing Winifred was pregnant and then went through with the trip anyway. Or did my father's birth not go that well and Grandma wished to have a genuine "home" birth, with the home being in England. I don't know what the truth is but I am sure that my grandmother was incredibly brave–especially if her sea voyage included rounding Cape Horn during the middle months of her pregnancy. It is testament to the spirit shared by many of my Gray ancestors, going about their adventurous lives on the other side of the world.

After her rather eventful year in 1910 my grandmother remained in

| *William Gray* (1720-1795) | > | *John Gray* (1770-1830) | > | *James Gray* (1813-1880) | > | *Jesse William Gray* (1855-1894) | > |

England for quite a long period of time. I learned this from the 1911 census for "Greta Bank, Ash Mill, South Molton, Devon". Granny Gray filled out the form herself on the night of Sunday 2nd April, at least 6 months after Horace's birth:

As there is no mention of my grandfather, he had presumably returned to Japan after leaving his wife safely with her grandparents. Maybe he returned to Yokohama before his son Horace was even born in September. He was still

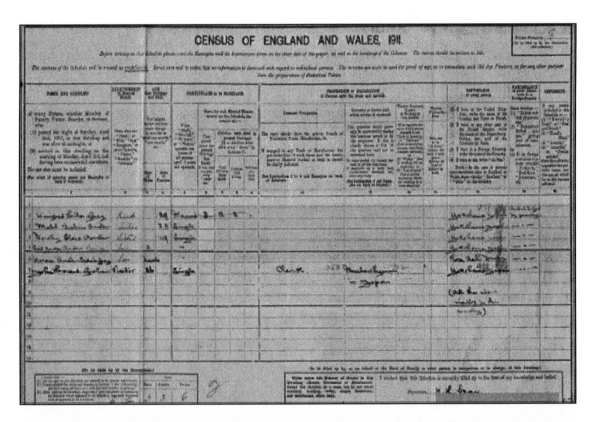

Name	Relationship to head	Age (m)	Age (f)	Marital Status	Where born
Winifred Leila Gray	Head		29	Married	Yokohama Japan
Mabel Beatrice Gray	Sister		23	Single	Yokohama Japan
Dorothy Elsie Gray	Sister		19	Single	Yokohama Japan
Cecil Jesse Austen Gray	Son	2			Yokohama Japan
Horace Austen Esdale Gray	Son	6mth			Rose Ash Devon
John Leonard Graham	Visitor	26		Single	Yokohama Japan

> *Jesse Esdale Gray (1885-1946)* > *Cecil Jesse Austen Gray (1908-1968)* > *Peter Nigel Austen Gray (1950-present)*

working and the two ship voyages alone between Japan and England must have meant a 4/5 months absence from work. I find it interesting that Granny Gray's two younger sisters Mabel and Dorothy are also entered on the Census return. They were both born in Yokohama so could hardly have had a strong emotional attachment to Devon. Their parents were still out in Japan and I am guessing this was probably their first visit to their grandparents back in "the old country". This is when family history research into events over a century earlier can be frustrating. In the absence of answers to the questions raised by one's discoveries, the best solution is simply to revel in knowing just a little more of their lives.

I must just say that I only knew of Horace's existence since becoming a family historian. All I knew from growing up was that my father was the eldest of four children born to Jesse Esdale and Winifred. I shall explain a little later why Horace was unknown to me.

It has just occurred to me that a secondary reason why Mabel and Dorothy may have travelled to England was to assist my grandmother make the return voyage back to Japan. Otherwise, Granny Gray would have had to undertake that trip alone–apart from my father as a 2yr old and my uncle as a babe in arms! Remembering what an ordeal the first journey had been, my grandmother probably could not face such a trip single handed. I have had to do some calculations to estimate when this return trip took place, but I am speculating it involved a party of 5–three sisters and two babies. Since they were included in the 1911 Census, the trip was definitely after April 2nd of that year.

Given my vague knowledge of the human gestation period and allowing time for a sea voyage of maybe two months duration, I calculate that the latest possible time for a "romantic reunion" between my grandparents was the spring of 1912. This is because my aunt, Stella Winifred Gray, was born in Yokohama on 14th February 1913–thankfully after a much less arduous journey than her brother Horace. And born on Valentine's Day; how romantic. Aunt Stella was my grandparents' first daughter and how typical of them to stick with the tradition of family names being passed down the generations. Hence the "Winifred" as her middle name. It certainly makes research easier for genealogists but, in this case, I knew of Stella from my father and am sure I met her at least once.

The family unit in Yokohama was completed on 3rd July 1916 with the birth of my uncle Norman; the last child, my aunt Yolande, was not born until after the family moved to Shanghai. He was baptised Norman William Hoskyn Gray and meant that the family now comprised father Jesse Esdale, mother Winifred Leila, son Cecil (8), son Horace (6), daughter Stella (3) and baby son Norman. I shall return to my grandfather's story later but now I want to continue introducing great grandfather Jesse William's children to you. The next one of his offspring to be married was his only daughter, my great aunt Amy.

Amy Gray (1888–after 1954; great aunt)

She was born on 16th January 1888 when the family were still living in Yokohama. However, it is later that year that Jesse William's career path takes him to the Kobe branch of Strachan & Co., an insurance agency. He relocates

the family to #30 Kobe.

I found myself struggling to fill in the blanks when trying to tell Amy's story, especially when having to research it from scratch through the Internet. Whilst the latter is an amazing resource for modern family historians, it can only reveal information that has been recorded in some way. The first lengthy blank of Amy's story is her childhood. I think this is partly due to her being a girl born at the end of the 19th century. It is probably fair to say that the next milestone in such a girl's life after her birth would have been her marriage, if indeed she did actually marry. With boys there might have been some information about their schooling or maybe an apprenticeship they followed. With girls I believe they were mostly educated at home and, at the risk of stereotyping, "schooled" by way of preparation for marriage and then motherhood. Therefore, I am actually pleased that my aunt did marry and did become a mother, so that I can at least share something with you, my readers.

This is why I now fast-forward Amy's story to her marriage. It was on 9th May 1912 and was yet another wedding solemnised at HBM's Consulate General, Yokohama. Just like at her elder brother Walter's wedding nearly three years earlier, JC Hall was His Britannic Majesty's Consul General presiding over the ceremony. My grandfather Jesse Esdale was a witness, together with a B. Farrer.

Amy was the 24yr old bride, taking 26yr old bachelor Herbert Vernon

---

William Gray *(1720-1795)*	>	*John Gray* *(1770-1830)*	>	*James Gray* *(1813-1880)*	>	*Jesse William Gray* *(1855-1894)*	>

Hawley to be her husband. He was a Pharmacist and his residence is given on the register as 60 Yokohama (Settlement). The wording of this is significant because it means Herbert Hawley is not living in the Bluff, the residential quarter of Yokohama populated by the non-Japanese. From Bernd's set of Japan Directories, I learned that Herbert only came to Yokohama in 1909, after qualifying as a Pharmacist. He was employed at

Brett's pharmacy–the listing in the directories is for Brett and Co., Chemists and Druggists, with premises at Yokohama #20 and #60. Yes, the groom is actually living on the premises of the pharmacy where he works! Not much of a commute for him then. He was not totally averse to a bit of travelling though, because he pops up in the 1911 Census back in England. He is shown as working in Yokohama so he must have just been visiting his parents and siblings at the family home in Merton, Surrey.

Amy's residence was given as no 48, The Bluff. This is not actually revealed as a Gray residence, in my overall analysis of where my ancestors lived in Yokohama. It is in fact the residence of a Mr Charles Thwaite and his wife. They had a large pianoforte business (import, export, manufacturing, etc.) located at Yokohama #61. It was quite common for employees to lodge with their employers, which would suggest that Amy was working in some capacity within the pianoforte business. If she took after the rest of her family, it would probably be something clerical. Dare I even suggest within accounting? Those readers amongst you who are actually following this tale closely, with an eye for detail, will have now arrived at the conclusion that Herbert Vernon was a chemist definitely working at #60 Yokohama and Amy Gray could possibly be an accounts clerk working "next door" at #61 Yokohama. My suggestion is that their romance blossomed during shared lunch hours! My wife has another possibility: Amy was a sickly individual and their romance blossomed over the counter at Bretts when she collected her medication! It's entirely your choice.

I have to make another assumption now as to where the newly-weds might have lived after their nuptials. I am guessing that neither "over the chemist shop in town" nor "with the Thwaites out in the Bluff" were suitable alternatives for the young couple. It may have been a little while after their wedding that they set up home together, because it was 5 years before they had an addition to their family.

Their only child, a daughter Verna, was born on 25th October 1917 in Yokohama. This date takes me past the period covered by Bernd's work in the Meiji Portraits so I am dependent upon other sources of information to flesh out Amy's story. One coincidence with this year 1917 as when Amy starts her family is that it coincides with her brother (my grandfather) Jesse Esdale moving his whole family to Shanghai, China the very same year. With Jesse Esdale's departure, I make it that Amy was the only one of Jesse William's children left living in Japan. This is because her eldest brother Walter left in about 1912 for Australia, and her youngest brother William was doing service

with the Indian Army between 1914 and 1918! "What!" I hear you cry. "Where did that come from?". I shall get to William's story in due course but for now, Amy is the last of these 4 siblings in Japan.

Amy's husband Herbert is described in a passenger listing in 1938 as a Consulting Chemist, suggesting quite a progression in his career from being just a "chemist" at Bretts at the time of his wedding. It was quite difficult to track the Hawley family movements after the birth of Verma in 1917, as it was largely governed by Herbert's career path. As I discussed earlier when considering Walter's move to Australia and as illustrated by Jesse Esdale's relocation to China, there was something of an exodus of Westerners from Japan going on in the 1920s. This was due to the impact of post Meiji period policies on Japan generally and her international relations in particular. One surprising discovery I made whilst researching this period was that Japan was actually allied with Britain during the Great War, even though flexing her military muscles in a series of conflicts with Russia and China.

The Hawley family themselves definitely travelled to other countries, including China, before their final move in 1938 which was to England. The passenger listing for the SS *Glenapp* travelling from North China to London showed Mr H V Hawley aged 53, Mrs A Hawley aged 50 and Miss V Hawley aged 21 all boarding at Shanghai. It is quite interesting to note the ports of call for this voyage; these were Shanghai, Hong Kong, Singapore, Penang, Suez and Port Said. In other words, it was the route via the Suez Canal, reducing travel time compared with the trip taken by my grandparents in 1910 via the Pacific and Atlantic oceans. The ship arrived at London on 19th September 1938. China was given on the passenger list as the family's "last country of permanent residence", showing that they had been living in China until this final trip. On the same listing they had entered England as their "future intended country of permanent residence", showing their plans to relocate there. I hesitate to say "come back to England" since both my aunt Amy and her daughter Verma were born in Japan and had never previously lived in England.

Earlier that year there is a passenger listing for Herbert Hawley only departing London on 22nd January on board the SS *Flintshire*, travelling to Shanghai. My imagination obviously leads me to thinking that perhaps he was returning home after a house-hunting trip, ahead of the family's move to England. How exciting that must have been. By the 1939 Register (a kind of mini-census carried out at the start of the Second World War for administrative purposes), all 3 Hawleys were living at 24 Deepdene Vale, Dorking, Surrey. I am guessing that this was the property that Herbert found during his January visit and that all the family were very pleased with his "choice" because it was to be the family home for the rest of Herbert's life. As a piece of speculation, I believe Amy probably remained in Japan until after the death of her mother Sarah Anne. I have not been able to put a date to that particular event but you may recall that my great grandmother Sarah (known as Annie Gray) had been

| *William Gray* (1720-1795) | > | *John Gray* (1770-1830) | > | *James Gray* (1813-1880) | > | *Jesse William Gray* (1855-1894) | > |

widowed aged 36 in Kobe. She went on to raise her four children alone, see them all marry between 1907 and 1915 in Yokohama, and then say goodbye to her three sons in turn, as they emigrated from Japan–my two great uncles to Australia and my grandfather to China. Thus by 1917 this amazing woman was nearly 60 years old, with only her daughter Amy remaining in Japan for company. My guess is that Herbert Hawley probably delayed his own career move away from Yokohama, to allow Amy to "be there" for her mother until the end.

As my great aunt Amy settled in England with her small family in 1938, she had arrived just in time to endure the impact of the Second World War on the civilian population. And she was very much on her own in terms of her nearest and dearest, as her two remaining brothers were still "overseas". Eldest brother Walter had died tragically in New Zealand, middle brother Jesse Esdale (my grandfather) was in Shanghai and youngest brother William was in Australia. She would have had to turn to her husband's family for any support she needed.

The family did survive the war. In fact, there was at least one happy wartime event for them, because in October 1942, the Hawleys' only daughter Verna married Cecil A. White, who owned a butcher's shop in nearby Wescott. Verna White was still living with her parents at 24 Deepdene Vale, Dorking in 1945 and she had her first child–Michael–in 1948. The Whites had their second child Anita in 1957. These two White children are thus my 2nd cousins, since we all share a great grandparent, namely Jesse William Gray. I introduce Anita

---

> *Jesse Esdale Gray*
(1885-1946)   >   *Cecil Jesse Austen*
Gray (1908-1968)   >   *Peter Nigel Austen Gray*
(1950-present)

into my story here because, at the time of writing, I am in contact with her cousins, Jill and Joanne, sisters who are both keen genealogists. They have helped me explain what happened to Amy towards the end of her life; more on that later.

In summer 1953 the Hawleys had a visitor to their home in Dorking. On the passenger list for the SS *Strathnaver* departing London on 2nd July 1953 bound for Sydney, Australia was a certain Mary Isabel Cropper. On the passenger list this lady gave "last address in the United Kingdom" as 24 Deepdene Vale, Dorking, Surrey! Now I am not necessarily expecting you, the reader, to remember exactly who this lady was, so here is a little reminder. Mrs Cropper was her second married name; she had previously been married to Amy Hawley's eldest brother, Walter Gray. After Walter's tragic death in the boarding house fire in 1930, Isy (as she was known in the family) remarried–a certain William Henry Cropper. However, they divorced in 1950. I find it quite interesting that, relatively soon after her divorce, she chooses to travel to England to visit her former sister-in-law. The romantic in me likes to think that my great uncle Walter was Mary Isabel's first true love, and that she had formed quite a bond in Yokohama with her then sister-in-law Amy. Enough to travel half way around the world to meet up with her anyway!

Less than a year after Mary Isabel Cropper (formerly Isy Gray) had returned to Australia, Amy herself was widowed. Herbert, her husband of 42 years marriage, died on 7th July 1954. Probate was completed in September and his estate, recorded as worth £9,601, was left to Amy. In the 1950s, the

---

average cost of a house was just under £1,891 and the average worker took home around £10 a week; so, this was a substantial amount of money. The 4-bedroom detached house at 24 Deepdene Avenue currently has an estimated value of between £768k-£849k. Amy was now 66 years old and would have been considered a wealthy widow.

Amy's daughter Verna, and son-in-law Cecil were living a few miles from Dorking in Westcott. Cecil's mother Alice White lived a short walk from them and had a lodger Archibald Bertram Du Feu. Presumably, Amy must have met him at some point and, despite their age difference (Archie was 25 years younger), Amy became besotted with him. Verna's daughter Anita remembers her mother telling her about it many years later; about how Verna and Cecil had tried to make Amy see sense but to no avail. Amy and Archie were married within a few months of her being widowed. Their marriage was in the Quarter 4 records for 1954 i.e. Oct-Dec. What happened next is unclear, but Amy must have gone to Australia as there is a record of Amy arriving in England on a ship from Australia (on her own) on 5th March 1955. This was definitely Amy, as her address in England is recorded at 2 School Lane, Westcott, which is the address at which Verna and Cecil lived. In 1955 Amy's younger brother, my great uncle William Gray was living in Tasmania and it is highly possible she had travelled there to investigate emigrating with her new husband. Amy and Archie then set up home in Worthing. Anita believes that Amy re-wrote her will in 1955, leaving everything to her mother Verna.

On 24th May 1956 Amy and Archie emigrated to Tasmania on the SS

Oronsay (Tourist B Class). Archie's occupation is recorded as "Farmer". In Tasmania, they bought Wilmot Farm, near Forth; it meant Amy was definitely living just a few miles from her younger brother William, who lived in Spreyton, near Devonport. The farm is described in a letter from a local solicitor to the Immigration Office as "comparatively isolated" and the house as being old but with renovation plans. No further records have been found about their time in Tasmania, but there is a record of an Amy Du Feu dying in 1958 in New South Wales in 1958. Her granddaughter, Anita, recalls her mother Verna saying that they suspected Archie had tried to murder her. but there is no evidence of this. After what I have discovered about so many of my ancestors, a possible murder plot does not seem beyond belief!

Now I shall turn my attention to the last of my great grandfather's offspring, the youngest son William Maxwell Gray.

William Maxwell Gray (1889–1960; great uncle)

The baby of Jesse William's 4 children was William, born on 1st March 1889 in Kobe, Japan. You will no doubt recall that his father had moved there just the previous year to start work for WM Strachan & Co., Insurance Agency. Walter's birth followed on quickly after that of his sister Amy,  who had been born on 16th January 1888. Considering she had given birth and moved house in the same year, my great grandmother was obviously made of sturdy stuff to start another pregnancy in that same year, 1888.

The family unit of father, mother, 3 sons and a daughter did not remain together for long. My great grandfather Jesse William died suddenly on 6th December 1894 in Kobe. He was buried in the Yokohama Foreigners Cemetery (YFC), where his father James Gray is also buried. He was only 39, and now left a 36yr old widow with four children ages ranging from 9 down to 5. I have described earlier the effect this tragedy must have had on my great grandmother. She was "alone" now in Japan in terms of living Gray family members and had to turn to her Esdale family for support. She left Kobe with her young family in 1896, returning to Yokohama to live with her parents at #179 the Bluff. More tragedy struck the family in 1902 when both Sarah Anne's parents died—within 8 days of each other! They were buried in the YFC, along with her husband.

Now my great grandmother really was the head of the Gray family living in Japan. She remained in #179 The Bluff until about 1905 when she moved the family into #87B The Bluff, presumably a larger property to accommodate her four adult children and herself.

Having lost his father at age 5 only, young William had to grow up fairly quickly through this difficult time for the family. "Home" for him changed several times, from the family home in Kobe to living with his grandparents in Yokohama to the bigger house at #87 The Bluff. I have no proof of where he was educated, although an entry into Who's Who in Australia 1921-1950 claims it included time at the Bedford Grammar School, England. I have not been able to verify this on the Old Bedfordians database and I remain highly dubious about this claim. How could a young widow in Japan afford to send the

> *Jesse Esdale Gray*   > *Cecil Jesse Austen*   > *Peter Nigel Austen Gray*
> *(1885-1946)*   *Gray (1908-1968)*   *(1950-present)*

youngest of her 4 children to a private school in England? My wife had a theory that her Esdale parents may have funded William's overseas schooling, by way of practical assistance to their daughter. Certainly, her father James Esdale had a successful business as Tailor and Outfitter, established on his arrival in Japan in 1867. In 1869 he had been appointed HBM–Army & Navy Tailor & Outfitter, a highly significant post in terms of contracts for his business.

My great uncle obviously received an education of some sorts, because he started work aged 15 for the International Banking Corporation, Yokohama#75 in 1904. I imagine that he followed the well-trodden path of my other Gray ancestors into a clerical job related to accounting. In 1908 he joined Healing and Co., Electrical and Mechanical Engineers, Yokohama #22. By then he is living at yet another Gray house on the Bluff–no 57-A, along with his mother, his sister Amy and his eldest brother Walter. They will soon be joined there by Walter's wife Mary Isabel. The middle brother, my grandfather Jesse Esdale is close by, at no 64-B The Bluff with my grandmother and the newly born Cecil Jesse Austen Gray. Yes, readers, we have now worked our way together right up to the birth of my father! This was 9th July 1908. That means, as I am writing this, there is over a century of travelling my Gray family timeline to reach the present day.

As I have mentioned earlier, my fantastic "treasure chest" of Gray genealogical data aka The Meiji Portraits only covers me to around this date. Thereafter the relevant jigsaw pieces of family history become spread out, with a lot of pieces missing. The element of luck comes into play much more, as does the need for some skilful detective work. However, it is such great fun and extremely rewarding when pieces fit together to reveal enough of the picture one is trying to discover.

I now take a bit of a leap forward along my great uncle William's timeline–to his wedding. He was the last of the four siblings to marry. On the 3rd August 1915 William married Helen Forsyth at the British Consulate General, Yokohama. There were no Gray relatives among the official witnesses (signatories) at the Consulate General ceremony; these were a Mabel P Morris, a D Thompson and a "new" HBM Consul-General, A M Chalmers. However, I believe there may also have been a more traditional ceremony, maybe a blessing in church, alongside the civil ceremony at the Consulate General.

This wedding saw the last and youngest of my great grandfather's four children get married. His bride Helen was the daughter of Donald Forsyth from Banff, Aberdeenshire in Scotland. On the wedding certificate Donald's profession is given as "merchant", the same as the groom's father Jesse William. I get the feeling that this may have been quite a generic term, used to describe most Westerners involved in trade or commerce in Yokohama in the early 20th century. William, the groom, is down as a "Mercantile Assistant" which I guess makes him a trainee merchant! His "residence at the time of marriage" in certificate-speak is shown as the Cherry Mount Hotel, Yokohama.

His bride Helen's profession is given as "Trained Nurse" and her residence is the Severance Hospital, Seoul! I was genuinely surprised to read this when their certificate arrived by post from GRO but, on reflection, I thought "why am

I surprised at that?". After all, it was my Gray family ancestors I was researching and it was a wedding in Japan. South Korea is a kind-of neighbouring country. Great uncle Walter's wife came from New Zealand. I should have known William wouldn't just meet someone in Yokohama–not nearly exotic enough to be part of this global adventure the Grays were living through.

Thanks to good old Google, I discovered that the Severance Hospital of the Yonsei University Health System is a hospital located in Sinchon-dong, Seodaemun District, South Korea. It is the oldest Western-style hospital in the country, founded in 1885 as a royal hospital by Horace N. Allen, an American doctor and medical missionary. Both Presbyterian and Methodist medical and educational missionaries from the United States were active in Korea for decades. This was renamed Severance Hospital on 3 September 1904 after a generous American donor, Louis Severance, of Standard Oil. In the same year, the hospital added Severance Hospital Medical School and the attached School of Nursing. After 1910, when Japan took over rule of Korea, it added new requirements for hospitals and staff which the missionaries, in some cases, struggled to meet. In 1947, after the end of World War II and Japanese rule of Korea, the medical school was upgraded to "Severance Medical College". On 5 January 1957, the Severance Medical College was united with Yonhee University under the name of "Yonsei University". Since 1957 it has been affiliated with Yonsei University College of Medicine, and is part of the Yonsei University Health System. The system has 7,000 employees, including 2,000 physicians and 5,000 other personnel. A total of 24,000 students have graduated from its

---

medical schools.

Given the discovery of a School of Nursing being attached to the Severance Hospital and the fact that Korea was under Japanese rule from 1910, I am guessing that my great aunt Helen had only recently completed her nursing training at the time of her 1915 wedding. So now all I have to do is come up with a plausible scenario as to how my great uncle and aunt actually met and fell in love.

I found out that Helen had lived in Canada between 1905 and 1911. The address was 130 Dunn Avenue, Toronto. Given that she only turned 16 in 1905, I was interested to learn the circumstances that found her in Canada. Who was she living with? Why was she there? How did she get there? Some of the answers came to mind when I researched this address in Toronto. I discovered that it was the address of an institution called the Toronto Home for Incurables; basically, it was a hospital for long-term care patients, those with untreatable forms of consumption (TB), heart disease, and paralysis. The first Home for Incurables was established in the early spring of 1894, moving the institution into larger premises on Dunn Avenue in suburban Parkdale five years later, and continued to expand several times over the next few years. Several name changes have occurred since its' opening more than 120 years ago and the present Queen Elizabeth Hospital has grown and evolved into a 601-bed specialized chronic care and rehabilitation centre.

My theory is that my great aunt Helen trained to be a nurse at this facility in Toronto. This is based upon another piece of information gleaned about her

---

movements in 1911. This was in a letter printed in the American Journal of Nursing dated Jan 1911, written by Esther Lucas Shields, a nurse working at the Severance Hospital, Seoul. The relevant passage reads:

"...Nurse ??? left us in May... we were so sorry to have her leave us. Miss Helen Forsyth, of Toronto, has been appointed to this hospital, but she is taking a six months' post-graduate course at Bellevue before coming. We shall be glad indeed when she comes."

Therefore, great aunt Helen had obviously spent the period 1905–1911 qualifying as a nurse and reaching a standard of proficiency that made her much in demand. Maybe she applied for the position at the Severance Hospital on the basis of securing her post-graduate qualification first. She was obviously very proud of her nursing skills–you may remember that her profession on her wedding certificate was given as "Trained Nurse". I think the Bellevue mentioned in the article above is a college in Washington DC, offering higher level nursing qualifications.

A later letter by the same correspondent to the same journal confirms that great aunt Helen did take up her appointment at the Severance Hospital, Seoul. The following is the relevant extract:

"...Dr Avison gave a very useful talk, then Miss Helen Forsyth put before the nurses some ideals and told of the inspiration she had received from Miss Rose Lucas, during her earlier training, and from Miss Ennis while taking a post-graduate course. Miss Forsyth and I placed the caps on the heads of the nurses who were to receive them, a graduate nurse of a sister training school

led in prayer, and we finished the service by singing the "Consecration Hymn" before congratulations were offered in the normal western fashion. The girls did look well, and we hope they may become thoroughly good nurses.

Miss Forsyth is at present living in the hospital–we hope before many years to have a nurses' home–and studying the Korean language and making use of it as she superintends the work in the hospital."

So, here is proof that she did complete her post-graduate course, and it sounds very much like she is in some kind of supervisory role at the Severance Hospital. I find myself feeling very proud of her, because she is just 23 years old at the time of this second letter–June 1912. The Gray extended family certainly has produced some strong characters over the years!

I hope you are still following the story of how this couple came to wed. Having established that great aunt Helen was busy nursing in Seoul, I now want to track great uncle William's movements leading up to August 1915. The edition of Who's Who in Australia 1921-1950 mentions him "engaged in commerce in Far East until 1924". However, it also states that he was "attached to the Indian Army 1914 -18; served in Persia with the 15th Lancers, as Capt.". I can only assume his business career was interrupted by the small matter of the Great War. It marked the first of his military services in two different armies as, in World War 2, he enlisted into the Australian Army.

More of that later, as I still need him to finally meet Helen. My guess is that it was at the Severance Hospital, since she was resident there at the time of the wedding. Surely a case of William's wanderings causing their paths to

---

> *Jesse Esdale Gray*
> *(1885-1946)*

> *Cecil Jesse Austen*
> *Gray (1908-1968)*

> *Peter Nigel Austen Gray*
> *(1950-present)*

cross by him coming to her. I have a notion it may have been an ancestral re-enactment of a well-known film, but in this case retitled "*The Japanese Patient*" with Helen the nurse caring for William the wounded hero! It's just my theory, and as likely as any other. Meet they surely did, as they got married in August 1915 in Yokohama.

They started a family in 1918 with the birth of their first son. However, I am going to explain how that came about in the next chapter which I am calling a family history research case study. I shall attempt to investigate whether my great uncle William was a spy!

WORLD HISTORICAL EVENTS	GRAY FAMILY HISTORY EVENTS
1894 Opposed to China's influence there, Japan sends troops and takes control of Korea	1894 **Jesse William Gray (great grandfather)** dies in Kobe
1895 In Germany, Wilhelm Roentgen develops X-rays	
1898 Britain obtains a 99-year lease of Hong Kong	
1901 Edward VII becomes King after death of victoria	
1903 First controlled "heavier-than-air" flight by the Wright Brothers	1907 **Jesse Esdale Gray (grandfather)** marries Winifred Leila Austen in Yokohama
1908 Ford Motor Company invents the Model T	1908 Jesse Esdale's 1st son **Cecil Jesse Austen Gray (father)** born in Yokohama
	1909 Walter Gray (great uncle) marries Mary Isabel Newbold
1910 George V becomes King after the death of his father Edward VII	1910 2nd son Horace Austen Esdale Gray born in Yokohama
1912 The Titanic sinks on its' maiden voyage, with over 1500 lives lost; Emperor Meiji dies in Japan, ending the Meiji Restoration period	1912 Amy Gray (great aunt) marries Herbert Vernon Hawley in Yokohama
	1913 Jesse Esdale's 1st daughter Stella Winifred Gray born in Yokohama
	1914 **Kathleen Kent Downton (mother)** born Erith
	1915 William Maxwell Gray (great uncle) marries Helen Forsyth in Yokohama
1916 The Royal Army Medical Corps carries out the first successful blood transfusion	1916 3rd son Norman William Hoskyn Gray born in Hakodate, Japan
1918 World War 1 ends with Armistice Day on 11th November	1918 Jesse Esdale Gray (grandfather) moves his family (wife + 4 children) to Shanghai, China
	1918 2nd daughter Yolande Gray born in Shanghai

WAS MY GREAT UNCLE WILLIAM A SPY?

My great uncle William and his family are the central characters on one of my favourite family history research documents. This is a Canadian Immigration Service form completed on entry into Canada in 1925. It follows the voyage they made on the SS *Yokohama Maru* in 1925, departing Kobe, Japan on 9th March and arriving in Victoria, British Columbia, Canada on 27th March. I have reproduced it in full to illustrate the fantastic amount of detailed information just one piece of original documentation can provide. However, it is not merely simple facts that it presents to me, when reading it nearly a century later. It sets my imagination racing in all directions. Firstly, I try to rationalise the circumstances that brought the family to be making such a trip in the first place. Then I try to relate to how they actually coped with the practicalities of such a journey. This sends me off into the realms of fantasy, as there can be countless scenarios to explain the personnel involved in this particular drama. It has the makings of an excellent contemporary thriller, and I could easily "go off on one" if I didn't curb my imagination. It is a fine example of how a set of "skeletal" facts gives the discovering genealogist a strong desire to "flesh out" the full body of the story they support. I shall attempt to illustrate this interpretation process, using great uncle William's voyage as the model.

Firstly, I considered the rationale behind the trip. How the various columns are completed suggest that this voyage is an actual emigration of the family from Japan, for a new life in Canada. For "trade or occupation in your own country" William put "underwriter" but for "Intended trade or occupation in Canada" he put "farmer". In the next column he has entered that he intends to live "probably in the Peace River District". This is a region in the north west of British Columbia and in 1925 was relatively young in terms of settlement. After a treaty that created four First Nation reserves, the government surveyed out its land as the Peace River Block in 1907 and opened it to homesteading in 1912. Early pioneers cut trails and opened stores and lodges to help incoming settlers. The first community of these settlers was established at Pouce Coupe, which only incorporated as a village in 1932, the first in the region to do so.

I find it fascinating that great uncle Walter actually named this area on the immigration form. How had he heard about this "promised land" in Canada whilst engaged in commerce in the Far East? My guess is that it may have been through his wife Helen. I have already explained that she had lived and worked in Canada. On the immigration form, against the question "Have you ever been to Canada?", she was able to show her period studying nursing in Toronto. Maybe she was the one in possession of first-hand knowledge of settlers moving west into British Columbia and the Peace River region in

CANADIAN GOVERNMENT RETURN

S.S.: Yokohama Maru   SAILING FROM: Kobe   9th March   19 27

Line	FAMILY NAME, GIVEN NAME	Relationship	Age M	Age F	Single Married Widowed Divorced	COUNTRY AND PLACE OF BIRTH	NATIONALITY (Country of which a Citizen or Subject)	RACE OR PEOPLE	IF IN CANADA BEFORE — Between what periods	IF IN CANADA BEFORE — At What Address	EVER REFUSED ENTRY TO OR DEPORTED FROM CANADA	DO YOU INTEND TO RESIDE PERMANENTLY IN CANADA	CAN YOU READ	WHAT LANGUAGES	BY WHOM WAS YOUR PASSAGE PAID
		3	4	5	6	7	8	9	10	11	12	13	14	15	16
1	Gray, William	Husband	35		M	Japan, Kobe	British	English	----	----	No	Yes	Yes	English Japanese	Myself
2	Gray, Helen Forsyth	Wife		36	M	Scotland, Banff	-do-	-do-	From 1905 to July 1911	130 Dunn Ave., Toronto	No	Yes	Yes	English French	Husband
3	Gray, William Graeme Forsyth	Son	7		S	England, Bournemouth	-do-	-do-	----	----	No	Yes	No	----	----
4	Gray, Nancy Kaye	Daughter		5	S	Russia, Vladivostok	-do-	-do-	----	----	No	Yes	No	----	----
5	Gray, Alan Duncan Forsyth	Son	1		S	China, Harbin	-do-	-do-	----	----	No	Yes	No	----	----
6	Gray, Malcolm Neil Forsyth	Son	1		S	China, Harbin	-do-	-do-	----	----	No	Yes	No	----	----
7	Balashoff, Claudia Gregravna			20	S	Russia, Moscow	Russian	Russian	----	----	No	Yes	Yes	Russian English	Accompanying Mr Gray and his family

> Jesse Esdale Gray (1885-1946)   > Cecil Jesse Austen Gray (1908-1968)   > Peter Nigel Austen Gray (1950-present)

CANADIAN IMMIGRATION SERVICE

ARRIVING AT: Victoria, B.C. 27th March 19 25

Line	OCCUPATION		DESTINATION	Give Name, Relationship and Address of your Nearest Relative in the Country from Whence You Came. If a wife or children are to follow you to Canada, give the Address to which you are going	Have you or any of your family ever been			Passport details	Money in Possession belonging to Passenger	Travelling Inland On	ACTION TAKEN AND CIVIL EXAMINER
17	What trade or occupation did you follow in your own country? (18)	What trade or occupation do you intend to follow in Canada (19)	20	21	Mentally defective (22)	Physically defective (23)	Tubercular (24)	Number, date and Place of Issue (25)	26	27	28
1	Underwriter	Farmer	Victoria, B.C, eventually and West, probably Peace River District	Uncle: H.G. Fox, Bradford, Yorkshire, England	No	No	No	#7/23 HBM Consul Harbin 24/2/1923	Gold Draft $5000		Landed Immigrant
2	Housewife	Housewife	-do-	-do-	No	No	No	#8/23 HBM Consul Harbin 24/2/1923	$300		Landed Immigrant
3	---	Scholar	-do-	-do-	No	No	No	#8/23 On Mother's P/P			Landed Immigrant
4	---	Scholar	-do-	-do-	No	No	No	#8/23 On Mother's P/P			Landed Immigrant
5	---	---	-do-	-do-	No	No	No	#8/23 On Mother's P/P			Landed Immigrant
6	---	---	-do-	-do-	No	No	No	#8/23 On Mother's P/P			Landed Immigrant
7	---	---	-do-	Father: Mr Gregory Nandritch Balashoff c/o Tchurin & Co., Harbin, China	No	No	No	No valid passport, carries P/P no 7.0 issued by Chinese Authorities at Harbin, visa by HBM Vice Consul Feb 1924 + authorising letter 15 Nov 1924			Landed Immigrant

---

William Gray
(1720-1795)   >   *John Gray*
(1770-1830)   >   *James Gray*
(1813-1880)   >   *Jesse William Gray*
(1855-1894)   >

particular. She could well have shared it with her husband during a family discussion about "making a new life together" in Canada.

So, what exactly was the couple's "old life" like before they headed out West? They were certainly quite used to travel. The same immigration form details the pattern of births of their four children, between their marriage in August 1915 in Yokohama and their arrival in Victoria, British Columbia in March 1925. And what a sequence of birth locations it reveals! I shall outline the basic biographical data first and then offer my probable interpretation of what appears a totally random set of place names.

First up is William Graeme Forsyth Gray, born 4th March 1918 in Bournemouth, England. Two years later, their only daughter Nancy Kaye Gray is born–in Vladivostok, Russia in 1920. The family is completed with the arrival of twin boys, Malcolm Neil Forsyth Gray and Alan Duncan Forsyth Gray, on 24th February 1924–in Harbin, north east China! My first reaction when reading this was "Crikey! How many Airmiles!!". Having gotten over this rather stupid 21st century reaction (I realised it was more likely to have been a Sea Knots scheme back then), I started to search for something that linked Bournemouth to Vladivostok to Harbin.

My atlas was my starting point. Whereas I knew for certain where Bournemouth was, I only thought I knew where Vladivostok was and hadn't got a clue where Harbin was. The answer was quite a surprise; Vladivostok and Harbin are only about 350 miles apart! I had correctly placed Vladivostok– my wife might say "top right corner of Russia", whereas I prefer "about as far east as one can be whilst still being on the Russian mainland". I have a bit of a hang-up about right, left, up and down being used for directions–when the points on the compass do the job very precisely! If the proverbial crow was to fly roughly south west from Vladivostok for those 350 odd miles, it would land in Harbin–presumably totally shattered! Now I knew where they were, I needed to discover how these locations were connected and why my great aunt gave birth in each of them. It must have had something to do with her husband's movements. I mean geographical of course, not physical! So, what was William doing in these places?

On doing some research into the history of Vladivostok, I discovered it was originally under Chinese rule with the name Yongmingcheng ("city of eternal light"). The area that is now Vladivostok was ceded by China to Russia under the Treaty of Aigun in 1858 and the Treaty of Peking in 1860. The first Europeans to visit the bay, later called Golden Horn Bay, were the crews of British warships HMS *Winchester* and HMS *Barracouta* in 1855. Vladivostok was made an official port after 1862 and designated a free port to encourage trade. It was officially made a city in 1880 and gradually expanded economically and culturally through the turn of the century. After the October revolution of 1917, foreign troops from Britain, America, Japan and Canada were landed in the city to protect their citizens caught up in the Russian Civil War 1917–1922. Bolshevik supporters conducted a partisan struggle in the city. Between 1916 and 1922 the city's population increased from 97,000 to 410,000 as opponents of the new regime, including the White Army, retreated to the east. From

1920 to 1922 cultural refugees from Moscow and St Petersburg founded two conservatories, two theatres and several symphony orchestras and published arts newspapers. After the Bolshevik victory, many of them moved abroad and by 1926 Vladivostok had a population of 108,000, about a quarter of its' peak as a haven for refugees from the internal struggles. So where did this mass exodus of marginalised Russians finally settle? You guessed it–Harbin in China!

Harbin is the capital of Heilongjiang province, and largest city in the north eastern region of the People's Republic of China. Holding sub-provincial administrative status, Harbin has direct jurisdiction over nine metropolitan districts, two county-level cities and seven counties. Harbin is the eighth most populous Chinese city according to the 2010 census, the built-up area (which consists of all districts except Shuangcheng and Acheng) had 5,282,093 inhabitants, while the total population of the sub-provincial city was up to 10,635,971. Harbin serves as a key political, economic, scientific, cultural, and communications hub in Northeast China, as well as an important industrial base of the nation.

Harbin, whose name was originally a Manchu word meaning "a place for drying fishing nets", grew from a small rural settlement on the Songhua River to become one of the largest cities in Northeast China. Founded in 1898 with the coming of the Chinese Eastern Railway, the city first prospered as a region inhabited by an overwhelming majority of the immigrants from the Russian Empire.

> *Jesse Esdale Gray (1885-1946)* > *Cecil Jesse Austen Gray (1908-1968)* > *Peter Nigel Austen Gray (1950-present)*

Having the most bitterly cold winters among major Chinese cities, Harbin is heralded as the Ice City for its well-known winter tourism and recreations. Nowadays, Harbin is notable for its beautiful ice sculpture festival in the winter. Besides being well known for its historical Russian legacy, the city serves as an important gateway in Sino-Russian trade today, containing a sizable population of Russian diaspora. In the 1920s, the city was considered China's fashion capital since new designs from Paris and Moscow reached here first before arriving in Shanghai. Learning these facts, especially this mention of Shanghai, started to drop possible clues into my thought processes for understanding this family mystery.

I now need to return to the Canadian Immigration Service form of 1925 that is at the centre of this chapter's case study, if only to assist you along its' complex trail. Accompanying my Gray ancestor family's immigration trip to Canada in 1925 was a 20-year-old Russian woman, Claudia Gregayna Balashoff. She was born in Moscow in 1905 and, on the same Immigration Service return, she states her intention to make Canada her permanent residence. So, what is her attachment to my great uncle's family? And when did it occur, so strongly that she is actually seeking to be classed as a legal immigrant along with all my ancestor family?

The most likely explanation is that she is the family nanny. At the time of their arrival in Canada, the children's ages were William (7), Nancy (5) and twins Malcolm and Alan (1). You may remember that Nancy was born in Vladivostok in 1920 but the twins were born in Harbin in 1924. Maybe my

William Gray	>	John Gray	>	James Gray	>	Jesse William Gray	>
(1720-1795)		(1770-1830)		(1813-1880)		(1855-1894)	

great aunt Helen employed Claudia in Vladivostok when Nancy was born, since she now had 2 infants to care for. If this was the case, Claudia would have been a young nanny indeed–aged 15 in 1920. I think it is more likely that she became the nanny four years later, when the twin boys were born. But they were born in Harbin, China; was this young Russian girl even in Harbin? A close examination of the Immigration form of 1925 shows that Claudia gives her father Gregory Nandritch Balashoff as her "nearest relative in the country from which you came" in the official language of this document. His address is "c/o Tchuriin and Co., Harbin, China". Bingo! That means Claudia was living in Harbin pre-1925, presumably with her father who is working there.

This scenario leads me back to my original theory that great uncle William's job holds the answer to the locations of the children's birthplaces. In particular, I believe he had some strong business link to Mr Gregory Balashoff and it was the latter's travels that set the course that William then followed. Going back to the Immigration form, William's profession is given as "underwriter". This seems to fit well with his early career history. From my "Meiji Portraits" information treasure trove, I know that he became an employee of the International Banking Corporation at Yokohama #75 in 1904. What a surprise! Another Gray accountant, just like his elder brothers Walter and Jesse (my grandfather). In 1906 he joined Healing & Co., Electrical and Mechanical Engineers at Yokohama #22, presumably in the finance department. As I said in the previous chapter, his entry in Who's Who in Australia 1921-1950 describes him as "engaged in commerce in the Far East until 1924". I'm

happy with that–Japan, China and even Vladivostok surely qualify as the Far
East! So, I believe William was doing business (with his "Underwriter" hat on)
with a company that Mr Balashoff worked for. Incidentally, I also think this
spelling of his surname results from an immigration clerk in Canada filling
in the form just as he heard the name spoken to him by Claudia in her strong
Russian accent. I have found Balashov as a surname when trying to research
these individuals.

I believe their working relationship began in Vladivostok and continued
after Gregory Balashov emigrated to Harbin sometime between 1920 and 1922,
as part of the massive influx of Russian political refugees to that city. In whatever
capacity William was working in these two cities, they were "accompanied"
assignments to use modern jargon, because the ever increasing Gray family
were with William along the way. This makes me believe that my great aunt
Helen may have known Claudia Balashov growing up in Vladivostok, almost
as a family friend. This may have given her the confidence to engage her as the
children's nanny, when she was faced with twin boys born on 24th February
1924, joining William aged 5 and Nancy aged 3! Whenever she actually became
the nanny, Claudia probably made herself indispensable, which was why she
accompanied the family to Canada in 1925!

I hope that offers you readers a credible explanation for these Gray births
in Vladivostok and Harbin. But what about the first born, William Jnr, who
was born in Bournemouth. I think this may have been a case of Helen going
to England just for her confinement. The date is key to this statement. Baby

William was born on 4th March, 1918. William Snr was seconded to the Indian Army during the First World War (1914–1918), including serving with the 15th Lancers in Persia. The fairly dormant mathematician in me calculates he must have been "practising night manoeuvres" during a period of leave around June 1917! The historian in me knows that Armistice Day was 11th November 1918 and so presumably William is away "on active service" until late 1918. So, Helen is heavily pregnant at the start of 1918, in Yokohama with no immediate family around her. Both her brothers-in-law have already left and I cannot say for sure if her sister-in-law Amy Hawley (nee Gray) is around or not. I am assuming any maternity help was only to be found in England.

The immigration form is also quite informative in terms of the travel documents required for entry in Canada. Both parents were issued with passports by His Britannic Majesty's Consul in Harbin, with consecutive numbers 7/23 and 8/23. All four children are included on Helen's passport. Things did not prove as easy for poor Claudia. The handwritten comments on the form state:

"no valid Passport; carries a passport (no. illegible) issued by the Chinese authorities in Harbin (date illegible), visa issued by HBM Vice Consul, Harbin (date illegible); also carries letter signed by the Commissioner for Immigration permitting her entry into Canada under certain conditions, with which she complies"

There are two official stamps dated 27th March 1925, one stating she passed a medical examination and the other from the Canadian Immigration office. I

> *Jesse Esdale Gray*
(1885-1946)

> *Cecil Jesse Austen*
Gray (1908-1968)

> *Peter Nigel Austen Gray*
(1950-present)

imagine quite a scene at whatever Immigration desk there was at the Victoria port office, as Claudia's "claim" to be admitted was examined. All ended well, as the final column states "Landed–immigrant" for the six Gray family members and their travelling companion, 20-yr-od Claudia! There is other information contained within the form including details of funds being carried by my great uncle and aunt, presumably to prove their ability to sustain themselves during their initial stay. The Dominion Hotel, Victoria is handwritten onto the form as their initial place of residence.

That covers this family history research case study and hopefully demonstrates the scope of information one such bureaucratic document presents to any diligent researcher. It provides so many clues to events, that require cross-checking against other evidence to try and form the true picture. It also provided me with a wonderful excuse to "trip out" into a parallel, fantasised storyline–with my great uncle William at the centre.

With his military experience during WW1, his language skills covering English and Japanese, and a ready-made "cover" profession as an insurance underwriter giving him free movement around some of the political "hotspots" of the time (Japan. China, Russia), he appeared to be an ideal candidate to be recruited into MI6! I would not be surprised if he actually carried "Double 0" status–if this existed at the beginning of the 20th century. It almost seems an easier story to believe than my interpretation of the actual facts. I mean– did a trainee accountant born into an ordinary family in Japan in 1899 really fight in the cavalry in Persia as a Captain in the 15th Lancers, marry a nurse

| William Gray | > | John Gray | > | James Gray | > | Jesse William Gray | > |
| (1720-1795) | | (1770-1830) | | (1813-1880) | | (1855-1894) | |

in Yokohama in 1915, carry out commerce across the Far East in the early 20th century living in Yokohama, Vladivostok and Harbin, "attach" a young Russian woman to his family, and then emigrate to Canada with a wife and four young children? Well actually, yes, he did. I suppose I have given you the answer by describing him as being "born to an ordinary family". The more I have researched into my ancestors, the more I find them to be anything but ordinary. And I suppose I should also own up to the fact that *True Lies* is one of my favourite films!

I shall now move on to the next chapter in my narrative, which tells how the majority of my Gray and Austen ancestors completed a mass exodus from Japan.

GRANDPA JESSE MOVES THE FAMILY TO CHINA

Earlier in this story I went to considerable lengths to explain why and how my Gray ancestors came to be in Japan. To summarise the main reasons, under the banner of the Meiji Restoration the Japanese basically invited as many entrepreneurs, tradesmen and professionals as possible into the country, as a way of "fast tracking" their knowledge of all aspects of Western technology, craftsmanship and commerce. In other words, they wanted to pick the brains of anyone who had experience of what the Japanese had missed out on by following an isolationist policy for the 250 years prior to 1867.

By the early 20th century Japan had rapidly re-invented itself as a modernised, industrialised country. It was having an ever-increasing influence on international affairs, and was even flexing its' military muscle through conflicts with near neighbours. As mentioned earlier, Japan actually had control of Korea at the time my great aunt Helen was working at the Severance Hospital in Seoul. Gradually, its' government moved away from awarding contracts to foreign companies in favour of encouraging its' own blossoming homegrown industrialists and native entrepreneurs. It started an expansionist policy and became a nett exporter of goods and services. In other words, it was telling its' large immigrant population, that had greatly facilitated this remarkable transformation, "Thank you very much but most of your work here is done. We don't really need you any more".

Obviously, it was not an overnight change of policy. But it did turn Japan from what I previously labelled "an opportunists' Klondike" into a far less welcoming proposition. It started to reverse the initial "flash flood" of immigration that saw my great grandfather Jesse William Gray and his siblings John and James Joseph surge into Yokohama in the 1860s and 1870s, bursting with youthful optimism and genuine hope of success. They were joined by the Austens, the Esdales, the Vincents, the Hawleys, the Newbolds, the Brearleys– all surfing into town on the vast wave of opportunity that Japan had created by its' open-door policy. The timescale of the turnaround is maybe best illustrated by using dates associated with my direct-line male Gray ancestors as examples. My great grandfather Jesse William was in Japan by 1875 and my grandfather Jesse Esdale left for Shanghai in 1918. Over 40 years and spanning three generations, since my father Cecil was accompanying Jesse Esdale, both of them having been born in Yokohama.

I believe the duration of any individual Gray ancestor's stay in Japan was governed by their particular skills set and how useful they made themselves to their hosts. To illustrate this, I shall use my 2xgreat uncle James Joseph as an example. He was relatively unskilled, being more "blue collar" than clerical.

> *Jesse Esdale Gray (1885-1946)*   > *Cecil Jesse Austen Gray (1908-1968)*   > *Peter Nigel Austen Gray (1950-present)*

He worked as a barman, then as a steward onboard ships, including contracts on the lighthouse tenders. He went on to be a storekeeper, a coal merchant and he even worked briefly in an ironworks. Basically, manual labour rather than clerical. He was one of the earliest of my ancestors to leave Japan, choosing to emigrate with his family to Canada around 1890. Thus, he had just over 20 years in Yokohama, working in jobs supporting the developing infrastructure of the city, whilst having a family. I believe he then thought it better to find a new location that was just beginning a similar pattern of settler development, where his talents might be more valuable.

In a similar way, John Gray (the eldest brother, so another 2xgreat uncle) proved himself "useful" working on the new railroads, so earned a succession of government contracts between 1873 and 1884. He was at a higher level than James Joseph, being in a managerial position, but he still reached the point where he was no longer required. Presumably he had passed on enough of his knowledge to a Japanese "replacement" by 1884, when his contract was not extended.

By contrast, their younger brother Jesse William chose a clerical career path, in particular the insurance business. I imagine this gave him more scope for progression and longevity, as his services would be in greater demand as the city continued to flourish commercially. Jesse William even relocated to Kobe, as he climbed his chosen career ladder before his ambitions were cruelly ended by his tragic death aged 39. His employment path however served as a signpost for others, especially his three boys. In turn they all became accountants and followed him into the financial sector of Yokohama's growing economy. Whereas the first generation of incomers found their prospects relatively short-term, due to being "developmental" in nature, subsequent generations adapted their career choices into more "continuity" roles that offered longer periods of usefulness to their Japanese employers. Throughout this period of transition for Yokohama, my Japan-based ancestors gradually decided their futures lay elsewhere and drifted away to many parts of the world. To stick to some kind of chronological sequence regarding these departures, I need to tidy up how and when my great grandfather Jesse William's four children all left Japan.

In a previous chapter, I have already explained the circumstances surrounding eldest son Walter's moves to Australia and China before returning to Australia, where he was living at the time of his death in 1930. I have also tracked youngest son William's moves as far as his emigration to Canada in 1925. I shall now complete great uncle William's story, as best as I can piece it together. I don't believe his emigration to Canada was much of a success because, within two years, the family had actually moved to Australia! They arrived there in 1927. In the 1938 edition of Who's Who in Australia, my great uncle William is listed as Secretary to a branch of the Australian Institute of International Affairs, with a business address of Kurrajong House, 177 Collins Street, Melbourne, Victoria. And when he enlists for military service with the Australian army at the outbreak of WWII, his place of enlistment is given as Melbourne. In the 1944 edition of Who's Who in Australia, his entry states that he served in Military Intelligence at Army HQ, Melbourne. I knew it!

Proof at last of my spy theory expressed in Chapter 7. In the 1954 electoral roll, William is shown living in Main St., Spreyton, Tasmania with his wife Helen. William is listed as Manager and he was actually running a button-making business in Spreyton, a small town south of Devonport. Two of his sons, Alan and Malcolm, were working in the business with their father, but living in Devonport itself according to the electoral role. William died on 19th November, 1960 and is buried in the Devonport cemetery; the inscription gives his age as 71 years and his rank as Lieutenant Colonel.

I have also explained that Jesse William's only daughter Amy returned to England as Mrs Herbert Vernon Hawley, living at 24 Deepdene Vale, Dorking, Surrey, England. The Hawleys had arrived there after departing Japan sometime soon after 1917, the year their only daughter Verma was born in Yokohama.

That only leaves one of Jesse William's children to follow out of Japan–my grandfather Jesse Esdale Gray. His emigration is central to my genealogical story, as it transports my direct male line to its' next key location, namely Shanghai in China. I shall briefly recap my grandfather's story, to bring you up to date with his family in 1918, the year of the move.

This is another of my favourite family photos. It is a professionally produced portrait of my grandfather's family on the eve of their departure from Yokohama in 1918. I have to

L-R: uncle Horace (7), my father Cecil (9), my aunt Stella (4), my grandmother Winifred (35), my uncle Norman (1)

assume my grandfather was busy at work! You see I have labelled the picture underneath including my Uncle Norman. Yes, the pretty little blond "girl" far right is a boy! More evidence of the old habit of safeguarding baby boys by dressing them as girls. It was when I first came into possession of this picture that I even knew I had an uncle Horace, which later research confirmed for me and brought him very much to life. More of that further on.

My grandfather was working for Lane, Crawford and Co. in 1907 at the time of his wedding. The description for this company in the Japan Directory reads "general store keepers, house furnishers, dressmakers, tailors and outfitters" which I interpret as some kind of department store. Having recently researched the company on the internet, I think the previous sentence may just be a slight understatement!

Under the simplified brand name of Lane Crawford, its' website reveals the company to being still very much in business today. Its' "About Us" web page is divided into 'Now' and 'History' so I dived straight into the history page. The company was founded in Hong Kong, as below:

"1850–Lane, Crawford & Co. opens for business in a Mat-shed on the waterfront on the north side of Queen's Road. Its first customers are the visiting ships' crewmen and the colonial staff and families of senior staff of the British Navy and Military establishments..." (A Mat-shed is usually a temporary structure with walls and sometimes a roof made of overlapping pieces of coarse matting stretched over poles)

"1862–Lane Crawford opens in Shanghai and expands to Japan, opening

---

> *Jesse Esdale Gray*   > *Cecil Jesse Austen*   > *Peter Nigel Austen Gray*
  (1885-1946)   *Gray (1908-1968)*   *(1950-present)*

shops in Yokohama and Kobe."

So that was a fascinating discovery. Far from my grandfather working for a solely Yokohama-based department store, albeit a largescale operation by Yokohama standards, the reality was that he was joining a well-established business founded over 40 years earlier. It was part of a chain of stores across the Far East, operated by a company that would go on to become "a global luxury fashion, beauty and lifestyle department store that offers the largest designer portfolio in Greater China", to quote the Now page on its' current website. With the company having its' origins in Hong Kong, I shall return to it later in my narrative when that colony was at the centre of my parents' lives.

It is quite frustrating that I have not been able to track my grandfather's career with 100% accuracy but, considering he died four years before I was born, I am excited how much I have learned about his working life. There is this short gap of roughly 10 years prior to his move to Shanghai that I have to make assumptions about. It appears to be a relatively settled time for the couple, as four children were born during these years. I know with certainty that the old joke applied then–they really didn't have a television!

First came my father Cecil Jesse Austen Gray, born 9th July 1908. No doubt any readers who have followed my tale so far will already know where the Jesse and Austen names come from–but Cecil? Before doing my research, it appeared to be a new name to the family. I now know that my grandmother had a brother called Harold Cecil Austen. My ancestors never seemed to stretch their imagination when it came to choosing their children's names, which is quite helpful whilst doing research but can cause some confusion with the similar sounding combinations. After my father's arrival, the sequence of births continued as follows:

1910–Horace Austen Esdale Gray

1913–Stella Winifred Gray

1916–Norman William Hoskyn Gray

After a lot of research, I did finally identify where Hoskyn fits into the family tree. I knew it had to be somewhere on the Austen branch, as two of my great grandfather William Thomas Austen's daughters passed it on to their children. My great aunt Dorothy Elizabeth Austen even managed to get it in as a forename for all three of her sons! It is actually the maiden name of Granny Gray's maternal great grandmother–a lady called Emma Hoskyn. She died in 1883, the year after my grandmother was born and eight years before my great aunt Dorothy was born! So why did these two sisters choose to give Hoskyn as a forename to their children born some thirty years later? It is interesting that it was added to only boys' names, which suggests it might have something to do with bequests made for their education. I have learned that it was fairly common for grandchildren or great grandchildren to be the beneficiaries of such bequests in Victorian wills, with the accompanying acknowledgement in the form of continuing the family name down the generations. It is a theory, in the absence of anything else, to "bridge" a 3-generation gap in regard to the name Hoskyn.

I have told the story already of my uncle Horace being born in England.

He was the exception, as Cecil, Stella and Norman were all born in Japan. I am making another assumption now, when I suggest that the family circumstances might have started to change following Norman's birth. The next year sees the whole family emigrate to China! Considering my grandparents had lived all their lives in Japan–32 years in Jesse's case and 35 years for Winnie–and their parents were still living there (except Jesse William, who had passed away), it has to be a highly significant change of circumstances to explain emigration. This leads me to the conclusion it was probably work related, and in line with my earlier explanations regarding Jesse's older brother Walter already having left. What I am really saying is that the very same motivation that took the earlier Grays to Japan in the first place was now leading my grandfather to China–the need to find work! Opportunities had been drying up in Japan due to its' evolving political circumstances, hence many of my ancestors were heading off to pastures new.

Australia was the preferred choice of a few of these emigrants, including Jesse's elder brother Walter in 1912 and his brother-in-law Harold Austen by 1910. This got me questioning why didn't my grandfather follow these relatives to Australia, favouring a move to China instead. I believe the answer relates to who my grandfather Jesse had been working for in Yokohama. I think the settled family life I alluded to earlier may have included working continuously for Lane, Crawford and Co. from 1908 through to 1918. This business had its' headquarters in Hong Kong with branches throughout China, including Shanghai. To deliver on one of their core values–sourcing quality goods for their stores–the company had incorporated a distribution business into the group. My grandfather moved to Shanghai straight into a position with the China Import and Export Lumber Company, whom he then worked for over the next 28 years until his death in 1946! And my next clue to explaining his move comes from one of my favourite pieces of family memorabilia. This is a letter written by my father aged 9 to his mother, asking her to find a nice home for the family–in Shanghai. What a chance discovery, actual documented evidence of a house hunting trip to Shanghai prior to the move. And the author of this vital mystery-breaking document was none other than my father! The letter was written from #60c The Bluff and dated the 19th November 1917.

I think my grandfather must have learned of a possible job opportunity in Shanghai because he was working for an organisation with its' headquarters in China. There must have been strong commercial links between Japan and China and maybe Lane, Crawford and Co. advertised career opportunities

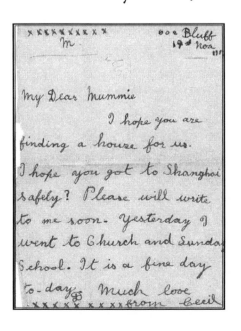

across its' group of subsidiary companies. Perhaps the China Import and Export Lumber company, who were to be my grandfather's future employers, were associated with Lane Crawford as part of their logistical supply chain. The fact of the matter is that Jesse had obviously secured his new position in Shanghai before leaving Yokohama. This is in strong contrast to some of my other

---

ancestors, whose emigrations from Japan were more like "leaps of faith", driven to uncertain futures more by a general notion of the grass was sure to be greener anywhere other than Japan! I think it probably reveals quite a lot about my grandfather's character. He does not seem to be a risk taker and obviously exercised a lot of caution before relocating his family of a wife and four young children. I suppose I should not be too surprised, as he was an accountant.

I think the actual career move might have been more like a present-day cross-border recruitment, with interview(s) in the future location and possibly a resettlement trip to Shanghai even involving my grandmother. Hence my father's letter to his mother hoping for "a nice house for us". Jesse, Winifred, Cecil, Horace, Stella and Norman all swapped 60 The Bluff, Yokohama for a new home in Shanghai in 1917. In terms of my direct paternal Gray line, this marked the end of living on Japanese soil. My great grandfather had come to Yokohama by 1875 and this was his son and grandson leaving over forty years later! This simple statement gives you some idea how eternally grateful I am for having stumbled upon the Meiji Portraits.

This amazing piece of archiving preservation has proved absolutely priceless to me and, I am sure, to a great many other family historians. In fact, as I have expanded my virtual network of Gray descendants around the world through my family history research, several have asked me "whether I have heard of a fascinating piece of work detailing the lives of westerners in Japan during the Meiji Restoration"! It makes me smile every time, because it is through this genealogical information source that I have contacted these individuals! Its' author Bernd Lepach continues to fine tune his fantastic project and share it online. Without his efforts in cataloguing and indexing thousands of biographical details unearthed from his Japan Trade directories, those forty years of my family history would have remained mostly blank to me. And I would not have been able to enrich this story with such interesting personal detail. Where and when my ancestors worked and lived would have remained a mystery to me. They would not have been brought to life for me, in the way that other family historians usually learn so much by talking to their elderly relatives. With my grandfather dying before I was born and my parents divorcing when I was quite young, those normal research tactics were never a possibility for me! But I am getting ahead of myself, "killing off" my grandfather when I have only just told you of his move to China. What happens to him and his descendants is probably why I wanted to write this book under its' particular title!

As described earlier, my grandfather Jesse went to considerable lengths to ensure the family's move to Shanghai was successful. In terms of his career history, joining the China Import and Export Lumbar Company was a success. It would eventually turn out to be his last job change. He worked as an accountant for that company continuously from 1918 until his death in 1946.

My wife and I had the good fortune to actually visit the premises of the company in Yangztepoo Road, Shanghai during a holiday to China in 2014. It was no longer operating as a timber merchants but we did meet an elderly gentleman who remembered the site as it was in its' heyday. We had

---

> *Jesse Esdale Gray*   > *Cecil Jesse Austen*   > *Peter Nigel Austen Gray*
    (1885-1946)   *Gray (1908-1968)*   *(1950-present)*

The modern-day road sign for Yangztepoo Road

The main office building of the old China Import &
Export Lumber Company where Grandpa Jesse worked

My wife Jenny and me outside the office block

The old warehouse building of the lumber company

Tong, an English-speaking guide, with us for this visit and she was able to
question this man on our behalf and interpret his enthusiastic responses. He
certainly painted a vivid picture of what must have been a very busy timber
yard, with a dock area, saw mills and warehousing. He actually told us that
the Accounts department was on the top floor of the main office building,
when Tong explained the purpose of our visit and what Grandpa Jesse's job
had been. He also showed us which building had been the warehouse, still
standing opposite the office block. This was a short distance up from what
would have been the quayside, where the imported timber was landed. We
had seen this area ourselves a couple of evenings previously, as it now forms

part of the magnificent Shanghai waterfront, with its' massive cruise ship terminal. Our elderly Chinese gentleman also told us that the sawmills of the original site, where all the cutting and preparation of the timber products was completed, were originally situated across the modern Yangshupu Road. The whole company site was obviously a considerable size when my grandfather worked there.

We were very lucky still to have Tong with us when we visited. She had been our tourist guide for the previous 3 days of general sight-seeing in the city and we had hired her and the driver to stay with us for our extra day of highly customised "touring". I shall make reference to the other places she "guided" us to, on what was a fantastic day of "following in my grandfather's footsteps", as and when I introduce them into my story.

I guess the move from Yokohama to Shanghai went quite well for the family because, within the first year of moving, the last addition to Jesse and Winnie's brood was born. This was the younger of the two daughters, my aunt Yolande Doreen Gray, born 28th August 1918. If you remember, that letter her elder brother Cecil wrote from Yokohama begging his parents to "find a nice house" was dated 19th November 1917. I hadn't picked up on it before now but maybe my grandparents "celebrated" finding that house, in the privacy of their Shanghai hotel whilst their 4 existing children were safely back home in Yokohama! After all, it was an adventure for them–moving the family from the country of their births to a brand-new life in a city that was fast becoming one of the most exciting in the world. Remember that my grandfather was a 33year-old accountant and my grandmother was an Anglican missionary's daughter!

What kind of place was Shanghai when my grandfather took his family there? In the next chapter I shall piece together some of the information I have researched about it and hopefully explain why Grandpa Jesse considered himself to be Scotch!

JESSE ESDALE WASN'T A SCOT, JUST A SHANGHAILANDER!

Shanghai owes its' significance as a city almost entirely due to its' location on the Yangtze River delta. It sits on the south edge of the estuary of the Yangtze, in the middle portion of the East China coast. The two Chinese characters in the city's name are 上 (shàng/zan, "upon") and 海 (hǎi/hae,"sea"), together meaning "Upon-the-Sea". The earliest occurrence of this name dates from the 11th-century Song dynasty, at which time there was already a river confluence and a town with this name in the area. There are disputes as to exactly how the name should be understood, but Chinese historians have concluded that during the Tang dynasty Shanghai was literally on the sea. During the Warring States period (475 BC), Shanghai was part of the fief of Lord Chunshen of Chu, one of the Four Lords of the Warring States. He ordered the excavation of the Huangpu River. Its former or poetic name, the Chunshen River, gave Shanghai its nickname of "Shen". Fishermen living in the Shanghai area then created a fishing tool called the hu, which lent its name to the outlet of Suzhou Creek north of the Old City and became a common nickname and abbreviation for

---

> *Jesse Esdale Gray*
> *(1885-1946)*

> *Cecil Jesse Austen*
> *Gray (1908-1968)*

> *Peter Nigel Austen Gray*
> *(1950-present)*

the city.

During the Tang and Song dynasties, Qinglong Town in modern Qingpu District was a major trading port. Established in 746 (fifth year of the Tang Tianbao era), it developed into what contemporary sources called a "giant town of the Southeast", with thirteen temples and seven pagodas. The port had a thriving trade with provinces along the Yangtze River and the Chinese coast, as well as foreign countries such as Japan and Silla, one of the three ancient kingdoms of Korea.

By the end of the Song dynasty, the centre of trading had moved downstream of the Wusong River to Shanghai, which was upgraded in status from a village to a market town in 1074, and in 1172 a second sea wall was built to stabilize the ocean coastline, supplementing an earlier dike. From the Yuan dynasty in 1292 until Shanghai officially became a municipality in 1927, central Shanghai was administered as a county under Songjiang Prefecture, whose seat was at the present-day Songjiang District.

Two important events helped promote Shanghai's development in the Ming dynasty. A city wall was built for the first time in 1554 to protect the town from raids by Japanese pirates. It measured 10 metres (33 feet) high and 5 kilometres (3 miles) in circumference. During the Wanli reign (1573–1620), Shanghai received an important psychological boost from the erection of a City God Temple in 1602. This honour was usually reserved for prefectural capitals and not normally given to a mere county seat such as Shanghai. It probably reflected the town's economic importance, as opposed to its low political status.

During the Qing dynasty, Shanghai became one of the most important sea ports in the Yangtze Delta region as a result of two important central government policy changes: In 1684, the Kangxi Emperor reversed the Ming dynasty prohibition on oceangoing vessels–a ban that had been in force since 1525; and in 1732 the Yongzheng Emperor moved the customs office for Jiangsu province from the prefectural capital of Songjiang to Shanghai, and gave Shanghai exclusive control over customs collections for Jiangsu's foreign trade. As a result of these two critical decisions, by 1735 Shanghai had become the major trade port for all of the lower Yangtze region, despite still being at the lowest administrative level in the political hierarchy.

Although Europeans had shown more interest in Canton than Shanghai early on for commercial advantages, the port's strategic position was key to British interests as the island nation declared war against China in 1839, later known as the first Anglo-Chinese Opium War. The first settlement in Shanghai for foreigners was the British settlement, opened in 1843 under the terms of the Treaty of Nanking, one of the many unequal treaties China incurred in opposition to its European trading partners. On the orders of Sir Henry Pottinger, first Governor-general of Hong Kong, Captain George Balfour of the East India Company's Madras Artillery arrived as Britain's first consul in Shanghai on 8 November 1843 aboard the steamer Medusa. The next morning Balfour sent word to the circuit intendant of Shanghai, Gong Mujiu (then romanised Kung Moo-yun), requesting a meeting, at which he indicated his desire to find a house to live in. Initially Balfour was told no such properties were available, but on leaving the meeting, he received an offer from a pro-British Cantonese named Yao to rent a large house within the city walls for four hundred dollars per annum. Balfour, his interpreter Walter Henry Medhurst, surgeon Dr. Hale and clerk A. F. Strachan moved into the luxuriously furnished 52-room house immediately.

It served as the consulate during construction of a Western-style building within the official Settlement boundaries just to the south of Suzhou Creek. This was completed within a year. This soon became the epicentre of the British settlement. Afterwards both the French and the Americans signed treaties with China that gave their citizens extraterritorial rights similar to those granted to the British, but initially their respective nationals accepted that the foreign settlement came under British consular jurisdiction. However, it must be clearly understood that Shanghai has been from the beginning a settlement, not a possession. The British Government annexed Hong Kong, which became British territory, and subject to British law. The land on which the Foreign Settlement of Shanghai was created was, on the other hand, only leased to the British Government. That is proved by the fact that all the landowners still pay ground rent to the Chinese Government.

The Sino-American Treaty of Wanghia was signed in July 1844 by Chinese Qing government official Qiying, the Viceroy of Liangguang, who held responsibility for the provinces of Guangdong and Guangxi, and Massachusetts politician Caleb Cushing (1800–1879), who was dispatched with orders to "save the Chinese from the condition of being an exclusive monopoly in the hands of England" as a consequence of the 1842 Nanking treaty. Under the Treaty of Wanghia, Americans gained the same rights as those enjoyed by the British in China's treaty ports. It also contained a clause that effectively carved out Shanghai as an extraterritorial zone within Imperial China, though it did not actually give the American government a true legal concession.

It was only in 1845 that Britain followed in America's footsteps and signed a land-deal to allow Britons to rent land in Shanghai in perpetuity. The American consular presence did not create a problem for the British because it was never intended to have a person in post. Since American traders in China were prohibited from engaging in the opium trade, their business transactions were conducted under the auspices of British firms. The only serious incident of political complaint against the Americans was in 1845, when the Stars and Stripes was raised by the acting US Consul, Henry G. Wolcott, who had just arrived in the city. Neither the British nor the Chinese governor approved of the display. In 1848, France established its own French concession under French consular jurisdiction, squeezed between the British settlement to the north and the Chinese walled city to the south.

During the Taiping Rebellion, with the Concessions effectively landlocked by both the Manchu government and Small Swords Society rebels, the Western residents of the Shanghai International Settlement refused to pay taxes to the Chinese government except for land and maritime rates (nominally because Shanghai's customs house had been burnt down). They also claimed the right to exclude Chinese troops from the concession areas. While the Settlement

---

had at first disallowed non-foreigners from living inside its boundaries, a large number of Chinese were allowed to move into the International Settlement to escape the Taipings or seek better economic opportunities. Chinese entry was subsequently legalised and continued to grow.

On 11 July 1854 a committee of Western businessmen met and held the first annual meeting of the Shanghai Municipal Council (SMC, formally the Council for the Foreign Settlement North of the Yang-king-pang), ignoring protests of consular officials, and laid down the Land Regulations which established the principles of self-government. The aims of this first Council were simply to assist in the formation of roads, refuse collection, and taxation across the disparate Concessions.

In 1863 the American concession–land fronting the Huangpu River to the north-east of Soochow Creek (Suzhou Creek)–officially joined the British Settlement (stretching from Yang-ching-pang Creek to Suzhou Creek) to become the Shanghai International Settlement. The French concession remained independent and the Chinese retained control over the original walled city and the area surrounding the foreign enclaves. This would later result in sometimes absurd administrative outcomes, such as needing three drivers' licenses to travel through the complete city.

By the late-1860s Shanghai's official governing body had been practically transferred from the individual concessions to the Shanghai Municipal Council (literally "Works Department", from the standard English local government title of 'Board of works'). The British Consul was the de jure authority in the

Settlement, but he had no actual power unless the ratepayers (who voted for the Council) agreed. Instead, he and the other consulates deferred to the Council.

The Council had become a practical monopoly over the city's businesses by the mid-1880s. It bought up all the local gas-suppliers, electricity producers and water-companies, then–during the 20th-century–took control over all non-private rickshaws and the Settlement tramways. It also regulated opium sales and prostitution until their banning in 1918 and 1920 respectively.

Until the late-1920s, therefore, the SMC and its subsidiaries, including the police, power station, and public works, were British dominated (though not controlled, since Britain itself had no authority over the Council). Some of the Settlement's actions during this period, such as the May 30th Movement, in which Chinese demonstrators were shot by members of the Shanghai Municipal Police, did embarrass and threaten the British Empire's position in China even though they were not carried out by "Britain" itself.

No Chinese residing in the International Settlement were permitted to join the council until 1928. Through an informal agreement, by the 1930s the British had five seats on the Council, the Japanese two and the Americans and others two. At the 1936 Council election, because of their increasing interests in the Settlement, the Japanese nominated three candidates. Only two were elected, which led to a Japanese protest after 323 uncounted votes were discovered. As a result, the election was declared invalid and a new poll held on April 20-21 1936, at which the Japanese nominated only two candidates, leaving the structure of the Council unchanged. The International Settlement was wholly foreign-controlled, with staff of all nationalities, including British, Americans, Danes, Italians and Germans. In reality, the British held the largest number of seats on the Council and headed all the Municipal departments (British included Australians, New Zealanders, Canadians, Newfoundlanders,

(above) The 1920s buildings on the Bund, taken on our 2014 visit to Shanghai (bottom left) the Bund skyline at night

William Gray   >   *John Gray*   >   *James Gray*   >   *Jesse William Gray*   >
(1720-1795)   *(1770-1830)*   *(1813-1880)*   *(1855-1894)*

and South Africans whose extraterritorial rights were established by the United Kingdom treaty). The only department not chaired by a Briton was the Municipal Orchestra, which was controlled by an Italian.

The Settlement maintained its own fire-service, police force (the Shanghai Municipal Police), and even possessed its own military reserve in the Shanghai Volunteer Corps. The SVC was created on 12 April 1853 during the Small Swords Society's uprising. It saw action alongside British and American military units in the 1854 'Battle of the Muddy Flat', when Qing imperial troops besieging the rebel-held city ignored foreign demands to move further away from the foreign concessions. Concerned that the Qing forces were drawing rebel fire into the settlements, the foreign consuls and military commanders authorised an attack on the Qing forces to dislodge them. The operation was successful, and the battle was thereafter commemorated as an important event in the history of the SVC. The Corps was disbanded in 1855 but re-established in 1861. In 1870 the Shanghai Municipal Council took over the running of the SVC.

The unit was mobilised in 1900 for the Boxer Rebellion and in 1914 for the First World War. In 1916 the British recruited Chinese to serve in the Chinese Labour Corps for service in rear areas on the Western Front to free troops for front line duty. Many members of the SVC served as officers in the CLC. The SVC reached its maximum strength in the early 1930s when it consisted of the following units:

Light Horse (1882, American Troop)

> *Jesse Esdale Gray*
> *(1885-1946)*

> *Cecil Jesse Austen*
> *Gray (1908-1968)*

> *Peter Nigel Austen Gray*
> *(1950-present)*

Field Artillery Battery

Light Artillery Battery (prior to 1924 it was the Scandinavian Company)

Field (Engineers) Company

Armoured Car Company (1928)

"A" Company (British)

"B" Company (1890, Eurasian)

"C" Company (Chinese)

American Company (1900)

Japanese Company (1907)

"H" Company (1932, Jewish Company)

Philippine Company (1932, under American Officers)

Portuguese Company (1906)

Shanghai Scottish (1914)

American Machine Gun Company (1932)

Transport Company (1932)

Signals Company (1932)

Interpreter Company (1932)

Air Defence Company

Public School Cadet Company

White Russian Regiment (1932)

With the exception of the White Russians, the Corps were all unpaid Volunteers with the SVC financed by the Shanghai Municipal Council. Many of these national contingents wore distinctive parade uniforms at their own expense, modelled on those of their respective armies. This was particularly true of the Scottish regiment, as seen in this photograph of my grandfather Jesse, who served in it for a considerable time.

The Shanghai Scottish unit had only been formed three years prior to Jesse's arrival in Shanghai. Maybe they were having a recruitment drive at the time, which attracted my grandfather to them. It certainly had a profound effect on his self-identity; more about that later!

The need for its' own "army" says a lot about the International Settlement's status within China during this period and helps to understand how and why the British settlers of Shanghai developed their own identity and character. The total British presence in China comprised four overlapping but clearly differentiated groups: settlers, expatriates, missionaries and officials. The largest sector was the settler community, centred in concessions (with elected British-controlled municipal councils) like Hankou, Jiujiang, Tianjin, Shamian, etc., British-dominated International Settlements in Shanghai and Xiamen and the more formally colonial Weihaiwei and Hong Kong. Shanghai was much the largest settlement in China.

Settlers typically fell into three categories of occupations. First, there were those who worked for the treaty port service industries, the Shanghai

Municipal Council or the Shanghai Municipal Police. Foreign missionaries and mission workers would also fit into this first category. The bulk of people in the service trades were working class or lower middle-class. Others in this category were local recruits into the expatriate China companies. I would probably include my grandfather Jesse in this group, having been recruited into the China Import and Export Lumber Company as a junior accountant. The second group were property owners and land speculators; the entrepreneurs busily growing the city through their enterprises. Thirdly, there were the small businessmen and women, they ran boarding houses or shops, tuned pianos, sold books or ran dairies.

None of these jobs or opportunities, or possibilities of access to them, would have existed without the treaty port system. By far the greater proportion of the British community in Shanghai at any one time was comprised of settlers. It was the difference in the "political" status of the Shanghai settlers from that of their counterparts in Hong Kong that fashioned their identity. Whereas Britons in Hong Kong were under the direct control of British colonial staff across all aspects of their lives, the Shanghai settlers were very much "on their own", under the governance of the SMC. They shared a sense of earning everything they had through their own efforts, almost despite any official British governmental interventions. They believed they deserved any rights they had won through their working interactions and the latter had in turn created their independence from British influence.

However, the settler community maintained their distance from the

---

William Gray   >   *John Gray*   >   *James Gray*   >   *Jesse William Gray*   >
(1720-1795)   *(1770-1830)*   *(1813-1880)*   *(1855-1894)*

Chinese people. They restricted contact to their business interactions or, at the lower level, to employing natives as servants. They had a policy of segregation across all their social, cultural and religious institutions. Chinese were not welcome in their clubs, masonic lodges, theatres, churches, parks and gardens. There was a myth circulating through the settler community and its' press and literature that an actual sign reading "No dogs or Chinese" was posted at the entrance to one of Shanghai's larger "public" gardens. Despite being often referenced in much propaganda material around the issue of the treatment of Chinese, later research, including that of Chinese scholars, failed to prove the existence of such a sign.

I hope you readers have managed to plough through that rather heavy-going "combined geography and history lesson" on Shanghai! All I was trying to do was "set the scene" in terms of what life was like for the average Brit arriving in Shanghai in the early 20th century. My grandfather Jesse Esdale arrived in 1918 but here I have identified a significant difference between him and the "average Brit" mentioned previously. I doubt that my grandfather considered himself particularly British, and definitely not English. After all, he was a second-generation immigrant in Japan, having been born there in 1885. His father Jesse William G. had arrived in about 1875 and, apart from "delivering" my grandmother to her grandparents in Devon in 1910 so that she could safely "deliver" her son Horace, I don't believe my grandfather ever set foot on English soil! He was raised in Japan, educated in Japan, married in Japan, had his first 4 children in Japan, qualified as an accountant in Japan, and

> *Jesse Esdale Gray*   >   *Cecil Jesse Austen*   >   *Peter Nigel Austen Gray*
> *(1885-1946)*   *Gray (1908-1968)*   *(1950-present)*

started his working life in Japan! On a passenger list in 1922, his original entry in the nationality column is illegible, because it has been over-typed with "Gt Britain". I would love to know what it read initially. The next column is for race and this clearly states "Scotch". You will have seen some quite convincing evidence for this statement in the picture earlier in this chapter. My wife has her own theory about it—she believes Grandpa may have been confused between this form and his drinks order!

It is true that, throughout the International Settlement, its inhabitants were keen to carve out their identities along national lines, if only to draw clear distinction between themselves and their "hosts" outside the boundaries,

L-R (back row): uncle Bill, grandfather Jesse, unknown
L-R (front row) father Cecil, unknown, aunt Stella, grandmother Winifred, 6 unknown, (2nd from right) aunt Yolande, (far right) uncle Norman

both geographical and social. Hence there were ceremonies and traditions on all the patron saints' days–St George, St Andrew, St David and St Patrick– for the British community. As the Scottish community actually numbered the most, maybe it was natural that Jesse slowly metamorphised from a Japanese caterpillar into a Scottish butterfly. He certainly became a Shanghailander! I found this fabulous picture that shows how much this Scottish influence affected the whole family! It shows them attending a St. Andrews Ball in Shanghai. Although it is not shown in the picture, I am sure my grandfather is wearing a kilt just like his two sons–but my grandmother is standing in front of him! Judging by the stripes on my father's sleeve, the Gray men all appear to be wearing the mess kit of the SVC.

Of course, on parade with the SVC was another occasion the two boys could don their kilts, as seen in the smaller pictures below. Dad is 3rd from left, front row in the L/hand photo; uncle Norman on left in R/hand photo slightly sideways on.

GRAY FAMILY LIFE IN SHANGHAI

Hopefully you will recall that the my Gray family in Shanghai was completed with the birth of my Aunt Yolande in August 1918. I shall always be grateful to my grandparents for this name choice, because it has meant that I know at least one when my family play "girls' names beginning with Y" as part of a variety of word games we enjoy.

L-R: Uncle Horace, Uncle Norman (now actually dressed as a boy!), Granny Gray (Winifred), unidentified baby doll, Dad. Aunt Yolande, Aunt Stella

| William Gray | > | John Gray | > | James Gray | > | Jesse William Gray | > |
| *(1720-1795)* | | *(1770-1830)* | | *(1813-1880)* | | *(1855-1894)* | |

I love this photograph, as it matches the one taken in Yokohama of "Winifred and her 4 children" before the family moved to Shanghai. Yolande was a younger sister for my father Cecil, my uncles Horace and Norman and my aunt Stella. "Home" for this growing family was at 80 Yangtzepoo Road, Shanghai; this was the same road as Jesse's work premises and I am assuming was the property that my grandparents found on their 1917 house-hunting trip. At least it made my Grandpa's commute quite easy in those early days! It was to serve the family well until they moved to their only other house throughout their time in Shanghai. This was 104 Columbia Road (now called Panyu Road), which was in an area just outside the western "boundary" of the International Settlement, where a lot of foreigners and wealthy Chinese lived.

104 Columbia Road, Shanghai—the Gray family home

As mentioned earlier, my wife Jenny and I had an enjoyable visit to China in 2014. Whereas it was mainly a family holiday visiting many of the "must-see" tourist attractions (Beijing for the Forbidden City, Temple of Heaven, Tiananmen Square and the nearby Great Wall, Xian for the Terracotta Warriors,

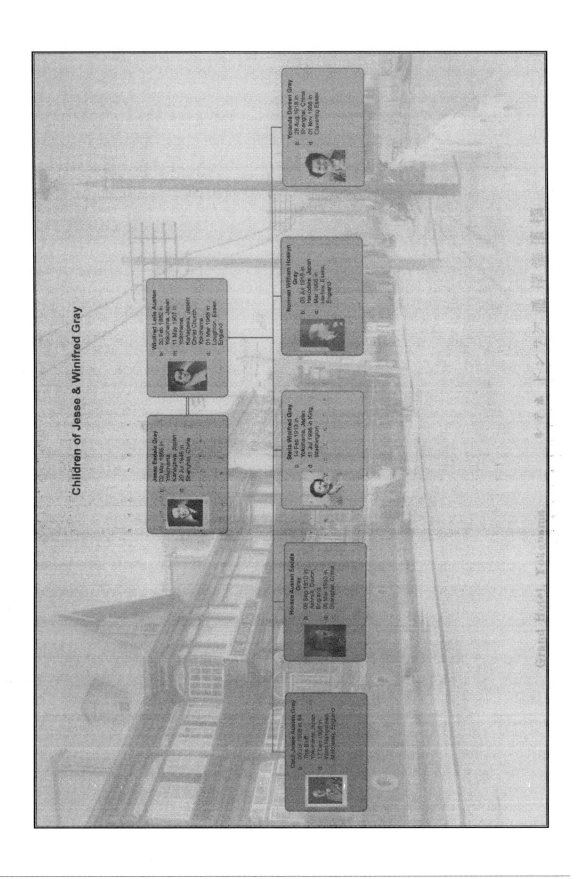

Children of Jesse & Winifred Gray

Chong Ching for the Yangtze /Three Gorges river cruise), we made sure that our itinerary included Shanghai! I have described earlier how we visited my grandfather Jesse's place of work on Yangtzepoo Road. We also walked the entire length of Panyu Road (which was previously Columbia Road) in search of No. 104, the Gray family residence but to no avail. To say things have changed in the intervening century since the youngest sibling Yolande was born there in 1918 is an understatement. There was a substantial property in approximately the right spot assuming the numbering had remained unchanged. But I have no idea if it was the original building from my grandfather's time. I do know that I felt very privileged just to be standing outside where no. 104 Columbia Road had previously stood. It did make me feel close to Jesse Esdale, even though he died before I was born!

Trying to write about Jesse's day-to-day life in Shanghai has proved difficult, without having had the chance to hear about it from my father. With my grandfather's death pre-dating my birth, I suppose my father saw little point in talking to me about him when I was a young child growing up. By the time my parents got divorced when I was about 7 years old, I guess the moment had passed. The whole "family" dynamics change after one's parents stop living together, especially if you add in the extra dimension of being away at a boarding school. Gone were family events like birthdays and Christmases, when conversation might easily centre around the extended family gathered to celebrate together. As an adolescent growing up during this period, I cannot actually remember celebrating a single birthday of mine with parents,

---

> *Jesse Esdale Gray*
(1885-1946)

> *Cecil Jesse Austen*
Gray (1908-1968)

> *Peter Nigel Austen Gray*
(1950-present)

grandparents, aunts and uncles all present. Of course, a lot of this is due to the fact that this particular "cast list" didn't live in the same country as me, never mind the same county! This is in stark contrast to my own experiences, first as a parent to my three daughters and subsequently as a step-father to two more girls! As for the role of grandparents in one's life, mine was not exactly the typical child's experience. The reasons for this are varied–including death, divorce and distance, as in hundreds of miles! Again, as I am a grandparent to seven granddaughters and three grandsons, I cannot imagine not interacting with my extended family, as was the case with myself. One learns so much about one's own pedigree and roots by such family interactions, and I regret their absence from my formative years. I think this may have a lot to do with why I have become a family historian. I have always been fairly inquisitive with a strong desire to gain knowledge, and filling in the gaps in what I knew about my ancestry has become a latter-day obsession. At least, my wife uses this "O" word to describe my fascination with who I am and where I came from.

Back to telling my grandfather's story and the fact that I have to interpret a lot, based on a few key facts unearthed by research. These tend to be the "bare bones" of a life story, such as the births of children, change of location, changes of profession, etc. These are usually obtained from censuses but, in my grandfather's case, we are researching after the last published census i.e. 1911. Even if there were later censuses, they wouldn't have covered Columbia Road, Shanghai! So, it really was a case of looking for clues in any scraps of evidence discovered. For Grandpa Jesse, this was from "fringe" record collections like

| William Gray | > | John Gray | > | James Gray | > | Jesse William Gray | > |
| (1720-1795) | | (1770-1830) | | (1813-1880) | | (1855-1894) | |

passenger lists and freemasonry registers. I shall use some examples to illustrate how I came to interpret the meaning of one sequence of events

On a list of all alien passengers landing in a port of mainland United States of America, he appears as a passenger on the SS *Berengaria*, sailing from Cherbourg, France on 29th July 1922 with a final destination of Shanghai, China. The ship arrived at New York on 4th August 1922. He is listed as aged 37, an accountant by profession, able to read and write English and French. He is travelling alone, with my grandmother Winifred listed as "nearest relative in country from whence alien came". Her address is given as 80 Yangtzepoo Road, Shanghai which is actually on the same road as the premises of the China and Japan Import and Export Company, my grandfather's employer. Jesse states that he paid the fare himself, he has the required $50 in his possession and that he had been in the US before–in 1910 in transit to England. You may remember this was the trip when my grandmother was going to her grandparents (the Shapcotts) in Devon for the birth of my uncle Horace in 1911. Grandpa also states he is in transit to Shanghai, China and intends to remain in the US for "about a month".

I have recounted earlier how my research has "brought my grandfather to life for me". Surely there can be no better example than some of the other answers on this wonderful immigration form from the Ellis Island processing procedure. In summary, I learned that my grandfather Jesse didn't intend to become a US citizen, had never been in prison or an alms-house, had never been supported by charity, had never been in a mental institution, was not a polygamist or an anarchist, nor was he wanting to overthrow the US government by force or violence, nor was he entering the US to work or had not been deported from the US! That is quite a lot to learn about one's grandfather. Mind you, I don't know that Grandpa would have answered "yes" if being asked was he an anarchist or terrorist–even if he was! To complete the revelation into what he was like, his general health (physical and mental) was good, he was not deformed or crippled, 5ft 11inches tall, fair complexion, brown hair, blue eyes and no identifying marks. Wow! I guess I probably could have identified him in a line-up without having seen his photo–if it turned out he had been arrested by the CIA! I don't really know why he was making this trip. He states on the form "in transit to Shanghai" and regarding the duration of the stay in the US, it states "about a month". Jesse was travelling alone, maybe because my grandmother had three children under 10 years old at home with her in Shanghai, with the elder two sons receiving their education back 'home' in England. It may have some connection with his brother-in-law's wife Nancy Austen (nee Grose) whose parents were living in West Virginia at that time. His brother-in-law Albert had himself made a trip to the Grose family home in 1919 after marrying their daughter Nancy in Yokohama in September 1914. The Grays and the Austens were obviously quite close, due to my grandparents' marriage and maybe Albert just said "Be sure to look up Rev. and Mrs Grose on your way through New York"! Yes, you read that correctly–Albert Austen had gone and got himself a father-in-law who was a vicar, just like his own father!

| William Gray | > | John Gray | > | James Gray | > | Jesse William Gray | > |
| *(1720-1795)* | | *(1770-1830)* | | *(1813-1880)* | | *(1855-1894)* | |

Winding the clock forward some 17 years, it is a different story altogether regarding another trip to the US. This time it is my grandparents travelling together and the details come from a US Border Crossing document, recording entry into the US from Canada in 1939. The ship was the *Empress of Japan*, which departed from Manila, Philippines on July 3rd, 1939. Jesse and Winifred embarked from Shanghai on 10th July 1939 and the vessel landed at Vancouver, British Columbia on 25th July. The Immigration form was completed on entry in the US at Seattle, WA on 27th July.

Cecil Jesse Austen Gray (1908 -1968; father)

Again, the bureaucracy of the form provides a lovely lot of detail. In answer to the question "Name and address of nearest relative in country from whence alien came" they gave "Son c/o Yeo Taoong Tobacco Company Ltd., Shanghai, China". From the dates etc., I can safely say this was my father Cecil Jesse Austen Gray. I give his full name like this deliberately, by way of introducing him formally to you readers. He would have had a job denying he was their son, with his father's name as a second name and his mother's maiden name as his third name. Thus, his name was actually a summary of his full birth certificate!

The other clue to my father being the son referenced on the form is who

---

he is working for. A tobacco company fits in exactly with my father's career, as one of the few things I did know about him was his career working for BAT (British American Tobacco). My guess is that working for the Yeo Taoong Tobacco Company was the first tobacco business he worked for in his career. In terms of age, he would have turned 31 in July 1939 when he was given as my grandparents' next-of-kin.

Sorry about that slight digression–it was my grandfather Jesse's journeys we were following. From the immigration paperwork for this 1939 trip to America, I learned that the duration was to be for "less than 60 days". This time I am sure that the purpose of the visit was to visit close family, namely his brother-in-law (and hence my great uncle) Albert Austen. Albert was born in Yokohama on 5th October 1880 which makes him about five years older than my grandfather. They obviously first met when my grandfather was courting Winifred in Yokohama, leading up to their eventual wedding in 1907. Albert was actually one of their witnesses at the ceremony, performed by his father– Rev. Austen who was, of course, also "father of the bride". The two men were to become close friends, such that they were still in touch over forty years later. I know this because of another "treasure chest" of priceless supporting evidence that came to me via my 1st cousin Tony, when I met him for the first time ever only in 2019. I knew him as the only son of my aunt Stella but, as will become clear from later on in my story, our paths never crossed until now. Amongst these hidden family history gems are a number of letters between my grandparents and Albert and his future wife Nancy.

Nancy Virginia Grose was born in Clay County, West Virginia on 4th June 1880 and arrived in Yokohama on 2nd October 1908, to work as a teacher. I don't really know how large the pool of eligible young ladies as potential brides was for a young Westerner growing up in Yokohama during this period. However, this latest recruit, and an American citizen to boot, must have attracted the attention of my great uncle Albert, for they were duly married on 19th September 1914. Their wedding photograph here is one of the few I have from the Yokohama period and is one of my favourites, as there are so many of my relatives in the picture. The bride Nancy Grose and the groom Albert Austen are seated on the front row. The young boy dressed in the sailor suit to the left of the groom is my father Cecil and his "shipmate" standing to the right of the bride is his younger brother, my uncle Horace. He is standing next to my great grandmother Leila Ada Austen, the older lady just to the right of the bride. The lady carrying the young child in her arms is my grandmother Winifred Leila Gray, and the child is my aunt Stella Gray. Also, on the middle

---

row, are my two great aunts; Mabel is second from the right and her sister
Dorothy is second from the left, both obviously part of the bridal party as
they are carrying bouquets. The older gentleman with white hair and a white
beard towards the left of the middle row is my great grandfather, Rev. William
Thomas Austen. The groom's elder brothers are on the back row; furthest right
is my grandfather Jesse Esdale Gray; 2nd from the right is my great uncle
Walter Gray.

I really love this picture, as it acts like my own time machine. It immediately
transports me back over a century to the other side of the world, such that I
feel like a "fly on the wall" at this amazing family occasion. It was probably
the first time my father had a role to play at a wedding, as a pageboy with
his young brother. He wasn't to know then that he would actually play the
groom's role at three weddings in the future! But more of that later. I have a
little chuckle to myself, seeing him in a sailor suit–as he did actually join "the
Senior Service" as he called it much later in his life! I get the impression that
the two couples–my grandfather Jesse, his wife Winifred, her brother Albert
and his wife Nancy–became good friends and socialised together in the busy,
bustling city port that was Yokohama in the early 20th century.

However, it was also a time of change in Yokohama as Japan had achieved
its' transformation from an isolated country with a feudal-like system to a
modernised, industrialised nation beginning to wield greater influence on the
international stage. It had become a world power and begun an expansionist
policy, that saw it controlling areas beyond its' national border in the wider

| William Gray (1720-1795) | > | John Gray (1770-1830) | > | James Gray (1813-1880) | > | Jesse William Gray (1855-1894) | > |

Far East. The opportunities for Westerners in Japan were reducing, as they outlived their usefulness and overstayed their welcome. Against this changing backdrop, both my grandfather Jesse and my great uncle Albert began to realise their long-term futures probably lay elsewhere. I have explained that Jesse's answer was to emigrate to Shanghai in 1918, which meant he was the first of the pair to leave. I originally thought the catalyst for Albert's emigration related to one of the most devastating acts of nature ever to strike the world, namely the Great Kanto earthquake of 1923. But now I am not so sure, due to some incredible first-hand information about this tragedy, contained in a letter written by my great grandfather, Rev. Austen–who was very definitely caught up in this disaster

The earthquake struck the Kanto Plain on the Japanese main island of Honshu at 11:58 am on the 1st September, 1923. Varied accounts indicate the duration of the quake was between four and ten minutes. There was a total of 57 aftershocks, with six registering a magnitude of 7.0 M or more. It created a tsunami of up to 12 metres depth. The timing of the original shockwave, at lunchtime when people were cooking over open fires, caused widespread fires which the associated typhoon turned into fireballs that engulfed the city. The earthquake devastated Tokyo, the port city of Yokohama and the surrounding prefectures of Chiba, Kanagawa and Shizuoko. The earthquake's force was so great that in Kamakura, over 37 miles from the epicentre, it actually moved the 84-ton Great Buddha statue almost two feet. The overall death toll, including 40,000 missing people presumed killed, totalled 142,000. Over 570,000 homes

---

were destroyed, leaving an estimated 1.9 million homeless. The damage is estimated to have exceeded $15 billion in today's values.

These facts and figures concerning the tragedy are "in the public domain" to use current journalistic language; I researched them across the internet including Wikipedia. If this had happened nowadays, I can imagine the intense scramble amongst any on-the-spot news reporters to get that "Holy Grail" of scoops–an eye witness interview. Imagine my excitement when I discovered the letter below amongst my grandparents' documents held by my cousin Tony. It is written by my great grandfather, Rev. Thomas Austen to his daughter-in-law Nancy:

80 Yangztepoo Road, Shanghai,

24 October 1923

Dear Nancy

On the 1st of Sept. I went into the village at Kanuikawa and when returning I was halfway to the house just about noon when the earth began to quake all about me severely and I had to stand squarely with my feet well apart and both hands on my walking stick to prevent myself from being thrown down. The earth was swaying all about me and the people in the house near me were grouped together greatly alarmed, and I distinctly heard the noise of breaking crockery inside their house. When I reached Greta Bank the guests, ayahs, Mother and Mabel were all outside. Bishop Welch came towards me saying "this is the severest earthquake I have experienced". I went upstairs into the

---

various rooms, and found a good deal of plaster had fallen from the walls, and broken crockery in most of the rooms. For some time after minor shocks were felt, also through the night, so that most of the guests would not go upstairs to sleep, but slept or dozed about anywhere downstairs.

We got no news of what had been happening in Tokyo and Yokohama till the next day & then nothing definite. It was several days before we heard what awful destruction had been done in those cities and many other districts. We could learn no news of Mr Sheriff, 60c and 234d, until Thursday noon, when Mr Sneyd brought us a letter from Otomisan, and the news that 60c was all gone & the whole compound practically in the street, the sustain wall having broken down. As soon as ladies were allowed to travel Mother, Mabel and Mr Sheriff who had arrived from Kobe, visited Yokohama and Kamakura, sleeping on Mr Robson's lawn one night, and among the debris of the two Kamakura Cottages the next night. They told me on their return that the whole thing was indescribably sad and awful. The whole city, the Bluff included was gone, the only buildings standing in the City were the Kencho(?) and the Y.Specie bank, and the latter was gutted inside. 234d was burnt to ashes, portions of the Bluff were down on the reclaimed ground below. Those on the Bluff who were not killed escaped with the help of ropes from the R.M.Hospital also down the cliff to the reclamation ground. Ferris Somenary(?) totally collapsed & part went down into Motomachi, Miss Kuyper was buried under the ruins. Retz's(?) flats building also toppled over and fell down the adjoining hill, all the churches were a mass of ruins. The Cemetery likewise, the memorial Arch broken to pieces, & most of the gravestones and monuments all down and broken, the various roads to the Bluff all broken and in big fissures, and unpassable. In fact, I might write hundreds of pages and yet you would get but the faintest description of the awful calamity. Yokohama as you knew it is nothing now but a wilderness of debris everywhere and unrecognizable. Even when Mother went down they were still burning hundreds of bodies every day as they were recovered from the ruined City.

As soon as we got the definite news that we had lost everything we had and that you also were both in the same position I sent you a wire, also Winnie, Harold and Dorothy. Unfortunately, neither yours or our silver were in the Bank strong room which escaped, yours according to Albert's instruction was in the godower(?) at No 100, and ours in Mr Sheriff's godower. As I wrote the other day we are here at Winnie's, the Sheriffs included, and shall probably remain through the coming winter. I shall D.V. try to arrange to see you both next spring. Leaving this by the E. of Australia about the middle of March, I hope it won't be too cold for me in East Orange early in April?

Do let me have a letter I have not had one for at least three months past. Yesterday Mother gave me one to read that you had sent her, very many thanks for the loving sympathy it contained & also the offers of help re-clothing etc.

With fondest love to you both, I remain as ever yours affectionately
Father.

Reading this letter, some 96 years after my great grandfather wrote it, absolutely blew me away. Talk about bringing my ancestors to life for me! I

| *William Gray* | > | *John Gray* | > | *James Gray* | > | *Jesse William Gray* | > |
| *(1720-1795)* | | *(1770-1830)* | | *(1813-1880)* | | *(1855-1894)* | |

have used this expression many times regarding information I have discovered doing my research but I think this illustrates it perfectly. He puts the address from where he sent the letter–this is my grandparents' house in Shanghai which is his first stopover on his return journey to England after the disaster. He talks about arriving at "Greta Bank"–this was the name of his in-laws' property in Devon where my grandmother stayed after giving birth to my uncle Horace; he obviously chose to use it for a hostel-type premises near Kanuikawa in the hills inland from Yokohama. He talks about the Bluff, the residential area in Yokohama where so many of my ancestors lived, particularly at nos.60 and 234. He tells what happens to my great grandmother (Mother) and my great aunt (Mabel) as well as mentioning all his other children (Winnie–my grandmother, Harold and Dorothy). He writes so expressively that I felt I was sharing his emotions surrounding this catastrophic event in the family's history. That's what you call a "first-hand account"!

So, this is how I knew that my great grandparents, Rev. William and Leila Austen, definitely were among the 1.9 million left homeless by the earthquake. He was chaplain at the Yokohama Seaman's Mission, located permanently from the beginning at #82-B Yokohama. The family was living at #60 The Bluff, also known as "Sunnyside". They lost everything in the earthquake–except their lives which, given the scale of the disaster and the number of deaths, was itself a minor miracle. They left Yokohama in the aftermath of the disaster, returning to England. My great grandfather eventually became the vicar of the parish of North Shoebury, near Southend-on-Sea, Essex.

	Jesse Esdale Gray		*Cecil Jesse Austen*		*Peter Nigel Austen Gray*
>	*(1885-1946)*	>	*Gray (1908-1968)*	>	*(1950-present)*

The exact timing of my great grandparents' trip to England is unclear but it would appear that Rev. Austen started his voyage in Shanghai with a stopover in the US on his way. The timeline of events after the quake goes like this:

1/9/1923   *the earthquake strikes Yokohama; my great grandparents are in Yokohama*

22/2/1924   SS **Empress of India** *departs Hong Kong, bound for London; my great grandfather Rev. Austen boards at Shanghai; he is travelling alone. He had been staying with his daughter Winifred (my grandmother) and the family–her husband Jesse and their 3 younger children Stella, Norman, and Yolande. The 2 elder boys were at school in England*

20/3/1924   *Great grandfather enters the US from Canada, as the ship had landed at Vancouver; he states he is in transit, intending to remain in US for 14 days; his visa (or the immigration paperwork at least) classifies him as a tourist;*

12/4/1924   *Rev. Austen departs US from New York to complete his voyage to England; perhaps he took the train across America to save the sea voyage*

As with most such passenger listings, they provide me with lots of details but still present lots of questions. Bearing in mind my great grandfather was 77 years old at the time of this trip, it seems there has to be more to the trip than tourism! Who was he visiting in the US? I have tried to solve this riddle but again I am left guessing from a few clues. I have explained how my grandfather

Jesse had been to New York two years earlier, probably visiting his brother-in-law's in-laws! By that I mean the Groses in West Virginia. The brother-in-law in question was Albert Austen, eldest son of Rev. Austen, so maybe he was just visiting them in West Virginia on his way home to England.

It is extremely difficult "placing" my much-travelled ancestors at any one moment on their timeline. For instance, where were my great uncle Albert and his wife Nancy when the earthquake struck Kanto? They were married on 19th September 1914 in Yokohama. They gave Nancy's parents in West Virginia as the address they were staying at in 1919. Their next definitive movement was their emigration trip in August 1926 to California. They made the crossing on the SS *Carmania*, which departed Southampton 21st August 1926 and arrived in New York on 29th August. On another of the wonderfully detailed Immigration documents covering this trip, they gave Rev. Austen and the Vicarage at North Shoebury, Essex as "relative and address from whence the alien came". Albert had obviously visited his father in this new "post-earthquake" home. On the same form, Albert details two earlier trips to New York–March 1919 and February 1925. I have already informed you readers about the earlier trip, to see his Grose in-laws in West Virginia. I assume the 1925 trip was an exploratory visit, in preparation for emigrating. My great uncle gave his occupation as relief worker and gave an organisation called Near East Relief at 151 Fifth Avenue, New York as the contact address in the US, with the note "business".

The next obvious Google search for me was into Near East Relief. Wow!

What a discovery that was and it has informed me greatly of a shocking episode from world history that had essentially passed me by. I discovered that the Near East Foundation (NEF), formerly the American Committee for Armenian and Syrian Relief (ACASR), then the American Committee for Relief in the Near East (ACRNE), and later Near East Relief, is a Syracuse, New York-based American international social and economic development organisation.

Founded in 1915, it is the United States' oldest non-sectarian international development organisation and the second American humanitarian organisation to be chartered by an act of Congress. Near East Relief organised the world's first large-scale, modern humanitarian project in response to the unfolding Armenian and Assyrian genocides. Known as the Near East Foundation since 1930, NEF pioneered many of the strategies employed by the world's leading development organisations. In the past 100 years NEF has worked with partner communities in more than 40 countries. The foundation had organised the world's first great humanitarian project of the United States, in the beginning of the 20th century. From 1915 to 1930, Near East Relief saved the lives of over a million refugees, including 132,000 orphans who were cared for and educated in Near East Relief orphanages. Near East Relief also mobilized the American people to raise over $116 million for direct relief. Nearly 1,000 U.S. citizens volunteered to travel overseas. Workers from Near East Relief built hundreds of orphanages, vocational schools, and food distributions centres. Overseas relief workers were responsible for the direct care of orphans and refugees, including the organization of vast feeding and educational programs.

Thousands of Americans volunteered throughout the U.S. by donating money or supplies and hosting special events to benefit Near East Relief's work.

I find it astonishing that I had previously known nothing of the events that led to this early 20th century genocide. The Armenian Genocide, also known as the Armenian Holocaust, was the Ottoman government's systematic extermination of 1.5 million Armenians, mostly citizens within the Ottoman Empire. The starting date is conventionally held to be 24 April 1915, the day that Ottoman authorities rounded up, arrested, and deported, from Constantinople (now Istanbul) to the region of Ankara, 235 to 270 Armenian intellectuals and community leaders, the majority of whom were eventually murdered. The genocide was carried out during and after World War I and implemented in two phases–the wholesale killing of the able-bodied male population through massacre and subjection of army conscripts to forced labour, followed by the deportation of women, children, the elderly, and the infirm on death marches leading to the Syrian Desert. Driven forward by military escorts, the deportees were deprived of food and water and subjected to periodic robbery, rape, and massacre. Other ethnic groups were similarly targeted for extermination in the Assyrian genocide and the Greek genocide, and their treatment is considered by some historians to be part of the same genocidal policy. Most Armenian diaspora communities around the world came into being as a direct result of the genocide. Raphael Lemkin (a lawyer of Polish-Jewish descent) was moved specifically by the annihilation of the Armenians to define systematic and premeditated exterminations within legal parameters and coin the word

---

> *Jesse Esdale Gray*
(1885-1946)

> *Cecil Jesse Austen*
Gray (1908-1968)

> *Peter Nigel Austen Gray*
(1950-present)

genocide in 1943. The Armenian Genocide is acknowledged to have been one of the first modern genocides, because scholars point to the organised manner in which the killings were carried out. It is the second most-studied case of genocide after the Holocaust, and yet I have only learned of it as part of my only family history research. If my great uncle Albert had not joined this organisation as a relief worker, I might have remained ignorant of the facts forever.

It was another case of "genealogical jigsaw pieces" fitting together after further research. On his application form seeking US naturalisation in 1926, my great uncle Albert had given Beirut, Syria as his last place of residence! Syria was one of the focal points of the humanitarian relief efforts being undertaken by Near East Relief, and I am guessing maybe both Albert and his wife Nancy were active "in the field" in Syria. Nancy had gone to Japan originally as a teacher, so maybe she was teaching some of the thousands of Armenian orphans being cared for by Near East Relief workers like her husband.

If you readers are still with me, this evidence of Albert and Nancy having lived in Syria prior to 1926 leads me to believe that Albert had been a relief worker for Near East Relief from around 1919. I am suggesting that he heard of that organisation's formation whilst visiting his Grose in-laws that same year and was one of the first to join the fledgling humanitarian group. He was probably one of the earliest relief workers to be posted to Syria. So, I think I have finally placed him in Syria in 1923, when he heard that his own parents had lost everything and were now themselves homeless as a result of the

| *William Gray* *(1720-1795)* | > | *John Gray* *(1770-1830)* | > | *James Gray* *(1813-1880)* | > | *Jesse William Gray* *(1855-1894)* | > |

Kanto earthquake. This strikes me as greatly ironic, that his obviously strong humanitarian instincts were now being redirected from helping Armenian orphans to worrying about his own parents' welfare.

Albert Austen

Nancy Austen (nee Grose)

Again, I am speculating but it would appear that the timing of the earthquake in some ways coincided with a change in Albert and Nancy's career plans, because they emigrated to America within 3 years of its' occurrence. Albert's parents (my great grandparents) had made it back to England by mid-1924 and in fact the Rev. Austen had become the new vicar at North Shoebury. Letters between my grandmother Winifred and her brother Albert confirm he was job hunting in the US in 1924. Albert and Nancy must have travelled from Syria to England, maybe in 1925, because it was from my great grandparents' house The Vicarage, North Shoebury that they departed for a new life in America. As I have recounted earlier, Albert still gave his occupation as relief worker on the Immigration paperwork but also stated his wish to reside in America permanently. From this information I assume he was intending to do

> *Jesse Esdale Gray*
(1885-1946)
> *Cecil Jesse Austen*
Gray (1908-1968)
> *Peter Nigel Austen Gray*
(1950-present)

less work "in the field" and maybe pursue more of an administrative, support role for Near East Relief. The couple eventually settled in California, as this is where my grandparents Jesse and Winifred visited them in 1939.

I appreciate that has taken the long way around but we are now back following my grandfather Jesse's life story. It was necessary to explain how my grandmother Winifred came to be separated from her elder brother Albert, who had also been quite close to my grandfather, as young businessmen growing up in Yokohama. My grandparents went to Shanghai in 1918 and Albert and Nancy to Syria (via the US) after 1919. Therefore, the two couples had a lot of catching up to do when they met up in California some 20 years later. There is a chance that Jesse and Albert may have met in New York in 1922 when my grandfather had made his previous trip to the US but my grandmother hadn't accompanied Jesse on that occasion.

One of the things Winifred may have updated her elder brother on was how well "my Jesse is doing at his firm". This is because my grandfather had obviously had a promotion, because his occupation on the passenger list was Company Secretary. So, he had made it onto the Board. I think I know how he may have achieved this elevated status at the China Import and Export Lumbar Company–by becoming a freemason.

Jesse had several role models who obviously thought being a mason was advantageous–both for their careers but also socially. His father Jesse William became a member of the O. Tentosama Lodge in Yokohama in 1875 and even transferred to the Rising Sun Lodge in Kobe after moving his family there in

1890 when he changed employers. His elder brother Walter joined the Royal Sussex Lodge in Shanghai in 1916, whilst his uncle James Joseph was also in the O. Tentosama Lodge. James Joseph's father-in-law Henry Vincent was also a freemason in Yokohama. Despite all of these influences, my grandfather chose to make his way "on his own", initially in Yokohama and then for the first 13 years of his career in Shanghai. But things changed in 1933 when he decided to join the Cosmopolitan Lodge in Shanghai.

The actual joining process was obviously quite involved, and prompted me to research what the various stages my grandfather had to complete to become a freemason. The levels (degrees) of freemasonry match those of the medieval craft guilds, namely Apprentice, Journeyman (now called Fellow) and Master Mason. Progress through these grades is by a series of degree ceremonies at the Lodge. Candidates for Freemasonry are progressively initiated into Freemasonry, first in the degree of Entered Apprentice. Sometime later, in a separate ceremony, they will be passed to the degree of Fellowcraft, and finally they will be raised to the degree of Master Mason. My grandfather Jesse was 'initiated' on 29th April, 'passed' on 18th May, 'raised' on 19th October and 'made his mark' on 16th November 1933. He must have made his mark in more ways than one, because he actually became Master of the Lodge on 19th December 1940. He officially held this position until his death in 1946 but I am not sure how active the Lodge was in that period. More on that later. Back to my theory about my grandfather's freemasonry helping his career progression. By the time of his visit to America in 1939, Jesse had become the Company

---

>   *Jesse Esdale Gray*   >   *Cecil Jesse Austen*   >   *Peter Nigel Austen Gray*
     (1885-1946)   *Gray (1908-1968)*   *(1950-present)*

Secretary after years as an accountant. Assuming his core skills improved with experience within the company such that he steadily climbed his personal career ladder, he was a one company man throughout his time in Shanghai (1918–1946). Becoming a Freemason is the most significant change in his circumstances between his two trips to America in 1922 and 1939. He was just an accountant when making the former trip but was Company Secretary for the latter. There are plenty of precedents for membership of a Lodge proving to be the necessary "door opener" to both social and career advancement. I believe my grandfather was a hard-working, self-made businessman who tried to achieve professional success on his own merits, but was forced to "play the game" prevailing at that time to secure the final step-up in the company to whom he wanted to stay loyal. I know it is just a theory and really wish I had met my grandfather, to discover the truth of the matter. But that wasn't to be the case, as I shall explain later.

Apart from carving out success in his career and as a Freemason, my grandfather had a fairly uneventful life through the 1920s and into the 1930s.

My wife and I outside the Masonic Hall building, Shanghai

The lobby area of the Lodge's Masonic Hall

William Gray   >   John Gray   >   James Gray   >   Jesse William Gray   >
(1720-1795)   (1770-1830)   (1813-1880)   (1855-1894)

I find it strange trying to understand just what his life might have been like, given that Shanghai itself was far from ordinary. The city was at the centre of a chain of events throughout China as the power struggles of the various political factions raged across the country. However, much like the International Settlement in Shanghai was an island of stability among the stormy political seas of mainland China, my grandfather kept himself mostly isolated from much of the cosmopolitan hubbub of 1920s Shanghai. Service in the Shanghai Volunteer Corps was about his only activity that could be considered political. Other than that, his life centred around providing for the family, raising his children and giving them with an education.

My father Cecil was the eldest son and he began his schooling at Shanghai Public School, founded in 1886 by freemasons. You could say this might have been the earliest influence of freemasonry on his life! As was common practice at the time, for boys anyway, he was sent to England for his further education. In his case this was to Blundell's, a public school near Tiverton, Devon founded in 1604.

My father's entry in the Blundell's alumni archives reads:

No. 6427–GRAY, Cecil Jesse Austen, age 15yrs 1mth, son of Jesse Esdale GRAY, accountant, and Winifred Leila Austen GRAY, of Fair Oaks, Tiverton; attended from September 1923–Easter, 1927 as a Day Boy; previous school Shanghai Public School

This simple factual record is another example of a document both asking and answering questions about one's ancestors. It suggests my grandparents

were living at Fair Oaks, Tiverton which is close enough for my father to be a Day Boy at Blundell's. But, between 1923 -1927, I thought my parents were in Shanghai! Knowing my uncle Norman also went to Blundell's, I turned to his record for help.

No. 6989–GRAY, Norman William Hoskyn, age 14yrs 2mths, son of Jesse Esdale GRAY, manager of lumber company, and Winifred Leila GRAY, of 80 Yangtzepoo Road, Shanghai; attended from 1930 to 1934, boarding at North Close; previous school Norwood School, Exeter

So, did this help me or not? It confirms they were brothers–same parents! The address is right in Shanghai and my grandfather was a manager of a lumber company. I found a story of an Old Blundellian who had attended Norwood School, a preparatory school nearby before moving to Blundell's. This showed this route to be a well-trodden path that Norman had obviously followed. But it says he boarded at Blundell's, whereas my father was a Day Boy? There was an 8-year age gap between Cecil and Norman, with another brother Horace in between. Horace was just two years younger than my father, so maybe his schooling would provide the answer. Wrong! Uncle Horace's education followed a different path altogether, as I shall now explain.

The detail of Horace's education comes from a sad source, namely his obituary in a Shanghai newspaper article following his death in 1930, aged just 19 years old. I have explained earlier that I only learned of Horace's existence through doing my family history research. Whilst he would have always remained in my father's memory, being just 2 years younger than the latter, I find it strange that he was never mentioned forty years later when I reached the age at which Horace died! Of course, I come from a family that wasn't exactly close (emotionally or geographically) in terms of keeping in touch and my own father had actually died when I was still only 18 years of age!

Anyway, the obituary states that Horace attended a different school altogether, namely Kings School in Taunton. I have no idea why the change from Blundell's but it reinforces the fact that my grandfather's three sons were all sent back to England for their further education. This must have proved something of a strain on the family budget but no doubt my grandfather considered it necessary to advance their career prospects. It is quite revealing about the attitudes of the period that such an education was not deemed necessary for his two daughters.

I am left pondering on whether my father was actually a day boy at Blundell's and, if he was, it seems unfair that he inflicted the emotional nightmare of "boarding" at school on both of his sons. In due course, the three boys returned to Shanghai to commence work, albeit in Horace's case for only a tragically short period. I have attached Horace's obituary in full because it summarises all I really know about my "mystery" uncle, whose very existence was unknown to me until I discovered him on an early family photograph that my Grandma had actually annotated on the back. If only all the old photos I have in my possession had been so carefully "written up" by their original

> *Jesse Esdale Gray (1885-1946)*   > *Cecil Jesse Austen Gray (1908-1968)*   > *Peter Nigel Austen Gray (1950-present)*

owners, my family history research would have been greatly simplified.

The obituary also describes how popular my uncle had made himself at only 19 years and 6 months old and its' list of mourners is virtually a roll call of my family and their circle of Shanghailander friends in 1930. It was a tragedy that a life of such potential should have been cut short by a form of meningitis, such a life-threatening condition even today. I believe Horace's early death must have hit my father quite hard. After all, they were only two years apart in age, had grown up together through their childhoods, firstly in Yokohama and then through the move to Shanghai and their early schooling. It seems likely that they were very close and losing his brother would surely have dampened my father's youthful optimism and exuberance. He had his younger brother Norman for companionship but there was an eight-year gap between them, so my father probably missed Horace as someone with whom to enjoy the Shanghai

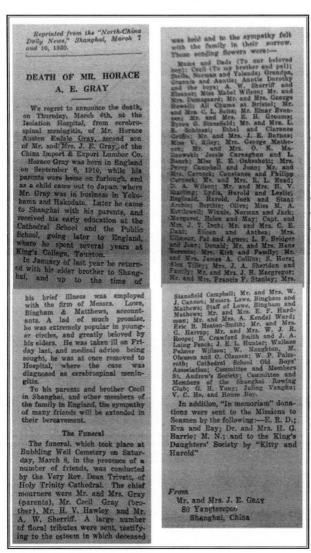

social life. I imagine the latter to have been in full swing during the 1930s, and I'm guessing my father threw himself into it with considerable gusto.

Front row L-R: Doreen (father's 1st wife), my father Cecil; next row, 4th from left: aunt Stella (with 3-droplet necklace)

After Horace's funeral in 1930, the next big Gray family event in Shanghai was a more joyous occasion altogether. This was my father Cecil's wedding to Doreen Beldon on 22nd May 1934.

As you can see from this copy of their marriage certificate, they were married in Holy Trinity Cathedral by the Very rev. Dean Trivett, the same Dean who conducted my uncle Horace's funeral. My grandparents (Jesse Esdale and Winifred Leila Gray) were witnesses along with Doreen's mother–Florence

No.	When Married.	Name and Surname.	Age.	Condition.	Rank or Profession.	Residence at the time of Marriage.	Father's Name and Surname.	Rank or Profession of Father.
163.	22nd May 1934	Cecil Jesse Austen Gray	26	Bachelor	Accountant Shanghai Race Club	Shanghai	Jesse Esdale Gray	Company Manager
		Doreen Myrtle Beldon	20	Spinster	-	Shanghai	J. Pattison Beldon	Deceased

Married in the Cathedral of the Holy Trinity, according to the Rites and Ceremonies of the Church of England, by me, *A.C. Truett M.A., D.D. Dean*

This Marriage was solemnized between us, *Cecil Jesse Austen Gray / Doreen Myrtle Beldon* in the Presence of us, *F.... Beldon / Winifred C. Gray / M. Gray*   PRECEDED BY CONSULAR CEREMONY.   NOTICE BY BANNS.

Elizabeth Beldon (nee O'Connor). Sadly, the bride's father, James Pattison Beldon had died at Flanders in 1917, a WW1 casualty. My father's profession is shown as accountant at the Shanghai Race Club, with my grandfather Jesse Esdale shown as a company manager.

2nd from left—my aunt Yolande; 4th from left—my aunt Stella; right of Stella—bride's mother Florence Beldon; groom—my father Cecil; bride—Doreen; to the right of bride—my grandfather Jesse; next right—my grandmother Winifred

As with all these overseas weddings, there is a need to try and understand how the future married couple came to meet. Whilst it is easy to place my father in Shanghai in 1934, it is trickier to explain how the 20-year-old Doreen was there, given that her father had been killed in the Great War. The fact that her mother was a witness to her marriage poses more questions than answers. Her mother was Mrs Beldon, so she was still a widow. My best guess is that another relative or family friend was living in Shanghai, and that the young widow travelled there with her daughter from their previous location. I have found a shipping record that shows James and Florence Beldon arriving in England in 1916 from South Africa (stated on the form as their "last place of permanent residence"). First question–where is their baby Doreen, born in 1914? James's profession was "Accountant", and it demonstrates he was living and working abroad. His elder brother William Burt Pope Beldon (that is an easy set of names to trace through records!) was also an accountant; at least he was when initiated as a freemason into the St Blaize Lodge, Mossel Bay, South Africa in January 1921! So, this is when doing "genealogical jigsaws" is so much fun. I have two brothers in South Africa within 5 years of each other, both accountants. The younger brother returns to England in 1916 in the middle of the Great War, joins up and is killed about 3 weeks before Armistice Day in Flanders. How does Florence, as a young widow with a daughter, find her way to Shanghai whilst her brother-in-law goes to South Africa? Did William Beldon maybe apply for the accountant's job that his deceased younger brother had been doing in SA? Did his freemasonry connections inform him of an opportunity in Shanghai? If not directly for himself, maybe for his sister-in-law Florence and Doreen? It is intriguing to speculate how it came to be but, however it occurred, my father Cecil did meet Doreen sometime in the early 1930s. Their friendship grew in what I imagine was a pretty lively social scene in Shanghai, culminating in their marriage in 1934. The North-China Daily News covered the wedding thus:

"A popular wedding took place yesterday afternoon when Miss Doreen Myrtle Beldon, daughter of Mrs F.E. Beldon and the late Mr. J Pattison Beldon of Cape Town, became the wife of Mr Cecil Jesse Austen Gray, son of Mr and Mrs J E Gray of Shanghai. The ceremony was held in the Holy Trinity Cathedral, Dean Trivett officiating. Following the ceremony a reception was held at the Cathay Mansions where a very large number of friends gathered to drink the health of the bride and bridegroom and to wish them happiness. Mr and Mrs Gray are leaving on the **Empress of Japan** *for their honeymoon which will be spent in a round trip to Manila"*

Notice the reference to Cape Town in the newspaper report. So now, even the press of the day is joining in on the mystery of where Doreen Beldon moved from, to be there marrying my father in Shanghai.

My two aunts, Stella and Yolande, were bridesmaids at this wedding of their elder brother. It was not long before Stella swapped the role of bridesmaid for that of bride. For Stella was the next of the Gray siblings to be married, as her wedding to William Dudley Ward-Smith took place on 11th May 1937. They were married at a civil ceremony at HM Consulate-General in the morning

| *William Gray*
(1720-1795) | > | *John Gray*
(1770-1830) | > | *James Gray*
(1813-1880) | > | *Jesse William Gray*
(1855-1894) | > |

Back row: (L-R) unknown male; Jesse (my grandfather); Cecil (my father); Norman (my uncle)
Middle row: (L-R) 3 unknown males; Winifred (my grandmother); William Dudley Ward-Smith (my uncle); Stella (my aunt); unknown; Doreen (my father's 1st wife); unknown
Front row: (L-R) 4 bridesmaids; Maid of Honour–Yolande (my aunt); bridesmaid Verna Hawley (my 1st cousin, once removed); unknown

and then at the German Church, Shanghai in the afternoon. The wedding was described in a newspaper covering the event as "Coronation Week Wedding"– as it took place in the same week as the coronation of King George VI in England.

The article covered the main facts of the event as follows:

"The German Church provided the setting yesterday afternoon for the pretty Coronation Week wedding of Miss Stella Gray, eldest daughter of Mr and Mrs J. E. Gray of Shanghai and Mr William Dudley Ward-Smith, the son of the

late Mr and Mrs Harry Ward-Smith. The bride was given away by her father and attended as maid of honour by her sister, Miss Yolande Gray. Bridesmaids were Miss Peggy Sayle, Miss Anthea Inch, Miss Verna Hawley, a cousin of the bride, Miss Doris Gilbert, Miss Frances Engler, and Miss Betty Hargreaves. Mr J.O.Pote-Hunt attended the bridegroom as best man and the ushers were Mr Norman Gray, the brother of the bride, Mr Dennis Box, Mr W MacKenzie, Mr H L Bridges, Mr D van Brandeler and Mr F W Sutterie III. After the ceremony a reception was held at the home of the bride's parents in Columbia Road. Mr and Mrs Ward-Smith will spend their honeymoon making a world trip. After two weeks in Japan they will sail from Yokohama in the Empress of Japan *for Seattle where a motor car awaits them. They will motor across the United States, cross the Atlantic in the SS.* Queen Mary, *motor across England and the continent before returning to China"*

On reading this wedding report and comparing it with the one on my father's wedding just 3 years earlier, I had to have a little chuckle to myself about the contrasting honeymoons described. The Ward-Smiths' world trip, including an Atlantic crossing on THE *Queen Mary*, seems somehow to eclipse the round-trip voyage to Manila enjoyed by my father and his bride! The *Empress of Japan* is the only thing the respective journeys have in common!

This wedding of my aunt Stella was quite a grand affair, judging by its' coverage in the "About Shanghai" gossip column of the local newspaper. It gives some interesting insights into the occasion as follows:

"Interesting Wedding Takes Place

One of the largest and loveliest of the season's weddings was the Ward-Smith–Gray nuptials, held yesterday afternoon. A large group of friends of the bride Miss Stella Gray, and groom Mr William Dudley Ward-Smith witnessed the ceremony performed by Dr. E. W. Luccock at the German Church, which was beautifully decorated with pale pink carnations, daisies and ferns for the occasion. Mrs. B. R. Bryant sang two selections during the service, one being the familiar "Ave Maria". A large number of guests attended the reception which followed at the home of the bride's parents at 104 Columbia Road. Small tables were set out in the garden and tea and refreshments were served from a specially erected marquee, where most of the guests gathered. A three-piece orchestra played light music throughout the afternoon. The couple received the congratulations of their friends inside the house under an arbour of bamboo and white flowers with a wedding bell of white flowers overhead. Mr R. F. Barrie, an old friend of the family, proposed a toast to the bride and groom, to which Mr Ward-Smith responded suitably, also thanking his best man and ushers and thanking the bridesmaids. Mr. J. O. Pote-Hunt, the best man, replied on behalf of the bridesmaids, after which Mr. Barrie once again spoke, informing the guests that in addition to being an occasion for celebration of one wedding, the day was also the 30th wedding anniversary of the bride's parents, Mr. and Mrs. J. E. Gray, and the guests then drank a toast to that couple also, Mr Gray expressing his and his wife's thanks. Later in the evening, Mr. and Mrs. Ward-Smith left on their honeymoon, which is taking them around the world, with their return to Shanghai scheduled for late November..."

> *Jesse Esdale Gray*
> *(1885-1946)*

> *Cecil Jesse Austen*
> *Gray (1908-1968)*

> *Peter Nigel Austen Gray*
> *(1950-present)*

Note the confirmation of the honeymoon being over six months duration. If this had been set in the present day, my guess is that the Shanghai equivalent of OK magazine might well have been involved! In a way, it is a shame they weren't, because I might have been able to track down a copy, to see what my grandparents' house in Shanghai looked like. But I did get an unexpected treat relating

to this wedding, again courtesy of my cousin Tony, the happy couple's son. When I visited him last year, he gave me a digital file of some old cine footage taken at the wedding! Amazing for me, since here was my grandfather Jesse Esdale "in the flesh" helping Stella out of the bridal car and walking her into the church. Remember that I never even met my grandfather, as I was born some four years after his death. This still photo shows the proud parents of the bride–Grandpa Jesse and Granny Gray, with my father appearing between their shoulders. I am guessing they were only allowed to film outside the church but that shows me a few minutes of the bride arriving, having her dress sorted out by her bridesmaids, before entering the church on her father's arm. Then walking out of the church on the arm of her husband, with the wedding procession following on, and then other guests. Marvellous to have it, with glimpses of my grandparents, my father, Uncle Norman and Aunt Yolande. Plus, of course, shots of numerous other people whose identities remain frustratingly unknown. This is very often the lot of so many family historians when presented with any such media. "Who are these people?" we all shout. If ever there was a gap in the Apps market, it is for one that could conduct virtual seances, for genealogists to connect directly with "the departed" for help with identifying people in old photos.

The gossip column article, that I have quoted from above, also refers to the "bride's sister-in-law, Mrs C. J. A. Gray", describing the outfit she was wearing at the wedding. This of course is Doreen Myrtle Gray (nee Beldon) who married my father three years earlier. She is in my aunt Stella's wedding picture but unfortunately in the second row. I only say this because it means I have not got visual evidence to support vital information I discovered in one of Grandpa Jesse's letters. In autumn 1937 he writes that Doreen is "nearing her time and I shall soon be a grandparent for the first time". However, I have not been able to discover any record of a child born to Doreen and my father. And, in a letter written some years later welcoming my older brother Ian, my grandma Winnie describes him as our first Gray grandchild. It is quite a coincidence that a lot of this correspondence was passed to me by my cousin Tony because, when it is all studied together like a detective in a TV series would do, it actually demonstrates that Tony was the first grandchild born to Jesse and Winnie. It is as though fate ordained him to be the custodian of the evidence proving him to hold that "title" amongst us nine grandchildren still alive today. Knowing him as I do, I can say Tony would dismiss this "claim to fame" in the Gray family story as nothing, but I think he deserves to have the

---

> *Jesse Esdale Gray*   >   *Cecil Jesse Austen*   >   *Peter Nigel Austen Gray*
> *(1885-1946)*   *Gray (1908-1968)*   *(1950-present)*

fact recorded here.

I shall now return to Doreen and the mystery of what happened to the expected child. I can only conclude she lost it, although what the actual circumstances were remains unanswered. It may relate to the date, Autumn 1937, when Shanghai was at the centre of the Second Sino-Japanese war, of which much more later. I can only speculate that it had a considerable impact on the couple (Doreen and my father) because, some three years later in 1940, my father actually married my mother in Hong Kong. How is that for "Breaking News". I am going to have to tell more, as this is the next wedding in the Gray family history timeline. Overall and speaking personally, it is probably THE most important wedding–because yours truly is the second child of this particular union.

Much like I did with my father and Doreen, I need to explain how my parents came to meet. If you have been following "the story so far", you just know this is going to take some explaining don't you. I shall start with my mother, since my father is already there in Shanghai and I have to explain how Mother came to be there as well. Actually, I am going to let her tell you. This is an extract from a little piece she wrote for me, after one of the occasions we were talking about her colourful past. I shall be returning to these notes of hers later in this book, but for now she explains how she came to be in China:

"The reason I went out to China was because when I was 19 I had months in bed suffering from rheumatic fever so my sister and brother-in-law invited me to stay with them in Shanghai and kindly paid my passage out as a 21st

birthday present."

That's some 21st birthday present! My mother's notes read a bit like the screenplay for the opening scene of a movie, so I need to explain a bit more about the characters she has just introduced. Her sister is Marjorie Ellen Bannister (nee Downton), the middle of my Downton grandparents' three daughters, born in 1911 which makes her three years older than Mother. She married Thomas Roger Banister in Dartford in December 1933, when he was probably on leave in England, as he was working as a customs officer for the Chinese Maritime Customs in Shanghai. "Ban", as he was called by my maternal family, was born in Preston, Lancashire in 1890, the only son of William Banister and Mary Alice Grieve. His father was a clergyman and a pre-eminent missionary in China, eventually becoming the Bishop of the Church of England in Kwangsi and Hunan, the first diocese created in China. Baby Ban lived in China from an early age, since his only sibling, Maud Violet, was born in Fucheng, China on 19 December 1891 when he was still under two years old. I need you readers to just remember Maud Violet Banister for a short while, as she appears later in "the movie". Marjorie's husband was 21 years older than her, which I imagine was a significant factor in Marjorie wanting her younger sister Kathleen to join her in China. We are talking about two sisters aged 24 and 21 joining the social scene that was Shanghai in the 1930s. Hence the couple's extremely kind gift of my mother's passage to China.

As it was her 21st birthday gift, it places Mother in Shanghai in late 1935. To recap, that is only the year after my father and Doreen were married and two years before the loss of their child. There is now a short time gap in terms of hard facts about my parents' lives. From her own notes, Mother got a job with the Shell Company *"which I left in 1940 to go to Hong Kong to get married. My fiancé had left Shanghai to join the RNVR"*. So, in her own words, she is now engaged to my father sometime in late 1939. Again, I find myself having to surmise how to explain the real story behind the bare facts. One theory is that losing her child had an extreme effect on the marriage and Doreen and my father became estranged as a result. Another possible explanation is that my father was captivated by the beauty of the young Kathleen Downton who had recently arrived on the Shanghai social scene, and that was the cause of the marriage failure. Because fail it did, and a divorce must have occurred quite rapidly, given the short timescale involved before Mother writes about "my fiancé".

Of course, external factors always play a major part in any unfolding drama and they don't come much bigger than one's country going to war. With Britain declaring war with Germany in September 1939, "normal life" ended for so many families around the world. My father, although born in Japan and raised there and in China, obviously thought himself to be totally British, unlike his father Jesse's lifelong struggle with knowing his nationality. My father was quite clear that he wanted to enlist, even though the conflict initially was centred upon Europe. And naturally his choice of service was the Navy. I don't know where my father's love of all things nautical actually came from, but it was a lifelong passion of his and central to my memories of his character. I have not

| *William Gray* | | *John Gray* | | *James Gray* | | *Jesse William Gray* | |
| *(1720-1795)* | > | *(1770-1830)* | > | *(1813-1880)* | > | *(1855-1894)* | > |

discovered any seafarers among our ancestors but making trips by sea was a regular occurrence for the family, and his birthplace Yokohama was probably one of the busiest ports in the Far East at that time. He did make the voyage from Japan to England aged two for his brother Horace's birth. And the two boys did wear sailor suits at their uncle William's wedding. And he made the voyages to England for schooling. I guess it wasn't really any surprise after all!

In one of Grandpa Jesse's letters, he writes how desperate Dad was to gain acceptance into the navy, worrying whether he would pass the examinations and whether his family background would be a problem. Jesse writes that my father had studied so hard that he was confident Cecil would succeed, which he eventually did. I have a Navy List from 1941 which lists my father as a Sub-Lieutenant in the Hong Kong Royal Naval Volunteer Reserve; it gives an enlistment date of 2nd May 1940. Incidentally, it lists his younger brother, my uncle Norman, lower down the page as an Acting Sub-Lieutenant, enlisted on 22nd May 1940. In another letter Jesse writes about "the two boys doing their bit". This places my father and his brother in Hong Kong in time for the wedding. My father's message on this photo of him in his first uniform reads *"To dear Dad–Cecil; February 1940"*. He looks extremely proud of himself, and wanted to share the feeling with his father Jesse back home in Shanghai.

> *Jesse Esdale Gray*
(1885-1946)   > *Cecil Jesse Austen*
Gray (1908-1968)   > *Peter Nigel Austen Gray*
(1950-present)

My cousin Ann Banister has helped fill in some detail about my mother's arrival in Hong Kong. Ann was born in Shanghai in 1936, the only daughter of Thomas Roger and Marjorie Banister. You may recall that I asked you readers to remember Maud Violet Banister, who was born in China and was the brother of my aunt Marjorie's husband Ban (Thomas Roger). Maud met and married a diplomat working in China called Norman Lockhart-Smith. The latter gradually worked his way "up the ladder" in his civil service career, such that he was Acting Governor of Hong Kong in 1940. My mother was now engaged to my father at this time and waiting for the divorce to be settled. Cousin Ann explained that it was not considered "quite right" in Shanghai society for this young girl to be seen in a relationship with a gentleman not yet divorced and, to keep up appearances, my mother was sent to "stay with family" in Hong Kong, namely her sister's brother-in-law. Because he happened to be the Acting-Governor, my mother was staying at Government House. I shall return to my parents' actual wedding in the next chapter, since it occurred during the period in the family's history when events in Shanghai were beginning to turn nasty in terms of relations with the Japanese.

This chapter is entitled "Gray family life in Shanghai" so I had better return from Hong Kong and continue with my story in the correct chronological order. The newly-weds Stella and Bill returned from honeymoon at the end of 1937 and settled into married life in Shanghai. My aunt Stella gave birth to her first child on the 21st September 1938; thus, my cousin Tony became my grandparents' first grandchild. On discovering his date of birth, I initially felt slightly envious of him, thinking he knew our grandfather Jesse. However, this was not the case, because Tony arrived in America in July 1941, together with his mother Stella and new baby sister Dawn, who was only born on 5th March of that year. Therefore, he would hardly have known our grandfather, since he was only 2 years old when he left Grandpa Jesse behind in Shanghai. The reason for the family's rapid exit was the ever-changing political situation in the Far East at that time, which leads me nicely into the next chapter of my story.

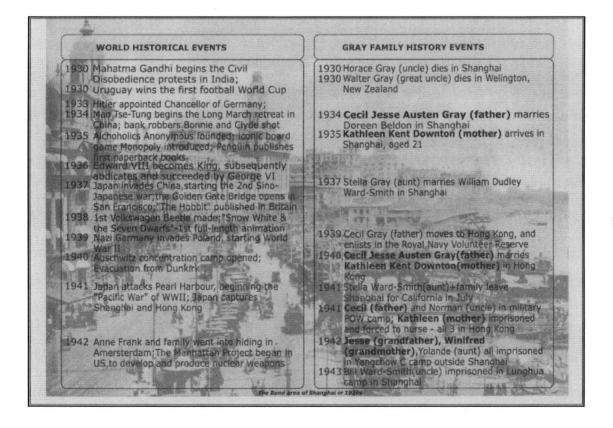

WORLD HISTORICAL EVENTS	GRAY FAMILY HISTORY EVENTS
1930 Mahatma Gandhi begins the Civil Disobedience protests in India;	1930 Horace Gray (uncle) dies in Shanghai
1930 Uruguay wins the first football World Cup	1930 Walter Gray (great uncle) dies in Welington, New Zealand
1933 Hitler appointed Chancellor of Germany;	
1934 Mao Tse-Tung begins the Long March retreat in China; bank robbers Bonnie and Clyde shot	1934 **Cecil Jesse Austen Gray (father)** marries Doreen Beldon in Shanghai
1935 Alchoholics Anonymous founded; iconic board game Monopoly introduced; Penguin publishes first paperback books	1935 **Kathleen Kent Downton (mother)** arrives in Shanghai, aged 21
1936 Edward VIII becomes King, subsequently abdicates and succeeded by George VI	
1937 Japan invades China, starting the 2nd Sino-Japanese war; the Golden Gate Bridge opens in San Francisco; "The Hobbit" published in Britain	1937 Stella Gray (aunt) marries William Dudley Ward-Smith in Shanghai
1938 1st Volkswagen Beetle made; "Snow White & the Seven Dwarfs"-1st full-length animation	
1939 Nazi Germany invades Poland, starting World War II	1939 Cecil Gray (father) moves to Hong Kong, and enlists in the Royal Navy Volunteer Reserve
1940 Auschwitz concentration camp opened; Evacuation from Dunkirk	1940 **Cecil Jesse Austen Gray (father)** marries **Kathleen Kent Downton (mother)** in Hong Kong
1941 Japan attacks Pearl Harbour, beginning the "Pacific War" of WWII; Japan captures Shanghai and Hong Kong	1941 Stella Ward-Smith (aunt)+family leave Shanghai for California in July
	1941 **Cecil (father)** and Norman (uncle) in military POW camp; **Kathleen (mother)** imprisoned and forced to nurse – all 3 in Hong Kong
1942 Anne Frank and family went into hiding in Amersterdam; The Manhattan Project began in US, to develop and produce nuclear weapons	1942 **Jesse (grandfather), Winifred (grandmother)**, Yolande (aunt) all imprisoned in Yangchow C camp outside Shanghai
	1943 Bill Ward-Smith (uncle) imprisoned in Lunghua camp in Shanghai

The Bund area of Shanghai in 1930s

HOW AND WHY THINGS CHANGED FOR THE FAMILY IN SHANGHAI

I have been pondering on how best to start explaining what changed for the family in Shanghai and decided a good start point might be to recap with a "who was where when" section! I shall set the date at the beginning of 1939. The family is living at 104 Columbia Road. My grandfather Jesse (54) is working at the China Import and Export Lumber Company. My grandmother Winnie (57) is running the home and keeping a maternal watch over her "children". My father Cecil (31) is working for the Yeo Taoong Tobacco Company, a BAT-owned business in Shanghai. As explained earlier, he is going through a divorce from his first wife Doreen and becomes engaged to my mother Kathleen (24) sometime in that year. I am guessing slightly as regards timing but I think Kathleen starts 1939 living with her sister Marjorie and brother-in-law Ban, the customs officer working for the Chinese Maritime Services in Shanghai. My aunt Stella (26) is in Shanghai as Mrs Ward-Smith, with baby Tony only 18-months old. My uncle Bill (42) is working as an Export Manager for Foster

McCellan, an American company based in Buffalo, New York. My uncle Norman (23) and aunt Yolande (21) complete the Gray family living at home.

Now I shall start to detail the political situation prevailing in China at the time. The Shanghai my family knew was actually still the International Settlement administered by the Shanghai Municipal Council, with America, Britain and Japan amongst the numerous countries represented on the council. Japan had actually grown its' influence within the council and held an equal number of voting members as Britain and America. Shanghai outside the SIS and China generally had experienced the rise of Imperial Japan from the beginning of the 20th century. Japan entered the century as a rising world power, having obtained extraterritorial rights with China under the Treaty of Shimonoseki signed in 1895. In 1915, during the First World War, Japan overtook Britain as the country with the largest number of foreign residents in Shanghai. In 1914 they sided with Britain and France in the war and conquered all German possessions in China. By the beginning of the 1930s, Japan was swiftly becoming the most powerful national group in Shanghai and accounted for some 80% of all extraterritorial foreigners in China. Much of Hongkew, (a suburb of Shanghai), which had become an unofficial Japanese settlement, was known as Little Tokyo. In 1931, supposed "protection of Japanese colonists from Chinese aggression" in Hongkew was used as a pretext for the Shanghai Incident, when Japanese troops invaded Shanghai. From then until the Second Sino-Japanese War (1937–1945) Hongkew was almost entirely outside of the SMC's hands, with law and protection enforced to varying degrees by the

Japanese Consular Police and Japanese members of the Shanghai Municipal Police. In 1932 there were 1,040,780 Chinese living within the International Settlement, with another 400,000 fleeing into the area after the Second Sino-Japanese War broke out in 1937. For the next five years, the International Settlement and the French Concession were surrounded by Japanese occupiers and Chinese revolutionaries, with conflict often spilling into the Settlement's borders. In 1941, the Japanese launched an abortive political bid to take over the SMC: during a mass meeting of ratepayers at the Settlement Race Grounds, a Japanese official leapt up and shot William Keswick, then Chairman of the Council. While Keswick was only wounded, a near riot broke out.

It seems quite incredible to me now, researching these details, that my family were going about their daily lives in the middle of what was essentially a war zone. In one incident on 14 August 1937, the Chinese dropped four bombs intended for the Japanese Navy's flagship, the cruiser *Izumo*; they fell in the Shanghai International Settlement; 700 civilians were killed outright, with a total of 3,000 civilian deaths and injuries. The *Izumo* was moored on the Huangpu river, adjacent to the Bund area, but the four errant bombs fell in the SIS; two exploded in Nanking Road and two in front of the Great World Amusement Centre on Avenue Edward VII, killing an estimated 2,000 shoppers and passers-by. My wife and I actually visited these areas during our stay in Shanghai and so I know exactly the distances involved, between where the bombs fell and my grandparents' house! Depending what time of the day it was, if my grandfather was at his office, he would have been even closer to these scenes of utter devastation. This incident was in August 1937; you may remember that the whole family only celebrated Aunt Stella's wedding in the May and my father's wife Doreen was about to deliver my grandparents' first grandchild. I can only liken it to families living through the blitz of WW2 or "the troubles" in Northern Ireland or, much more recently, war-torn Bosnia or Syria. There is a lot more to tell in terms of direct impact on my family, so I shall continue to describe how some of the family chose to leave, while they could.

As I related earlier, my father was among the first to leave Shanghai, though only as far as Hong Kong. He enlisted into the Hong Kong Royal Navy Volunteer Reserve, along with his younger brother Norman and were both on active service by 1941, albeit against the only official enemy then–Germany. My maternal aunt Marjorie also moved to Hong Kong by 1940, presumably into the care of  her sister-in-law Maud Lockhart-Smith or, more probably, Maud's husband Norman. If you remember, Norman Lockhart-Smith was the Acting-Governor. My mother was certainly living in Government House in the lead up to her wedding in 1940. In the next chapter I shall return to these members of the family and how subsequent events impacted on them.

There was obviously a sense of fear about being a Westerner in Shanghai in

---

>   *Jesse Esdale Gray*
(1885-1946)   >   *Cecil Jesse Austen*
Gray (1908-1968)   >   *Peter Nigel Austen Gray*
(1950-present)

those days, and that pressure increased steadily right up to "the boiling point" of 8th December 1941–the attack on Pearl Harbour. However, on 25th July 1939 my grandparents Jesse and Winnie disembarked from the SS *Empress of Japan* in Vancouver, Canada and crossed over the border into Seattle, Washington on 27th July. On the Immigration form Jesse stated they will be in the USA for "no longer than 60 days". They were on their way for a holiday, staying with Albert and Nancy Austen in California. This picture shows them visiting Treasure Island, which Google tells me is an artificial island in the San Francisco Bay built in 1936-1937 for the 1939 Golden Gate International Exposition. By going on vacation to America at that particular time, I think they are making quite a statement about their confidence in their future back home in Shanghai. How all that was about to change!

My grandfather's optimism was certainly not shared by his son-in-law Bill Ward -Smith. I am now going to let my uncle Bill explain his interpretation of the unfolding events in Shanghai, by quoting from the opening section of a memoire he later wrote for his son Tony:

"It was the summer of 1941. I was 42 years old. I had come to Shanghai twelve years earlier as Far East manager for Foster McClellan Company, a Buffalo, New York pharmaceutical company, makers of the familiar Doan's Pills. I met Stella here, we married in May, 1937 on her parents' 30th wedding anniversary. Anthony, my first-born, was almost three; my daughter Dawn was five months. We all lived together quite comfortably in Shanghai's "International Settlement," with my wife's family nearby. But it was a time of

turmoil in Shanghai. Skirmishes between Japanese and Chinese locals were frequent. And all the while, rumours that the allies would be involved in a war against Adolph Hitler's Nazi Germany persisted. I was entitled to "home leave" every three years, so on the advice of our consular officials, I had a packing company come to our home, carefully wrap several choice pieces of Chinese silver, some priceless porcelain and other valued wedding gifts, and pack them away in wooden cases. I then sublet our house with the rest of our furniture in place, turned control of the company's business over to my understudy, and booked passage to San Francisco, U.S.A. on the American President Line's President Hoover. My one objective at the time was to get self and family out of China!...It was a safe, peaceful trip. We landed in San Francisco, and immediately took the Southern Pacific Train across the continent to Buffalo, New York, so I could report to my corporate superiors on conditions in China affecting the company's business. After a few days of this, we left again for the west coast to visit some relatives in San Jose, California. We all were looking forward to a much-needed vacation. But such was not to be."

So, there we have another of my grandfather Jesse's children leaving Shanghai. My aunt Stella was now in America, with her two young children. Her two brothers (my father Cecil and my uncle Norman) were in Hong Kong, serving with the Navy. Only my aunt Yolande, the youngest of their children, remained with her parents in Shanghai. As I write their story now, with the benefit of hindsight and "knowing what comes next", I feel like trying to intervene and offer some counsel as to their best course of future action.

> *Jesse Esdale Gray*
> *(1885-1946)*

> *Cecil Jesse Austen*
> *Gray (1908-1968)*

> *Peter Nigel Austen Gray*
> *(1950-present)*

However, as a fan of some contemporary "time-travelling" fiction, I know that no time-traveller is allowed to change the course of history! So, I shall continue relating this fascinating saga just as I have pieced it together from eye-witness accounts, namely letters written by members of my family. As indicated in the preceding chapter, there was one more big event in the Gray family story before international events overturned family life completely–my parents' wedding.

For this we have to return to Hong Kong in the summer of 1940. This next quote is from my mother's short memoire note, and I love the understated way she recalls the happy event:

"...My sister's brother-in-law was Acting Governor at the time and he gave me away, and held a reception for me at Government House, which was pleasant but quiet, being war time and the evacuation of Dunkirk..."

My mother arriving at her wedding, with her replacement "father-of-the-bride"

The guard of honour greets the happy couple

L-R: Maud Lockhart-Smith; Sub-Lieut. F.R.L. Carey, RNVR; Sub-Lieut. C.J.A. Gray, RNVR; Miss Kathleen Kent Downton; Mrs Marjorie Banister; Norman Lockhart-Smith

> *Jesse Esdale Gray*   >   *Cecil Jesse Austen*   >   *Peter Nigel Austen Gray*
(1885-1946)   *Gray (1908-1968)*   *(1950-present)*

Now I know her father was back home in Erith, Kent at the time but come on, the Acting Governor as stand-in "Father of the Bride"! And the reception– OK, maybe it was small, but Government House? Oh, and they did walk out under an arch of swords formed by naval officers in whites! It does look a bit like "*An Officer and A Gentleman*" to me, even if my father isn't quite Richard Gere!

The Hong Kong newspaper covered the happy occasion thus in its' 19th June 1940 edition:

PRETTY WEDDING

Acting Governor Gives Bride Away

GRAY–DOWNTON

His Excellency the Acting Governor, Mr. N. L. Smith gave the bride away at yesterday's pretty ceremony at the Union Church, Kennedy Road, and Mrs. N. L. Smith acted as hostess at a small reception held at Government House. The marriage was between Sub.-Lieut. Cecil Jesse Austen Gray, R.N.V.R. and Miss Kathleen Kent Downton.

The bride is the youngest daughter of Mr. and Mrs. W Downton, of Erith, Kent, England. In place of the conventional wedding gown, she wore a smart white sharkskin suit with hat made of the same material, trimmed with a white spotted veil. Her corsage was of African daisies.

There were no bridesmaids, the bride's sister, Mrs. T. Roger Banister attending as matron-of-honour. She wore a turquoise blue dress and jacket, with white hat and corsage.

| William Gray | > | John Gray | > | James Gray | > | Jesse William Gray | > |
| *(1720-1795)* | | *(1770-1830)* | | *(1813-1880)* | | *(1855-1894)* | |

The Rev. K. MacKenzie Dow officiated at the ceremony.

The bridegroom is the eldest son of Mr. and Mrs. J.E. Gray, of Shanghai.

In peace time he is connected with British American Tobacco Co. Ltd., and

was last stationed at Shanghai.

Sub.-Lieut. F.R. L. Carey, R.N.V.R., undertook the duties of best man.

Mrs. N.L. Smith received the guests in a dress of old-rose and

white printed silk.

I am left with mixed feelings on reading this newspaper report of my parents' wedding. Whilst it sounds quite grand in terms of location and "celebrity" participants, neither the bride's nor the groom's parents were present to help the happy couple celebrate. Obviously, it took place in wartime and so was not unlike many weddings across the world during those troubled times. I also imagine that there wasn't a honeymoon at all, given these comments that my mother wrote in her short memoire of the time:

"...Ten days after the wedding, the Hong Kong government decided all women and children should leave the island if they did not have essential jobs. A colleague of mine, who was Marine Superintendent at Shell before joining up (he was an ex naval officer), gave my husband an order that I should become this man's secretary–he was Sea Transport Officer and Flag Lieutenant to the Commodore! Then, when he managed to get back home, my husband took over his job. Because of this, we mixed socially with all the top brass but, in spite of being a very shy person, I found them easy to talk to, as they were so pleasant and natural."

> *Jesse Esdale Gray* *(1885-1946)*	> *Cecil Jesse Austen* *Gray (1908-1968)*	> *Peter Nigel Austen Gray* *(1950-present)*

Reading this again later and putting it in its' context, I find it another revealing insight into my mother's personality. You must remember that she was only 25 years old, just married and thousands of miles from her family in Kent, and yet here she was, mixing with "the high society" of a Hong Kong that was embroiled in war. Of course, things were about to get a whole lot worse, but I am beginning to understand something about my mother's character, that was going to sustain her through her coming ordeal.

Back in Shanghai, my grandparents were facing their own challenges. I shall try and illustrate the contrasting views on the situation there by quoting from a couple of letters I have from this period. The first is from my grandmother Winnie to her sister-in-law Nancy in California. At the top of the letter she gives the address for my father and my uncle Norman as "c/o Fleet Mail Officer, Hong Kong":

104 Columbia Road

Shanghai

July 18th 1940

My dear Nancy,

I was delighted on returning home this morning, to find your letter waiting for me, so hasten to answer it at once or else I shall get busy on something else and this letter won't get written. There is always something waiting to be done.

So glad to hear you are better. Jess received a letter from Mr C. Griffin the other day and he mentioned that you had fallen over your dog & we

| William Gray | > | John Gray | > | James Gray | > | Jesse William Gray | > |
| (1720-1795) | | (1770-1830) | | (1813-1880) | | (1855-1894) | |

understood had hurt your back again. This time you thought you would have a change and try your hip instead!!! Give up trying after this my dear. So glad you are able to get about once more.

Jess wrote you a long letter the other day with all the news, so there won't be much for me to say. We returned here Dec 6th & it was a rush for me to get settled and ready for Xmas and the New Year, then Jess started being unwell & laid up, until he got so bad that on April 20th the doctors put him into hospital & to bed for 6 weeks and the next 2 weeks he was allowed up a little each day, and came home just 8 weeks after he went in, that was June 15th and even now he still has to go slow.

It appears he had hernia of the heart quite a rare thing & it was touch and go with him; at first they did not tell me how serious, only after he had improved a little and there was a chance of getting over it. It has been quite a worrying time & also busy time for me, as I went to the hospital from "15 to 2" and stayed with him until 6.30 or 7 p.m. so had to be extra busy at other times to get all my work done.

I do war work 2 mornings a week Tuesday and Friday from "15 to 9" to 12.30. We make garments & sheets & p.slips for the sailors and soldiers & send several cases home every two or three weeks. Our exchange is so bad now it is not worth much to send money home, so we buy the material here and we ladies make the things, so can send quite a lot in that way.

The exchange has been as bad as $24 for 1 gold dollar & $76 for a pound so we can do very little to help others at home these days

Our expenses too have gone right up, and we have to pay 4,5 or 6 times as much now, as we did two years ago or less. I hate to go shopping now, it seems wrong to have to pay so much for things now, you feel you ought to go without rather than pay so much.

Yes Cecil joined up in December, he left soon after we arrived back & now Norman has gone too; he went in May (22n) so both our boys are doing their bit and all three of Dorothy's have gone.

Yes we have written and asked Mabel several times to try and rent her place & come out here with us, but that was all some time ago, but she did not want to then but now she would like to, just when the exchange has gone to pieces and Jess can't do it now. It would cost 7 to 9000 dollars to get her out via Suez or Africa, and via America much more, so it is out of the question for the time being. She will have to rent her home and take up War Work.

Often think of you and of the very pleasant days we spent with you last year and all your friends we met and were kind to us. Mr Sinclair and that lovely drive he took us for.

Cecil was married again on June 18th to such a nice sweet girl, Norman writes Cecil so improved since 2nd marriage.

Stella and Anthony with amah gone to Japan for 6 weeks to Miyanoshita for a rest and change.

Next Sunday week Yolande will be 21, our baby. We are giving her an "At Home" on the 27th, about 80 people.

Have not been very well myself lately, tummy trouble and this hot weather tries me a lot, but have to keep going on.

Sent our house boy-cook off on May 31st as he was stealing so much and now cannot get one to suit. Hope we get settled soon, the servants are awful these days, far worse than they used to be, do much less and want much more, so cheeky and independent.

Please remember us kindly to all we met. Much love to Albert, trust he keeps fit and well. Must go and see about tea now. Much love to your dear self, thanks for writing, take care of yourself,

Love

Winifred

Isn't that just the best letter? I immediately feel my grandmother's joy as she remembers her trip over to California the preceding year. I also feel the anxiety she must have suffered, worrying about my grandfather's health, the financial situation impacting on her housekeeping budget and the quality of her domestic servants! She is even worrying over the safety of her younger sister Mabel back home in England suffering through the horrors of the war in Europe, and trying to scheme a way of bringing her to Shanghai for her safety! In other words, she seems to be thinking about others far more than her own situation, despite living in Shanghai surrounded by an invading Japanese army who pose a real threat to her own way of life. More on that presently.

I now want to share the second letter with you. It is from the same Nancy that Granny Gray had written to a year earlier, since this one is dated November 1941. It goes quite a long way in expressing the contrasting view of matters in

Shanghai and my grandparents' safety held by Nancy and Albert Austen:

Box 73, Catawba Avenue,

Fontana, Calif.

Nov23/41

Dear Winnie and Jess,

We were happy to have two letters from Jess and to hear you were all well. Needless to say, we are quite anxious about you now, not knowing whether you have left Shanghai or not. Do let us know where you are and how things are going over there.

Last week I had a letter from Stella, the first line from her since Anthony was born. It was a happy surprise to hear from her and especially to hear that she is in San Jose. She did not say how they happened to select San Jose. While it is a pleasant place yet I am sorry she isn't further south. We hope to go up to see her but I do not know if it will be possible or not until Albert can get more work. Isn't it ridiculous to have to consider such items!

Have you heard that Dorothy has been flat on her back six weeks with a strained heart? She is up now and allowed to exercise a little each day, but must be very careful for a long time.

At last letter Mabel was safe but her feet are very bad and she has to work until midnight every day to get all her housework and gardening done. Has to iron at night she says. We have never heard a word from Aunt Jane and family.

We are quite thrilled that Michael is on patrol duty in the Atlantic from

Iceland to the West Indies, with a base at Halifax, Nova Scotia. I've written to friends in New York and Boston to look out for him should he ever get leave there. He seems very near us. He must be a darling boy, judging from his good letters.

Have you good news from Cecil and Norman? Please give me their addresses. I wrote them at the addresses you gave in Hong Kong. But do not know whether they received my letters or not, as I did not hear from them. Give them our best wishes & love when you write them.

I won't write much today as I am not sure you will receive it. But I hope it reaches you and that you will know how often we think of you and pray for your safety and happiness.

We hope that world conditions will take a better turn before long and that you will be able to stay in Shanghai until you can pack your things and find a ship to take them out. Let me know where you do decide to locate. We hope it may be near us. Wherever it is, may God bless you all. We shall be thinking of you at Christmas and hoping you are all safe and happy.

Was Bill able to get to Shanghai? Do hope he can get their things out before trouble comes. Our best wishes to him too.

Lovingly

Nancy

This is another fantastic letter which immediately reveals so much about the tension and stress building up in families around the world. It is just brilliant to be told it in my own relatives' words, as they lived through it all.

> *Jesse Esdale Gray*   >   *Cecil Jesse Austen*   >   *Peter Nigel Austen Gray*
  (1885-1946)   *Gray (1908-1968)*   *(1950-present)*

My great aunt's hope–"that world conditions take a better turn"–would never be realised, as the pressure build-up would finally be released so dramatically on the morning of 8th December, 1941. How, and where, and with what devastating outcomes, is to be told in my next chapter, again by my family members who were cast centre stage in this unfolding drama.

MY "MAGNIFICENT SEVEN"– DETAINED BY THE IMPERIAL ARMY

When I was growing up in suburban Kent, living in my Downton grandparents' house, I used to love going to the cinema. One of my favourite films of the time, and it still remains in my top 5 all-time favourites, was "*The Magnificent Seven*". This 1960s western was a re-working of a Japanese classic called *The Seven Samurai*. It tells the story of the heroics of 7 mercenary gunfighters hired by the farmers of a small Mexican village to protect it from bandits. It was this Japanese connection that led me to adapt the film's title for this chapter–the story of seven of my close family, who showed great heroism themselves in the war-torn Far East. And, once again, I am going to enlist the help of three of them, to tell a lot of their stories in their own words. The table below introduces My Magnificent 7 to you, with their locations when their whole world changed on that fateful day in December 1941:

Having "positioned" all of these 7 family members geographically in the last chapter, I can conclude that they were all "in the wrong place at the wrong

| > | *Jesse Esdale Gray (1885-1946)* | > | *Cecil Jesse Austen Gray (1908-1968)* | > | *Peter Nigel Austen Gray (1950-present)* |

"MY MAGNIFICENT 7"						
Kathleen (my mother)	Cecil (my father)	Norman (my uncle)	Jesse (my grandfather)	Winifred (my grandmother)	Yolande (my aunt)	Bill (my uncle)
Living in Hong Kong, working as a civilian for the Navy	Serving with the RNVR as a naval officer	Serving with the RNVR as a naval officer	104 Columbia Road (their house in Shanghai)	104 Columbia Road (their house in Shanghai)	104 Columbia Road (their house in Shanghai)	Just returned to Shanghai, after evacuating his wife and children to USA

time". The time in question was 8th December 1941, because that was the date of the attack on Pearl Harbour. The latter was a surprise, pre-emptive military strike by the Imperial Japanese Navy Air Service upon the United States (a neutral country at the time) against the naval base at Pearl Harbour in Honolulu, Territory of Hawaii, just before 08:00, on Sunday morning, December 7, 1941. The attack led to the United States' formal entry into World War II the next day. Japan intended the attack as a preventive action to keep the United States Pacific Fleet from interfering with its planned military actions in Southeast Asia against overseas territories of the United Kingdom, the Netherlands, and the United States. Over the course of seven hours there were coordinated Japanese attacks on the U.S.-held Philippines, Guam and Wake Island and on the British Empire in Malaya, Singapore, and Hong Kong.

The attack commenced at 7:48 a.m. Hawaiian Time (18:18 GMT on 8th December). The base was attacked by 353 Imperial Japanese aircraft (including fighters, level and dive bombers, and torpedo bombers) in two waves, launched from six aircraft carriers. All eight U.S. Navy battleships were damaged, with four sunk. All but USS *Arizona* were later raised, and six were returned to service and went on to fight in the war. The Japanese also sank or damaged three cruisers, three destroyers, an anti-aircraft training ship, and one minelayer. 188 U.S. aircraft were destroyed; 2,403 Americans were killed and 1,178 others were wounded. Important base installations such as the power station, dry dock, shipyard, maintenance, and fuel and torpedo storage facilities, as well as the submarine piers and headquarters building (also home of the intelligence section) were not attacked. Japanese losses were light: 29 aircraft and five midget submarines lost, and 64 servicemen killed.

Japan announced a declaration of war on the United States later that day (December 8 in Tokyo), but the declaration was not delivered until the following day. The following day, December 8, Congress declared war on Japan. On December 11, Germany and Italy each declared war on the U.S., which responded with a declaration of war against Germany and Italy.

There were numerous historical precedents for the unannounced military action by Japan, but the lack of any formal warning, particularly while peace negotiations were still apparently ongoing, led President Franklin D. Roosevelt to proclaim December 7, 1941, "a date which will live in infamy". Because the attack happened without a declaration of war and without explicit warning, the attack on Pearl Harbour was later judged in the Tokyo Trials to be a war crime.

Let's pick up my ancestors' stories, starting with my uncle Bill Ward-Smith. His is probably the worst case of bad timing, as he explained in his memoir

---

> *Jesse Esdale Gray*
> *(1885-1946)*

> *Cecil Jesse Austen*
> *Gray (1908-1968)*

> *Peter Nigel Austen Gray*
> *(1950-present)*

written for his son, my cousin Tony:

"Within weeks the company's Vice President was calling with word from my understudy that conditions in Shanghai had deteriorated considerably since my departure. He asked what I thought of turning the China business over to some neutral national outfit.

"Do you want me to go back and see what I can do?"

"Well Bill," he said, "I'm not asking you–or telling you to go. But we'd sure like it if you would."

I was foolish. I agreed to do it. And so it was that, just days later, I kissed my wife and kids good-bye... and, yes, headed back to Shanghai.

The normal course of the voyage would be Frisco to Hawaii, to Yokohama, to Shanghai. The ship would then go on to Hong Kong, Manila, Singapore and onward from there.

We got to Honolulu without incident, but our departure was delayed several hours. At just that time, Japanese military authorities were visiting at the White House, shaking hands with officials there, telling them how peaceful were the Japanese intentions towards the Americans. In Honolulu the ship was quite peacefully taking on some U.S. military personnel, trucks and heavy equipment, along with six young Japanese men. But the scare must have been on even then because instead of proceeding west to Yokohama, we discovered on the fourth day out that we were actually heading south, towards Australia, skipping the Solomons and other Japanese mandate islands.

The captain came on the loudspeaker, "Please go easy on fresh water...our next port of call will not be reached for sixteen days!"

When we reached Sydney, Australia, the ship's radio opened up enough for a message to have a pilot come and take us up through the Torres Straights. We could see the Australian coast on one side, and New Guinea on the other. There was much debris in the water, the result, apparently, of a typhoon or storm around the New Guinea area. I remember seeing tree branches floating by with snakes crawling over them.

We dropped the pilot off at Cape York, the north tip of Australia, and continued on to Manila.

When we arrived, two U.S. military officials greeted us with "...Everybody gets off here!" Not good news for those of us destined for Shanghai and Hong Kong. We had no means of support in Manila; we'd be stranded there. And... the cargo for Shanghai and Hong Kong would have to be removed before they could get at the Manila cargo. A Shanghai-American friend, Judge Hemlick, and I decided to take the matter up with the authorities. We told them they should take us to Hong Kong and from there we would find our own way to Shanghai. It took about nine hours before we got them finally to agree.

Three days later we reached Hong Kong, but instead of off-loading the cargo, the ship pulled out within an hour of its arrival. Hemlick and I debarked and were able to get passage to Shanghai a few days later on a small coastal steamer. As it turned out, our arrival in Shanghai harbour was but hours before the very last evacuation ship was due to depart with a number of our good friends aboard. One of them, Barbara McIntyre, pregnant (and

---

due shortly) had agreed to take back a few things I managed to buy hurriedly for my wife. But I learned later that she went ashore when her ship reached Manila… the ship pulled out hurriedly, leaving her and a lot of others behind. She had to sell the things I had given her to get money for herself and her baby. As our journey to Shanghai had taken so long, I went straight to the Reuter office to cable my wife of my safe arrival. Little did I know it was to be the last word she would have from me for quite some time.

Things at the office were going normally, but buyers were holding off on orders and sales were almost at a standstill. I did make a few inquiries to see about turning over the business, but with rumours of the impending war, even the neutrals were timid. There was little interest even in the very generous terms I offered. But it mattered not, for all such efforts were soon frustrated once-and-for-all by the declaration of war between Japan, Germany and the allies. I saw it on my way to the office one morning–Japanese soldiers were everywhere on the street, fully armed, peeking around corners as though expecting trouble at every turn. They appeared ready to shoot without hesitation at anyone who might make even a questionable move"

Talk about hard luck! Out of a sense of duty to his employers, my uncle used all his influence towards negotiating his return to Shanghai, only to miss the last ship evacuating Westerners to safety on the very day of his arrival back there!

Anglo-American influence effectively ended after 8th December 1941, when the Imperial Japanese Army entered and occupied the British and

---

American controlled parts of the city in the wake of the attack on Pearl Harbour. The British and Americans troops taken by surprise surrendered without a shot, except the only British riverboat in Shanghai, HMS *Peterel*, which refused to surrender: six of the 18 British crew who were on board at the time were killed when the ship was sunk when the Japanese opened fire at almost point-blank range. The French troops did not move from the preserved French Concession, as the French Vichy government considerate itself as neutral. Western residents of the International Settlement were forced to wear armbands to differentiate them by nationality, were evicted from their homes once the internment camps were set up, and–just like Chinese citizens–were liable to maltreatment. The Japanese eventually sent European and American citizens to be interned at a number of internment camps in and around Shanghai. Uncle Bill eventually found himself at the Lunghua Civilian Assembly Centre, a work camp on what was then the outskirts of Shanghai, thus becoming the first of "My Magnificent Seven".

I shall now let Bill continue the story:

"Large posters appeared throughout the city instructing "enemy nationals" to remain calm, go to our businesses, and carry on as usual. In due course, they said, we'd be contacted by Japanese authorities. We were also instructed to go to various control centres and turn in any American and English money in our possession, as well as any arms, ammunition or binoculars. I had a revolver, as did my in-laws who were still in Shanghai. But instead of turning them over to the Japanese, possibly to be used against our own people, we decided to

---

dump them in a muddy, smelly creek near my father-in-law's residence. I think they still must be there today. We also had to give up our autos... for which there was no longer any gas anyway. Some of these had to be pushed in with the help of Chinese coolies. I lost a good one.

And, we were instructed to register at the Japanese centre and be given a red armband–"A" for American, and "B" for British nationals. I don't recall what was on those for the French or for others. Next, we had to obtain specially printed forms on which to list, tag, and estimate the cost or value of every piece of household furniture–tables, chairs, carpets, bed and bedding, crockery, utensils–everything. My wife and I owned valuable pets and pieces of made-to-order furniture, including some choice pieces of intricately carved Blackwood opium tables, stools, stands. When we turned these lists over to the Japanese authorities, they came to our home and stuck a proclamation notice on the premises saying that nothing, from then on, could be touched.

By now all our bank accounts were frozen and balances were reduced significantly. We were allowed to draw no more than $500 each month–equal to about $20 U.S. at the time–so very soon everyone needed money for food and other living expenses. Most of us found ourselves obliged to contact our home governments through the neutral Swiss consulate for relief funds. Having been treasurer of the Shanghai Relief Organization, a charitable group which distributed funds obtained from the Race Club and other donating sources to various Shanghai charitable institutions, I was appointed Treasurer of the British relief organization... the "BRA". A committee of seven prominent *citizens from the British community was formed to interview applicants and dictate the amount of funds I would requisition from the Swiss consulate each day. About fifteen people assisted me in distributing the funds and getting from the applicants their "promise-to-repay-after-the-war" receipts.*

Fresh and canned good prices in the Chinese grocery stores were rising sky-high. The compradors (Chinese grocers) were instructed by the Japanese authorities that canned goods sold to anyone wearing a red armband had to be pierced open at the time of purchase to prevent hoarding. To avoid this, I bought canned goods, cigarettes and tobacco through my Chinese business friends who were more than willing to help, some even refusing payment, and a few even offering to loan or give me money. One friend, Simian Woo–my advertising manager–offered to give me ten thousand U.S. dollars, a sizable amount at the time, even on the very real probability that he would never see me again after the war!

During the next couple of months (early 1942) the situation was more or less static. Then the Japanese began to call in some of the younger able-bodied men and took them to areas which were to be future internment camps. They put them to work doing repairs to the buildings and stringing barbed wire around the compounds. It was clear what was coming.

An old warehouse at Chapei, across the Whangpoo River from Shanghai City, was the first of the internment camps. Another was in the north end of Shanghai known as Honan Road. One other, up the Whangpoo River at a place called Hangchon, is where my in-laws were sent. Finally, there was

Lunghua, an old abandoned and dilapidated Chinese university, about twelve miles west of Shanghai, near a previously used airport. It comprised a number of substantially constructed concrete, one, two and three-story buildings and several single-story wooden huts, all very neglected... with doors, windows, floors and toilets in much need of repair. As soon as these camps were readied, the Japanese determined whom to call in from their lists of registered persons. Each of us was required to bring a bed and bedding, but only as much clothing or whatever else as could be carried. Most stuffed whatever they could in the way of canned goods, personal treasurers and such into bedding bundles.

Because of my position as Treasurer with the Relief Organization, the Swiss Consulate wanted to keep me out of internment to assist with hospitalized British nationals, but the Japanese refused. They did allow me to choose which camp I would be sent to (* March 1943). I chose Lunghua since many friends were there. It was a good choice. The camp commandant, Tom Mayashi turned out to be a decent and compassionate bloke who treated us all reasonably well and therefore was liked by most of the internees. The official designation of the camp was "Lunghua Civil Assembly Centre." A friend of ours, Ken Miller, now also living in the Seattle area, was there as well. His memory of the layout is better than mine; I do not recall any lawn bowls area or tennis court, but I do remember there was a fair-sized creek on the north side in addition to the pond on a sketch he did. I know we had to use water from this creek for the vegetable garden.

The entrance to the camp had a path leading from the gate at the guardhouse up to the main three-story concrete building known as F block which housed a number of families with small children. Here, too, is where the commandant's office was located. I was appointed monitor of E Block, a three-story concrete building that housed about four hundred men whom the Japanese considered of military age and therefore very dangerous. Guards frequently patrolled this particular building at night.

E Block had a stairway leading up to a large flat concrete roof on which, with the kind consideration of the commandant, ladies were allowed. This was our social hall and we had some very enjoyable dances here. Someone had the foresight to bring along a gramophone and records to provide us with music on various occasions. Unfortunately for us, about mid-way through our stay, our commandant Mr. Hayashi was transferred and a new commandant was appointed to replace him. The new man put the roof of E Block out of bounds for all of us and that put the end to our evening fun.

The camp was run by a committee of twelve internees, under the control of the Commandant. All chores and activities–such as kitchen, garbage and garden work–had to be done by us. At first both men and women prepared and cooked the meals, then later teams of six or seven of the younger men took on the job. These teams took turns getting up at five in the morning to start the cooking fires and cook the congee (rice gruel), amounts of which were doled into a large Dixie container for each block or hut according to the number of occupants in each. These huge pots were then toted on a flat, two-wheeled pushcart. Upon delivery to the huts, the occupants had the job of doling congee *out to each inmate on his or her own plate. Nearly all utensils–plates, cups or mugs–were enamel; crockery could not be replaced. Breakfast over, all dixies were returned to the kitchen to be cleaned along with the gaws (large circular containers in which the gruel was cooked).*

At 8am, all internees had to be in their rooms for the roll call. Roll was taken again at 8pm every night. We stood in rows to be counted by the guards; the number of people assigned to each room was checked against the records and reported to the Commandant. When this was done, one of the guards would walk out on the steps of F block and blow a whistle–the all-clear signal; we could leave the buildings and go about doing whatever we had to do… work in the kitchen, tote water for laundry, clean toilets and, of course, work the vegetable garden in the spring, summer and fall months. Water in the pond creeks and the well was very brackish; it could be used only for washing clothes and utensils, cleaning, flushing toilets and gardening. Water for cooking, drinking and tea had to come from Shanghai on a motorized water cart. This required several trips each day, and the dilapidated cart frequently broke down. The Chinese drivers were mechanically inept (totally inept might be a more accurate description) and could not do the repairs, so we managed to persuade the commandant to let a couple of our chaps who knew about motors do the driving–accompanied, of course–by two guards. This, as it turned out, was a very satisfactory arrangement as, after the first few trips, the guards would leave our boys to fill the tank and go off to buy cigarettes or whatever else they did, and return in time to ride back to camp. One of our drivers had been employed in the Shanghai Police Department and, during the time the guards were away he was contacted by a couple of young Russian men who were former co-workers. These fellows were getting all kinds of news by underground shortwave radios and would pass it along to us. Their reports were written in minute letters on small sheets of toilet paper; we almost needed a magnifying glass to decipher what was written. This was all very hush-hush... only eight of us had access to it and were told how, if at all, we could pass any of the news on to other camp inmates. This is how we got word of the threatened bombing of Japanese cities, and the actual bombings of Hiroshima and Nagasaki.

Then there were the two homemade radio receivers in the camp... one in my room and one in F block. They were made from elements out of Hotpoint stoves. The one in F block was actually built in a small toy horse on wheels; its owner would tell his small daughter to play with it–pull it down the passageway–whenever the guards came along on one of their many inspection tours. We had a special hiding place under the floor for the one in my room. All we could get on these radios was local Japanese news from Shanghai. The receiver in my room was brought in by one of the men transferred from the Chapei camp when the Japanese felt we needed more strong laborers.

My barrack was long and had doors at each end. At radio time we would station someone at either door to watch for guards. "Tally Ho!" was the warning call in such an instance; the receiver would be clicked off and hidden quickly away. One day someone assigned to guard a door missed doing so, and, sure

---

enough, that was the time for a guard to walk in on us. But in proper form, he shouted "Tally Ho!" before entering, presuming it to be the appropriate courtesy on such an occasion. It was a close call, but we were able to hide the radio in time. It would have meant big trouble had we been caught. Instead, we had many a chuckle over the incident.

It was shortly before the evacuation took place that we had our first escapee from the camp. He was a guy by the name of Condor. None of us knew much about him, but word was he was having domestic problems with his wife, and decided to crawl under the barbed wire and hustle off to Shanghai to hide himself there, away from her.

Often, we played cards. Our time for this was during the evening before lights-out and whenever daily routines and personal chores were done. Bridge, poker and cribbage were the favourite games. We had a ladder of cribbage players in our room, each player could challenge the one whose name was above his. The top player was "champ," the bottom man was the "schlemiel." Our delightful Jewish friend, Ike Levy, ironically, held this less-than-honoured position, with great consistency. Cribbage may not have been his game; he was, however, one powerhouse of a bridge player. We were playing poker in my room one evening. The chap next to me looked at his cards and announced graciously to one and all "...I'm not going to bet this hand" and then showed us what he held–a royal straight in spades! He asked us each to sign our names on the pack of cards that, henceforth, he claimed, belonged to him. No problem with that, we thought. But the next night he had the audacity to escape from the camp—and take our best pack of cards with him! They must have held their luck, for he made it safely back to England. Lewis Murry-Kidd was his name. Once home, he sent a message back to his sister still in the camp, "Siwel arrived safely." Siwel—Lewis spelled backwards.

After the replacement of the friendly Mr. Hayahsi, three more of our number managed to escape. Carole Pate from my room, and Tommy Crosstwaite and Tom Hurley from upstairs. They took quite some time preparing their getaway. They managed to get a supply of indigo dye from somewhere, and colored all their clothes to look like those of the local villagers. They gathered what canned foods they could from trusted friends, saved up bits of bread and made melba toast in the sun. These were all packed in carrying sacks and stashed in the long grass near the barbed wire at the edge of the compound… the wire they had carefully cut early in the evening of the night they planned to make their move. Now, before the war my company made and sold toothpaste to the Chinese market, and I had obtained a number of empty toothpaste tubes, each with just a little paste in the screw-cap end. Having previously converted all my Chinese money into U.S. $50s and $100s, I rolled these bills into bundles, wrapped them in grease paper and pushed them into the tubes which were then clamped shut with the little metal strips. If anyone ever opened and squeezed one of the tubes, just a bit of toothpaste would come out! No one would suspect a thing. I had shown the tubes with the money inside to my roommates, in case anything ever happened to me. So when Carole and his buddies were finally ready to go, he asked if I'd let them have some of the money in case they needed

---

> *Jesse Esdale Gray* *(1885-1946)*	> *Cecil Jesse Austen* *Gray (1908-1968)*	> *Peter Nigel Austen Gray* *(1950-present)*

it along the way. I gave them $350 and assumed I was saying good-bye to it. They promised to make good someday but I never expected to see the money or my campmates again. I was just pleased to play a small role in their venture. So, it was–a night or two later, after roll call, they climbed out of the building and crawled away in the long grass, recovered their bundles at the edge of the compound... and were gone. I did meet Carole again after the war. He told me about their get-away. After taking off to the west, they ran smack into a creek too wide and deep for them to cross without getting everything they were carrying wet and spoiled. They laid up in a paddy field the rest of that night and all next day–no more than a mile from the camp! Eventually they moved south and met with an aid group of American-Chinese servicemen whose job it was to rescue any of our pilots the Japanese may have shot down. So, their escape from Lunghua, as it turned out, was a complete success. When they eventually reached New York, they contacted my wife in California and sent her the cash I had given them in Shanghai. For her it was more than a pleasant monetary surprise, it was her first actual word, after about two and a half years, that I was actually still alive and O.K.

Food in the camp was never good. In truth it was pretty lousy, and as days went on it got worse. There was never enough to eat; what we did get was far from appetizing. At first our fare was fish and rice for the main meal; the Japanese, of course, thought this to be the choicest of selections. Most of us, however, did not. It was adequate, and not too difficult to get down, but nothing at all like what we had been used to. Later we got a little meat and some

---

occasional vegetables. But following the replacement of our Commandant, everything, including the food, really started to deteriorate. The rice, one of the main constituents, became nothing but sweepings, not fully de-husked and often smelly and caked with urine, droppings and other dirt. We washed it for hours before cooking it. The meat was also very smelly and at times unfit to eat. Often it had to be burned or thrown away. On a number of occasions, we got a batch of sweet potatoes. We would wash these and cut the rotten parts away, but what was left was a welcome change to our simple diets. Once we were given what we thought were small goats. We cooked them up and ate them, only to discover, a little later, that we had been issued carcasses of greyhounds from the racetrack. They had been slaughtered and delivered to us because food for them had run out and they could no longer be kept. Oh, but had they only been goats–there is very little meat on a greyhound! On another occasion three or four half-cured small pig carcasses were delivered to our kitchen. I jumped on the truck to help unload them, and a leg of one of the animals came off in my hands. It revealed a mass of blue maggots chewing away at the pig's innards. The others were all in the same condition. We quickly burned them and buried the remains.

Several parts of the camp had, at one time or another, been used for growing vegetables, so upon receiving a supply of seeds through the Red Cross, we formed two garden work groups. I was in charge of one because I happened to know a little more than most about vegetable gardening. Tilling that soil was a real chore. It was heavy work using heavy Chinese four-pronged picks that were the only implements, other than a few rakes, available to us. But we did harvest some tasty goods–carrots, beets, cabbage, lettuce, tomatoes, and cucumbers–for our efforts. Most of it was delivered to the camp hospital. Some was taken by the Commandant, and any surplus was rationed by rotation to the rest of us. In time we became quite adept at using the Chinese picks, but because of malnutrition and, at times, extremely warm and humid temperature–at one time it was 108 degrees in the shade–we could only work about 10 minutes or so before having to a rest. My usual get-up for the job was a pair of khaki shorts, tattered tennis shoes, no socks, no shirt and a Chinese straw hat. Anything more would have been excessive.

We were in our garden patch one morning when someone began yelling– "Hey! Hey! Rabbit… rabbit…!" I looked up in time to see a small brown hare streaking by, fifteen yards away. In a completely spontaneous move, I hurled my rake at that bunny and, sure as shooting, caught it a glancing blow. Before it could recover its' senses I pounced upon it and held on for dear life… only to find that the bang on its head had indeed done it in. A French lady in the camp offered to do up a fancy meal if she could partake of it, too. She had a few prunes and spices to add to the cooking, and did a superb job. Altogether, nine of us dined off that one little rabbit… by far one of the tastiest meals we'd had in a long time. The episode earned me a new nickname–from then on, I was "Safari Bill".

Though the food provided by our captors was so meagre and unappealing, those of us who were fortunate to have brought in or received parcels of canned food sent in by neutral friends or on a few occasions by the Red Cross were able, occasionally, to augment some of our meals. The canned goods generally needed to be warmed up–a problem until someone came up with the brilliant idea of making what was called a "chatty"…an apology for a camp stove, which was nonetheless quite serviceable for our purpose. The best chatties were those made out of a four-pound tin with an opening on the side and about four or five stout wire bars inserted from one side through the other near the base of the can and a couple of bent hoops of iron inserted a few inches above the top of the can to hold a cooking pot or frying pan. The inside was packed with mud, leaving room in the center for a small fire. Fuel, of course, like everything else, was scarce, so every little scrap of wood was collected; ash heaps were religiously scraped through by all and sundry for whatever little scraps of unburned coal might be retrieved.

Our drinking water was hauled into camp from Shanghai. None but the Chinese would ever drink any of it without first boiling it. Everyone, Thermos bottle in hand, attended to a shelter known as "Waterloo"–where the water was boiled–to receive their daily water ration of two pints per person. Coffee was very scarce but most of us had small stores of Indian or Chinese tea, a tiny bit of which we'd drop into our Thermos before drawing the daily supply of boiling water.

I don't know whether it was while they were scratching in the ashes for coal or what, but two of my friends, (the afore mentioned) Ken Miller and Sylvia Walker fell in love. Sylvia had a choice job in the Commandant's office–administering to the twenty-five-word letters inmates were allowed to send or receive via Geneva on occasion. When Mr.Hayashi first heard of their engagement, he was opposed to their being wed in the camp. But later he relented and even allowed them to use the private and secluded part of the assembly hall for a few days of honeymooning! Many of the short letters that came in never reached Sylvia for distribution. They were simply dumped into a wood box in one of the camp offices by the replacement Commandant. We found them, with mixed pleasure and disgust, after VJ day.

There's no way to say this gently. Our kitchen was inundated with rats. So, we decided one day, after cooking chores were done, to have a serious rat hunt. A set of wooden shelves stood against one wall of the kitchen and we suspected some varmints to be hiding at the back of them. We pulled the shelves away from the wall and to our great surprise–out came not one or two, but umpteen rats. The more we pulled the shelves away, the more they came. The doors and windows had all been closed and all of us, armed to the teeth with brooms… paddles… anything we could swing, gave chase. In a half-hour we must have killed over two or three dozen of the rodents. Not one, as far as I know, lived to see another day. After the evening meal and clean-up of the gaws (the large Chinese cooking bowls), we heated some water remaining in one of the bowls over what was left of the fire, scooped it out into buckets and ceremoniously poured it over our naked bodies… a very welcome bath!

Life in the camp was not just doing chores and sitting around wistfully afterwards. Some of us visited friends in other buildings. We would chat

---

and share a cup of tea at "elevenses", even if it meant bringing one's own tea and eats. On occasions, when the weather permitted, it was pleasant to take a stroll with a friend of the opposite sex around the paths of the camp. The buildings and camp area had previously been used as a Chinese university and the paths laid out when it was built. On occasion we could hear and see pheasants sitting on Chinese grave mounds just a short distance outside the barbed wire enclosure. They were most plentiful and very good eating, but we had, of course, no way of shooting or trapping them.

There were several mynah birds in and around the camp. Under the eaves of the dining building must have been a good place for nesting for several pairs settled in there and hatched broods of chicks. Some of the young boys in the camp captured chicks too young to fly and taught them to talk. These birds became very tame. I remember seeing one whose young master would let it out the window to fly around freely. When it had had enough of the great outdoors, it would fly back and tap against the window to be let in for feed and bed.

There were some extremes of weather that we found tough. The heat and humidity of summers, and the severe cold Siberian wind of winter which brought frightful chillblains, tested us unmercifully. None of the buildings had any heating of any description. Typhoons were also a problem. I remember the night that none of us in our room got a bit of sleep.

We had no windows, which was fine in the summer. A typhoon hit us at about 8:00 one night, and continued through until the next morning. We used every towel we collectively possessed to mop up the water that poured through the window openings and flooded the floor. Six of the gents would squeeze the towels into buckets, the rest of us would empty the buckets and hurry them back to be refilled. We took turns throughout the night squeezing towels and toting buckets. We were all dead-tired by the time morning came and the typhoon ended.

OK, camp life certainly wasn't beer and skittles, but there were good times. But good or bad, we managed, with only a few exceptions, to keep ourselves plugging along. There were two or three deaths, but from what causes I don't know.

Our kitchen gang was busy preparing and cooking the chow one afternoon when we heard shooting and the noise of several planes. I jumped through the kitchen window to see what it was all about. A dogfight was in progress overhead and I watched as several of our planes chased and shot down three or four old Japanese planes that tried to take off from the airfield close by. This generated quite a bit of excitement for all of us. One bright sunny morning we were absolutely elated to see about five of our big silver airplanes flying high in the sky over our camp. Everybody cheered at that beautiful sight... which only brought the Jap guards running. They shooed us back into our buildings and the planes flew off westward. But it gave us all a tremendous thrill and a renewed sense of hope. It was about a month or two later that the atomic bomb was dropped on Hiroshima and then on Nagasaki. The long war came to an end. Within a few days of the bombing, an American plane landed at the Shanghai airport and a team lead by an American Major visited our camp.

He informed the Japanese commandant that they would be held responsible for our safety; he warned us to be careful and observe the protection of the Japanese until such time as allied forces could officially take over. A number of deserters from the Chinese army had turned bandit. They were armed and roaming the countryside, intimidating whomever they came across and pillaging anything they could find. We, of course, didn't have much to warrant their attention except a bit of food and some clothes. A few days later American planes appeared overhead again. They circled the camp and dropped barrels of food and supplies by parachute. America! I began, for the first time in a long time to have vivid thoughts of Stella and my babies again. I couldn't help but wonder who would I be to them? And who would they be now... after all this time?"

Wow! Isn't that the most amazing "eye-witness" account! When I first read my uncle's story, I felt as though I was watching an episode of *"Colditz"* combined with *"The Great Escape"*, with even James Bond's quartermaster Q featured, showing Bond the wireless concealed in the toy horse on wheels and dollar bills inside tubes of toothpaste! And I could hear the English squaddie  shouting "Tally-Ho", to stop the guards finding the escape tunnel entrance. And yet this wasn't Hollywood; nor was Steven Spielberg involved in any way.

>   *Jesse Esdale Gray*   >   *Cecil Jesse Austen*   >   *Peter Nigel Austen Gray*
>   *(1885-1946)*   *Gray (1908-1968)*   *(1950-present)*

This was true life, and the action hero wasn't Tom Cruise or Harrison Ford. "Safari Bill" was none other than my uncle, Bill Ward-Smith. The supporting cast were just ordinary folk, caught up in the drama. I find myself full of respect and admiration for the bravery and fighting spirit shown by my uncle and all his fellow internees.

My uncle mentioned his in-laws in his memoir, which brings us to the next three of My Magnificent 7–my grandfather Jesse, grandmother Winifred and their younger daughter, my aunt Yolande. As I have explained earlier, they were the only other members of my immediate family living in Shanghai in December 1941, when the Japanese seized control of the International Settlement. As Uncle Bill explained in his memoir, the Japanese eventually interned all the British and Americans living in Shanghai, including my grandparents and my aunt. For a detailed account of how this occurred, I shall handover to my second "on-the-scene reporter", namely my grandfather Jesse. This is a reproduction of a letter he actually wrote to his daughter Stella (Safari Bill's wife) at the end of their internment. It is a fascinating insight into their plight leading up to their arrival in Yangchow C, as well as their actual period of captivity:

Yangchow, China

September 4, 1945

Our very dear Stella,

At long last this ghastly nightmare, which has lasted about three years and

eight months, is over, and there are prospects that we shall soon be leaving this Interment Camp and resuming a more or less normal life. The collapse of the Japanese is so utter and complete as to leave me aghast. While I had no doubt whatever of the ultimate outcome, I never expected such an early and sudden finish–fully anticipating the war to continue until next spring at least. Thanks chiefly to America, the dreadful Japanese menace has been squashed for all time, I hope. They have done nothing but disturb the peace of the Far East for years past and we have good cause to remember the arrogance, tyranny, bullying and looting we have suffered in their hands, in common with most other foreigners in China. I ceased, as you will remember, criticising the USA after our gorgeous tour there in 1929; my respect for them has grown and the entire civilised world owes them the deepest gratitude.

I will try to cover the entire position for the last three years eight months in this letter, and will put each item under a separate heading so as to ensure clarity.

OUR INTERNMENT:

We were notified early in March 1942 that we were for Yangchow. The majority of British Americans were interned in Shanghai. Why we were chosen for this place is a mystery. There are several people here of our own type, but the majority are of very poor class. Very mixed–Eurasians–out and out Chinese, Ilios (Europeans and Asia Minor), many Russian women who are wives of British men in China. The camp spirit has not been good–and that, coupled with the neglect shown by

---

| Jesse Esdale Gray | Cecil Jesse Austen | Peter Nigel Austen Gray |
| (1885-1946) | Gray (1908-1968) | (1950-present) |

the Japanese, has made the past 2 ½ years an unpleasant memory. There are 650 people here of whom 40 are Belgians from Tientsin, who arrived nearly 1 ½ years after us. The Japanese Commandant and guards have not been actively cruel or beastly, but we were made to feel our position. Mums has acted as one of the interpreters and got on well with them. For reasons which will appear later, I did very little of this. Food was scanty, and for weeks at a time we were not actually on the verge of starvation, but pretty close to it. The camp made its own bread. We got fragments of pork five days weekly with horrible Chinese vegetables. Other days vegetables only, and very little too, of bad quality. Water arrangements were dreadful; always a shortage–and, what we had, came mostly from the Grand Canal, brought in on wheelbarrows (buckets on them), or just pumped in. During the last few months there was an improvement as the Japanese dug a couple of wells. Baths were unknown–you could get a bucket of hot water for a washdown when water rationing was not in force. Sanitary arrangements horrible and inadequate. Almost indescribable. The compound itself is nice, plenty of room with grassy plots and fine shade trees. Housing pretty poor, each person allowed 40 square feet of floor space, and usually from 4 to 8 people in one room. Some families had rooms to themselves–mostly in threes–men and women together. We have been fortunate in having our room to ourselves, the three of us, for the first nine months on an upper floor. After that we were given a ground floor room in the Hospital building so as to avoid my having to climb stairs. We were strictly confined to the compound, and I have not set foot out of it for the entire period, nor has Yolande, but Mums went into town twice under guard, to do interpreting work for sick Japanese. To sum up, grounds good, no actual tyranny as such from the Japanese, appalling food, foul sanitation, intense mental stress, housing rotten (the place is bug-ridden), insufficient water (one shudders to think what would have happened in case of a fire)... and so on.

OUR PERSONAL CONDITION ON LEAVING SHANGHAI:

The year spent in Shanghai before coming here was awful. Our office which had almost been liquidated before coming here, or rather before the Japanese war broke out, was taken over by the Japanese, like all other British And American concerns. I had to work for 14 months under Japanese control. They paid me 25% of my salary and conditions were most humiliating, although not brutal. They took our car away in the first months of the war, so I had to tram and walk to the office from Columbia Road–one hour and a half each way, and most exhausting. Regarding our house at 104 Columbia Road, we stayed in it until we were interned, but the fiendish Japanese–gendarmes, soldiers, civilians, officials– were frequently in and out, asking the aggravating and tiresome questions only a Japanese can ask–on every aspect of our private affairs–financial, family, political–and so on. I have recently been informed that the house is vacant, but do not know if it has been so since we left. While our personal possessions, bric- a-brac, curios, etc., are still there, we fear most of our heavy furniture, etc., has been confiscated, with scant chance of return. However, we cannot be sure of this until we have an opportunity of checking up ourselves.

> *Jesse Esdale Gray (1885-1946)*   > *Cecil Jesse Austen Gray (1908-1968)*   > *Peter Nigel Austen Gray (1950-present)*

OUR HEALTH:

As far as I personally am concerned, this is rather a grievous subject. On leaving Shanghai, my heart trouble was dormant and I could move around and act almost normally but with great care. Immediately after coming to camp, I took a severe chill, got bronchitis which is now more or less chronic, my heart condition got worse, giving me long spells of exhaustion and sometimes considerable distress. I had dysentery (mild) twice–had a very painful hernia caused by much coughing, which finally necessitated an urgent operation under local anaesthetic. All in all, I have had six spells in hospital and while I have not kept exact count, I think I have put in nearly half my camp time therein. The camp hospital is staffed with excellent personnel, mostly missionaries, and I have had devoted and unceasing attention and owe a debt of gratitude which can never be repaid. I am now actually in the hospital, but as our room is just across the passage, I see quite a lot of Mums and Yolande. Mums has been most loving and devoted, waiting on me hand and foot, and I am deeply grateful. Yolande also has been very kind and loving, and I am fortunate, indeed, in having them with me. Yolande has done a lot of camp work, chiefly cooking, but lately teaching small kids. In addition to household work, Mums has done a lot of interpreting and has given valuable assistance with the Sale and Exchange Department. I started to work in the canteen, in charge, but had to give it up because of the rotten crowd I was associated with. They were largely instrumental in getting me into serious trouble with the Japanese camp authorities, who violently abused me on several occasions. I narrowly escaped being beaten up and being sent to a real prison camp. I must admit that a part of the trouble, albeit a small one, may have been due to the fact that I refused to be obsequious or abject to the Japanese. I was always courteous, but cold and would not do any bootlicking, which some other Japanese-speaking people did. I have good cause to hate the Japanese! Now in regards to Mum's and Yolande's health–they are both well but naturally, both show the effects of the miserable life we have led here. What with malnutrition, cold, last winter was indescribable and with no heating, hot in the summer, monotony, etc., there is hardly anyone in the place who does not show the effects. In the winter we were three months without lights, no coal to run the power company. There was always something wrong in the camp–no fuel, no bread, no water, sometimes no chow...all because the Japanese were neglectful or unable to provide for us. About my own camp work, I might mention I did a few spells of teaching– French, etc., and English to the Belgians, but I could not keep it up. You may be interested to know that I have learned the Spanish language while here in camp.

WHEN ARE WE GOING TO LEAVE HERE FOR SHANGHAI:

This is the question we cannot answer. Although the war as now been over for nearly three weeks, they are just beginning to start work on the evacuation, and an American Mission (four officers) arrived yesterday to commence to make arrangements. I know that Sassoon's have provided quarters for our temporary accommodation in Shanghai and funds will be available, so we

---

> *Jesse Esdale Gray (1885-1946)* > *Cecil Jesse Austen Gray (1908-1968)* > *Peter Nigel Austen Gray (1950-present)*

may be amongst the first crowd to return to Shanghai. The whole thing is an enormous problem and I am afraid that a month or more will elapse before the camp is finally broken. Shanghai is said to be in a dreadful state–sanitary, PWD, money, housing–all in a fearful state of chaos, and it will be years before the place recovers. In any case it will never be the place we used to know–no more SMC or Extra'lity–all will very likely be under complete Chinese control.

OUR FUTURE PLANS:

These are most indefinite. I have told the company that I will give them one year of my time to help them to reorganize the company, but no more. After that I want to retire and get away from the East–quite enough of it! Future residence–Australia? Canada? California? Cannot say, but the former most likely. In addition to the work I may do for the office (only if health permits, however), I shall have many personal affairs to attend to and adjust. I should have mentioned earlier that the doctor will not permit me to go to work when I get back to Shanghai. I shall have to lay up in hospital for three to four weeks before I attempt to do anything. Yolande proposed to go to India as soon as she can get in touch with her fiancée, so Mums and I shall be left on our own.

OUR TWO BOYS:

As you know, they are prisoners-of-war in Hong Kong, unless the Japanese have moved them. No news from them since July 1944. They may or rather, must, have been liberated by now, so we are momentarily and anxiously awaiting to hear. We also naturally want to hear from Cecil's wife who was a civilian internee in Hong Kong.

BILL:

You have heard from him regularly of course, so no need for me to say anything. He has written to us three times, I think, no four, since we were put in. As he is of the British Relief Association Committee, which has been reorganized, he has probably been released from camp, and I am hoping we shall hear from him soon.

YOUR DEAR SELF:

We have been very pleased, indeed joyful, when we got your letter. God grant that you and the kids are safe and sound. I do not, of course, know what you are going to do, whether Bill will go to USA to collect you, whether you will continue to stay there, or whether you will come out to re-join Bill, who will no doubt have to get to work soon. The latter seems to me to be the most likely, but whatever is done–I hope, nay, WE hope we shall meet again soon.

GENERAL:

I think I have covered almost everything, dearie. If not, it will have to wait and will no doubt keep until we meet. Although I have written this letter, it is from all three of us, and our united love goes with it, with an earnest longing to see you again soon. Since the Japanese caved in, the Red Cross and the Chinese

---

| > | *Jesse Esdale Gray (1885-1946)* | > | *Cecil Jesse Austen Gray (1908-1968)* | > | *Peter Nigel Austen Gray (1950-present)* |

authorities have flooded us with good things, and now there is feast instead of famine. The Chinese are very friendly and kind and so they should be. The International Red Cross has been very good, and has frequently sent us up good things–Jam, tinned goods, etc. On two occasions we got parcels from the American Red Cross with magnificent contents. How grateful we were–tears of gratitude all over the camp when these were distributed. It is not too much to say that, had we not received these things, we would have been nearer to starvation than we want to think about.

Goodbye for today, dearest girlie. Our united fondest love–and here's to "The Day"!

Your ever affectionate

Dads, Mums and Yolande

A FEW THINGS WHICH HAVE SINCE OCCURRED TO ME:

The Japanese left us our radios until the end of November 1942, so we kept in touch with the news. After that, we got news from neutrals until March 1943, when we were interned. In camp we got newspapers published by the Japanese in English, so we kept in touch with the situation–but had to ignore lies, and read between the lines. All work in the camp was done by inmates, no servants of any kind. We had a fair library. Can't think of anything else.

I had intended writing to Amy in England and to Nancy and Albert in California, but time lacks and the effort to triplicate this letter would be too great. Will you, therefore, dear, try and get a couple of copies made, and send them to the two enclosed covering notes. You know Albert's address; Amy's is

Mrs. H.V. Hawley, 24 Deepdene Vale, Dorking, Surrey, England.

Dear Albert and Nancy–I have neither the time or the energy to write you at any length, so have asked Stella to send you a copy of my letter of today. I understand it is going from Hong Kong by air, so I hope delivery will be pretty prompt. What indescribable relief at the end of this horror and how complete the collapse of the arrogant Japs who have been such a menace to the peace of the world for years! I always knew it would end the right way but expected a long and grim fight. We are so grateful to the USA for their magnificent efforts–they did the lion's share of the work, at least in the Far East. The British are not in evidence in Central or North China, but they are very busy in the South, taking over Hong Kong, Singapore, A.E.I. and other places. Do write us soon and tell us your news which I hope will be good. Better write c/o China Import Export Lumber Co. Ltd, 1426 Yangtzepoo Road, Shanghai. Not 104 Columbia Road, the situation there is very doubtful. All the best, and we hope we shall meet again soon. Love from us both–or rather, three, as I am including Yolande. Yours affectionately, Jess

I came into possession of this letter quite a few years ago, soon after my introduction into family history by a distant cousin on the maternal side of my family. It came from one of my Reynolds cousins, the four sons of my aunt Yolande. She is another of my Magnificent Seven, and Jesse's letter serves to describe her ordeal alongside my grandparents in Yangchow C camp. It is

---

> *Jesse Esdale Gray*
> *(1885-1946)*

> *Cecil Jesse Austen*
> *Gray (1908-1968)*

> *Peter Nigel Austen Gray*
> *(1950-present)*

wonderful to read of my grandfather thanking Yolande for her love and care during their time in the camp. I believe her presence with him through their shared experience was vital for him to be able to endure his suffering. And she was only 24 years old when her whole world was turned upside down–from "living the life" in Shanghai society, to being incarcerated by the Japanese with her elderly

parents. And, almost hidden in her father's letter, is the fact that she became engaged just before being taken captive; Jesse writes of her getting in touch with her "fiancée". So, she had to endure her internment separated from the man she had fallen in love with.

I have very mixed emotions about this letter. I was thrilled when I initially read it, as it was the first time I had "heard" my grandfather's voice. It was when he truly came alive for me; a real person with a character, feelings and emotions, rather than just a name on my tree. In a way, it was my grandfather introducing himself to me personally, albeit about 60 years after his death. It prompted me to wonder what he was like, would I have liked him and, rather selfishly, would he have liked me. But then, when I stopped thinking about me and focussed on what he was actually writing about in his letter, my initial sense of joy at forming an emotional attachment to my grandfather turned to a feeling of sadness and loss. Additionally, armed with the few genealogical facts of his life, including the date of his death, I soon realised the full significance of the date his letter was written. Basically, this was probably the last letter he wrote. So, when he writes of his future plans regarding where he hopes to live–*"Australia? Canada? California? Cannot say, but the former most likely"*–it is heart breaking to read, knowing that he died just ten months later.

In the letter my grandfather wrote *"I have good cause to hate the Japanese!"*. This simple sentence was the most intriguing for me, because my wish to understand it is probably why I wrote this book. I felt a need to know the full story behind it. Why would my grandfather express such hatred for the people of the country of his birth? I shall return to this question later, when I try to summarise what I have discovered of my family's history and answer the book's titular question–*"Too Far East?"*.

But I am getting ahead of myself; back to the plight of "My Magnificent 7". My uncle Bill is in Lunghua camp; my grandparents Jesse and Winifred and my aunt Yolande are in Yangchow camp. Jesse names the other three in his letter and places them in their respective locations. "Our 2 boys" are my father Cecil and his brother Norman, who were in the Military Prisoner of War camp in Hong Kong, because they were serving in the RNVR. "Cecil's wife" is my mother, also in Hong Kong but in Stanley Interment Camp as she was a civilian when captured. I am now going to let my mother pick up their stories, as the third of my eye-witnesses:

"On the morning of the Pearl Harbour attack we were also attacked and the Commodore phoned us and told us to bring a change of clothing, as he did

---

not know when we might get back home.

The shelling and bombing of the Dockyard was so heavy the Commodore sent me and the cypher ladies to the Naval Hospital and that is where we were captured by the Japanese Navy. A few days later I went with one of the naval sisters to their house which they had had to evacuate, to see if she could find any of her belongings. We were upstairs when two Jap army privates walked in, they nattered to each other in Japanese, which we did not understand then one put his hand up above his head and we realised he was referring to our height–so being tall saved us from being raped. We shot back to the safety of the hospital as quickly as we could. Some of the nurses in the outlying hospitals were raped and bayoneted. We were sent to two other hospitals during the first eight months of our captivity.

The first move was to Stubbs Road Convent where we mixed with army medical services. We had not had any nursing training other than taking temperatures and giving bed baths so we just had to learn the hard way. During the fighting whilst we were in the Naval Hospital, I felt so sorry for the patients who were getting shelled in their beds, so I just walked up and down the ward with my tin hat on and smiled at the men to make them feel safe whenever there was a raid.

A strange thing happened before we left the Stubbs Road hospital because we were told that we would be going to Stanley Camp the following day. At the time we had some tea to drink and six of us had our tea leaves read by a lady. Five of us were told that we would see our husbands but would not be able to talk to them and the sixth that she would be able to talk to hers. We thought it was a lot of nonsense as our husbands were in the Officers Camp on the mainland. To our surprise the next day we were taken to the Ferry Landing stage and left waiting for hours in the rain until they took us across the harbour to Kowloon by ferry and then in an open truck to St Theresa's Hospital which was opposite the Officers camp, so we could see our husbands across the barbed wire but were not allowed to talk to them. The one could see and talk to hers because he was a patient in the hospital!

In that hospital we had a diphtheria epidemic and the Japs would only bring enough medicine to treat two or three people and the doctors had to decide who, out of the large number of patients, was most likely to live after taking the medicine.

The guards used to come on duty quite tight at times and yell "We want nurses" and the doctors would send a message to us to stay on the wards whilst they calmed the devils down, they were very brave because they could easily have been bayoneted.

I did a long spell of night duty in that hospital and we had so many dysentery patients and the only medicine we had for them was Epsom salts so you can imagine what a dreadful time we had trying to keep them as clean and comfortable as possible. Twelve hours duty with only a cup of tea for sustenance. If any patient came into hospital with a bar of coal tar soap there would be a cheer. I gave my first injection to a dying patient as I was told it would not hurt him but would make his going easier and then I had to sit

---

with him until he died, that was the first time I had seen anyone die and I felt terrible and so sad.

At the end of eight months I was taken to Stanley camp and so I did not have to do any more nursing.

Our diet was down to starvation levels with two bowls of rice a day and stewed vegetables including chrysanthemum leaves. For a ten-day period, we were each given 3 oz of peanut oil, 2 dessert spoons of soya beans, 2 teaspoons of sugar and 2 teaspoons of tea. We only received 4 Red Cross parcels during the whole of our captivity.

Necessity is the mother of invention, as any nail varnish available was used to repair spectacle frames. I had a box of Lux soap flakes and I kept them to use as a shampoo for the 3½ years. For washing our clothes, we had lye made from the wood ash from cooking our rice and vegetables. We only had cold water for washing and showering etc.

The Japanese did bring in plenty of books for us to read, but all of them gave descriptions of meals which did not help our hunger. We had some very good concerts with pianists and singers. Our windows were such a bad fit that we had to sleep with an umbrella when it rained. We were three people to a room, which in peace time was occupied by two Chinese students. The rooms were so bug invested we had to periodically take our camp beds outside and run a lighted taper over them to kill the blighters.

I had a lovely gold Rolex watch which kept going all through our captivity and everyone used to ask me the time. Just a few weeks before the end of the war my gums were so bad with no vitamins that the doctor advised me to sell any gold I had and so my watch had to go. All I got for it was half a pound of lard and some dried egg yolk. When I arrived home ten years after my 21st birthday trip I weighed 6 stones and had to have all my teeth taken out. My poor parents did not know that I was alive for the first two years of our captivity.

We had to line up and be counted every day and we were supposed to bow to the wretched guards but we just nodded our heads very slightly. Some people who were good with their hands made clogs for us and we made ourselves shorts and tops out of hospital screen covers but it was very cold in the winter months with no fat inside us. We did have some army trousers and tops which were wool and helped.

There were over 2000 of us in the camp mixed [between]men, women and a few children. We were allowed to send 25-word notes once a month to our husbands and parents but I think only two arrived in England.

When the war was over our husbands commandeered a ferry and came across to our camp to see us; they saw the Japs dumping RX parcels into the harbour. We had a very worrying ten days at the end because we did not know how the Japs would react to losing the war. We had already gathered from Chinese newspapers that, had there been a landing on the China coast, all prisoners were to be put into caves round the island and the fronts blasted down. We heard them blowing out the caves so we know it was true. Thank heaven for the atomic bomb otherwise we would never have survived. Naturally

---

I will not hear anything against the bomb.

One good thing to come out of my years of captivity was learning to play bridge which has stood me in good stead ever since. Whenever I had any worries, I found that I had to concentrate so much while playing that I forgot my troubles. Also, it has been a social asset for the 16 years I have been a widow.

When we were rescued by our Navy, they thought we had the hoarding instinct as we did not eat all the food they gave us but, after being starved for so long, we could not eat much at a sitting. They put a notice up to tell us there was more where that came from. All the food tasted so rich to us.

It took us seven weeks to get back to England and the ship's officers thought we looked a lot better by the end of the voyage but my family thought I looked dreadful.

The Admiralty and the Hong Kong government told us to put in a claim for all we had lost but we received nothing. My pay for the four years was £216 after they had deducted the amount I had signed for the purchase of soap and toothpaste on board. The Admiralty wanted to cut my husband's marriage allowance because the Japs had been feeding me all that time!

When I returned to China, I went to our house on the Peak in Hong Kong to see if I could find any of our belongings but there was no front door, floors or ceilings, all had been stripped for firewood. We never did get back home while the war was on."

As you can imagine, this autobiographical account of my mother's war

---

experiences makes me very emotional whenever I read it. I am so glad I asked her to write it for me, as it provides me with an everlasting memorial to her. It reveals so much of her spirit and personality, and it is a story of such courage that it deserves to be retold. From her vocabulary, her style of writing, and even her grammar, I can hear her calmly telling the story to me, with her phlegmatic acceptance that "it was what it was".

I treasure this short summary of my mother's ordeal, written by her many years later with the benefit of hindsight maybe changing her view on what had happened to her. However, it is not the only source of information I have from this chapter of my parents' lives. Far from it, because Mother kept an amazing collection of memorabilia from her war time experiences, including correspondence between her and my father, her parents, her brother-in-law, and fellow internees. She even wrote a daily diary during her time in captivity. I knew of the existence of this material towards the end of her life, and we had talked about it in the context of it "being a story deserving of a wider audience". She even met with a young lady researcher from the Imperial War Museum in London, discussing a possible solution as to where this splendid resource should be archived after her death. However, events overtook these loose plans and I became the guardian of this particular family history "treasure trove".

> *Jesse Esdale Gray*   >   *Cecil Jesse Austen*   >   *Peter Nigel Austen Gray*
> *(1885-1946)*   *Gray (1908-1968)*   *(1950-present)*

It was only when I examined in detail just what I had inherited that I got the notion to include it in any family history book I might write. This is because it covers so much detail of her "life" as a Japanese prisoner-of-war and it contains my parents' love story, played out across barbed wire! I shall try to precis these events in my next chapter.

MY MOTHER'S REAL-LIFE "TENKO" EXPERIENCE

Hopefully those of you readers who have made it through from Chapter 1 will recall that my daughter Ann was able to inform her classmates that "Grandma Katie ate fried banana skins! And she is only alive because they dropped an atomic bomb!" Both fairly random statements to drop into a school discussion in Leicestershire, but both possessing genuine impact and, more importantly, a healthy amount of "street cred"! She was armed with this information because they are the essential facts of Grandma's life that I had shared with her as a teenager, which in turn was about all I knew of that period of my mother's life as I grew up. I only learned more much later on, when I started my quest to know as much as possible about my family history. And, by writing this book, I can hopefully pass on some more equally- interesting gems to Ann and the rest of my family. If I'm being honest, I want to pass it all on–to anyone who might be the slightest bit interested!

I am guessing the majority of you readers haven't got a clue about the Tenko reference in this chapter's title. "*Tenko*" was the name of a television

---

drama, co-produced by the BBC and the Australian Broadcasting Corporation (ABC), which was broadcast between 1981 and 1984. The series dealt with the experiences of British, Australian and Dutch women who were captured after the Fall of Singapore in February 1942, after the Japanese invasion, and held in a fictional Japanese internment camp on a Japanese-occupied island between Singapore and Australia. Having been separated from their husbands, herded into makeshift holding camps and largely forgotten by the British War Office, the women have to learn to cope with appalling living conditions, malnutrition, disease, violence and death. *Tenko* was created by Lavinia Warner after she had conducted research into the internment of nursing corps officer Margot Turner (1910–1993) for an edition of *This Is Your Life* and was convinced of the dramatic potential of the stories of women prisoners of the Japanese. Aside from the first two episodes, set in Singapore, which were written by Paul Wheeler, the series was written by Jill Hyem and Anne Valery.

"What has all this got to do with your mother?" I hear you ask. Well, unlikely as it sounds, *Tenko* was one of Mother's favourite television programmes! She watched every episode and told me how much she enjoyed it. My guess is that it was a very close re-enactment of her own experiences and she was "safe" to watch it retrospectively, secure in the knowledge she had survived the real thing, so a fictional TV show couldn't harm her. This is in sharp contrast to a researcher for the series, War hero and prisoner of war Dr Margaret Thomson, who did not like to talk about her experiences and never watched the programmes! Much of this chapter could essentially provide the material

| *William Gray* | > | *John Gray* | > | *James Gray* | > | *Jesse William Gray* | > |
| *(1720-1795)* | | *(1770-1830)* | | *(1813-1880)* | | *(1855-1894)* | |

for an alternative *Tenko* script, only Stanley-style.

So, back to Hong Kong and my mother's record of her internment. To summarise much of what you have read in the last chapter and to put my mother's account in its' context, I have detailed the key dates and locations of the internments of "My Magnificent 7" in this updated table below:

DATES	"MY MAGNIFICENT 7"						
	Kathleen (my mother)	Cecil (my father)	Norman (my uncle)	Jesse (my grandfather)	Winifred (my grandmother)	Yolande (my aunt)	Bill (my uncle)
Jan, 1942 – after Japanese take Shanghai and Hong Kong	Stubbs Road Hospital, Hong Kong	North Point POW camp, Hong Kong	North Point POW camp, Hong Kong	104 Columbia Road (their house in Shanghai)	104 Columbia Road (their house in Shanghai)	104 Columbia Road (their house in Shanghai)	Shanghai (not yet interned)
25th February 1942	St. Theresa's Hospital, Hong Kong	North Point POW camp, Hong Kong	North Point POW camp, Hong Kong	104 Columbia Road	104 Columbia Road	104 Columbia Road	Shanghai (not yet interned)
March 1942	St. Theresa's Hospital, Hong Kong	North Point POW camp, Hong Kong	North Point POW camp, Hong Kong	Yangchow C Internment camp, Shanghai	Yangchow C Internment camp, Shanghai	Yangchow C Internment camp, Shanghai	Shanghai (not yet interned)
18th April 1942	St. Theresa's Hospital, Hong Kong	Argyle Street POW camp, Hong Kong (opposite St Theresa's)	Argyle Street POW camp, Hong Kong (opposite St Theresa's)	Yangchow C Internment camp, Shanghai	Yangchow C Internment camp, Shanghai	Yangchow C Internment camp, Shanghai	Shanghai (not yet interned)
10th August 1942	Stanley Internment camp, Hong Kong	Argyle Street POW camp, Hong Kong	Argyle Street POW camp, Hong Kong	Yangchow C Internment camp, Shanghai	Yangchow C Internment camp, Shanghai	Yangchow C Internment camp, Shanghai	Shanghai (not yet interned)
July 1943	Stanley Internment camp, Hong Kong	Argyle Street POW camp, Hong Kong	Argyle Street POW camp, Hong Kong	Yangchow C Internment camp, Shanghai	Yangchow C Internment camp, Shanghai	Yangchow C Internment camp, Shanghai	Lunghua Internment camp, Shanghai
August 1945 (just before release)	Stanley Internment camp, Hong Kong	Sham-shui-Po POW camp, Hong Kong	Sham-shui-Po POW camp, Hong Kong	Yangchow C Internment camp, Shanghai	Yangchow C Internment camp, Shanghai	Yangchow C Internment camp, Shanghai	Lunghua Internment camp, Shanghai

I have a small lined notebook in which she kept a full diary for 1942, her first full year in captivity. She drew her own calendar on the front page, on which she has crossed the days off. It is strange what thoughts it evokes in me. I remember another of my favourite films was *"The Man in the Iron Mask"* where the captive scratches the days off on the prison walls. Here was my mother recording each day spent without her liberty.

She even used this calendar as the equivalent of any woman's diary, in that she marked her menstrual cycle on it. Whilst I would definitely class this as TMI in modern parlance, it helped me to understand a phrase that keeps cropping up in her diary entries. Take the 13th January for instance–"Susie arrived and I felt rotten so stayed in bed all day". A quick glance at her calendar shows a ring around the 13th. There was a ring around the 25th February and sure enough this same person arrived on that day! What Mother actually wrote as part of her entry for 25th Feb. was "Of course all the upset caused Susie to come". Even her slow-witted son finally understood that there was no internee called Susie with special privileges, that allowed her to come and go in the camp as she wished! Whilst I am joking about this revelation through her diary, it illustrates how much normal life still goes on for females in captivity, though without the resources to cope with it. It seems to bring home to me the full extent of what having one's liberty removed actually means, down to the smallest detail. I have reproduced the diary in full in Appendix 1 at the end of my book, to allow you to "hear" my mother's thoughts, as she recorded every detail of a year in captivity. However, I am going to quote extensively from the diary, to give you a sense of how the human spirit copes through such trauma. It fills me with such pride and admiration for her and, indeed, for all the internees and prisoners-of-war who shared similar experiences.

So, it begins in January 1942 when Mother is still at the Naval Hospital, being forced to carry out nursing duties, despite not being a trained nurse:

JANUARY 1942

Jan 1st   *So unused to late nights that I felt quite tired after seeing the New Year in. The terrific rush of casualties having eased we were able to have organised times of duty. Had the afternoon off and was glad of the rest.*

Jan 6th   *Long day duty. Made the calendar on the front of this book during my short off-duty spell and brought same up-to-date. Mr Longyear & his two assistants have put up curtains in the mess and it looks quite homely now. The big dining table was also brought up for us from the Sisters' mess so we have more room for feeding. The usual four played Mah-jong and Jean and Christine went next door to play bridge. I lost at Mah-jong.*

Jan 9th   *Miss Franklin asked me to go into Ward 6 to work instead of Miss G. because she had been upset by one of the stewards. I was so fed up because all our really bad cases are in ward 6 and I am scared to touch them. It is so depressing too and gets me down rather. Half day spent in the sunshine*

Jan 13th   *Susie arrived and I felt rotten so stayed in bed all day.*

Jan 18th   *(Sunday) Most eventful day when we had to leave the R.N.H. and*

>   *Jesse Esdale Gray*   >   *Cecil Jesse Austen*   >   *Peter Nigel Austen Gray*
>   *(1885-1946)*   *Gray (1908-1968)*   *(1950-present)*

go to St Albert's Convent on Stubbs Road

Jan 21st   We were told we could send a card home to England. I got up but felt awfully dizzy, filled in my card to Mummie, poor darling I do hope she receives it as quickly as possible as I am sure she will be most frantically worried. Went on duty in the afternoon, felt very weak but much better. Good concert at 7p.m.

Feb 1st   Usual day but in the evening we were told to pack our luggage ready to send to Stanley early the next morning, as we were to follow the day after

Feb 2nd   Sent off our luggage and bedding. Mrs Greenwood went dashing off in the ambulance to Stanley and we were very glad to have a peaceful night, unfortunately we could not sleep as our mattresses having been sent away we had to sleep on the wire bed

Feb 3rd   Jeff managed to find enough biscuit mattresses for Mrs Tomlin, Wexie and self and so we managed to have a better night. No word about Stanley.

Feb 15th   Usual day. No news of going to Stanley. Very damp weather

Feb 24th   In the evening we were told we should be moving the next day, not to Stanley as we had thought but over to Kowloon, most likely to St Theresa's Hospital

Feb 25th   The Japanese arrived with the news that everybody but the Indians were to leave the Hospital. Cleave and the Naval Sisters were sent to Bowen Road. All our Naval stewards were sent to

North Point. Drs. Page, Gunn and Jackson, Mums, Wexie, Jean and I were to go with the Army and the VADs [The Voluntary Aid Detachment was a voluntary unit of civilians providing nursing care to military personnel during both World Wars] to Kowloon. Of course, all the upset caused Susie to come and we were waiting around for so long in the grounds of St. Albert and then on the HK side of the harbour and longer still on the Kowloon side where we had to sort out all our luggage and then we were crowded into one lorry and driven to St. Theresa's. We had been 1p.m. hanging around and moving and we arrived at St. Theresa's at about 9:30pm. I was of course soaked through and so fagged out and in such pain that I was in tears. We slept on the floor, 11 in one room.

Feb 26th   *Everyone was put straight on duty–Mums was very sick and I asked if I might stay off the wards for one day because of Susie. Matron very grudgingly allowed me to stay off but I spent most of the day looking after Mrs, T. Got a bed for her & the rest of us slept on the floor again*

Feb 27th   *Went on duty in the hospital. Very well-built hospital. Quite a lot of work to do. All had beds to sleep on thank goodness. The mosquitoes were frightful.*

Mar 4th   *Long day and we moved to a larger house, which indeed was a lucky thing or we would all have been mad as our rooms had been far too crowded and 30 women sharing one bathroom is no joke. We are now 7 in our room and it is a room with plenty of windows so we should be alright for keeping cooler in the summer*

Mar 8th   *Our luggage arrived from Stanley. Long day duty, after tea I sorted my clothes. Wexie day off. Mums very sick brought to the hospital and we had a frantic day of bedpans*

Mar 9th   *Short day duty, Allison Black off. It was such a joy to have a change of clothing, Mums still very ill*

Mar 26th   *My day off, did a lot of washing and scrubbing, washed my hair and packed all my odds and ends and moved out of my corner so that Jean could move in as I was going on night duty. Tried to sleep in the afternoon but could not. Had tea, moved into the night staff sleeping room then Wexie and I had a quick bath each and went on duty at 8 pm. During the day 4 VADs were taken to hospital, 2 of which had dysentery and I had them all on my floor. Consequently, I had a ghastly night. Thirty bedpans between the 2 dys. patients. Another patient was vomiting and had a high temperature so she was not allowed out of bed. Day staff forgot to send a relief on by 7.30am so I had to go on till 8 am and was nearly dropping with tiredness. Then, having had our breakfast and taken over breakfast to the lazy people who were about to have a day off and could not drag themselves out of bed to go to the bungalow for theirs, we staggered across for roll-call only to find the corporal had not arrived and so there would be no roll-call. That is why I cannot understand why people want to stay in bed for breakfast when they have to get up immediately afterwards for the roll-call*

Mar 27th   *Slept on and off during the day–had a most frightful headache when I got up and had an even more hectic night on duty with a total of 38 bedpans to deal with*

Mar 28th   *During the day 4 more VADs went into the hospital sick. Sister Morgan took over night duty from Sister Hills. I was very nearly left with the top floor alone but for Wexie saying it was impossible for me to do it. We had a total of 46 B.P.s*

Mar 29th   *Did not have nearly enough sleep during the day and awoke with a splitting headache and aching all over. Wexie was the same. We decided that we would get up for tea. Before tea Wexie had a jolly good cry because she was feeling so rotten and after tea, which consisted of plain rice and hot water, I also had a good cry. Fortunately, the B.P.s slackened slightly during the night so we did not have quite so much to do. Day staff played tennis*

Mar 30th   *I slept a bit more but Wexie felt very rotten. She came on duty but felt too rotten to do anything, had a temperature of 100 and a very troublesome tummy. At 5.30 she went back to the house and went to bed and was brought to the hospital as a patient at about 10am on 31st Mar*

Mar 31st   *I had a much better sleep. Mrs Simpson came on duty to help me in Wexie's place but was only with me during the quietest parts of the night as Sister took her onto the 2nd Floor at 5:30 am when all the washings, temperatures and beds had to be done, so I had a lot to do. The Major was demoted and sent to Sham-po and Dr. Jackson was made Commanding Officer of the hospital. So, we now have a Military hospital run by 3 Naval Doctors entirely*

Apr 1st   *Got to sleep at 11am. Had to get up at 10 to 1 for an inspection by the Japanese Governor of Internment Camps who was due at 1:30 pm–having dressed ready we were told it would not be until 2:30 and when I first got up I had a frantic pain in my tummy and consequently could not sleep when I eventually got back to bed–the result being a total of 3½ hours sleep. Mrs Mills and Dr Jackson admitted to hospital on day floor. At 8:20 Betty M. staged a faint in the bathroom and was sick afterwards–good beginning to my night's work. Dr Page came up and chatted for a short while and offered to loan me $10 so that I could buy some sugar to share between Mums and Wexie and self–our finances having been nil for so long I must say I felt extremely thankful and grateful for the offer. Slightly easier night.*

Apr 2nd   *We ordered 5 lbs. of sugar, a tin of cocoa and a tin of jam after Parade. I do hope they will arrive quickly as we are feeling so dreadfully weak from lack of sugar. This rice and water diet is*

| *William Gray* | > | *John Gray* | > | *James Gray* | > | *Jesse William Gray* | > |
| *(1720-1795)* | | *(1770-1830)* | | *(1813-1880)* | | *(1855-1894)* | |

certainly awful when you have to work so hard. It was such a glorious day it seemed a pity to go to sleep but I had 4½ hours and then got up for a bath and tea. Did some scrubbing after breakfast and some washing in my bath. Had an operation case during the night, apart from which everything was as usual, Mrs Rudolf left hospital

Apr 3rd   *Had about 5 hours sleep and then got up about 4:30 in time for a bath before tea. Betty Longbottom left hospital. Generally, a quieter night with fewer bedpans. The only troublesome patient was Betty Mills suffering from illusions and I had a most unpleasant 10 minutes with her. Good Friday.*

Apr 4th   *Hardly had any sleep during the day, got up at 4:30 for a bath and tea. Went on duty at 8 pm and received profound apologies from Betty who was much better and slept all night thank goodness. Everyone was greatly improved but my hopes of getting a sleep were spoiled because the mosquitoes were so bad.*

Apr 5th   *Easter Sunday which I could hardly believe. I slept better and had the quietest night on duty since I started nights and managed to rest quite a bit.*

Apr 9th   *Moved Wexie's and my belongings to our new quarters which was pretty hot work as everything had to come downstairs from the Night staff sleeping room. Then I made up our beds and arranged all our goods and it was 12 o'clock. After lunch I tried to have a sleep but could not as people kept coming in and out of the room, being the main entrance to the house. Wexie came out of hospital about 3 pm. Felt dreadfully tired and went to bed early but in our room it was impossible to sleep until 10:30 or 11 because of disturbances. People coming in and out and the Burnie crowd having their nightly feast and laughing and screaming in the next room*

Apr 11th   *Started work on the 1st Floor of the hospital–all new patients to me having been on the 3rd for 6 weeks. Long day duty. I asked Matron if we might have the red screen from the ward as we were going to be left with one only to screen us from the eyes of all and sundry walking through the room but of course because we are just Naval people and not Brigadiers' and Colonels' wives we cannot have it. All we want is a screen frame as we have a cover and she has a frame which she hangs her washing on–but still one cannot expect anything else from the Army*

Apr 12th   *Short day duty. Had a church service in the morning. Rested and had a bath in the afternoon and made covers for my locker and cushion in the evening and so to bed. Mums taken to hospital pm. Mrs Rudolf very kindly took pity on us and said we might have a screen frame from the laundry if Sgt. Roberts fixes some lines for hanging clothes.*

Apr 14th   *Short day duty. Rested in the afternoon having scrubbed and*

---

cleaned frantically at the hospital all morning. We got our screen from the laundry and returned the Ellis' to them. Visited Mums after tea.

Apr 15th   *My day off. Did some washing in the morning, rested after lunch and saw Mums after tea. Four R.A.F. officers amongst whom were Sullivan the C.O., Bennett and Gray, were brought in by the Japanese but locked in a room and nobody was allowed to see them or speak to them. Jean started duty 3rd Floor*

Apr 16th   *Long day duty–Sgt. Roberts and Morgan fixed up a very snappy light for me in my corner so that I can read in bed, I was very thrilled with the result. Saw Mums morning during my off time and after 8 pm when I came off duty. Wexie started duty but on the dining room staff while Mrs. Burnie has a week's leave. Alison Black's 21st birthday–she did not do at all badly in the way of presents and a cake was made for her & decorated with flowers by the Matron. Most people gave what little things they could find amongst their few possessions*

Apr 18th   *Long day–rather a long afternoon with the new patient who is very likely to die. The Army officers arrived at Argyle Street Camp from Sham-shui-Po in the afternoon and then, to our great joy, the Navy arrived in the evening but we did not see them at all as it was dark before we heard they had arrived.*

I need to break off from my mother's diary to explain the significance

---

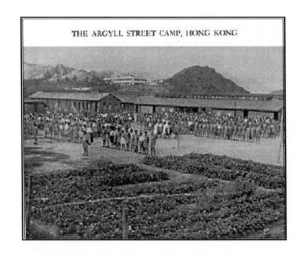

THE ARGYLL STREET CAMP, HONG KONG

of her statement "*…and then, to our great joy, the Navy arrived*". For this, I am going to switch to a letter written by my father. I have transcribed the whole letter from a copy of Dad's actual note, which my mother actually typed onto a piece of cloth when she was doing secretarial work later in Stanley camp. It is dated 10th February 1942 and sent from North Point Camp. It is perhaps the most precious letter of my father's that I have in my wonderful collection of memorabilia and fills me with emotion every time I read it, since it starts to reveal my parents' love story, that would unravel over the next 15 years:

North Point Camp, 10th Feb 1942

My darling precious Kathy,

I was so glad to hear Winter of the "Cornflower" answer the first of the two questions which I have been asking you to myself every day since I saw you last on Xmas eve and heard your voice last on Xmas day just after the surrender. It was "How are you Kathy darling?". I am grateful to know that Winter saw you in a window looking well and reasonably cheerful. Thank you for sending your love back by him and also thank you so much for the blanket, shirt and toothbrush. It was very kind and thoughtful of you dear and the gifts are all very much appreciated. Winter told you where I am and that I am quite well.

So today we both know where the other is and that we are well. I had heard over at Shamshuipo that the R.N.H. had been closed and that you had been shifted somewhere but I did not know where and it was worrying. The Naval personnel was all moved over to this side again to the above address on the 24th January and we are now all together with the two Canadian regiments. I was thankful to get away from the army crowd. They have given me and all of us a pain in the neck. I'll tell you all about it one day. I did not come over until the 29th January–I was left behind because I was so weak after a very bad attack of ear trouble. An abscess formed behind the drum and I was in absolute agony for four days, until it burst and then I was laid out for ten days because it took it out of me so much. I am perfectly alright again now though darling, so don't worry. My only troubles in the Camp (of course leaving missing you out of it) are insufficient food and smokes. It's the same with others though and moral courage must see us through for the time being.

The other question that I mentioned above and which I am always asking myself is "Do you still love me darling Kathy?". Oh, darling say "Yes"–"More than ever". I have made a big discovery since I have had so much time to think about things deeply and work and sort things out and that is that I now realise that I am really still falling in love with you and that I am not likely to love you as much as I think I can for years yet. It is a grand feeling. I know that I love you today more than I did yesterday and yesterday more than the day before. It will take me all my life to show you just how much and how deeply I love you. You are absolutely everything in this life to me Kathy–absolutely

---

everything and without you I'd die. Truly dearest. I have said that before but I mean more than ever now. I absolutely worship you dearest and all that you say and think and do. Do you see now just how it is that you are everything in life to me? Love me for ever Kathy–please love me and want me for always and increasingly too. I have always tried to be loving and kind to you since we came into each other's lives some time ago now but I am going to treble my efforts in those respects when this is all over and live only for you more so than ever. In the meantime, keep your pecker up and look forward to Blue Skies (I often wish I could hear you humming that tune) and our new home and family life together. If only I could see you for half an hour, I have so much to say to you. No, one hour–I'd need a whole half hour for kissing you. We have probably lost everything up at the house. I hope some things are left like photos and things. I'll have lots of backpay waiting for me at the Admiralty though and compensation and a gratuity when demobbed so we'll have some grand shopping in London to do and lots of money besides. Did you take your jewellery down with you that morning darling? I worry more about the things we've probably lost which have intrinsic value or sentimental value. Never mind dear, if we've still got each other when this is all over it's more than 99% of the battle of starting again over right away. Do you see what I mean?

When you are no longer required–I hope you will be required for some time yet–at St Albert's, I expect you will have to join other Britons and Americans of the Civilian class out at Stanley. Though we won't be so near we'll still be on the same island. I wonder if we will ever be allowed to see each other for a

---

bit before the war ends. I don't say they will but it's by no means certain that they won't transfer Service prisoners somewhere–Formosa or something and you might even go somewhere else. By then I presume letters will be allowed regularly and, if we get separated by hundreds of miles, we'll have to rack our brains to let each other know where to meet out here on release before going home together. If that's not possible then we meet at home I suppose. I'm talking now IF we get separated in different Camps in different lands out here. I'd like for us to go home together though very much. I somehow want to finish with the Far East after this altogether–what do you think about it precious? That's one of the things we must have a long talk about. After this more than ever I am going to do nothing without our both being in complete agreement.

I'd love to get a chit from you on the Q.T. if it is at all possible, but be careful, make sure that the person is coming to this camp and that he will tuck it away carefully. Several people have been lucky already but from different hospitals. Don't get yourself into trouble you precious darling but surely some of the officers who are nearly ready to come here would oblige or even a better class rating. Use your discretion.

Are you kept pretty busy these days? Thank goodness I believe that dreams go by opposites. I dreamed the other night that you had an affair with someone who was getting better at the hospital and it got so bad that you belonged to each other and when the war finished you left me flat and, because I would not divorce you, you lived with this chap openly and you broke my heart and yours and my people's and the chap was chucked out of the Army. Yes–he was a

---

	Jesse Esdale Gray		Cecil Jesse Austen		Peter Nigel Austen Gray
>	(1885-1946)	>	Gray (1908-1968)	>	(1950-present)

pongo! Wasn't that a nasty dream?–I'll say it was, and I woke up and could not sleep for hours afterwards–not because I doubted you or thought that there might have been something to it but because I had a nasty feeling of having insulted the dearest, purest and most loveable girl in the world by dreaming such a thing. It must be the hard board that I sleep on! Anyway, forgive me. You know that the day I have to stop trusting you and having all my faith in you is the day that my world ends as suddenly as the breaking of a plate and I suppose that's why I got that feeling of insulting you because you don't want to break my heart I know. I feel I could go on writing to you for hours but I must not make this too bulky. Keep your pecker up my sweetheart and love me in absence until we meet again or are re-united. The reunion may be sooner than we dare hope. I pray for that day and I pray for you and us every day. I love and adore you more than I can hope to tell you in words. Keep well and strong, take care of yourself and be mine and only mine forever. I'm completely yours for ever and a day. All my love Kathy my darling wife,

J.J.

Phew! That still gets me, no matter how many times I've read it. Thinking about it, I don't suppose many people have read their parents' love letters, even ones originating from an "ordinary" relationship in a sleepy little town or village in peacetime England–never mind a letter exchanged between young newly-weds who are both prisoners-of-war in the Far East, not knowing if they'll ever be together again. The fact that I know "what happens next" gives an extra layer of poignancy to nearly every paragraph that my father wrote all those years ago. More on that later. I introduced this letter just at this point in the story to explain the "J.J." reference my mother makes in the next entry in her diary. It is my father and I need to explain how and why he became JJ. His full name is Cecil Jesse Austen Gray and, somewhere along the line, the Jesse part became linked to the gunslinger from Wild West legend–Jesse James. Remembering that his father was called Jesse, maybe there was a need to distinguish between the two Jesses. This in turn was changed to Jimmy James or just even "J.J.". Even later than these war years, he was actually just called Jimmy; hence many of my parents' post war friends knew them simply as "Jimmy and Kay"–rather than Cecil and Kathleen! All quite easy to follow really.

Now my mother continues the story:

Apr 19th *Whoopee! I saw J.J. before breakfast which was a wonderful start to the day. Saw him also when I went across to the house during the morning and after lunch. Rested in the afternoon, Saw him in the evening. Very sick patient died and we nurses had to form a guard of honour for the funeral.*

Apr 20th *Mummie's Birthday. Saw J.J. before breakfast. Long day duty. I saw him while I was off in the morning also from the verandah in the afternoon and evening. Mrs Tebbutt gave me a dress length. Saw Mums in the evening after duty at 8pm*

Apr 21st *My day off. Saw quite a lot of J.J. It really is most dreadfully* *tantalising being able to see him & not be able to rush over and hug him and kiss him as I should so love to do–but still it is grand seeing him and knowing that he looks so fit and well. Did some washing and sewing, rested in the afternoon. Saw Mrs Tomlin in the evening * Mrs Macleod*

Apr 22nd   *Long day duty. Did not see J.J. before breakfast but after I came off in the morning. Missed him at lunchtime but saw him at 4:30pm and 6:15pm * Mrs Simpson*

Apr 23rd   *Short day duty. Saw quite a lot of J.J., Mums came out of hospital.*

Apr 24th   *Long day duty. 4 very sick patients were brought in from Argyle St. Camp hospital one of which came to our floor–he had a wee note for me also Mrs. Newnham. Very busy time, saw little of J.J.*

Apr 25th   *Leo Ellis' birthday–we had a piece of cake and a lovely cup of coffee with milk and sugar in it. Saw quite a lot of my darling as it was my half day*

Apr 26th   *Long day duty. Morning uneventful but the afternoon was hectic with one mental patient and McGill the new patient delirious. I spent most of the time with McGill–the Matron who has a wounded hand asked me to give him an injection and showed me how to do it.–I was afraid I might make a mess of it but managed very well and she told me I had, so I was quite pleased with myself. She knew that it was too late to save his life but it was all we could do for him & then I stayed with him for the rest of the afternoon.*

Matron relieved me whilst I dished out the other patients' teas and then Cpl. Elliott took over whilst I had my tea and then I took over again. He eventually died at 7:30 and I helped to wash and dress and lay him out. So, after that & dealing with the mental patient who wanted to commit suicide all afternoon, I felt absolutely done in. Found notes in a pocket of McGill's for Betty Long & Muriel McCaw also Y10 for Muriel. I wish J.J. could send me some money.

Apr 27th   Short day duty, did a spot of washing after forming a guard for McGill's funeral then rested a wee while & had a bath and spent the evening looking at J.J. till 7:30 then went to see Mrs Gubbey & Rosie in hospital. Saw Gorman for a few minutes–he came in last Friday with pneumonia

Apr 28th   Long day–Alison started night duty so I had the whole floor to myself–Moore the mental patient was extremely trying and nearly drove me mad but still we got through all right. Only saw J.J. in the morning whilst ironing and once walking round from the verandah as I was so busy.

Apr 29th   My day off–washed my hair, brought this diary up to date and did some sewing. Saw a lot of J.J.

Apr 30th   Long day–Moore was terribly ill, in fact dying all afternoon and evening and we had to sit with him all the time as he was trying to get out of bed. He eventually died at 10.10pm * Mrs Richardson

---

> Jesse Esdale Gray
(1885-1946)
> Cecil Jesse Austen
Gray (1908-1968)
> Peter Nigel Austen Gray
(1950-present)

May 1st   *Lt. McGee's 21st birthday–he was made a small cake–a hot roll with butter and marmalade, and also a boiled egg that was produced by one of our 13 chickens that were bought a week ago. Moore was buried and we had to form a guard again. My half day–I did a spot of washing in the afternoon and saw a quite a lot of my darling. Rations came in at last including bread, also in the evening our stuff came from the Comprador. Matron says I may start my weeks' leave on Monday if no V.A.D.s go sick before then. Saw my darling.*

May 4th   *Started my week's leave–Whoopee. Did some sewing, rested in the afternoon. Saw J.J. in the evening. Went visiting patients in hospital. Margie's birthday (her sister Marjorie, in America)*

May 5th   *Did some washing & ironing, also sewing and ironing. Rested after lunch*

May 9th   *Mrs. McLeod went to hospital as she was very worn out and needs a good rest. Today is the second anniversary of my arrival in Hong Kong to be married*

May 12th   *Found out that my poor darling has an abscess in his ear, and I know what agony he suffers. I love him so dearly and hate to think of him suffering and me not being able to comfort him. I wish they would send him to the hospital. Long day duty, saw Ovans after 8 pm, don't much like him. Mrs Richards had an operation*

May 13th   *Poor darling J.J. has both ears bad now. Oh, how I wish they would let him come over here. Short day duty*

May 14th — *Long day duty. Saw J.J. in the morning but not in the evening. Poor darling, I feel for him so much, I know how he must be suffering.*

May 15th — *J.J. spent the day in bed so I did not see him. I did miss the sight of his darling face, I love him so. Short day duty*

May 16th — *Did not see my darling before breakfast but, to my joy, he appeared at 10:15 am. Long day duty, saw him from the verandah*

May 17th — *My day off–washed my hair and clothes, towels, pillow cases etc. Saw my darling one. Mums read my cup and said the gates will be opening on July 28th & my darling Jimmy James will be outside waiting for me. Mrs Gubbay died*

May 18th — *Long day duty, very busy. We have 22 patients, some of whom are very ill indeed. Saw my darling J.J. Wexie started on the 1st Floor so as to get to know the patients before starting night duty.*

May 20th — *Long day duty. Saw my darling one, I wonder how much longer we will have to endure this strain when we long for each other so much. Very busy afternoon and evening*

May 21st — *My day off, had a sore throat and cough just before tea. I lost my voice after tea. Matron told me to get the inhaler from the hospital and inhale before retiring and stay in bed the next day, which I did*

May 22nd — *In bed all day, Saw J.J. at 10:15 and pointed to throat,*

May 23rd — *Stayed in bed until 4pm, got up for tea, saw my darling after tea.*

May 24th   *I was given a day's convalescence–lovely weather*

May 25th   *Started work on the 2nd floor–very nice and peaceful after the hectic work on the 1st Floor. Long day duty*

May 27th   *Long day. Everybody received a present from the Japs consisting of a towel, toilet paper, a toothbrush, some foul-smelling tooth powder and 3 cards for writing home. We were allowed to write a letter or card home which had to be printed on one side of the paper only. No bread or rations came in so we were down to starvation diet again. I received 100 yen from my darling J.J., what a thrill it was to see the writing of his signature too, sweet thing. I shall now be able to settle my debts and buy some more necessaries.*

May 28th   *My day off–washed my hair, saw J.J., helped Jean with her diary and the morning was almost over*

May 31st   *Short day–Barbara Hills birthday–news came then that V.A.D.s with relations at Stanley who wanted to go and join them could do so*

Jun 1st   *Short day duty–we were given permission to open the windows facing the Camp in the Mess. There was a terrific hullabaloo with the sentries who came around in the evening as they had not been told about it.*

Jun 2nd   *Still a certain amount of trouble re windows. Long day duty*

Jun 5th   *My day off–did odd jobs of sewing. Saw plenty of J.J. Poor darling seems to be suffering with his ears. More canteen arrived thank goodness. Expected excitement did not occur*

Jun 8th   *Long day duty–no rations in, consequently meals absolutely punk*

Jun 9th   *My day off–Betty Mills 1st wedding anniversary. Started new meal hours–which meant we had to get up earlier as breakfast is now 7:30 instead of 8 am*

Jun 10th   *Started working on the 1st Floor again (Bed Pan Alley as we call it), not so nice. Long day duty, my darling J.J. came out at 7.25 thanks to Jock calling him*

Jun 13th   *Susie arrived as soon as I got up. Felt pretty lousy. Sister Buckle very kindly sent me off at 12:20 instead of 1 pm. As I was looking wretched. Rested a lot*

Jun 17th   *Sleep was impossible as all the Stanley people left and volunteer replacements arrived. Amongst the new arrivals were 5 trained sisters making us 4 short on the nursing staff and more people to give orders which I feel is going to be a very bad thing. I was alone on Bed Pan Alley the whole night which kept me very busy.*

Jun 18th   *Having only had ¾ of an hours' sleep yesterday, I managed to sleep from 10 until 4 without waking–what a day to spend one's wedding anniversary–but still it was grand being able to see each other. Mums put flowers on the table for me by way of a celebration. Mrs. Crabbe joined me on night duty and we had a reasonable night.*

Jun 19th   *Did not sleep so well–6 new patients in and we broke all records, having 126 BPs in 11½ hours. It really was a ghastly night and we were thoroughly exhausted at the end of it*

Jun 27th   *Had a better sleep–some new patients have come in & I hope I shall not have too bad a night, being my last–Had a very bad night as I was greeted with a death immediately I got on duty. It was one of the new patients and another one was very ill with diphtheria and the mental patient was worse. Also, to crown everything I had awful pains*

Jun 29th   *Had a day off–Westwood, the mental patient, died and one patient came in with typhoid and died during the night*

Jul 2nd   *Damp weather caused me to suffer very badly with rheumatics. Half day thank goodness*

Jul 3rd   *Long day duty–Bosco's birthday, was sorry I could not wish him many happy returns. Big inspection by Japanese "Big Noises" and Swiss representatives of the Red Cross. Things must have been going against them outside because they were particularly B-minded. The affair finished up by us having to bow by way of showing our respect and we are going to be starved for 10 days*

Jul 4th   *Sisters and nurses are to be trained to parade properly. Amusing joke by Sister Morgan re dressing*

Jul 5th   *Mitchell was brought down to our floor–he is dreadful ill with dysentery, jaundice and a very infectious skin disease. I doubt very much if he will live through the day–Long day duty, two new patients in; one, Cripps, very ill*

Jul 6th   *Short day duty–Canteen arrived thank goodness. Mitchell slightly improved, but I don't think he will live. Funeral for two diphtheria patients, I had to stay on the ward as Mitchell and Cripps could not be left.*

Jul 7th   *Long day duty–We had a dreadful afternoon with Mitchell and Cripps who were both incontinent the whole time. At 8pm we had a diversion by way of a "Quiz and Spelling Bee" which was good fun and just what I needed to make me forget BPs etc. for a while. I did very well and answered most of mine correctly*

Jul 8th   *My day off, for which I was truly thankful as both Mitchell and Cripps died. Went to see Muriel in the evening. 6 more patients came to our floor*

Jul 9th   *My darling J. J's birthday–he got his fags alright I am pleased to say. It looks as though I am in for a bad afternoon on the wards… Yes I was very busy. We had a cup of coffee in the morning and a spot of lunch left over with one Oxo between the three of us to give it flavour by way of celebrating*

Jul 10th   *Half day–was very worn out with rheumatics and hard work, lugging heavy screens around the ward every two minutes of the day. Had a very sleepless night with a fever feeling hot and cold and aching badly*

Jul 11th   *Got up but felt like death with a raging headache & aches all over and went over to breakfast but just could not make it and somebody told Matron who came to see me and took my temperature and pulse. After she had seen Dr, Gunn she came back and told me I was to go into hospital and the stretcher would be sent for me in 15 minutes. Well, knowing that J.J, would be expecting to see me at that time I decided to get over before the stretcher so as not to scare him too much. Poor darling, he looked so staggered as it was and here I am with acute rheumatism and have to lie still & flat all the time or I might get a weak heart. My "sweet adorable Beast" sent me more money. Oh my darling one, if only I could thank you properly*

Jul 12th   *Having been dosed with Sodii Sal 2 hourly I felt horribly sick and dizzy*

Jul 13th   *The medicine has been cut down to 4-hourly, still feel wretched. 8 more diphtheria cases came in, and 2 previous diphs died during the night*

Jul 14th   *Muriel and I are now surrounded by diph cases and there is talk we will have to be moved to the house to be nursed which will be dreadful as we won't be able to see Henry and J.J.*

Jul 15th   *Still feeling wretched*

Jul 16th   *Still feeling wretched*

Jul 17th   *We were shifted down to the 2nd Floor which we don't like so much as the screen has to be in front of the window. I am next to it though so can peep round the corner. My poor darling did not know where I had got to and it was heartrending to watch him walking up and down looking so depressed.*

Jul 18th *Thank goodness J.J. has found me and so he looks happier*

Jul 19th *Feeling a wee bit better*

Jul 20th *Allowed to sit up for a short time & the most important thing, allowed to use the commode*

Jul 21st *Wexie's Birthday–Mums and I gave her 3 pkts of cigarettes, Miss Ellis made her a small cake*

Jul 22nd *Gradually improving, was able to get up to wash myself and potter around the room*

Jul 23rd *Same sort of day*

Jul 24th *I went to the staff bathroom and had a bath in one bucket of hot water which was a terrific event. 15 new patients came in–9 dysentry, 1 septic sores and 5 diphtherias; one diph and one dysentery died during the night*

Jul 25th *Dr Gunn tested my heart and seemed quite satisfied with it and says I may leave hospital tomorrow morning. Mrs T. is coming at 4 o'clock to read Muriel's and my tea cups*

Jul 26th *Came out of hospital at 4:30 pm, had tea at the house, saw J.J. before parade*

Jul 27th *I managed to go on parade but was feeling very week and was excused drill. Had an excellent show in the evening consisting of 4 sketches which were very well done indeed*

Aug 3rd   *Started nursing again. Felt very weak, my pulse is 106 and I really should not be working. Heard the news that we are all to be sent to Stanley (the Civilian Internment Camp at Hong Kong) on Monday 10th August. Long day shift, Morgan tried to commit suicide*

Aug 6th   *A buzz that we might be leaving for Stanley within 48 hrs so I spent the afternoon packing*

Aug 7th   *J.J., the pet, sent me Y30 but unfortunately the canteen did not come*

Aug 8th   *Saw as much as possible of my darling when I was off duty*

Aug 9th   *Long day which was my last day of duty; finished nursing for good I hope at 8pm when we were told we would not be allowed to take beds or even mattresses with us only clothes*

Aug 10th   *The awful day for parting from my precious has arrived again and how I hated waving goodbye but it is better for me at Stanley and I don't think it will be for too long. The trip out to Stanley was not bad and the arrangements for our arrival and billeting were extremely well done. Had a few callers & was grand seeing new & familiar faces. Tommy, Wexie and I together in one room, grand*

This is the ideal opportunity to share some of my research into Stanley Civilian Internment Camp with you all, as it is necessary to put Mother's diary entries into a context that will allow you to make more sense of her "life" there. Stanley Internment Camp was a civilian internment camp in Hong Kong during the Second World War. Located in Stanley, on the southern end of Hong Kong Island, it was used by the Japanese imperial forces to hold non-Chinese enemy nationals after their victory in the Battle of Hong Kong. About 2,800 men, women, and children were held at the non-segregated camp for 44 months from early January 1942 to August 1945 when Japanese forces surrendered. The camp area consisted of St Stephen's College and the grounds of Stanley Prison, excluding the prison itself which was used by the Japanese authorities to hold what they considered "criminals" from Hong Kong. Several hundred internees lived at St. Stephen's, while the majority of them lived on the prison grounds. Prior to Japanese occupation, St. Stephen's was a secondary school whose facilities, in addition to classrooms, included an assembly hall, bungalows for teachers, and science laboratories. Over twenty internees occupied each bungalow, which was built for one family, and more than that occupied each science laboratory, living between partitions of sacking and old blankets. Almost all the buildings in the camp were used for housing.

Certain buildings and areas on the prison grounds had specific functions: The Prison Officers' Club was used for multiple functions, including as a canteen, a kindergarten, Catholic church, and recreation centre.

Two main divisions of quarters existed–the Warders' Quarters and the Indian Quarters. Before the war, the Warders' Quarters housed European warders, with large flats designed for one family each, and the Indian Quarters

---

> *Jesse Esdale Gray*
(1885-1946)
> *Cecil Jesse Austen Gray (1908-1968)*
> *Peter Nigel Austen Gray (1950-present)*

housed Indian prison guards, built with smaller flats. An average of thirty internees lived in each Warders' Quarters flat, and an average of six internees lived in each Indian Quarters flat. A building which had housed single Indian warders before the war was turned into a hospital called Tweed Bay Hospital. Two houses, originally used as homes for the prison superintendent and the prison doctor, were turned into the Japanese headquarters for the camp. The cemetery on the grounds became a popular spot for quiet relaxation as well as a place for intimate meetings between male and female internees.

Of the 2,800 internees, an estimated 2,325 to 2,514 were British. The adult population numbered at 1,370 men and 858 women, and children 16 years of age or younger numbered at 286, with 99 of whom were below the age of 4. The camp was under the control of the Japanese Foreign Affairs Department, but the Japanese forces had not made plans for dealing with enemy civilians in Hong Kong. As such, the camp was provided with few necessities, and the internees were left to govern the camp themselves. Committees were formed for such matters as housing, food, and medical care. The national groups remained mostly independent of each other except for matters of welfare and medical care. Very few government servants were selected to serve on these committees, due to anti-government sentiment; most internees blamed the government for the quick surrender of Hong Kong.

The biggest concern was food; ensuring there was enough food occupied most of the internees' time. Little food was provided by the Japanese authorities, and it was of poor quality–frequently containing dust, mud, rat and cockroach excreta, cigarette ends, and sometimes dead rats. Every day, the internees were served rice congee at 8 am, and meals consisting of rice with stew at both 11 a.m. and 5 p.m. Additionally, they relied on food mailed from friends or relatives in the city, Red Cross aid, garden-grown vegetables, and bought food from the canteen or the black market.

Another concern was the health and medical care of the internees. Although medical facilities were inadequate, the internees counted amongst them about 40 doctors, two dentists, six pharmacists, 100 trained nurses, and a large number of volunteer auxiliary nurses. Because of this, no major epidemic occurred. The most common sickness amongst the internees were malaria, malnutrition and its associated diseases, beriberi, and pellagra. The shortage of medical supplies and equipment posed a challenge for those in charge of medical care, with the lack of soap and disinfectant being a particularly troublesome concern.

The women and children contributed to a sense of normality as their presence provided conventional social, family, and gender relations. The internees believed the children's presence made them less selfish, as it forced them to think of the latter's welfare. The women organised Christmas and birthday celebrations. Other diversions such as musicals, plays, recitals, and variety shows were also staged. Although the camp lacked books and educational supplies, the teachers and educational administrators amongst the internees were able to provide lessons for the children at the primary and secondary levels. Additionally, extensive educational opportunities were

> *Jesse Esdale Gray*
(1885-1946)   > *Cecil Jesse Austen*
Gray (1908-1968)   > *Peter Nigel Austen Gray*
(1950-present)

available for the adults: language courses for Chinese, Malay, and French, and also lectures on photography, yachting, journalism, and poultry-keeping.

Stanley Civilian Interment Camp, Hong Kong

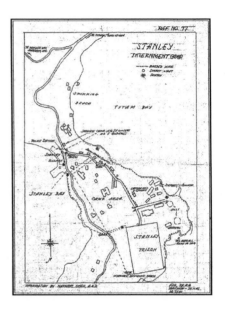

Having armed you readers with this background information and the above sketch map of the camp, I shall return you to my mother's diary, starting with the day after she arrived at Stanley. It saw her re-uniting with many people she knew before being forced to do her nursing and it was to be her home for the next three years:

Aug 11th   *Busy settling in. Went to tea with Sheila down in the slums*

Aug 12th   *More settling in. Went for a walk with Sheila around Stanley after tea*

Aug 13th   *getting more homelike after having a few odd jobs done. Having discovered a worm, I went to the doctor & got a prescription and set to de-worming. Did a spot of typing for Mr. Webb, the Block*

Representative, who looks after me and is snowed under with lists he has to complete

Aug 14th   *Stayed in after all my dosing. Did some more typing. Went down to the slums to watch a very amusing soft ball match with the men dressed up as girls*

Aug 15th   *Ray Mabb and I went to tea with John Stenker and he stuffed us up with waffles & sandwiches & coffee, it really was a wonderful feed and then Tommy, Wexie and I went to see Mrs. Dawes and she also fed us up with cocoa & jam tart and currant pasties*

Aug 16th   *Bunty Green had Wexie and I down for cocoa & bread & jam and we met her Mother and Father. Went to church in the morning.*

Aug 17th   *Made more improvements to our home. Got camp beds for Tommy and me*

Aug 18th   *A marvellous Tea Party was given by the Women of Stanley as a welcome to all the nurses and sisters who arrived on the 10th August. There were turns from a concert which had taken place before we arrived which were excellent*

Aug 19th   *Had to stay indoors all day as we had a typhoon which blew all the rain into our window which was most trying. I did a lot of typing*

Aug 20th   *Rained most of the day. Did sewing and went for a walk after our evening meal.*

Aug 21st   *Pottered around. Yvonne and Christine came to see me in the*

---

morning. Weighed ourselves–my weight 117 lbs. Went walking in the evening

Aug 22nd   *Went swimming in the afternoon, it was grand. Went to a Minstrel Concert in the evening which was jolly good*

Aug 23rd   *Swam in the morning and then went to church. Had Mrs. Dawes and Mrs. Greenwood to tea. Went for a walk in the evening*

Aug 24th   *Spent a quiet day as Susie arrived. Did some typing and checking cigarette money. Had 2 shares in the canteen*

Aug 25th   *My name was officially sent in as Secretary for Block 10. Did some work, had a good rest in the afternoon. Went out for a spot of air in the evening.*

Aug 26th   *Did plenty of work and did not travel far from home because of Susie but went to see Sheila*

Aug 27th   *Went to see Mrs. Dawes who gave me a beautiful pair of Gordons shoes. Tommy and Wexie went swimming with Mrs. Dawes and Smalley. I could not go of course so I rested*

Aug 28th   *Did some work and sewing, Watched a soft ball match in the evening.*

Aug 29th   *Concert in the evening which was very good*

Aug 30th   *Went to church, Cyril Brown preaching, very good indeed. Was frightfully windy again so we did not bathe as we had intended*

Aug 31st   *Very busy arranging the Welfare draw, also did a lot of machining*

Sept 1st   *Did a lot of work and went to a piano concert in the evening*

Sept 2nd   *Carried out the Welfare draw and filled in all the Welfare chits*

Sept 3rd   *Cholera inoculations*

Sept 4th   *My birthday started off wonderfully with grapefruit for breakfast, also toast with marge and jam on it. Tommy gave me a cute green buckle and Wexie gave me 2 diamante slips and Webb flowers, a hankie and toilet soap. We received $5 from the Pope. Had Sheila to tea and Tommy told our cups. Some of the musicians in the Block played "A Happy Birthday to you Mrs Gray" and other tunes outside my window which was very pleasant indeed. We played the "Spooks" game which was really uncanny*

Sept 5th   *An excellent "Pierrot" concert in the evening which we thoroughly enjoyed. Had a lovely bath in the afternoon. List of money sent from Argyle Street; none for me, very worried*

Sept 6th   *Went to church in morning and when I got back to the Mess received a message to go to "The House on the Hill" and collect some money. Whoopee so my darling had not forgotten me after all. T, Wexie and I went out to tea and so much to eat we could hardly eat our 5 o'clock meal*

Sept 7th   *Went to the beach for a bathe which was grand. Tommy, Wexie and I went to see Mrs. G and Mrs. Dawes. It was Mrs D's Birthday and we had a pasty and a piece of cake each. Walked back through the cemetery.*

Sept 14th   *Spent a quiet day and worked in the office. Went to listen to*

>   *Jesse Esdale Gray*   >   *Cecil Jesse Austen*   >   *Peter Nigel Austen Gray*
>   *(1885-1946)*   *Gray (1908-1968)*   *(1950-present)*

Elizabeth Brown and Heath playing on two pianos, it was really wonderful, it makes me feel very sentimental and long for my darling more than ever. Inoculated cholera and typhoid

Sept 18th   *Did a lot of sewing, completely made a swimsuit and cap. Went for a walk after tea, looked in on Sheila who could not walk with us as she was typing Norwegian verbs.*

Sept 19th   *Swimming Gala on the beach which went off very well. We took our tea with us and had a good time. Evelyn Kilber, Dorothy and Sheila joined us on the beach. Concert in the evening.*

Sept 20th   *Was going to church but my ear went deaf so I went to the doctor and had it syringed. Went to the beach in the afternoon. Did some office work in the evening.*

Sept 26th   *Spent afternoon on beach–swarms of Jelly fish and Jelly bugs so we did not stay in the water long. Sunbathing was super. Usual concert was cancelled because of the 'V' signs made whilst being filmed last Saturday. Had a lovely message from J.J. thro' Spooks.*

Oct 1st   *Very windy day so we stayed in. Played Bridge in the evening. Had a bad typhoon consequently did not sleep all night.*

Oct 2nd   *Typhoon still continuing. Received a certificate of nursing duty period from Miss Franklin. Played Bridge in the afternoon. Betty Long's 21st birthday.*

Oct 5th   *Susie turned up so spent a quiet day and went to hear the Monday Piano concert in the evening.*

| *William Gray* | > | *John Gray* | > | *James Gray* | > | *Jesse William Gray* | > |
| *(1720-1795)* | | *(1770-1830)* | | *(1813-1880)* | | *(1855-1894)* | |

Oct 6th   *Ann's birthday. Felt rotten and spent all day lying down was stung by a beastly centipede–gosh how they sting.*

Oct 7th   *Still suffering agonies, played Bridge during the afternoon. Very windy blowing up for another typhoon, curse it.*

Oct 8th   *Having gone to bed prepared for rain it did not–thank goodness. Still windy but sunny. Still feeling lousy so did not do much apart from sewing and reading. Played Bridge in the evening.*

Oct 9th   *Quiet day–Susie still troublesome–did a little work. Mums and Wexie went to the beach. Played Bridge in the evening.*

Oct 12th   *Went for a walk after 10 o'clock meal and heard the awful news that the "Lisbon Marn" had been torpedoed and that 900 out of 1,800 of our 'prisoners of war' from H.K. had been lost. We suffered a dreadful shock and felt thoroughly sick. Could get no definite news as to who had left HK. Went for a picnic which was already arranged as we felt the need for fresh air having been in the house for so much thro' bad weather and Susie. Listened to Mrs Brown and Heath in the evening and took ages to get to sleep.*

Oct 13th   *Wrote my postcard to J.J. and read. Weather foul again, rainy and windy all day. Heard that at present there is no hope of getting postcards delivered to camps.*

Oct 19th   *Went to the doctor as my mouth was full of ulcers and hurt badly–been bad for about 5 days. Went to music evening.*

Oct 20th   *Doctor's afternoon–walked evening.*

> *Jesse Esdale Gray*   > *Cecil Jesse Austen*   > *Peter Nigel Austen Gray*
> *(1885-1946)*   *Gray (1908-1968)*   *(1950-present)*

Oct 21st   *Doctor's afternoon–walked round the camp–went into St. Stephens and listened to Hyde-Lay paying the piano.*

Oct 22nd   *Doctors p.m.–had tea with the Ritchies, heard about Ban. Very kind they were–listened to Betty Brown and another lady playing–jolly good. Sent R. Cross letter forms, M and Margie.*

Oct 23rd   *Took a walk. Doctor visit. Red Cross letter message to Margie.*

Oct 24th   *St. Stephens do in the evening. Doctor's visit.*

Oct 25th   *Went to doctor–mouth much improved–picnic afternoon, Beryl swam–C.R.H. evening listening to music. 1st Allied raid over H.K. Great excitement in the camp.*

Oct 26th   *Went out on the rocks reading in the sunshine, very hot in the sunshine. Could hear planes all the time. Evening music.*

Oct 29th   *Money from Jimmy & Bosco = Y30. Grand and I hope it means they are both still at Argyle Street or I should say H.K. Went to the doctors in the afternoon and walked back through the cemetery. Two Piano concert evening. (Y10 was not from Bosco, not for me. I had to return it to a Mrs Cath Gray).*

Oct 31st   *Last day at the beach–closing for the winter. Took our tea and books with us. Very amusing and enjoyable evening at St. Stephens.*

Nov 2nd   *Oddment canteen–I drew a ticket but most unlucky as the only things I wanted sold out before my turn and so I spent the whole morning buying for other people. Usual Monday piano concert.*

Parcels arrived.

Nov 3rd   *Our Red Cross parcels were supposed to be given to us today having arrived yesterday but of course that was too much to expect and there is a hitch. Whoopee I received a letter from Yolande–what a relief to know the family are O.K.–today is definitely my lucky day because I managed to get a pair of slacks sent in from town through a friend of Bill's.*

Nov 4th   *Beryl Farrah came to tea and we played Bridge. Canteen draw– we were not very lucky as far as sugar was concerned but O.K. on dates and nuts. Walk p.m.*

Nov 5th   *Went out for air in the morning, took our books. Tommy and I went to hear the music p.m. and took a brisk walk round.*

Nov 6th   *Went for a picnic in the afternoon–men between the ages of 21 and 40 of Police and 21 and 35 other civilians had to spend the night in the gaol–this practice is to continue for 3 weeks. Poor devils lights out at 8 p.m. and stone floors to sleep on.*

Nov 7th   *The lads came out of gaol at 7 a.m., apparently they did have lights until 10 p.m. which was not so bad. Worked in the morning. Went to the canteen in the afternoon. Went to listen to a 'Quiz'–"Church v Lawyers and Medical v School Teachers"–very amusing.*

Nov 8th   *Went to church–good service. Parcels due tomorrow at 10 a.m. Listened to Heath playing in the evening.*

Nov 9th   *"Parcels" arrived safely–grand excitement–mine contained–1 tin*

10oz tomatoes, 2 pkts sugar, ½ lb bacon, 1 lb curried beef and rice, ½ lb Peek Freans biscuits, 2 oz cheese, ½ lb Golden Syrup, 1 lb Creamed Rice, 2 oz Maypole Tea, ¼ lb Margarine, large tin Nestles Condensed Milk, 1 Apple Pudding, 1 tin Lusty's Galantine, ¼ lb Vitamanized Chocolate. Wexie swallowed a tooth eating her biscuits. Sheila came along full of beans having received a message that her fiancé wishes to know if she is willing to marry him if her release can be obtained–thrilling. Played 4 sets Deck Tennis.

Nov 11th   *Susie arrived, felt rotten took things quietly. Beryl came to tea and Bridge. Mouth very sore again with ulcers.*

Nov 12th   *Took plenty of rest–Marjorie Buckle asked us in to tea and Bridge.*

Nov 13th   *Rested–did a spot of sewing and ironing. Few people in from town.*

Nov 14th   *Did nothing all day except lie with my feet higher than the rest of my body and managed to get across to the "Gilbert and Sullivan" show which was grand. (note at top of page–Sat Nov 14th at 10.55 a.m. dentist)*

Nov 15th   *Mouth still terribly painful but unable to visit the doctor–rested all day.*

Nov 16th   *Weather terrible so unable to see the Doc. Rested morning and played Bridge in the afternoon.*

Nov 17th   *All the bulk goods were taken from the Go Down and we received dried fruit, raisins, cocoa, corned beef and meat and veg.*

Nov 18th   *Weather still foul–went to see Dr. Dean-Smith who was not in. Beryl came to tea and Bridge. Started fruit juice. 1st mail arrived from England–none for me worst luck.*

Nov 19th   *Raining and windy still–went to Dr. who was again out. Went to the dentist. Told that my gums were badly infected. Tommy received a Welfare parcel, she and I went to collect in the rain– great excitement. Played Bridge p.m.*

Nov 20th   *At last Dr. Dean-Smith was in, so I was able to get my prescription for medicine. Went to Dr. Hackett who advises that I have my crowned tooth extracted. Went to tea with Greenwood. Played Poker at St, Stephens. (note at top of page–Thurs Nov 20th 11 a.m.)*

Nov 21st   *The best show yet at St. Stephens–had tea and played Bridge with Mary Wilson.*

Nov 26th   *All day in the sun. Had a Welfare Parcel–whoopee contained Pineapple, Bloater Paste, Tomatoes and Mixed Ginger. A show given by Blocks 8,9 10 and 11–quite good.*

Nov 27th   *Went out in the sun during morning–Sheila gave a tea party in celebration of 1 year being engaged. Jolly good party, grand eats, 11 of us all together.*

Nov 30th   *Had a foul cold so stayed in all day.*

Dec 6th   *Tommy's birthday–Beryl came to tea after which Wexie and self went out into the sunshine for a while then went to usual Sunday music.*

Dec 7th   *Nothing much doing. Went to music evening. Spent most of day in sun. Played Deck Tennis.*

Dec 8th   *Nothing unusual doing.*

Dec 9th   *Nothing unusual doing. Beryl to tea and Bridge*

Dec 10th   *Very busy day, went to the Go Down checking clothes a.m. and collected and distributed same during afternoon, being slightly late for evening entertainment at St. Stephens.*

Dec 12th   *Susie arrived and Sheila came to tea. Did not go to concert.*

Dec 17th   *Busy writing Christmas card and making up a parcel to send to Jimmy. I sincerely hope he receives same.*

Dec 18th   *Went to canteen for flask a.m. Saw Doctor and went to library. Afternoon played Bridge with Goley next door–had a lovely tea. Went for a walk afterwards Susie having gone.*

Dec 19th   *We had to have our Xmas Parcels ready for despatch. Jolly good show given by Police.*

Dec 20th   *Went to church. Were going to play Deck Tennis but one of 4 had bad cold so we played Bridge instead. Listened to music. I went to see Nellie and Sheila.*

Dec 21st   *Tommy and I managed to get a seat at St. Stephens but to our great disappointment they cancelled the show because of a case of diphtheria in the camp. Spent all morning drawing and dishing out clothing.*

Dec 22nd *Grand news, to go to the house on the hill for money from my darling J.J. so feel a wonderful relief knowing that he is in the Colony still. It was Nov. & Dec. allotment in one amounting to Y45. He also sent Nellie Y5.*

Dec 23rd *Lots of Xmas Cakes arrived in Camp but I did not get one from J.J.–Marjorie Buckle had one from Vernall, Muriel had one from Henry and heaps of other people received them. Lots of people came from Town and people were collecting from the Hill after 10 p.m. Tommy and I went for a walk called in on Nellie.*

Dec 24th *People took all day leaving for S'hai. Carols evening on the bowling green. Did up parcels–I did not go to the Carols on the Green as I had to help Bill arrange the Block Party and dress him up as Father Christmas with a cotton wool beard etc. The Party was a success songs and carols.*

Dec 25th *Paid a call to Block 9 with small gifts of sweets and cigarettes. Had people dropping in on us all morning. Had a wonderful Xmas dinner at 1 p.m. consisting of:–mince, Corned Beef Pasties and fried veg, fruit tarts and Xmas Pudding with custard. Our capacity for eating large meals having decreased we could not go farther than the Pasties on the menu, leaving the tarts for evening and pudding for next day. Tommy, Simmie and I went for a walk but halfway we met a friend of Simmie's who took us back to C.*

> *Jesse Esdale Gray (1885-1946)*   > *Cecil Jesse Austen Gray (1908-1968)*   > *Peter Nigel Austen Gray (1950-present)*

Bungalow for a drink. Had Sheila and Simmie to tea also Bill came in. Wexie brought Jimmie Bendall in to play cards.

Dec 26th   *We heard that our presents and cards had arrived at the camps and lots of lucky people received cards from their husbands etc. Tommy had 6, I had one from an ex patient & 1 from a Corporal in R.A.M.C, Wexie did not get one at all unfortunately. There were a few in from Argyle St. but I did not. Oh, how I would love just 10 words from my darling.*

Dec 27th   *Went to church–MacKenzie-Dow preaching grand. Played Deck Tennis p.m. with Wexie and her friends; they stayed to tea.*

Dec 28th   *My first effort with the P.T. class was good fun. Went to pay Bridge with Mary Stirling. Muriel McCaw's birthday party after 8 grand fun.*

Dec 29th   *Jimmie's birthday–he gave a tea party for which Tommy made a cake and we supplied lots of food stuff.*

Dec 30th   *Did a lot of work arranging New Year's Eve party. Got our costumes ready. Nativity Concert very good.*

Dec 31st   *Had a very good party in the evening. Betty Brown's concert beforehand which was excellent. Tommy, Wexie, Simmie, Marjorie and I went as the "Quins".*

Wow! I feel that same reaction every time I revisit this amazing, highly personal memoir of what was surely one of the most difficult years of my mother's life. For me, it is a unique insight into my mother as a person. I perhaps know more about her character and personality from the 365 "autobiographical snapshots" written in the diary than what she actually revealed to me through much of the 51 years she mothered me. I am so glad she "talked" to me through the pages of a small lined notebook–and I am truly glad that she kept it safe, for me to "hear" her, over seventy years after she wrote these words.

I bet I can guess some of your reactions to reading the second half of Mother's diary, when she is at Stanley Camp. Or should I have said "holiday camp"? I mean–swimming at the beach, sunbathing on the rocks, picnicking with tea and sandwiches, bridge, poker, deck tennis, piano concerts, theatre shows, birthday parties, Christmas parties! Sounds OK really? I am pleased I shared the general background information about Stanley with you before you read Mother's version. It was collected across numerous memoir-type books written by other internees and my mother's account merely adds to the picture of how a mixture of the "British Bulldog" spirit and women's natural "homemaker" instincts can triumph over an Imperialist imprisonment regime. Maybe not "triumphed" exactly–more like "survived". You may recall that Mother weighed herself within 2 weeks of arriving at Stanley, tipping the scales at 117lbs (about eight and a half stone). This in itself seems underweight, as my mother was quite tall, probably 5' 8". On her release in August 1945, she weighed 84lbs (six stone), so the "holiday camp" diet caused her to lose a further two and a half stone. And she lost all her teeth, aged only 31. It was a very poignant visual reminder of what she had endured when I, as a teenage boy, caught a glance of her dentures in a glass beside her bed. And it always struck home when comedians cracked their "old people and dentures" jokes, because I felt I had to inwardly defend Mother, thinking "it wasn't her fault" to myself. I think the expression most closely relating to their situation has to be "making the best of a bad job"!

Having read this personal account of Mother's first full year in captivity, I find myself in awe of the strength of character, courage and sheer bravado she reveals about herself. The contrast between the two distinct phases of her captivity is a stark one. Her time in the two hospitals as a trainee nurse made great physical and emotional demands on her. She witnessed death for the first time, even having to administer an injection to ease the pain of a dying patient and comfort him through his passing. She required hospitalising herself, suffering from an apparent re-occurrence of the rheumatic fever she endured back in England which initiated her Far East "journey". She was separated from her husband of only 18 months on Christmas Day 1941, not knowing where he was or even if he was alive. Then she was taunted by the mixed blessing of being able to see him in the POW camp opposite the hospital, without being able to talk to him or, in her own words *"hug and kiss him which I so long to do"*. This sight-only relationship is given to her for six months, only to be snatched away by her transfer to Stanley, commencing another period of worry about her husband's whereabouts and state of health. It breaks my heart each time I read her diary entry for 10th August 1942 when she rationalises to herself *"how I hated waving goodbye but it is better for me at Stanley and I don't think it will be for too long"*. She obviously did not think it would be anything like the three years their separation actually lasted. It is hard to summarise her Stanley years subjectively but I feel they left deep-rooted emotional scars which affected her for the rest of her life. And she never had the same physical strength ever again. She had the regime of "going for a lie-down rest after lunch" for the remainder of her life.

My mother changed her record-keeping method after her 1942 daily diary. She appears to have followed a different pattern for the rest of her internment, in that she kept a record of the correspondence between her and various family members. These included copies of the "postcards" she was allowed to send to family etc., together with copies of cards she received in. My father was allowed to send a monthly card from whichever camp he was in; his brother Norman was in the same camps with him and was another of Mother's correspondents. News from the extended family was very sporadic, relying very much of the postal services of the Red Cross and other neutral services. These other correspondents included her parents (Daddy, Mo), her in-laws (Dads, Mums), her sister-in-law (Yolande), her sisters (May, Marjorie).

I am sure this "contact" with her family played an enormous part in getting my mother through the long years of separation. She obviously worried about them all; sometimes it appeared she was more worried for her loved ones than for herself. To receive the messages of reassurance that they were all "alright" or "fine" or "OK" helped to ease her worries. And being sent love from so many quarters must have eased the sense of loneliness she surely felt sometimes, despite the hectic "social" life she pursued so enthusiastically, particularly in

Stanley. I have transcribed these precious communiques in a separate Appendix at the end of this book, so that they are not "lost" from my mother's story. But I am conscious that they are not central to the bigger picture of her captivity nor that of the rest of my extended family held prisoners by the Japanese.

I have not specifically covered my father's period of captivity, other than his own references in correspondence he exchanged with my mother. He did not keep any record of his time in the POW camps but I have got a fair insight into it because his brother, my Uncle Norman, shared it with him–and he did keep a record. My cousin Stuart (2nd eldest of Yolande's four sons) has it amongst another fascinating collection of war memorabilia that Norman left with him. Stuart kindly shared a lot of it with me during my research for this book.

Norman kept a diary of his and my father's captivity. It began at North Point POW camp on January 24th, 1942. They were transferred to Argyle Street POW camp on 18th April, 1942 where they spent the rest of their time, before moving to Shamshuipo camp immediately before their release in 1945. Unlike my mother's daily diary, my uncle recorded events as and when they seemed key to his experiences. These included the transfer dates, days when he received any letters from family etc., receipt of Red Cross parcels, "milestone" dates (e.g. *"March 18th 1944–completed 100 months at Argyle Street"*), and days when he witnessed air raids over Hong Kong by the Allies. The latter must have been highly uplifting in terms of morale for all the service personnel in the camp. Unfortunately, a lot of his diary entries charted his poor health during his captivity, when he was continually in and out of the camp hospital.

This was partly as a result of very harsh treatment by the Japanese including torture. More of that later, when I return to the circumstances of his release.

Perhaps the most fascinating aspect of his "diary" was his unique record of the books he read, to pass the long days of captivity. Prolific is the only word to describe his appetite for reading, since his notebook diligently lists over 360 books that he read in those three years and eight months. These must have been his only "weapons" with which to combat the treatment he received from his gaolers and survive his ordeal. From my reading of the correspondence he sent to my mother, he comes across as optimistic, cheerful and calm, which was probably a very good "act" he presented to her in place of the reality. He was also continually reassuring her about my father, saying he was "OK" or "fine", just to stop her worrying.

It isn't much but my uncle's records are the best insight I have into how the two brothers survived their long spell as POWs, and really completes my account of how My Magnificent 7 survived their captivity. I now want to move forward to the next chapter in their lives–freedom.

FREEDOM AT LAST-BUT EVERYTHING HAD CHANGED

Now I shall fast track forward through the last three years of My Magnificent 7's captivity–to the summer of 1945 and the events leading up to the Japanese surrender. Remembering my mother's comment to her granddaughter Ann–"*Dropping the nuclear bombs saved my life*"–I need to explore with you the context in which that happened.

The war in Europe effectively ended with VE Day on the 8th May 1945, with the Allies acceptance of the unconditional surrender of its' armed forces by Germany. After VE Day the Allies turned their full attention to the Pacific theatre. The Allies called for the unconditional surrender of the Imperial Japanese armed forces in the Potsdam Declaration on July 26, 1945, the alternative being "prompt and utter destruction". Japan ignored the ultimatum and the war continued. By August 1945, the Allies' Manhattan Project had produced two types of atomic bombs, and the 509th Composite Group of the United States Army Air Forces (USAAF) was equipped with the specialised Silverplate version of the Boeing B-29 Superfortress that could deliver them from Tinian in the Mariana Islands. The Allies issued orders for atomic bombs to be used on four Japanese cities on July 25. On August 6, one of the modified B-29s dropped a uranium gun-type bomb ("Little Boy") on Hiroshima. Another B-29 dropped a plutonium implosion bomb ("Fat Man") on Nagasaki three days later. The bombs immediately devastated their targets. Over the next two to four months, the acute effects of the atomic bombings killed between 90,000 and 146,000 people in Hiroshima and 39,000 and 80,000 people in Nagasaki; roughly half of the deaths in each city occurred on the first day. Large numbers of people continued to die for months afterward from the effects of burns, radiation sickness, and other injuries, compounded by illness and malnutrition. In both cities, most of the dead were civilians, although Hiroshima had a sizeable military garrison. Japan surrendered to the Allies on August 15, six days after the Soviet Union's declaration of war and the bombing of Nagasaki. The Japanese government signed the instrument of surrender on September 2 in Tokyo Bay, which effectively ended World War II.

Scholars have extensively studied the effects of the bombings on the social and political character of subsequent world history and popular culture, and there is still much debate concerning the ethical and legal justification for the bombings. As I have already explained, one such debate took place at my daughter Ann's primary school over 30 years after these bombs were dropped, and it was during her research for it that she learned of her grandmother's firm belief that they were totally justified!

To give some timings as to how significant the nuclear bombings were

---

> *Jesse Esdale Gray*
(1885-1946)
> *Cecil Jesse Austen*
Gray (1908-1968)
> *Peter Nigel Austen Gray*
(1950-present)

in hastening the release of My Magnificent 7, I shall jump straight to a letter written by my father from Sham-shui-Po POW camp on 17th August, 1945. (By some spooky coincidence, I was born exactly five years later)

Shamshuipo Camp

Friday 17th August 1945

Oh Kathy, my beloved, my precious wife,

Here I am, my sweet adorable one, quite well, all things considering, and absolutely longing to see you. How marvellous that the war should be over and wow, how glorious that the ghastly three years and eight months since we last met and kissed are ended and that we, you and I, are on the eve of our release and reunion! I am so excited and want to say so much which of course I can't hope to do in this note–I haven't got the time to start with, such short notice of being able to get this off to you having been received. But I will be seeing you very soon now, only a day or two–glory be! I trust you are alright Kathy–I've heard nothing of you since your May 25th card. Stout work, girlie, you are coming through so well.

Needless to say, those of us concerned have begun immediately to agitate for facilities for meeting our wives at Stanley but it has been pointed out (and quite right I suppose) that a few days must elapse before transport etc. can be arranged. It is on the cards that all of us, service and civilian personnel, will be promptly shipped off to some assembly centre (Philippines, Australia, who knows yet?) and then sorted out and sent to various desired destinations for

| *William Gray* | > | *John Gray* | > | *James Gray* | > | *Jesse William Gray* | > |
| *(1720-1795)* | | *(1770-1830)* | | *(1813-1880)* | | *(1855-1894)* | |

leave and recuperation. Even if we can't travel to that assembly point together in the same ship my darling, we will have seen each other before sailing and will have talked it all over. It may be possible to go from here together but I don't know yet and don't think much of the chances. Here's hoping and anyway– after that I never want to be separated from you again, not even for a day.

How we are all longing to see the arrival of the relief forces–they must be very close now, maybe tomorrow?

It's getting very dark we have no light and it is nearly time to hand this in so I must stop darling. Oh dearest, our life together is about to start again and in a peaceful new world–how I am looking forward to it and to my first sight of you once more and to that long talk.

Good night my beloved,

Ever your adoring–Jimmy James

Xxxxxxxx and thousands more

P.S. We are no longer prisoners–we kicked the nips out and are running the camp under the senior officer under British military law. No going out or anything like that yet on account of wanting to present to relieving forces a clean bill of health. Understand?

Another amazing piece of memorabilia that I treasure. To hear one's own father express such excitement and eager anticipation of his reunion with "his beloved" after nearly four years apart is emotional enough, and yet it is done in such a controlled, dignified, very "gentlemanly" way as to reveal a kind of reserve and awkwardness. I guess it is quite understandable, considering they

---

> *Jesse Esdale Gray*
(1885-1946)   > *Cecil Jesse Austen*
Gray (1908-1968)   > *Peter Nigel Austen Gray*
(1950-present)

were relative newly-weds when they were parted in December 1941. Their relationship was still very much in its' infancy and still being tested by these final moments of separation.

I am going to continue my narrative with a series of letters penned by my father over the next 14 days, which testify to the range of emotions he continued to experience over his agonisingly long wait for release. To read of these expressed in his own words was utterly compelling for me, so once again I hope you shall indulge me in my desire to share them with you, as they also detail the events that occurred over those last few days in camp:

Shamshuipo

Saturday 18th August 1945

Kathy my darling,

I've just been informed of another chance of getting a chit over to you–again with very short notice though. I hope you have received my note of yesterday's date and that a reply is en route now. We have just had a very welcome visitation by ten or so of our planes which dropped leaflets addressed to all allied prisoners of war and civilian internees. This was most satisfactory to my nerves and it has served to ease all our minds considerably. Briefly, we must hang on for a day or so yet when a "pre-occupational representative", with full official powers to work for humanitarian purposes, will arrive for yours and mine and others benefit. You will have probably been visited today by planes in a similar manner and will either have seen and read for yourself or else heard about the two kinds of leaflets dropped. So hang on, my cute beast and, of course one of those humanitarian purposes will be arrangements for our early meeting. How I look forward to it–I am so impatient. In a month or so we should be well on our way out of this hell hole with at least six months of peaceful bliss ahead of us in the form of a recuperation holiday at home followed by years and years of peaceful bliss living together wherever it may be.

I have been having very uncertain and mixed feelings about Mum's and Dad's welfare–goodness only knows when we can expect word through about them. Please God that they have survived, only they were both pretty shaky when Hell on Earth, in other words being prisoners of Japanese, began for them. Here's hoping they and Yolande and Bill will be following us home closely.

Norman is as well as can be expected I have not seen him today–perhaps he has sent you a chit. Forgive writing, (in haste and a lousy pencil) and I hope I have been coherent both in yesterday's and this note only I am a mixture these days of nerves, excitement, and goodness knows what not.

How I love you my dearest and how I long for you.

good night Kathy, always your own

Jimmy James

xxxxx–thousands of them

(You said you had no paper–writing I mean!!!–here is some)

Tuesday, 21st August 1945

My darling,

When I got back last night (9:30–quite good going) I found that I was the recipient of a quarter share of a "victory parcel" which the BAT comprador had sent in during the day. Accompanying this are a few items ex this parcel which I send with my love. I don't know what the tin contains and I took some matches out of the box. The toothpaste will probably be nicer than any nip issue stuff which you may be using now–I can make do on present stock of issue powder.

Yesterday was absolutely grand–the best day without any question of doubt I have had in three years and eight months. Au revoir Kathy–I'll come over again as soon as I can and in the meantime you know that I love you dearly and am thinking about you always.

Your own forever

Jimmy James

Shamshuipo

Friday, 24th August 1945

My precious darling,

I was so pleased to get your chit from John Bodeno last night–I had a feeling that you had written it and so anxiously awaited the party's arrival back in camp. I hope this bad weather is not going to last. It looks brighter now. Yes, we had a rough passage home on Wednesday thanks to efficient nip transport–we got back here at about 11:45. I don't know yet when I can come over again Kathy–I am afraid not before Monday or Tuesday–so many who are not as vitally interested as the married men are being allowed over that our turns will not come round as quickly as they should. Let's exchange chits though each day that we don't see each other. I have nothing to send to you today my dear by way of a present but I send all my love and tell you that I ache for the day when we are together again for good, and all these enforced separations are ended.

It was lovely on Wednesday (as of course it was on Monday) and I tell you truthfully that I am more in love with you than ever.

Au revoir my darling wife and here's hoping that perhaps it will be Sunday and not Monday when I see you again. I am sure anybody will bring chits back even if you don't know them.

All my love

Jimmy James

Awful pencil!

Good morning my sweetheart

Saturday, 25th August 1945

Yesterday's cancellation of the Stanley excursion was a great disappointment and of course it has served to put my next visit back one day. I hope this weather clears soon. I was thinking about your window yesterday and hope you were not too troubled by rain beating in. The wind was not in the East very much so it could not have been beating straight in on you.

A revision of the roster for Stanley visits is being made and it appears that husbands will have the opportunity of going over every three days. I should be seeing you next on Monday or Tuesday and you know don't you how I am longing to see you again. I am getting more and more impatient each day for our permanent reunion and very thankful to realise that that day is not very far off now. I think we still have a week or ten days to wait for the R.N. and relieving forces to arrive according to various broadcasts that I heard.

Cheerio Kathy for today–how I love you my adorable, precious, lovely wife–you are my everything. Write to me tonight.

Ever your own loving husband

Jimmy James

Sunday, 26th August 1945

My precious cute beast,

Another cancellation of the excursion yesterday and I am damned if it is not raining like hell again this morning! What bad luck. If today's crowd goes and there are no further upsets my turn will apparently be on Tuesday–I will be able to confirm that in tomorrow morning's chit. Not for a long time have I experienced such long dreary days as these that have elapsed since last Wednesday. This period of waiting I am finding very trying on my nerves and I seem to be growing increasingly impatient. As a matter of fact nothing matters to me now except one thing, yours and my permanent reunion. There are one or two very important things I want to talk about when I see you again–perhaps Wexie can be persuaded to leave us alone for longer on Tuesday (or Wednesday)? See what you can do about it with your usual sweetness and tact.

I had a nasty dream last night which gave me the creeps and has left me with an almighty headache this morning–remind me to tell you about it.

Oh, my darling Kathy, never stop loving me or wanting, as you are my everything–my very life, and I love you and want you more every day. I am very much in love with you this morning in spite of the hour!

Cheerio my darling wife–write to me

Ever yours Jimmy James

Monday, 27th August, 1945

Precious Kathy

It seems pretty definite now that I am in tomorrow's excursion so we must be patient for another twenty-four hours. I was very bucked to get your note last night–it was additionally pleasant because I did not expect it, not being aware of a post on days that the trip is cancelled. Tommy sounds very silly to me–I should have thought her best bet was to go home by hospital ship and well looked after. Anyway if she is out when I come, we must simply go away for a walk in the hills and find a quiet spot–I want at least two hours alone with you tomorrow. Everything in this lousy hut is damp and clammy this morning–

how sick I am of this place and it's dirt and squalor. So nice to hear you say that from now on you want to look after only me. How I love you my darling, my precious wife.

Forever yours, Jimmy James

29th August, 1945

Good morning my sweetheart

We got back in good time last night–the anchor was up at 20 to 8 and Bob and I walked into our hut at 10.0 exactly–not bad going. I am down for tomorrow as I half expected I would be and I have fixed for your birthday as well, between tomorrow and then another trip too either Saturday or Sunday. I had a good sleep last night and feel fine this morning. The numbness of the last 10 days is gradually wearing off and I am becoming aware instead of a glowing of happiness, gratitude, thankfulness and other things all mixed in a delightful way. Do you understand what I am driving at my darling? Yesterday was lovely and I am looking forward to tomorrow. No love offering today but I hope to bring you out a few things tomorrow. Oh, how I love you, adore you, worship you my precious.

Au revoir, your own

Jimmy James

Friday, 31st August'45

Good morning my sweetheart

Here I am starting off in a flap calling the day Wednesday! We had a marvellous time in the dockyard last night and I will tell you all about it when I am next over which I think will be tomorrow.

Yesterday I enjoyed thoroughly and I shall always look back on and vividly remember our delightful long talk in the cemetery under the trees.

Oh, my darling thank you, thank you for everything–you make me so happy and I am so terribly in love with you. What's in store for us today I wonder, both here and out your way? Things won't take long to come to a head now and we will soon be on our way.

Au revoir my darling Kathy, see you tomorrow if all goes well, I absolutely adore you.

Ever your very own

Jimmy James

That was the last in this very personal and emotionally-charged series of letters. My father's prediction of "*...and we will soon be on our way*" was to be proved very accurate. You may recall from my mother's summary memoir earlier that it took seven weeks for her to travel back to England following her release. Well, she arrived at Liverpool on board the SS *Empress of Australia* on the 26th October 1945, travelling straight home to her parents' house, 3 Lesney Park Road, Erith, Kent. I calculate that to be fifty-six days from Dad's last letter above, so she must have finally gotten out of Stanley camp about a week after his letter! And his fears that they would not be able to travel home together were also borne out by the shipping record detailing Mother's passage, as she

---

was travelling "alone" in terms of
no family members accompanying
her. It seems so cruel that the
couple were given those few brief
encounters during her last fortnight
of captivity, only to be parted again
for their different journeys home.

I guess my father, as still a serving officer in the RNVR, had to be officially
demobbed through the correct naval channels involving a lot of red-tape. I
don't know the exact date or location of their reunion as plain old "Mr and Mrs
Gray" but I imagine it couldn't come soon enough for either of them.

To lighten things up a little, I shall share with you some "advanced"
genealogical detective work I did to narrow down the possible date of this
meeting. I can say with reasonable certainty that they "got together" sometime
between October 1945 and mid-March 1947–because my brother Ian was
born on 18th December 1947! Now you mustn't go jumping to any conclusions
that their continuing story is as simple as resuming their married life in some
little house in suburban England and starting their family close to the proud
new grandparents. If I say that Master Ian Robert Downton Gray was born
in Tsingtao, China, you might just think "and so it goes on!" I shall pick that
thread up later but now back to "releasing" the rest of My Magnificent 7.

My uncle Norman's entire period of captivity mirrored that of my father,
as he was also serving in the Hong Kong Royal Navy Volunteer Reserves. They

---

| *William Gray*
(1720-1795) | > | *John Gray*
(1770-1830) | > | *James Gray*
(1813-1880) | > | *Jesse William Gray*
(1855-1894) | > |

were captured together when the Japanese seized control of Hong Kong in December 1941 and they were "inmates" together in several POW camps. The first was North Point, then Argyle Street and finally Shamshuipo Camp at the time of the Japanese surrender. Norman's release must also have been processed through the Naval channels in Hong Kong, but it was different from that of my father, due to his poor health. The exact timings of it are a bit sketchy but I knew from my Reynolds cousins that there was a potential "love story" at the heart of it. If it was the synopsis of a filmscript, it might go something like this–"Injured POW falls in love with his nurse on hospital ship voyage to freedom". Now that is enough to capture the interest of an old romantic like me and, of course, totally in keeping with the kind of stories my family history research continues to reveal to me. So, I had better introduce the central characters of this drama to you in a little more detail.

Most of you have already "met" my Uncle Norman and so I shall give this short recap of his life so far. He is almost a clone of my father, in that their lives followed a strikingly similar pattern. Norman William Hoskyn Gray was born in 1916, the third son of Jesse and Winifred, and eight years younger than my father. Cecil and Norman were both born in Yokohama, both went to Blundell's School, both were accountants, and both enlisted in the R.N.V.R. in Hong Kong soon after the outbreak of WW2. The death of

---

their brother Horace in 1930 must have brought them even closer together and their joint captivity ensured they remained inseparable throughout the war. In fact, it was probably their differing "release" journeys that caused their respective paths through life to separate for the first time. One significant difference between them was that Norman was single, and hence he was not involved in the "re-union excursions" between Shamshuipo and Stanley camps. Of course, being single was a pre-requisite of Norman being cast as the leading man in the upcoming seaborne romance!

So, who was his "co-star"? Joyce Trevellion Sexton was born on 7th July 1914 in Taihape, Wellington, New Zealand, the daughter of William Edward Sexton and Alethea Rachel Sinclair. After a childhood growing up in New Zealand, she trained as a nurse at Napier and qualified in 1938. I am assuming she enlisted into the New Zealand Auxiliary Nursing Service at the outbreak of the war in 1939. In Roll 3 of the New Zealand Army WWII Nominal Rolls for the period 1st July 1940–31st Mar 1941 her entry reads thus:

Name in full:	*Sexton, Joyce Trevellion*
Army No.:	*63392*
Rank:	*S/Nurse*
Unit:	*N.Z.A.N.S.*
Conjugal status:	*S*
Place of Enlistment:	*Auckland*
Occupation:	*Nurse*
Last New Zealand Address:	*9 Seaview Ave., Northcote, Auckland*

Name & address of   *Mrs A. R. Talbot, 29 Seaview*

next-of-kin (relationship):   *Avenue, Northcote, Auckland (Mother)*

Of course, the trained eye of an experienced genealogist (that's me folks– don't I sound grand!) will spot a different surname for the mother. Remarried, possibly? A quick check of her father's data shows that he died in 1918, four years after Joyce's birth date. Given the date of death and his age being only 44, one invariably supposes her father was a WWI fatality and Joyce's mother did remarry a Mr. Talbot. Incidentally, on a later Army Nominal Roll for 1942, she is again listed as Joyce's next-of-kin but she is now using her first married name–Mrs A. R. Sexton. I have to assume Mr Talbot died (possibly as a war casualty himself) between these two Army Roll entries, as Joyce's mother is listed as a widow in a later Electoral Roll record. She may have reverted to the name Sexton after being widowed to have the same name as her children. On this very same Nominal Roll, the name three lines below that of Joyce is "Sexton, Walter Ringwood; Cpl.; N.Z.M.C." with a Mrs. A.R. Sexton of 29 Seaview Avenue, Northcote, Auckland listed as his next-of-kin–and mother! So, Joyce had at least one sibling, who was a bank clerk before enlisting into the medical corps. This is when studying the various documents discovered in one's research is so much fun! A verification of one fact can quickly, almost by chance, set you off on another train of thought. In fact this brother, Walter, was the youngest of 5 siblings–Joyce had two elder sisters Margaret and Alethea, and two elder brothers James (died age 5) and Edward (died as an infant). My guess is that Joyce's mother was very worried when her only surviving son enlisted, but he did survive the war and in fact outlived his sister Joyce. It is highly commendable that these two siblings from New Zealand were "doing their bit" in a war that their country was not directly involved with. It was true of so many Commonwealth citizens and demonstrates the strong link felt with the "mother country".

Joyce gained promotion to the rank of Charge Sister and was awarded a medal–Associate Royal Red Cross–as reported in the London Gazette on 8th June, 1941. The Royal Red Cross medal was introduced by Queen Victoria in 1883 and is awarded to military nurses for exceptional services, devotion to duty and professional competence. The first recipient of The Royal Red Cross was Florence Nightingale for her work in the Crimea War. So, my aunt Joyce was following in some pretty illustrious footsteps!

She was serving on a hospital ship and my genealogical research lead me to think it was the NZHS *Maunganui*. She was a Union Steam Ship Company

A postcard of the HS Maunganui, personalised by staff and patients' signatures

liner converted to carry 390 patients accommodated in 100 swinging cots, 100 single fixed cots and 95 two-tier fixed cots. Emergency lighting, electric lifts and a 700 ton fresh water tank were fitted. One description I discovered online called her "the best fitted and finest hospital ship". After a voyage in which they brought back POWs from Hong Kong to Wellington in October 1945, this tribute was paid to the *Maunganui*,

"Wonderful work was done by the Nursing staff on board to restore these undernourished captives of the Japanese. Nothing was too good for these people and, to show their appreciation, they did their best to recover and after 5 weeks at sea several of the patients were able to assist in many small ways and help their own friends to regain some of their lost health."

I am now taking you all back to my uncle Norman's wartime diary, to correlate it with the information I have just shared above:

Sept 2nd (1945)   *Left Stanley at 5:30 pm for Shamshuipo*

Sept 3rd   ***Into hospital on board HMNZHS* Maunganui**

Sept 8th   ***Depart Hong Kong***

There we have it–my uncle Norman is on board the *Maunganui* for her voyage from Hong Kong to New Zealand! This hospital ship was the location of the romance between my uncle Norman and aunt Joyce. The first leg of the journey would have taken five weeks and, after a short spell at a military camp in New Zealand, HS *Maunganui* sailed on her final voyage in November 1945. Norman's diary states that she travelled by way of Port Said and Algiers, arriving at Southampton on 10th January, 1946–and his final entry reads "the end of a marvellous trip!". This surely refers to how their relationship had developed from that of "nurse and patient" to companionship and eventually love. Of course, this scenario is the stuff of many Mills and Boon novels or modern day "chick flick" but this was real life, with my close family members playing the central characters. But their story is not even unique amongst Gray family history. Those loyal, dedicated readers who have journeyed along this adventure with me from the start may recall that 'my' uncle Norman was only copying 'his' uncle–William Maxwell Gray–who fell in love with his nurse Helen Forsyth way back in… Chapter 6! Of course, this earlier "Gray hospital drama" was set against a different background; my great uncle William was recuperating from injury sustained serving with the Bengal Lancers during WWI. One tragic piece of information I learned about my uncle Norman's captivity came from another nephew of his, my cousin Stuart. Stuart was fortunate to get to know Norman quite well when they had both settled in England and Stuart learned that our uncle never could have children, because of the treatment he had received from the Japanese. One torture involved being made to sit naked astride a block of ice; the resulting injuries rendered him unable to reproduce. I include this horrendous event here, to add context to the nursing care given on board the hospital ship.

The exact timeline and locations for Norman and Joyce's ongoing romance are a bit sketchy, so I have to revert to actual record-based evidence. In a New Zealand Electoral Roll for 1946, Joyce is listed as living at 30 Seaview Avenue, Ponsonby, Auckland with her widowed mother Alethea and older

L-R: unknown, uncle Gordon (Yolande's husband), Norman, Joyce, aunt Yolande, great aunt Dorothy, unknown

sister Margaret Cecilia. Joyce is listed as "spinster" so it must have been from the earlier part of the year. This is because the couple were married on 27th November, 1946 in Bristol, Gloucestershire.

This wedding completes Norman's release story and brings the total of ex-captives up to three–my parents and my uncle. The remaining four of My Magnificent 7 were all held in Shanghai, so I need to turn your attention to how the Japanese surrender unfolded, both generally and in Shanghai particularly.

The surrender of Imperial Japan was announced by Japanese Emperor Hirohito on August 15 and formally signed on September 2, 1945, bringing the hostilities of World War II to a close. By the end of July 1945, the Imperial Japanese Navy (IJN) was incapable of conducting major operations and an Allied invasion of Japan was imminent. Together with the British Empire and China, the United States called for the unconditional surrender of the Japanese armed forces in the Potsdam Declaration on July 26, 1945–the alternative being "prompt and utter destruction". While publicly stating their intent to fight on to the bitter end, Japan's leaders (the Supreme Council for the Direction of the War, also known as the "Big Six") were privately making entreaties to the publicly neutral Soviet Union to mediate peace on terms more favourable to the Japanese. While maintaining a sufficient level of diplomatic engagement with the Japanese to give them the impression they might be willing to mediate, the Soviets were covertly preparing to attack Japanese forces in Manchuria and Korea (in addition to South Sakhalin and the Kuril Islands) to fulfil promises they had secretly made to the United States and the United Kingdom at the Tehran and Yalta Conferences.

On August 6, 1945, at 8:15 AM local time, the United States detonated an atomic bomb over the Japanese city of Hiroshima. Sixteen hours later, American President Harry S. Truman called again for Japan's surrender, warning them to "expect a rain of ruin from the air, the like of which has never been seen on this earth." Late in the evening of August 8, 1945, in accordance with the Yalta agreements, but in violation of the Soviet–Japanese Neutrality Pact, the Soviet Union declared war on Japan, and soon after midnight on August 9, 1945, the Soviet Union invaded the Imperial Japanese puppet state of Manchukuo. Hours later, the United States dropped a second atomic bomb, this time on the Japanese city of Nagasaki. Following these events, Emperor Hirohito intervened and ordered the Supreme Council for the Direction of the War to accept the terms the Allies had set down in the Potsdam Declaration for ending the war. After several more days of behind-the-scenes negotiations and a failed coup d'état, Emperor Hirohito gave a recorded radio address across the Empire on August 15. In the radio address, called the Jewel Voice Broadcast, he announced the surrender of Japan to the Allies.

On August 28, the occupation of Japan led by the Supreme Commander for the Allied Powers began. The surrender ceremony was held on September 2, aboard the United States Navy battleship USS *Missouri*, at which officials from the Japanese government signed the Japanese Instrument of Surrender, thereby ending the hostilities. Allied civilians and military personnel alike celebrated V-J Day, the end of the war; however, isolated soldiers and personnel from Japan's far-flung forces throughout Asia and the Pacific refused to surrender for months and years afterwards, some even refusing into the 1970s. The state of war formally ended when the Treaty of San Francisco came into force on April 28, 1952. Four more years passed before Japan and the Soviet Union signed the Soviet–Japanese Joint Declaration of 1956, which formally brought an end to their state of war.

My grandfather Jesse, my grandmother Winifred and my aunt Yolande were all in Yangchow C and Jesse wrote a letter from there to his other daughter Stella on 4th September 1945, some three weeks after the official surrender. He states "...*the collapse of the Japanese is so utter and complete as to leave me aghast. While I had no doubt whatever of the ultimate outcome, I never expected such an early and sudden finish–fully anticipating the war to continue until next spring at least.*"

He goes on to describe how 4 officers from an American Mission were in

---

> *Jesse Esdale Gray*
> *(1885-1946)*

> *Cecil Jesse Austen*
> *Gray (1908-1968)*

> *Peter Nigel Austen Gray*
> *(1950-present)*

the camp beginning to make arrangements for the family's release and expresses his thoughts about what kind of Shanghai they will be returning to:

"Shanghai is said to be in a dreadful state–sanitary, PWD, money, housing–all in a fearful state of chaos, and it will be years before the place recovers. In any case it will never be the place we used to know–no more SMC or Extra'lity–all will very likely be under complete Chinese control."

The next paragraph in his letter still fills me with great sadness, each time I read it:

"OUR FUTURE PLANS:

These are most indefinite. I have told the company that I will give them one year of my time to help them to reorganize the company, but no more. After that I want to retire and get away from the East–quite enough of it! Future residence–Australia? Canada? California? Cannot say, but the former most likely. In addition to the work I may do for the office (only if health permits, however), I shall have many personal affairs to attend to and adjust. I should have mentioned earlier that the doctor will not permit me to go to work when I get back to Shanghai. I shall have to lay up in hospital for three to four weeks before I attempt to do anything. Yolande proposed to go to India as soon as she can get in touch with her fiancée, so Mums and I shall be left on our own."

Far from giving his company one more year as he had said he would, my grandfather Jesse never even lived for a year after writing this letter. He died on 20th July 1946 in the Country Hospital, Shanghai, aged 61 yrs.

My grandfather had not enjoyed the best of health before the war, as testified to by numerous references throughout the memorabilia I have been quoting from. In her letter of July 1940, my grandmother Winnie wrote that he was admitted to hospital on 20th April, where he remained for eight weeks. She described his condition as "*a hernia of the heart*" and was obviously very worried by it, writing "*it was touch and go with him; at first they did not tell me how serious, only after he had improved a little and there was a chance of getting over it*". This was even reported in the paper, which I find fascinating and says something about Grandpa's standing in Shanghai at the time. My parents both expressed their fears about his health in their correspondence, upon hearing that he had been interned in Yangchow. And Jesse

MR. J. E. Gray, of the China Import & Export Lumber Co., who has been a patient in the Country Hospital for eight weeks, returned to his home at 104 Columbia Road yesterday. 15 6 40.

himself confirmed he had not been well during his captivity with this summary in his letter written immediately prior to his release–"*All in all I have had six spells in hospital and while I have not kept exact count, I think I have put in nearly half my camp time therein*".

I find it heartbreakingly ironic that my grandfather survived all the trauma of three years and eight months under Japanese control and was granted the potential of restarting his life, only for it to be snatched away from him less than a year later. And obviously I feel robbed of ever having him as a "real" person in my life, rather than a name on my family tree of whom I knew nothing. I would have much preferred tangible memories of times we had shared, good or bad, to a biography of his life that I have pieced together through doing genealogy. It is probably at the heart of my wish to share what I now know about him through writing this book.

My grandfather's short obituary in the Shanghai newspaper actually summarises quite nicely what I have been trying to say. I love the way it starts by recognising the esteem in which Grandpa was held by the Shanghai community. And it doesn't hold back on apportioning some of the blame for his health finally letting him down, when it states "… aggravated by his internment for nearly three years in Yangchow Camp". There can be no doubt that the last thing a man in his late 50s with a heart condition needed was imprisonment in very harsh conditions!

This was not the first Gray funeral at which Dean Trivett had officiated. He provided the very same service at the funeral of my uncle Horace sixteen years earlier in 1930. At least he had a rather more uplifting association with our family, since he also conducted the ceremony for my father's wedding to Doreen Beldon in 1934. I imagine this long association with the Grays brought some comfort to my widowed grandmother in terms of how he conducted my grandfather's committal.

Both Jesse's and Horace's funerals were held at the Bubbling Well Cemetery in Shanghai which was why my wife and I made sure we "visited" it during

| William Gray | > | John Gray | > | James Gray | > | Jesse William Gray | > |
| (1720-1795) | | (1770-1830) | | (1813-1880) | | (1855-1894) | |

Mr. J. E. Gray Laid To Rest

The esteem in which the late Mr. Jesse Esdale Gray was held was shown by the large attendance of Chinese and foreign friends at the funeral services (Cremation) held on Sunday afternoon at the Bubbling Well Chapel.

The Very Rev. Dean A. C. S. Trivett officiated.

The late Mr. Gray joined The China Import & Export Lumber Co. Ltd. in 1917 and served that Company to March of this year, when his health completely broke down aggravated greatly by his interment for nearly three years in Yangchow Camp, and he was compelled to go to the Country Hospital, where he passed peacefully away on 20th inst.

He was a prominent Freemason, at his death being Master of Lodge Cosmopolitan No. 428 S.C., was one of the most senior members of the Shanghai Scottish Company (S.V.C.) and in many other ways identified himself with social affairs in Shanghai.

He is survived by his widow, who is in Shanghai, two sons who served in the Royal Navy and were interned in Hongkong, and two daughters, Mrs. W. D. Ward-Smith (U.S.A), and Mrs. Reynolds (India), to all of whom deepest sympathy is extended.

our holiday trip there in 2014. In fact, the original cemetery was destroyed by the Chinese during the Cultural Revolution, when it was transformed into Jing'an Park. All that remains of the original cemetery layout is an avenue of yew trees, as seen in the photograph below. Nevertheless, our visit there was quite emotional, as it is the closest I have ever been to my grandfather Jesse.

I must return to my explanation of where the remaining members of My Magnificent 7 went to after their release. Obviously, my grandmother Winifred accompanied Jesse and their daughter Yolande back to the city of Shanghai but I am sure they never returned to the family home at 104 Columbia Road. Jesse was expressing grave doubts about what they might find, when they first saw it, in his last letter. The only information I can get about where they actually lived is from Granny Gray's letters but her first post-war letter was dated October 1946, after Jesse's death. So, there is an unexplained period of about 10 months between their release and Jesse's death. However, in his will which received probate in 1947, it refers to grandfather as "Gray, Jesse Esdale–of 615 Metropole

> *Jesse Esdale Gray* > *Cecil Jesse Austen* > *Peter Nigel Austen Gray*
> *(1885-1946)*   *Gray (1908-1968)*   *(1950-present)*

Hotel, Shanghai". The Metropole Hotel was owned by Sir Victor Sassoon, hence my grandfather's reference to "...*Sassoon's providing temporary accommodation in Shanghai*" in his letter. His will tells me he probably lived the last months of his life in a hotel, rather a tragic 'fall from grace' for a man seemingly proud of having provided for his family throughout his life.

The next definitive "sighting" of my grandmother is of her travelling to America. I found a shipping record from 1946 which has Grandma departing from Shanghai on the SS *General M. C. Meigs* on 2nd September ...and arriving San Francisco, California on 14th September. She gives her last place of permanent residence as Shanghai, with "Mrs A. Damsgaard, 30 Lucerne Road, Shanghai, friend" stated as who and where she has come from. My guess she has been staying with a family friend since my grandfather's death, as she is a widow alone in Shanghai, without the direct support of any of her family. She states she is planning to stay with her elder daughter "Mrs W.D. Ward-Smith, 283 South 10th Street, San Jose, California" for six months. This is my aunt Stella, whom you may remember was brought to safety in the US from Shanghai in 1941 with her two young children, my cousins Tony and Dawn. Prior to discovering it as a place where Gray family members lived, my only awareness of San Jose was Dionne Warwick asking directions on how to get there!

William Gray   >   *John Gray*   >   *James Gray*   >   *Jesse William Gray*   >
(1720-1795)   *(1770-1830)*   *(1813-1880)*   *(1855-1894)*

This is probably a good point to digress slightly from Granny Gray's story, to explain what happened to the last remaining member of My Magnificent 7–my uncle Bill. It is covered in this article from the San Jose Evening News, Friday December 7, 1945. It tells how he was finally released in late 1945 but discovered his office in Shanghai had been burned down. He left China on 17th November and was re-united with his wife Stella and the two children on 5th December, 1941. I quite like his summary of the events of his last few years–*"I've had enough of China to last me the rest of my life!"*. Hopefully you will see why I introduced my uncle Bill's return date at this point in the story–because it means he was there in San Jose when my grandmother arrived in September 1946 to stay with the family.

This visit was the first of a series of travels that Granny Gray made over the next ten years. Basically, she was a homeless widow, spending her time either staying with her family spread around the world or onboard ships travelling to get to them! The table illustrates how her extended family were gradually settling back into some kind of normality, after their ordeals during the war years. From her letters, Granny Gray was really unsure as to where she wanted to settle down and call home. After all, she was born in Yokohama, to parents who had made Japan their home many years earlier and hardly knew England as "home". Her parents did eventually make it to England, when her father Rev. Austen took over the parish of North Shoebury in Essex, but they were both deceased before the war. Her only family in England were her two younger sisters, Mabel and Dorothy. Her elder brother Albert was in America, a recent

---

> *Jesse Esdale Gray*   >   *Cecil Jesse Austen*   >   *Peter Nigel Austen Gray*
> *(1885-1946)*   *Gray (1908-1968)*   *(1950-present)*

PAGE 2   SAN JOSE EVENING NEWS, FRIDAY, DECEMBER 7, 1945

Britisher Held In China Joins Family Here

By GERRY REYNOLDS

While the two small children who were babies when he last saw them four years ago listen eagerly to his every word, British William Dudley Ward-Smith tells interesting tales of his experiences in a Japanese-controlled China.

Ward-Smith, who has been Far Eastern manager of the Foster-McClellan Co. of Buffalo, N. Y., for 21 years, brought his wife, Stella, and his two children, Dawn, then 8 months, and Anthony, 2 years, to San Jose in June, 1941.

In October of that year he started back to China, and, after a month at sea, he arrived in Shanghai just two weeks before war was declared. Realizing that the war was approaching, Ward-Smith attempted to get his business affairs straightened out in time to return to this country, but transportation was not available.

BUSINESS CLOSED

As soon as the war broke out, the Japanese closed all business and forced everyone to register. Ward-Smith was allowed to live in his Shanghai home, but he, like everyone else, was restricted as to the amount of money he could spend each month.

As the weeks passed, he reports, conditions became more difficult and the British and Americans in Shanghai opened relief organizations, under the supervision and control of the Japanese Consulate. Ward-Smith served as treasurer of the British agency, and therefore was not forced to go to an internment camp.

However, in June of 1943 he was placed in the Lunghwa internment Camp for civilians.

He served as head of one building and was responsible for its 350 occupants. Ten Britishers escaped in the early days of internment, and Ward-Smith has heard since that they are all safe.

He said that the prisoners were forced to do all the work in the camp, and that at one time he cooked as much as 800 pounds of rice in one day.

JUST SWEEPINGS

The rice, he added, was nothing but sweepings, and was mixed with bits of string, straw and dirt.

One of the most vivid recollections Ward-Smith has of his internment was the time he was threatened with imprisonment in the Bridge House, or "Butcher Shop," as the prisoners called it. It was there that J. B. Stowell, American newspaperman who spent 25 years in China, lost his legs, and it was also in the "Butcher Shop" that Jimmy Doolittle's flyers were tortured.

The Japanese commandant threatened to put Ward-Smith in the "Butcher Shop" when he heard that the Britisher had spoken insultingly of his wife.

"But I lied my way out of it after two and a half days of questioning," Ward-Smith declared.

Near the war's end, the internees at Lunghwa were able to smuggle radio parts into their rooms, and, by means of a well-hidden set, they followed the progress of the war. On Aug. 12 they heard rumors that the war was over, and on Aug. 15 they were called together and informed by a subdued Japanese commandant that the Allies had been victorious.

When he was finally released and returned to Shanghai, he found that his business establishment had been burned down. He left China on Nov. 17, and arrived in San Jose late Wednesday night.

"I've had enough of China to last me the rest of my life," he says.

British William Dudley Ward-Smith, a prisoner of the Japanese in Shanghai since 1941, arrived in San Jose this week. He is shown above with his two children, Anthony, and Dawn, and his wife, Stella.—San Jose News photo.

widower after Nancy's death in 1945. Her younger brother Harold was in Australia, the head of his own expanding family "Down Under". Her daughter Stella was the only one of her children not to have been a Japanese prisoner, and hence was Granny Gray's only child already established in a home of her own. And her only grandchildren were there in San Jose–my cousins Tony and

Dawn! These must have been the key factors in her choosing to go to Stella first, after losing Grandpa Jesse.

I am indebted to my cousin Andrew for helping me to understand the circumstances whereby my grandmother's other daughter Yolande, who had been with her throughout her internment ordeal, was finally re-united with her fiancé Gordon. Andrew explained that his father left Shanghai in August 1941 for Calcutta, where he joined the Indian Army. He was immediately sent to Bangalore for officer training before being posted to the 2/5th Royal Ghurka Rifles. As a 2nd Lt., he became the brigade transport officer and went through the retreat from Burma. Andrew tells me Gordon never spoke about this period of the war, something he had in common with many of his comrades. He was fairly quickly promoted to Lt., then Acting Capt. and even Acting Major for a short while. When the Battalion got back into India, my uncle joined a unit called the British Army Aid Group (part of MI9). Andrew speculates that his father's ability to speak Chinese may be the reason he was recruited into this unit, which was formed to go behind Japanese lines in China to aid escaped POWs. Part of their remit was also to persuade members of the Indian National Army who had joined the Japanese rather than being made POWs to desert and rejoin the Indian Army. The BAAG unit was formed by a Col. Ride, an Australian physiologist and soldier. He was appointed professor of physiology at the University of Hong Kong in 1928. With the fall of Hong Kong in December 1941, Ride was made a POW in Shamshuipo barracks but he escaped in January 1942 with the help of the Hong Kong guerrilla forces.

> *Jesse Esdale Gray*
(1885-1946)   > *Cecil Jesse Austen*
Gray (1908-1968)   > *Peter Nigel Austen Gray*
(1950-present)

This is the same Shamshuipo camp where my father and uncle were held immediately prior to their release. Gordon told Andrew that his intention in joining the BAAG was to try and reach Shanghai and find Yolande, but he never got close, as he was confined to the areas where the Indian troops were located. Andrew's understanding is that his parents were only re-united sometime after VJ Day (15th August 1945) in the UK.

They were married on 22nd December, 1945 at Boxmoor, Hertfordshire, near where Gordon's parents lived. The keen-eyed amongst you might have noticed both my aunt Yolande and Gordon were present at my uncle Norman's wedding in 1946. You will have noticed Gordon is wearing his army uniform, because he continued his military career for some time after the war. Andrew's information confirms that his father (and my uncle) Gordon was working for military intelligence and involved him "being behind enemy lines" both in Burma and China. So, I did get a spy in my family after all! You may remember my speculation regarding my great uncle William being a Gray-family version of James Bond!

In her October 1946 letter Granny Gray writes that Gordon has got a new job in the police force in Africa, expecting to go there early in 1947. She also writes that when he leaves the army, he is due a lot of leave which he plans to take in England. His wife is expecting their first child in February and she wants Granny Gray to be there with her. Sure enough, in her March '47 letter from her sister Mabel's home in Loughton, Granny Gray writes that Bruce Duncan Gray Reynolds was born on 16th February 1947, four days earlier

| *William Gray* | > | *John Gray* | > | *James Gray* | > | *Jesse William Gray* | > |
| *(1720-1795)* | | *(1770-1830)* | | *(1813-1880)* | | *(1855-1894)* | |

than his due date–her birthday! She adds she will miss them when they go, because Gordon, Yolande and 6-week old Bruce sailed from Tilbury on SS *Dominion Monarch* on 2nd April, bound for Mombasa. The record gives their "intended country of future residence" as Tanganyika, an East African country that in 1964 merged with Zanzibar to form modern day Tanzania. This was the start of a long career in the East African Police for my uncle, and a long stay in Africa for the family. Three more boys were added to that family in quick succession, each one carrying on the tradition of 3 forenames–and family names at that. They were Stuart Malcolm Jesse (07/07/49), Andrew Gordon Esdale (21/09/51) and Graham Keith Austen (02/08/53). Never could a genealogist have asked for a more helpful set of names in identifying a set of siblings! And I have to thank them for lining up in this later picture in age order, again simplifying the task of identifying them!

These are my Reynolds cousins whom I lost touch with for over fifty years for reasons that will become clear later in my story. Thankfully, we were re-united quite recently, when I started getting into family history research. It is probably the best part of doing personal genealogy, catching up with either long lost family or even unknown family! Now, each of these Reynolds boys have helped me in the writing of this book, along with other cousins discovered along the

> *Jesse Esdale Gray*
> *(1885-1946)*

> *Cecil Jesse Austen*
> *Gray (1908-1968)*

> *Peter Nigel Austen Gray*
> *(1950-present)*

LOCATION OF THE VARIOUS "GRAY" FAMILIES DURING THE IMMEDIATE POST WAR YEARS (as per dates of Granny Gray's letters to her brother Albert)

Date	Granny Gray	Mother & Father	Norman & Joyce	The Reynolds	The Ward-Smiths	Aunt Mabel (Austen)	Aunt Dorothy (Hume)	Albert Austen	Grandpa & Grandma Downton
					Family Member(s)				
3rd October 1946	Staying with Stella in San Jose	Dad is in Tsingtao; Mum in transit, left England 22/09 on Empress of Australia	Norman working for Lever Bros. in Bristol; Joyce due mid-Nov.; they marry 27/11/46; expects to go abroad in '47	In UK; Gordon has job in W. Africa, set to go there early '47; Yolande expecting in Feb '47, wants GG there	San Jose, California			Fontana, California – has been a widower since Nancy died May 7th, 1945	3 Lesney Park Road, Erith, Kent
20th March 1947	Kings Cottage, Kings Hill, Loughton, Essex (since Jan 13th)	Tsingtao, China	Left on 5th March en route to Shanghai	Gordon leaves from Hull for E. Africa on Apr 1st, Yolande and Bruce a few days later from Tilbury		Kings Cottage, Kings Hill, Loughton, Essex		Fontana, California	Erith, Kent
5th October 1947	Dunoon, Scotland — on holiday with Mabel	Tsingtao, China			Buffalo, New York			Fontana, California	Erith, Kent
14th December 1947	Brighton, Sussex – with Dorothy for Christmas & New Year	Tsingtao, China – Ian born there On 18th December				Brighton, Sussex – with Dorothy for Christmas & New Year	6A Chichester Place, Brighton, Sussex	Fontana, California	Erith, Kent
25th March 1948	Buffalo – with Stella & family				46 Highland Avenue, Buffalo, N.Y.			Fontana, California	Erith, Kent
2nd October 1948	Buffalo – with Stella & family	In transit back to China via Suez; had been on leave in UK since May 14th	In Shanghai	In East Africa – Gordon, Yolande, Bruce and new baby Stuart born 7th July	Bill is in Seattle with new job; house-hunting for family to move across after Pam's birth			Fontana, California	Erith, Kent
23rd September 1951	11030 Sands Point Way, Seattle, Washington – staying with Stella	Monghyr, India – Dad, Mum, Ian and 1yr old me!	Singapore	East Africa	Seattle, Washington			Fontana, California	Erith, Kent
12th December 1955	3 Lesney Park Road, Erith, Kent – staying with my Downton grandparents!	Calcutta, India. Had summer in UK; Mum + 2 boys 26/5 until 24/11 (flew); Dad 3/7 'til 1/11 (by ship)	Singapore	Gordon, Yolande + 4 boys - renting a house in New Barnet, North London while Gordon on police training; going back to Africa mid-May	Seattle, Washington			Fontana, California	Erith, Kent

William Gray (1720-1795) > *John Gray (1770-1830)* > *James Gray (1813-1880)* > *Jesse William Gray (1855-1894)* >

way. And it is so much easier questioning living people!

Back to the matter in hand. With both her daughters raising their families abroad, my grandmother maybe held out hopes of her sons "setting up home" in England. This was not to be the case however, as I continue my tale with my own family's travels. After her release from Stanley in September 1945, my mother was shipped back to England and to her parents in Erith, Kent. That really must have been some reunion, it being the first time they had met since Mother took her 21st birthday present trip to Shanghai ten years earlier. In between, she had married my father, survived eight months nursing and a further three years internment. Apart from re-uniting with her parents, she would also have caught up with her elder sister May and her two nephews Michael and Roger. She was still apart from my father, whom I believe had travelled to Shanghai after being discharged. The first positive "sighting" of him after the war is in Granny Gray's letter of 3rd October 1946, when she writes *"Kathleen is on her way out to Cecil, she left England on Sept. 22nd on the 'Empress*

of Australia'. She will tranship I expect at Singapore for Tsingtao direct". This is the first mention of Tsingtao in any correspondence or records relating to my father, and yet it is absolutely vital in tracking my father's movements after the war. I knew I had to get him to

---

Tsingtao somehow, because I have always known that my brother Ian was born there in December 1947. I now think my father returned to Shanghai to resume his career with BAT, and that Tsingtao was his first posting after re-joining the company. In her March 1947 letter, Granny Gray writes *"Cecil and Kathleen seem very happy and well in Tsingtao, want to know when I am coming to visit them"*. I think we can guess just how happy they were–because Ian's date of birth is 18/12/47! I have a shipping record that shows my father and mother arriving in London onboard the PO liner *Canton* on 14th June 1948–presumably to present their 6-mth old baby to their families. Certainly, my Granny Gray wrote very excitedly in a March 1948 letter about "my first 'Gray' grandchild". I hadn't fully appreciated that Ian actually held this title, nor that he and I had the responsibility of carrying on the Gray surname, since my uncle Norman couldn't have any children and both my aunts were–well, basically–women and women don't usually pass on surnames! Come to think of it, I haven't actually taken this responsibility seriously myself, since my three daughters are also basically–women!

Granny Gray's search for a suitable place to live was to continue for quite a few years after "meeting" her 1st Gray grandchild. When she was in England, she shared her time between her two younger sisters, Mabel and Dorothy. My great aunt, Mabel Austen, was living at Kings Cottage, Kings Hill, Loughton, Essex when Granny Gray came to stay with her early in 1947. She never married and, after leaving Yokohama in 1923 following the Great Kanto earthquake, she lived in England, either on her own or with Dorothy, the youngest of the

| *William Gray* | > | *John Gray* | > | *James Gray* | > | *Jesse William Gray* | > |
| *(1720-1795)* | | *(1770-1830)* | | *(1813-1880)* | | *(1855-1894)* | |

three daughters born to my grandparents William and Leila Austen.

Dorothy Elizabeth Austen was born on 6th September 1891 in Yokohama. She was the baby of the Rev. Austen's family growing up in Japan with her two elder sisters. She accompanied my grandmother to England in 1910 when the latter had her baby Horace near her Shapcott grandparents' home in Devon. She appears on the 1911 census as a 19yr old single woman, together with her elder sisters Winifred (29) and Mabel (23), and her nephews Cecil (2) and Horace(6mths). However, a shipping record for the SS *Kamo Maru* arriving in London from Yokohama on 14th May, 1919 shows her travelling as Dorothy Elizabeth Hume aged 27. Her entry is in the "not accompanied by husband or wife" column, which confirms her status as a married woman. Her "country of last permanent residence" is given as Singapore.

So, a lot has happened to her in those eight years between the two records. She is now married and living in Singapore–how and when did all that happen? This is when family history research is so much fun, because you have to turn into a detective, tracking one's ancestors' genealogical footprints through the sand of countless archived records.

Back to my great aunt then, now Mrs. Hume. On a later shipping record from that same year, she is travelling as "Dorothy Elizabeth Hume" with her age 28 in the "Accompanied by husband or wife" column. The date is October 1919 which means her age checks out, because she's had a birthday between the two voyages. She is listed between Thomas Josiah Hume (42) and Olive Mary Hume (8). Wait a minute–that doesn't quite check out. There's not enough time

> *Jesse Esdale Gray*
(1885-1946)

> *Cecil Jesse Austen*
Gray (1908-1968)

> *Peter Nigel Austen Gray*
(1950-present)

for her to have made her way back out to the Far East from Devon, met her "Mr. Right" aka Thomas Hume and got to know him well enough to give him an eight-year-old daughter! Back to work, Sherlock–there's got to be another explanation. Of course, there is

one–Miss Olive Hume was his daughter from his previous marriage. I don't know exactly when the previous marriage ended but my great aunt Dorothy had three sons with Thomas Josiah Hume or "TJ" as he was called. They were Colin Hoskyn Powell Hume born around 1918, Derek Greville Hoskyn Hume born 1920 and Michael Shapcott Hoskyn born 1921. I have already explained where the name Hoskyn came from. My theory is that Dorothy received a bequest in the will of her maternal great grandmother, Emma Hoskyn, along with her two sisters Winifred and Mabel. There was a tradition for Victorian ladies to leave money for the education of their grandsons or great grandsons, remembering that it was considered more important to educate boys than girls at that time. Mabel did not have children but my grandmother called her youngest son Norman William Hoskyn Gray.

Whilst doing my research for this book, I have made contact with my 2nd cousin Jeremy Hume, who is Dorothy's grandson through his father Derek. It was Jeremy who advised me of TJ's nickname and he also explained that TJ

William Gray   >   *John Gray*   >   *James Gray*   >   *Jesse William Gray*   >
(1720-1795)   *(1770-1830)*   *(1813-1880)*   *(1855-1894)*

was an adopted child. He was adopted by none other than a clerical brother of Robert Baden-Powell, founder of the Boy Scouts Movement, which explains his firstborn having Powell amongst his forenames. He also told me of the circumstances that saw my great aunt Dorothy divorcing TJ. It relates to the fact that he moved the children's nanny into the marital bed, during one of Dorothy's trips back to England! Jeremy also said everyone knew Dorothy as 'Betty' and that, after their divorce, she came to England with her three boys whilst TJ stayed in Japan with the two children of his first marriage. Maybe with the nanny as well!

Granny Gray's travels continued in 1947 with a trip back to the Ward-Smiths (my uncle Bill and aunt Stella) over in America, although this time it was to their new house in Buffalo, New York state, rather than San Jose, California. In her October letter to her brother Albert, she is still pondering about where best to live, even suggesting that the three siblings (widower Albert, spinster Mabel and her widowed self) should set up home together somewhere in the US. She returns to England in time for her and Mabel to spend Christmas and New Year at the end of 1947 with Dorothy at her home at 64, Chichester Place, Brighton, Sussex. Early the next year Granny Gray went back to America, to begin a long period of time spent with her daughter Stella. She wrote two letters to Albert in that year, the first on March 25th and the second on 2nd October. In the latter she writes that my uncle Bill has a new job in Seattle, Washington and he is busy house-hunting for the family to move there immediately after Stella has the child she is expecting. My cousin Pamela

---

| > | *Jesse Esdale Gray* *(1885-1946)* | > | *Cecil Jesse Austen* *Gray (1908-1968)* | > | *Peter Nigel Austen Gray* *(1950-present)* |

was indeed born in Buffalo, New York that October and soon afterwards the family did move to Seattle, including Granny Gray. She remained in Seattle until the following October, when she had something of an adventure–her first flight! In these letters I have been quoting from, she writes of her frustration trying to book passages on various ships for her transatlantic journeys. In one letter she wrote *"...Cooks said if I would fly they might be able to give me a passage in Nov. but could only give me a week's notice. But I am not keen to fly..."* So, I imagine it was quite an ordeal for her on 19th October, 1949 when she took off from Idlewild Airport, New York on board Pan American Airlines flight no. 100/19, bound for London, England! My guess is she only made the flight because she was accompanied by her daughter Stella with baby Pamela. Granny no doubt reasoned it out to herself that if a one-year-old can do it, a 67-yr old jolly well should be able to!

This trip to England was to make possible the most remarkable family reunion, that took place at my Downton grandparents' house in Erith, Kent.

In case it seems like there were no men folk from the Gray family at this wonderful reunion, these pictures show that my father Cecil, uncle Norman and uncle Gordon were all present as well. The only absentee was Stella's husband, uncle Bill, who was home in Seattle with the two older children, my cousins Tony and Dawn.

Another of my favourite photographs is this more formal portrait of my grandmother with her extended family, capturing the first time the siblings had been together with their mother for 10 years. They had obviously brought

| *William Gray* | | *John Gray* | | *James Gray* | | *Jesse William Gray* | |
| *(1720-1795)* | > | *(1770-1830)* | > | *(1813-1880)* | > | *(1855-1894)* | > |

L-R: mother Kathleen, brother Ian, aunt Joyce with cousin Stuart, great aunt Mabel, Granny Gray with cousin Pamela, aunt Stella and cousin Bruce

Inside looking out -great aunt Mabel) L-R: aunt Yolande, cousin Bruce, cousin Stuart, cousin Pamela, aunt Joyce, mother Kathleen, brother Ian (nearly!)

Uncle Norman & Aunt Joyce

Father Cecil holding Ian, Granny Gray with Pamela

Uncle Gordon with Bruce, Aunt Yolande with Stuart

Mother Kathleen with Ian, Yolande with Stuart, Granny Gray with Pamela, Stella with Bruce

L-R: aunt Stella, father Cecil, aunt Joyce, uncle Norman, uncle Gordon
L-R: brother Ian, mother Kathleen, grandmother Winifred, cousin Pamela,
cousin Bruce, aunt Yolande, cousin Stuart

a change of clothing for this wonderfully posed picture, maybe taken before an evening meal spent catching up on all their experiences during those intervening years. I can only imagine the emotions they all must have been experiencing.

There were other "firsts" being celebrated at this time. It was the first time my grandmother had ever met her daughter-in-law Kathleen or her grandchildren Ian, Bruce and Stuart "in the flesh", having "met" them through her correspondence. It was the first time five of the six surviving members of "My Magnificent 7" were together since their various captivities had started. Only uncle Bill was missing, presumably with his hands full–baby-sitting Tony and Dawn over in Seattle. Whilst the adults must have been going through a wide range of emotions, the four toddlers probably just thought "Cool party, but who are all these old people?" I also imagine that my mother gained some comfort, when first meeting her mother-in-law, from the presence of her own parents–since the latter were hosting the event! I really treasure these photographs, for they truly capture the overwhelming feelings of relief, gratitude, joy and optimism that the re-united family must have experienced together.

After playing their part in the re-union, aunt Stella and baby cousin Pamela flew back to the US on 15th December,1949 (another Pan-Am flight; no. 101/14 London to New York). But Granny Gray didn't accompany them, choosing to extend her stay in England awhile longer. The next definite journey I have discovered for her is covered in a shipping record, which is one of my favourite pieces of documentation from my research. It records that she sailed from London onboard the *Durango* on 30 August 1950, arriving in Seattle on 9th October, 1950. What I love about this record is the detail under the column "Number and Description of Pieces of Baggage". For my grandmother's entry reads: 4 suitcases, 1 hatbox, 6 hand packages. Simply fabulous! Never again shall I accuse my wife of overdoing things when it comes to packing! It says so much to me, not only about the fashion of those times but about my grandmother's sense of style. I remember her as always being impeccably dressed and well able to accessorise perfectly, whatever the occasion. Now we all know how such perfect personal presentation was achieved–with a hell of a lot of luggage! When I think that my wife and I can go for a month's holiday in Spain "hand luggage only", I am amazed by Granny Gray's requirements.

> *Jesse Esdale Gray*   >   *Cecil Jesse Austen*   >   *Peter Nigel Austen Gray*
> *(1885-1946)*   *Gray (1908-1968)*   *(1950-present)*

And I distinctly remember my grandmother only having two hands, so "6 hand packages"? What's that all about. Travelling must have been expensive for her, if only in porters' tips! It is just another wonderful piece of digital memorabilia, that brings a lady I hardly knew so vividly alive for me, over 69 years later. I am only so specific about this timing, because this trip happened just a fortnight after my birth. Sadly, I think she only had the pleasure of my company twice, three times at the most. One theory I have about this sea voyage across to Seattle is that it seems to suggest that one flight was quite enough for my grandmother, especially as she was travelling solo.

Granny's next letter was dated 23rd September, 1951 and is my next point of reference to help with locating the Gray tribe around the globe. She is writing it from the Ward-Smiths' home in Seattle, where she is staying with Bill, Stella, Tony, Dawn and Pamela. In the letter she writes that she is awaiting news of the arrival of aunt Yolande's third child, hoping it will be a daughter–"as they have two boys now". In fact, at the time she was writing, she had her numbers wrong–they had three boys! Andrew was born the day before, on 22nd September, 1951, in Tabora, Tanganyika. So that places the Reynolds family (i.e. that of my aunt Yolande) in Africa.

To complete this game of "Pick a Continent to Live In" that Granny's children appear to be playing, I turn to my father's family. Hopefully, you will all be up to speed with their travels from earlier in this chapter and have these Grays safely in Tsingtao, China–because that's where my brother Ian was born in December, 1947. Wrong! Do you really think my family could have remained in the same place for nearly four years! Shame on you, I thought you had come to know us better than that.

To be fair, it wasn't a completely voluntary choice that my father made to leave China. There was the small matter of the Chinese Civil War which had started in 1927 as a conflict between the Chinese Communists (CPC) and the Chinese Nationalists, called the Kuomintang (KMT). The opposing sides in the civil war ceased fighting between themselves, to conduct the 2nd Sino-Japanese War between 1937 and 1945. Chiang Kai-shek, the KMT leader, did not want to join forces with the CPC to fight the Japanese invasion because he believed the CPC was a greater threat. Chiang thought that his forces were not strong enough and wanted more time to build up his military so he could launch an effective attack on the Japanese forces. So, he ordered his KMT Generals Yang Hucheng and Zhang Xueliang to undertake the elimination of the CPC. His provincial forces sustained substantial casualties in their conflicts with the Red Army. Overall, the CPC had won popular support because of their guerrilla war efforts in the Japanese-occupied regions. The KMT suffered greatly in their efforts to defend China from Japanese assaults. In 1944, the Japanese launched their final major offensive called Operation Ichi-Go, which was against the KMT, during which Chiang Kai-shek's forces were seriously weakened. In the end, the CPC benefited politically from the Sino-Japanese War.

In March of 1946, the Soviet Union delayed leaving Manchuria because Stalin wanted to make sure the leader of the CPC, Mao Zedong, would have control over northern Manchuria. This led to more fighting for the control of this area. Chiang Kai-shek moved his KMT troops to recently liberated regions to stop CPC forces from receiving Japan's surrender. The CPC had more power when fighting resumed in the Chinese Civil War. Their main military force grew to over one million troops, and their militia had about two million soldiers. The CPC's "Liberated Zone" consisted of nineteen base areas, which included one-quarter of mainland China's territory (which had many important cities and towns) and nearly one-third of its population. In addition, the Soviet Union gave the CPC many captured Japanese weapons along with a large quantity of their own military supplies. The Soviet Union also gave them North-eastern China.

The KMT's defeat happened for many reasons and the main one was corruption, which had become a root problem in the party. Also, the CPC told the poor peasants they would be given their former warlord's farmland and this made them very popular with the Chinese people at the end of the war. No peace treaty or armistice was ever signed that officially ended the Chinese Civil War. Mao Zedong proclaimed on October 1, 1949, the capital for the PRC would be Beiping, later to be renamed Beijing. At this point the exodus, to Japanese-controlled Taiwan, of Chiang Kai-shek and around two million of his followers began.

Quite understandably, against the background of political instability prevailing in China at the time, my father decided that maybe Tsingtao was not the place for him or his wife or his new born baby (my brother Ian was born 18th December, 1947). I presume he asked his employer BAT (British and

| William Gray (1720-1795) | > | John Gray (1770-1830) | > | James Gray (1813-1880) | > | Jesse William Gray (1855-1894) | > |

American Tobacco) for a transfer or maybe the company itself saw 'the writing on the wall' regarding their presence in Tsingtao. Whichever it was, the family was living in Monghyr, in the state of Bihar, India with Dad working in the accounts department of their cigarette factory there, by August 1950–when I was born. Mother was actually moved to Calcutta for the birth; I was born in Room 4 of the East India Clinic at the Elgin Nursing Home at 5.24pm on 17th August. My mother signed as informant on the Daily Return of Births form sent to the Registrar's Office, 11 Belvedere Road, Alipore. This was because my father was still "up country" in Monghyr. He was advised of my arrival by the following hand-written note:

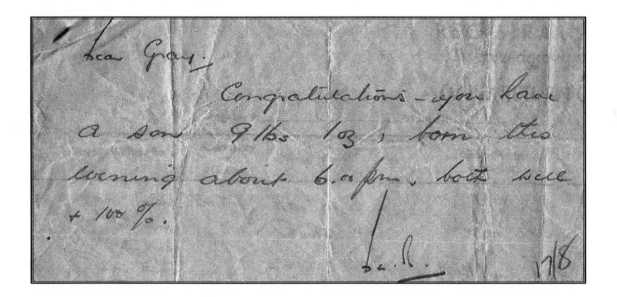

Peter Nigel Austen Gray (1950–present; the author)

Now, I am not sure who D.A.R. is exactly, my father's boss presumably, but his note is certainly business-like–concise and to the point. Seeing my father referred to as "Gray" took me right back to my boarding school days, and I

Jesse Esdale Gray
 (1885-1946)

> *Cecil Jesse Austen*
 Gray (1908-1968)

> *Peter Nigel Austen Gray*
 (1950-present)

can imagine Dad replying "Thank you, Sir"! Although, unlike a schoolboy, he probably celebrated hearing this wonderful news by "wetting the baby's head". Knowing of his fondness for a drink, I imagine it meant my nearly being drowned!

Having placed us (Dad, Mother, brother Ian and myself) in Asia, I am now only left with locating my grandmother's other son, my uncle Norman, on the world map. With his new wife Joyce, he sailed from Southampton on 4th March, 1947 onboard the P&O liner *Strathmore*, bound for Shanghai. So, both the Gray brothers are in Asia! I don't know exactly where Norman worked and lived but I know he was in Singapore as well as Shanghai. I am guessing he left China about the same time as my father, maybe after Mao proclaimed the People's Republic of China on 1st October, 1949. On a shipping record for a voyage to England in July 1959, he gives Singapore as his last "permanent residence" so I believe he and Joyce were based there for those intervening 10 years.

I am now going to reproduce in full a letter my grandmother wrote to her brother Albert on 12th December 1955, because it captures something of her continuing dilemma about where she was finally going to settle down, which had been a constant worry to her since she was widowed in 1946. She is writing it from my Downton grandparents' house in Erith, Kent.

William Gray		John Gray		James Gray		Jesse William Gray	
(1720-1795)	>	*(1770-1830)*	>	*(1813-1880)*	>	*(1855-1894)*	>

3 Lesney Park Road

Erith, Kent

12th Dec 1955

My dear Albert,

Now to try and write you a few lines, have been wanting to for some time, but have been so rushed and busy, never seem to get time to do half that I want to. Many thanks for the snap of yourself & the invitation to your B.D. Party. Sorry I could not attend, though I would have liked to.

I have had Cecil and his family home this summer, Kathleen and the two boys flew home on the 26th of May and Cecil came by P&O steamer on July 3rd. He arrived at Tilbury which is almost opposite here. Kay went down by car to meet him. The two boys went to boarding school & stayed there 'till a few days before they left. That left Kay and Cecil to do as they liked, so they got around and saw a number of friends. One weekend the 3 of us went down to Bristol and saw several of the Wise family. Later they went to Devon and Cornwall, and another time up north and to Scotland. They got about quite a little. Bought a 2nd hand car £60 and before leaving Kay sold it for £40, so they did not do too badly. Cecil left on Nov.1st by steamer and Kay and the boys flew on 24th and got there the next day. They are stationed now for good at Calcutta. Cecil has less than 8yrs till he retires, so he has been looking out for another job to take on then.

Last Thursday (8th) Yolande, hubby & 4 sons arrived in England, they have taken a furnished house in New Barnet, (North London). I am going to

---

> *Jesse Esdale Gray*
> *(1885-1946)*

> *Cecil Jesse Austen*
> *Gray (1908-1968)*

> *Peter Nigel Austen Gray*
> *(1950-present)*

stay with them for Xmas and New Year, & may stay on a while. Gordon has to
go to the Head Training site of Police near Coventry for 6-8 weeks & learn all
new methods etc. they will be in England till around the middle of May.

(14th) Now to finish off. Many thanks for a newspaper which arrived this
a.m. read about your B.D. party. Hope you have a very pleasant Christmas and
all the best for 1956.

How are things going with you? I am still looking for a home of my own
but do not know where to settle. Loughton is too hilly for me. If only one of my
families lived in England.

Have so many letters to write. Often think of you and wish we could meet.
Fond love, your loving sister,

Winifred

This last sentence seems so sad to me, reading it all these years later. Here she is, a widow aged 73, roaming the globe with no home, living out of a suitcase. Well, out of 4 suitcases to be pedantic, but you know what I'm saying. It is almost a cry for help when she writes "if only one of my families lived in England", as though that would save her the difficult task of deciding where to put down her roots. As late as April, 1957, she is arriving on the BI liner *Uganda* in England, from Mombasa where she has visited the Reynolds (aunt Yolande's family). For "country of last permanent residence" she still has to put China, albeit that was 12 years previously. She has put England as her "intended country of permanent residence", so she has apparently made her mind up that England is to be her home. She gives Kings Cottage, Loughton (aunt Mabel's house) as her future address. However, this is not where she puts down her roots–not to mention her 4 suitcases, 1 hatbox and 6 hand packages!

Her eventual home is a flat–12 Crescent View, High Street, Loughton, Essex. Yes, I know–Loughton! The same Loughton as in "Loughton is too hilly for me". I am guessing her dislike of hills related mainly to Kings Hill, where Mabel's house was situated, where she had been living off and on during the past decade. The High Street is obviously more manageable for her, for this is to be her home for the final years of her life. It is the only place at which I can remember visiting her, with my mother. In terms of when she actually moved in there, all I can say for sure is that it was before July 1959, because uncle Norman and aunt Joyce gave that as the address they were going to when they arrived back in England from Singapore. Incidentally, that trip marked the last voyage for Norman and Joyce, as they settled in England from that date. In terms of Granny Gray's families spread around the world, Norman and Joyce were not the first to answer my grandmother's wish recorded in her Dec.'55 letter–"*if only one of my families lived in England*". That honour befell to three-quarters of my own family, and the next chapter will explain how that came about.

| Jesse Esdale Gray | Cecil Jesse Austen | Peter Nigel Austen Gray |
| *(1885-1946)* | *Gray (1908-1968)* | *(1950-present)* |

THE INDIAN LEG OF THE GRAY FAMILY'S JOURNEY

I have told you of that memorable day in August 1950, when I finally made my entrance into this unfolding Gray family history drama. So, we have now entered the living history section of the story. Put another way, I am writing about events I actually have some memory of, rather than episodes recorded by members of my extended family or internet-researched background material.

Throughout most of my life, if the fact that I was born in India cropped up during a conversation with a stranger, it was usually followed with a question like "Was your Dad in the Army?" Apart from that particular question being guaranteed to annoy my father were he to hear it, due to his career in the "Senior Service", I usually had to answer it with a simple "No, he worked there for British & American Tobacco". After all, that is considerably easier than attempting to précis the 200-odd pages you have just read! Here is a lightning quick resumé of how Dad got to be working in Monghyr, India. After qualifying as an accountant in Shanghai, he joined BAT and worked at various locations in China either side of the war years, when he was a captive of the Japanese. He left China when it became the People's Republic of China in 1949, taking up an accountancy post at the BAT factory in Monghyr, a town located 268 miles northwest of Calcutta, in the state of Bihar.

So, the story starts again at the end of 1950, and our family comprises my father Cecil, my mother Kathleen, my brother Ian aged 3 and yours truly born mid-August. Dad's career with BAT seems to have consisted of postings to whichever site needed his particular skills at the time. In this respect, there is some similarity with a career in the services, where the serving individual gets posted to a particular location, and the rest of the family goes with them! Rather like 'married quarters' in the military, BAT provided company housing for the families of its' itinerant employees. The Gray family home in Monghyr was one of these company bungalows, in a compound on the factory premises. They were furnished and usually included servants' quarters for our live-in staff.

Whenever I have mentioned growing up in a household with servants in general conversation throughout my life, it usually promotes a reaction like "Ooh, get you, how posh!" from the listener. Maybe you readers have also immediately jumped to a preconceived view of domestic staff, somewhere between "*Upstairs, Downstairs*" and "*Downton Abbey*"! The reality is somewhat different. My parents were not the aristocracy, with servants looking after

---

> *Jesse Esdale Gray*   >   *Cecil Jesse Austen*   >   *Peter Nigel Austen Gray*
(1885-1946)   *Gray (1908-1968)*   *(1950-present)*

Master Ian and Master Nigel, with our ayah

their every need. But they were Westerners living, working and playing in a largely impoverished country, where the employment opportunities necessary to service Western staff accommodation were most welcome to the locals. And the way of life, built around numerous social and leisure clubs meant jobs for many more of the native population. I sometimes say that the only Indians I saw during my childhood in India were servants! It is definitely true to say that children like my brother and I saw more of our ayah (Indian nanny) than we did of our parents. After all, our parents weren't going to let the inconvenience of having children stop them "having a good time"!

Sometime in early 1952, my father was transferred to Bangalore, a city in the state of Karnataka in southern India. Of course, that meant the whole family moving from Monghyr to Bangalore as well.

I have learned quite a lot about the family's time in Bangalore since starting my family history research, but I was aware of having been there from quite an early age, thanks to a small trophy that has been in my possession since I have owned a house of my own. My mother decided I needed some artefacts to have on display, so she passed it on to me. It is the first athletics trophy I ever won, and it was for winning a running race around Bangalore Golf Club–

William Gray   >   *John Gray*   >   *James Gray*   >   *Jesse William Gray*   >
(1720-1795)   *(1770-1830)*   *(1813-1880)*   *(1855-1894)*

when I was three!

I have learned quite a lot about the family's time in Bangalore since starting my family history research, but I was aware of having been there from quite an early age, thanks to a small trophy that has been in my possession since I have owned a house of my own. My mother decided I needed some artefacts to have on display, so she passed it on to me. It is the first athletics trophy I ever won, and it was for winning a running race around Bangalore Golf Club– when I was three!

There is a plate on the base which is inscribed with the date of November 1953. The other interesting thing about this inscription is that I am called just "Nigel Gray", proving that 'Peter' was dropped as my name a very long time ago. When I say this was my first athletic trophy, I actually mean my only athletic trophy, despite that being my sport of choice as a teenager!

Knowing that I had lived in India as a child meant that I have always had it on my wish list for visiting "one day". Of course, India definitely fell into the 'long haul' category within our system for classifying future holiday destinations. As a category, 'long haul' had to wait until our children were no longer accompanying us on holiday, due to budgetary constraints. Then, even after we started doing long haul, India fell into a sub-category called "Far away as to need longer than two weeks to make it cost effective". I appreciate that's not the catchiest of category titles, but necessarily lengthy only to convey the financial criteria needing to be satisfied prior to booking. As a result of this secondary level categorisation, India actually had to wait until my retirement! But visit it we have now done; twice in fact, in 2016 and 2017, for a month each time. Both trips were absolutely amazing, and we still have a desire to return, because we consider there ls still unfinished business in that amazing country.

I am going to cross-reference places visited on both trips with their respective locations in my family history story, as I continue to tell it. We actually omitted Bangalore from our itinerary for the 2016 tour, because we had already filled our time with a wonderful balance of "following in the family's footsteps" excursions and the "must-see" places that might feature in every brochure offering Indian sightseeing. However, due to a most amazing sequence of coincidences that occurred on the first trip, Bangalore elevated itself to the top of our "things to see on a repeat visit" list and was probably the single most important incentive for sending us back to India the very next year!

To start our 2016 trip, we flew into Kolkata (previously Calcutta) and, after a fabulous day doing all the main tourist attractions with our private guide, we ventured out on our own in search of the Elgin Nursing Home where I was born. Fortunately, our destination was at 6 Elgin Road, very close to our hotel and we found it–even surviving a return trip on the Kolkata Metro! We left the following morning and travelled to Darjeeling, which involved an internal flight to Bagdogra, and a three-and-half hour drive, climbing up all the way to reach Darjeeling at 6000m. To help find another key location from my life story that we were planning to visit, on the first night in our hotel my wife asked a group of English tourists staying there how well they knew Darjeeling. In the conversation that followed, a lady called Gay Fegen told us she had been searching for the Elgin Nursing Home, on the day before we found it. It turned out she was also born there, in 1953–just three years after me! *What a coincidence!* We got talking to Gay and, of course, she asked those inevitable questions–"How come you were born in India? Was your father in the Army? ". When I gave my stock reply about my father working for BAT, Gay excitedly said "I don't believe it–my very good friend Pam's husband used to work for BAT". *What a coincidence!* Through our continuing conversation, I learned that this friend was Pam Boden, a surname that rang the faintest of bells with me as being one of my mother's friends. *What a coincidence!* Further discussion and an exchange of emails between Gay and Pam's son Simon back in England (Pam not having email herself) confirmed that my mother and Pam had been good friends, from when their husbands worked together for BAT in–Bangalore! *What a coincidence!* I am actually worried that I am going to wear out the exclamation mark on this keyboard before I complete my story! Even as I retell the story of this chance encounter, I can't quite believe it actually happened. What were the odds against my wife and I staying in the same hotel in Darjeeling as Gay? What were the odds against us both visiting the nursing home in Calcutta within one day of each other, over

> *Jesse Esdale Gray (1885-1946)*   > *Cecil Jesse Austen Gray (1908-1968)*   > *Peter Nigel Austen Gray (1950-present)*

sixty years after we were both born there? What were the odds against Gay
even being Pam's friend (Gay actually bought Pam's house in a small village
near Yeovil, Somerset)? What were the odds against Pam's husband working
at the same BAT location as my father? Oh dear, now I'm in danger of wearing
out the question mark as well!

To draw this remarkable coincidence to a conclusion, I should tell you
that we naturally maintained contact with Gay after going our separate ways
from Darjeeling and later that year, she actually hosted a meal for us at her
house–where we met Pam in person. What a wonderful occasion that turned
out to be. It was just before her 90th
birthday and yet, to quote one of my
mother's odd sayings, "she was all
there with her cough drops". She had
a wonderful memory and conversed
very well, making it seem like she

was telling us about events from a few weeks past rather than over 60 years earlier. The coincidences carried on at that meeting. I had taken a lot of my memorabilia "stuff" down with me, all collected in a large scrapbook that was itself a piece of memorabilia. It was approximately A3 sized, bound in a pale blue case, with a flysheet printed with *"Presented by the imperial Tobacco Company of India on the occasion of the coronation of Queen Elizabeth II, June 1953"*. As soon as I got my copy out to show Pam, she did no more than present me with an identical binder, which she had used as her scrapbook/diary from that time! It is not that often that I use this particular colloquialism but it seems totally appropriate–I was gobsmacked. Pam had been quite meticulous with her record-keeping and archiving skills and her binder was full of photos, letters, invitations, etc. Among my collection was a small, champagne flute-shaped card from the Bodens, inviting my parents to the christening of their son Simon (the one who helped during our email research from Darjeeling). It was checking this on our return from India that had clinched the deal regarding Pam and Mother being friends from Bangalore. In Pam's scrapbook, as a piece of directly collaborating evidence, she had recorded the names of all the guests who attended the christening party and a separate list captured what gifts they had given for Simon. It showed that my mother had given a silver spoon-and-pusher set, and Pam informed us that she was still using the same spoon in her sugar bowl at home! Amazing!

It is quite simply one of the highlights of my genealogical adventure that I met my mother's friend just at the time I needed so many questions answering but Mother was not here to answer them. It was incredible that Pam could fill in a lot of the gaps in my knowledge about life in India. In fact, she helped us plan our 2017 trip to Bangalore, as it gave an extra dimension to our visit, knowing she had shared some of my parents' experiences "back in the day".

It is back to Bangalore in the early 1950s that we go now, as I continue the Gray saga with Dad's spell there. Whilst my father's work was at the cigarette factory in the Peenya industrial district of modern Bengaluru, the family lived at 1 Richmond Road, a company house in the centre of the town. Perhaps the more significant fact about its' location was that it was within walking distance of the centre of my parents' life at that time–The Bangalore Club! My wife and I verified this fact by walking much of the route, when we visited in 2017. However, this walk is probably the only similarity there is between the 1950s Bangalore that my parents knew and Bengaluru, the present name for India's 3rd most populous city, behind Mumbai and Delhi. It is currently recognised as India's "Silicon Valley" because of its role as the nation's leading information technology exporter, and the city has experienced rapid growth in the decades 1941–51 and 1971–81. By 1961, Bangalore had become the sixth largest city in India, with a population of 1,207,000; by 2011 this had reached 8,443,675 and it was classified as a "megacity".

I was aware of Dad having been a member of The Bangalore Club and, after talking with Pam Boden about how it featured in my parents' life, I decided to contact the club before our holiday to explore the possibility of visiting it during our stay. I emailed the Club Secretary, a retired Indian Army officer, who said that such a visit was definitely possible and we fixed a date and time before leaving England. I was so excited looking forward to it but it got even better. During our holiday planning process with Travelbag, we received word that they were not happy with the hotel offered to us originally for Bangalore, asking *"….so would it be alright if we moved you to the Chancery Pavilion Hotel?"*. When we googled this hotel, it was on Residency Road and exactly opposite the main entrance gates of–The Bangalore Club. I think it took us about one nanosecond to agree to the move!

The Bangalore Club is the oldest club in the city, founded in 1868, and originally called the Bangalore United Services Club for officers of the British Empire. Membership was opened to Indian officers in 1915, and to civilians in 1946, when it was renamed The Bangalore Club. It counts among its' previous members the Maharaja of Mysore and Sir Winston Churchill. A ledger on display in the main building of the club is open to a page that has a list of "irrecoverable debts" that were written off by the club. One of these is the sum Rs.13, owed by Winston Churchill. Membership is by nomination and the waiting list for permanent membership is currently over 30 years. Thankfully, this was not the case back in the '50s, otherwise my father would not have obtained his membership, as his whole posting to Bangalore was for a couple of years only.

When we did make our visit in 2017, we could not have been made more welcome. The Club Secretary himself met us at the entrance exactly at our appointed time and took us straight to his office, after having shown us the

---

> *Jesse Esdale Gray (1885-1946)*   > *Cecil Jesse Austen Gray (1908-1968)*   > *Peter Nigel Austen Gray (1950-present)*

"Winston Churchill debt" entry in the ledger and telling us the story. You could tell how honoured they are to have that memento of his past membership! He gave us tea and refreshments whilst giving us a complete history of the club and how it operates today. He brought an old book that was a record of membership for the period that Dad would have been there, but apologised that he could not find the entry confirming my father's membership. He offered it for me to search and, whilst I couldn't find Dad's entry, I did find that of Pam's husband. The Secretary said his staff would keep looking, armed with all the details I could supply them, whilst he personally guided us on a complete tour of the Club. It was absolutely fantastic–we saw all the members rooms– restaurants, bars, libraries and the sports facilities i.e.: Badminton, Squash, Billiards, Table Tennis, Swimming Pools, Tennis courts, Bridge, Gymnasium etc. He showed us where the old swimming pool was in my parents' days; Pam had told me that she used to swim there with Mother, brother Ian and myself. One of the highlights of the tour was to see the original Ballroom (not used these days) which was a thrill for me, because I knew my parents had attended a Coronation Ball there on June 1st, 1953.

It was only seeing inside this splendid room that the penny finally dropped for me i.e. that, rather than watching all the spectacle of our Queen's coronation alongside the rest of Britain, my parents actually

celebrated at a function in The Bangalore Club, thousands of miles away! When we were finishing our tour, the Secretary actually offered us lunch at the Club which would have been amazing. Sadly, we had to decline his exceptionally kind offer, as we had already booked a driver and car for a half-day tour of family history-specific sights that afternoon. On our return to his office, one of staff had succeeded in her search, and we saw the actual entry in the register confirming my father's membership. I have to admit that, apart from being wonderfully exciting in its' own right, this discovery saved us any potential embarrassment about being "guests" under false pretences! Our visit lasted over three hours and had one last, glorious surprise–on leaving, we were presented with a copy of the bound souvenir book celebrating the 125th Anniversary of the Club. How cool was that!

Later that same day, Jenny and I continued following in my parents' footsteps around Bangalore. Our hotel had sourced a taxi driver on a fixed price 4-hour private hire, as we only had vague geographical clues as to where we wanted to go and needed a driver with "*The Knowledge*". It helped that he could speak the language as well, as there was still some detective work to be done in finding the places on our list. Our first destination was the house in Richmond Road but all we saw was "where it must have been"–since the whole area had been developed to build a huge roundabout called Richmond Circus. We had more luck with our second location–the Bangalore Golf Club which had witnessed my early athletic victory. Compared with the marvellous hospitality we were shown at The Bangalore Club, the official at the golf club was positively snooty. I accept that we were blagging our way in, based on the story of my parents having been members and showing him a photo of my trophy inscribed with Bangalore Golf Club. Having lectured us at length about how exclusive a club it was and it not being accessible to non-members, he finally allowed us to take one photograph with the course in the background.

Last stop on our very personalised sightseeing tour was the factory where my father worked. Finding it was not easy, as all I had to go on was the name of the company (The Imperial Tobacco Company of India) and details from an old letter addressed to Dad "c/o" a post office near to the factory. We asked our driver to take us to the post office first, where we had another huge stroke of luck. We met an English guy who was involved with an Anglo-Indian Historical group and he explained there had been a cigarette factory in the area but it had moved to new premises out near the new Bangalore airport. He gave us directions (to our driver actually!) to the original cigarette factory premises, which underwent a complete refurbishment into a software research centre in 1973 and now employs over 5000 IT staff on site. Armed with this new information, we set off for the site and our perseverance was rewarded with another excellent visit. We were hosted by the head of site security, a Major Subesh, ex Indian Army and equally as welcoming as the Secretary of the Bangalore Club had been. After giving us a snack lunch and tea, he handed us over to one of his senior officers, who knew the site when it was the cigarette factory. He gave us a full tour, explaining the full cigarette manufacturing flow process to us, building by building, even though each building we saw was full of programmers designing the latest IT innovations for ITC. We were particularly pleased to see the office block where Pam's husband had his General Manager office and where the Accounts Department was housed. We had to visualise where Dad's desk might have been, as there were no leather-bound ledgers or quill pens in sight! At the bottom end of the site was a large boarded-off area, behind which new tower block offices were being built. Back in his office at the end of our tour, Major Subesh confirmed that we would not have seen any of the original factory buildings had our visit been 6 months later–since they were all due for demolition after the Research Centre completed its' move into the new buildings. Fate or what! Thank heavens we had returned to India when we did!

My later research yielded the following "bigger picture" about the company Dad had worked for. ITC Limited is an Indian multinational conglomerate company headquartered in Kolkata, West Bengal. Established in 1910 as the 'Imperial Tobacco Company of India Limited', the first cigarette factory of the company was set up in 1913 at Bangalore. The company was renamed as the 'India Tobacco Company Limited' in 1970 and later to 'I.T.C. Limited' in 1974.

> *Jesse Esdale Gray*   > *Cecil Jesse Austen*   > *Peter Nigel Austen Gray*
> *(1885-1946)*   *Gray (1908-1968)*   *(1950-present)*

The dots in the name were removed in September 1974 for the company to be renamed as 'ITC Limited' where 'ITC' would no longer be an initialism. The company completed 100 years in 2010 and as of 2012–13, had an annual turnover of US$8.31 billion and a market capitalisation of US$52 billion. It employs over 30,000 people at more than 60 locations across India. I find it fascinating how the name changes have allowed the company to distance itself from all the bad press centred upon tobacco smoking, and yet make use of the initials I and T in exactly the right context for its' current corporate branding. These various visits, to The Bangalore Club, the golf club and Dad's offices, were really special because, like so much of my family history research, they brought my father to life for me during a part of his life that I was too young to fully share in.

Our family travels continued sometime in 1954, when my father was redeployed back to BAT's Monghyr site–and of course that meant the whole family moving with him. The next real 'sighting' I have of us is Granny Gray's letter of December 12th, 1955, which I shared with you all earlier, written from 3 Lesney Park Road, Erith–my Downton grandparents' house. It is slightly confusing when she writes *"they are stationed now for good at Calcutta"*, because I have other pointers that indicate the family was at Monghyr, at least some of the time before leaving India for good. Maybe my grandmother was confused in terms of what exactly my father's job entailed. BAT headquarters were certainly in Calcutta, so perhaps he had to make frequent visits there whilst his day-to-day duties were on site at the factory in Monghyr. Alternatively, he had received some kind of promotion, such that he was working in the Calcutta office, but with trips to Monghyr as required. I do remember one of these trips in particular, because I slept nearly all the journey–on the rear parcel shelf of Dad's Ford Consul car!

It is so difficult to pin down the exact sequence of events that unfolded over these next few years, which were to prove very challenging for our family. I was interested to read in Granny Gray's letter that *"the two boys went to boarding school and stayed there 'till a few days before they left"*, as the one she mentions must surely have been my very first school. Given that her letter gives the exact dates of when my brother and I were in England that year–26th May until 24th November–it means I had my 5th birthday in England but where did I celebrate it? It also confirms that I was sent to boarding school at a very early age, maybe before I turned five years old! I have tried to enlist my brother Ian's assistance in establishing a time line for our educational paths through these years, as he is that bit older than me. But I fear that I may have left it too late, as his memory is worse than mine. I also had a little smile to myself about having received a boarding school education as a young child. Whilst that would generally have been considered a privilege reserved for the well-to-do back then, one of my stepdaughters actually uses *"… or I will send you to boarding school"* as a threat against her young son, to improve his behaviour! How times change.

Back to 1955 and our family's long "summer" spent in England. Granny writes that, having packed us boys off to boarding school, my parents had a wonderful vacation travelling the country, visiting friends and family. These included trips down to Cornwall and Devon, and even north as far as Scotland. One trip was to Bristol, when Granny Gray actually accompanied them, recording it in her letter as follows–*"One weekend the 3 of us went down to Bristol and saw several of the Wise family"*. I knew of the Wise family from the hoard of Granny's memorabilia entrusted to me by my cousin Tony. My grandmother's "Auntie Emmie" was Emma Louisa Shapcott who married a Thomas James Wise. I discovered that this couple actually served a term as Lord Mayor and Lady Mayoress of Bristol in 1933! I also learned that Bristol is one of the sixteen cities whose principal civic officer is authorised to use the title of "Lord Mayor". Who says doing genealogy isn't educational! My mother evidently proved herself a bit of a "wheeler-dealer" on this holiday, as she bought a second-hand car for £60 at the beginning and sold it for £40 when she flew out in the November. She effectively had a 6-month car hire for only £20–Granny wrote that *"she hadn't done badly"*.

My family eventually arrived back in India late in 1955, to Calcutta and Dad continuing his career with BAT. Obviously, another boarding school had to be arranged for us boys. Heaven forbid that we should be at home with our parents. Oh no–that would never do. The solution to this threat to my parents' way of life was St. Andrews School. Unfortunately, this wasn't exactly local; it was in Darjeeling, 633 km. away by road. Whereas most children might use a school bus, we actually had a school plane! Even then we had to complete the journey first by train and then either coach or donkey!

But it was all to give us an excellent education so we mustn't grumble. We should have been grateful that our parents had made this generous sacrifice, both financial and emotional, to give us the best possible start in life! I always find it difficult to be subjective, viewing these events with a lifetime of hindsight, but I think my jury is still out on delivering its' verdict on a public-school education. I can see the practicalities of finding a good school but I think a lot of it had to do with the lifestyle choices made by ex-pat parents at that time. Their socialising was undoubtedly easier to continue, if their offspring were not 'on the scene'. How much of it was following the trend at the time I'm not sure but it must have been in my father's plan all along, because I was told as a child that he put Ian's and my name down for Blundell's from our births! It was probably well intended on Dad's part to provide the best education possible for his sons but I would argue that the educational benefits we gained have been exceeded by losses from our emotional stability. Both of our lives have suffered in different ways from the absence of a close, loving, family-based childhood, which robbed us of the opportunities to learn about relationships. Parents should not be strangers to their children at any point in their lives but especially not during those precious childhood years. Later in my life, people could never quite understand me saying I only felt the same for my mother that I might feel for an aunt or a family friend. This all stems from my never having spent "quality time" with either of my parents throughout my childhood. In fact, it is only through experiences with my own "families", as a husband, father and now grandfather, that I have understood what "quality time" even means to a child–and realise that I never had any as a child. I shall always be grateful to my wife Jenny, who acted as the catalyst for me to finally get close to my mother in the last years of her life. At least I actually felt the real love between mother and son for about ten of the fifty-one years she was my mother. It is a shame the same wasn't possible with my father, but more of that later. I must get you back on track with my story, which means back to 6000m. up in the foothills of the Himalayas, at St. Andrew's School.

My personal memories of the school are sketchy at best. I remember a lot of snow in the playground, which you may find strange about a school in a sub-tropical country. The answer is simple–its' location. Being at 6000m. above sea level in the foothills of the highest mountain range in the world, Darjeeling experiences a lot of heavy snowfalls each year. I remember a small slope in a corner of our playground that we used as a makeshift slide, presumably meaning our shorts were continually "in the wash". My memory of the place was severely tested in 2016, when my wife and I actually visited the school.

Prior to going there in person, we had done our internet research and knew the school had closed down. The premises were empty and very run down, having been bought by a Tibetan Institute for conversion into a Buddhist retreat and meditation centre. It was because we were trying to find out its' exact location that we quizzed our hotel guests, including Gay Fegen, and you already know where that led us! We had a car, driver Bedan and tour guide Naven for our 4-day trip to Darjeeling and they were really up for finding the school for us, once I told them my brother and I had been to school there.

| William Gray | > | John Gray | > | James Gray | > | Jesse William Gray | > |
| *(1720-1795)* | | *(1770-1830)* | | *(1813-1880)* | | *(1855-1894)* | |

As we looked around the place, both Jenny and Naven kept asking me if I remembered anything and, whereas I was desperate to say I did, I could not be sure of much of it at all, especially with it being so run down. I was trying to remember what I had experienced as a five-year-old nearly 60 years earlier! Naven took the picture below, because I knew I had a photograph at home amongst Mother's things that should confirm we were in the right place! It even has the snow!

Naven also helped us on a second, highly customised excursion in Darjeeling–to see the family home of perhaps its' most famous resident–Norgay Tenzing. More commonly known as Sherpa Tenzing, he achieved worldwide recognition when he and Sir Edmund Hillary reached the summit of Mount Everest on 29th May, 1953. This achievement propelled him to superstar status in the 1950s, which is why I went on a school trip from St. Andrew's to his house in Darjeeling. My memory of this marvellous encounter with the "local-boy-turned-worldwide celebrity" is of a little old man in a house surrounded by Pekingese dogs! To that extent, the visit was probably wasted on a six-year-old. But I was curious to see the house again, but was shocked at how big it was, when Naven duly took us there. It is quite near the centre of Darjeeling and one of Tenzing's sons still lives there. Incidentally, I find it cruel in a way that Hillary and Tenzing's moment of glory in the full glare of the world's press was short-lived, since the Queen's coronation was only four days later and must surely have replaced them in headlines around the world.

As far as my brother and I can remember between us, we were only at St. Andrew's for about eighteen months. The timings around this period of my story are vague but, to be fair, there was a lot going on. I remember starting at my preparatory school, St. Edmund's, Canterbury in early September 1958, just a few weeks after my 8th birthday. I know this, because that made me the youngest boy in school and the honour fell to me to propose a toast to the Queen in the school Dining Hall at some special dinner during my first term. My recollection is that I went to St. Edmund's at the end of the summer holidays, having left Steephill in the previous July. Ian says that he had a year at St. Edmund's before I arrived, which suggests I was at Steephill for the period September 1957 to July 1958 on my own. By that, I mean no big brother there with me. From our combined memories, Ian and I are agreed that Steephill must have been the boarding school that Granny Gray mentioned in her 1955 letter, which was when we were both there; only I had a second stint in 1957/8 as mentioned above.

Steephill School still exists today, as a coeducational independent day school, for pupils aged from three to eleven years old. It is situated in the beautiful Fawkham Valley area between Dartford and Gravesend in a quiet lane overlooking the thirteenth century St Mary's Church. Miss Bignold was the head teacher when my brother and I were there, assisted by one other, a Miss Francis. We were two of only a handful of boarders, as most of the children were day pupils and Miss Bignold and Miss Francis really were 'in loco parentis', being more like parents than ever our own were. For a start, they actually cooked our meals for us, and we sat around a table eating them together. Novel idea, don't you think, almost like families do. Since writing this book, I have been racking my brain, trying to think of any time when both our parents sat down for a meal at home with just us two boys–but it never happened. Consequently, my Steephill experiences hold some pleasant memories for me. The set-up allowed me to be what I was, a very young child just growing up and learning how to behave, albeit from substitute parents. I remember a rocking horse in the schoolroom that seemed huge to me as a seven-year-old. I remember us caring for guinea pigs in an outhouse next to our playground. If you have ever heard it said that the sense of smell is particularly powerful in retrieving memories, you should relate to the fact that, even now, smelling fresh hay can take me straight back to changing the bedding for our Steephill pets! I also remember spending a day in bed with twin sisters, Ruth and Dawn Chapman. I must clarify this was not sexually motivated–they had chickenpox and I wanted to catch it, so that I could miss classes too!

There was one not-so-good memory from this period however. On one occasion, we were collected from school by our parents and taken for a meal at

---

The Lion, Farningham, a 16th century country pub with views over the River Darent. My brother has a better recollection of it than me; he describes it as *"when they had that big fight and told us they were splitting up"*. I remember I cried a lot and it is a lasting memory as the last time I saw my parents together. I think my subconscious has deliberately confused the timing of this, because I don't think my young mind processed it at all. The exact chronological order of events is a blur, but somewhere along the line, my mother had brought us boys to England on her own, leaving our father alone in India. I know that was the "family" status when I started at my next school, St Edmund's, Canterbury in September 1958.

It may appear that I am jumping around between England and India in the telling of my story but it is only because there is overlap between the two countries during this period. I know the chapter was entitled "The Indian Leg of the Gray Family's Journey" but it isn't easy because 1957 sees our particular branch split in two directions. My mother returned to England with us, her two sons, and went to her parents' home at Erith, Kent. My father stayed in India, initially in Calcutta, before moving to Bombay (modern day Mumbai) sometime before the summer of 1959. I am sure of this date, as my brother and I travelled out to India on a 3-week trip to Bombay, arranged for the children of ex-pats during their long summer holidays from English schools. The journey itself was quite something, because Mother took us up to Heathrow and put us on the BOAC flight to make the journey to India ourselves. When I say that my brother was all of eleven years old and in charge of nearly nine-year-old me,

| William Gray | > | John Gray | > | James Gray | > | Jesse William Gray | > |
| (1720-1795) | | (1770-1830) | | (1813-1880) | | (1855-1894) | |

your reaction is probably something like "No way!". I cannot imagine two boys of that age being allowed to make such a journey unaccompanied nowadays. We were officially under the care of the stewardesses, because back then the term "cabin crew" hadn't yet been coined and all passengers were looked after by female flight attendants. Remember as well that this wasn't a direct flight; there were refuelling stops along the way at Frankfurt, Zurich, Beirut and Delhi. At each of these, passengers had to disembark the aircraft and walk to the terminal to wait for refuelling to be completed, then the process was reversed to reload the plane. So, one stewardess had to walk us, holding our hands, into the terminal, and then back out again for take-off at each of these stops.

On arrival at Bombay, we were met by Mistry, our father's man–which I suppose was preferable, in terms of safety, than us being met by a mystery man! The three weeks themselves were great fun; various trips and excursions had been arranged for us. There was even a party on the afternoon of August 17th, when I was presented with a birthday cake. Another trip was to a farm-type place, where we saw cobras being milked for their venom. I never even knew they made three-legged stools that small! Our Dad was working for most of the time, so Mistry acted as a chaperone for us on our trips and we spent the evenings with Dad. I seem to remember he took time off work, to accompany us on the day we visited a BI liner in dock at the time–how convenient. This trip was the first time we had seen our father for over a year, and the time went by very quickly. There was to be an even longer gap before we saw him again, as we returned to our mother in England and then back to St Edmund's whilst Dad remained in India. In terms of the Gray family in India, this chapter of the story

British India Steam Navigation Co

concludes with my father's trip to England in 1960. I have found the record of this journey, which was to be his last sea voyage. On 5th March, the BI liner SS *Uganda* arrived in London; under "whence arrived" the record shows East Africa. This suggests it was a record of the last leg of the voyage, from Dar es Salaam to London via the Suez Canal; this was certainly the route taken by BI ships. I am conscious of having used BI often without having introduced them to you properly. They were Dad's favourite shipping company called British India Steam Navigation, known as BI. The company was formed in 1856 and remained one of the largest companies in the British mercantile marine until it was finally absorbed into P&O in 1972. It was entirely fitting that Dad's last voyage should be on his favourite ship, the *Uganda*, pictured below. My guess is he booked the passage on it intentionally, thinking it might be his last. This statement is based on other information on the shipping record. For "country of future intended residence" it states "Not Known". For "Intended duration of stay in UK" it also states "Not known". He gives his mother's flat in Loughton as his address in the UK. I find it quite sad that here was my father arriving in England aged 51 and seemingly totally lost in terms of his future life. He was now divorced and on his own in terms of any Gray family living in the

Far East. His children, mother, and brother were all now living in England; Norman and Joyce had settled there the previous July. Maybe he had decided to follow their leads and make England his permanent home. But where would he live? Surely not with his 78-year-old mother in her Loughton flat.

Once again, I am left to guess the exact timing of his actions between his arrival in March 1960 and the next key date I know about him–23rd December 1960. That was the day he married Phyllis Parrott! Gosh, I think I heard your sharp intake of breath then! I can imagine that came as quite a surprise to you readers; I can almost hear you asking "Where did that come from?" or "Who's Phyllis Parrott?" or "That was quick, wasn't it?". Don't worry–it came as quite a surprise to me at the time as well; remember I was at boarding school (St. Edmund's) at the time. I actually learnt that I had a new step-mother in a letter from my father. By any stretch of the imagination, that has to fit the description of a "whirlwind romance"! From disembarking from the SS *Uganda* on 5th March as a divorced man to "tying the knot" in Hampstead on 23rd December–just over nine months. Incidentally, the date of their actual wedding was probably chosen deliberately–it was Phyll's birthday. I shall have to return to this part of my story shortly, because I have to back track slightly and explain how 1960 came to be an excellent year for me, as I doubled the number of parents I had!

| > | *Jesse Esdale Gray* *(1885-1946)* | > | *Cecil Jesse Austen* *Gray (1908-1968)* | > | *Peter Nigel Austen Gray* *(1950-present)* |

THE CIRCLE IS CLOSED-GRAYS ARE BACK IN LEICESTERSHIRE

My father's arrival in England completed the Far East chapter of my family's story. Recapping slightly, Granny Gray was in Loughton quite close to her sister Mabel; her younger sister Dorothy was in Essex. Of her children, the two daughters were abroad–aunt Stella's family in Seattle and aunt Yolande's in Tanganyika. Her youngest son Norman is in Essex with aunt Joyce. My mother was living with her parents in Erith, with my brother and I safely at boarding school.

St. Edmunds School, Canterbury was an independent day and boarding school, originally founded in 1749 for 'the sons of the clergy'. I am not sure quite how Ian and I qualified in that category, since Dad was never ordained to my knowledge. But it was still a boys' school at the time we were there, with a Junior and Senior school sharing the same site but quite separate in many ways. We were at the Junior School, with my brother starting in September 1957, twelve months before me.

As I mentioned earlier, I was the youngest boy in the school when I arrived, about three weeks after my eighth birthday. Although I was in a class of only eight (small class sizes were one of the supposed advantages of private schools), I struggled academically in that first year and it was decided I should repeat the first year's schooling again. So, when I returned for the autumn term in Sept.'59, instead of re-uniting with those eight classmates I had shared a full year with, I suddenly had another bunch of 'friends' to get to know. I remember feeling quite homesick through a lot of my first year, even though boarding was not a new experience for me and there was no great home life to be sick about. Nevertheless, losing all the friends I had shared a year with and being lumped in with new strangers could hardly have helped me emotionally; I was still only nine years old! Neither did the plan work in terms of my behaviour. Because I was repeating the year's schooling, I found it easy. I was coasting, top of the class, with too much time on my hands. Consequently, I got into mischief. That's how I would put it but the staff would probably say I was very naughty. Whatever the truth was, I managed to set a new record for "getting the slipper"–corporal punishment involving being beaten with a gym shoe across your backside. I got the slipper 118 times in the five years I was at the school! In my defence, it was not difficult to fall foul of the ridiculously inefficient disciplinary system in operation at the school. Basically, teachers, monitors and prefects could award A or B marks for breaking rules. A marks were given for minor offences such as running in the corridor, making too much noise, not making your bed properly, etc. If you got 3 A marks in a week, you had to see the Housemaster after lunch on Saturday, and were given

---

>   *Jesse Esdale Gray*
    (1885-1946)

>   *Cecil Jesse Austen*
    Gray (1908-1968)

>   *Peter Nigel Austen Gray*
    (1950-present)

your beating. Can you see the basic flaw in the system? You got a beating for three marks–or more! Assuming your scorecard reverted to zero when you received your Saturday lunchtime beating, I could easily get another three A marks by teatime the same day, merely by being a typical eight-year-old boy! So where was the deterrent, to cover your behaviour during the remainder of the week? You didn't get one beating per every 3 A marks collected; you got one beating–for 3 or 9 or 21 etc. My brother often tells the story that he only worried about me if he didn't hear my name read out in the list of boys 'invited' to the Housemaster's study at the end of Saturday lunch!

I am going to skip through the remainder of my St. Edmund's School career, other than to explain why it was never seen through to its' intended conclusion. A private boarding school education was meant to deliver excellent academic results, and prepare me to go on to university. Instead, I was a casualty of my father's financial situation. In brief, the kind of jobs he managed to obtain after coming to England in no way matched the salary levels he had enjoyed as a BAT accountant. We were aware from our mother that he continually struggled with his alimony payments on our behalf and things came to a head regarding the St. Edmund's fees. You remember that our names had been down to follow in Dad's footsteps to Blundell's but the reality of it all was that we had to make do with a second-choice cheaper alternative, as in St, Edmund's. Even then, the fees proved too much and Dad had the difficult choice of choosing only one of us to put through private schooling. It boiled down to a timing issue, because Ian had already commenced working for his O levels at the time, so it was decided that I should be pulled out, rather than following through from the Junior school up to the Senior.

There was only one small problem to that really, namely that yours truly had somehow managed to fail my 11-plus exam (this was then a requirement for entry into a grammar school). Thankfully, my mother wrote to the local education authority, pleading on my behalf for a place at Erith Grammar School. No doubt she gave it the full works–struggling to bring up two boys after divorcing my father, who was behind with alimony payments, but grammar school is the right level of education that my child deserves, etc., etc. Whatever she wrote it worked–and I started at the school in time for the autumn term in 1962. I shall always be eternally grateful for my mother's persistence in winning me this opportunity; it was undoubtedly better for my emotional well-being, to be attending a mixed school within walking distance of home rather than miles away in an all-boys private school. In addition, my academic progress was not hampered at all and it turned out Dad backed the wrong horse in terms of return on his investment. Continuing investment in Gray Major resulted in a total of 3 O-levels, whilst the state-funded Gray Minor showed a very healthy return of 9 O-levels. Given that both had the same pedigree, I think the contrasting performances had more to do with nurture than nature! I was certainly happier at the grammar school; there were girls there for a start!

Whilst getting my place at the grammar school sorted things out nicely in terms of O-levels etc., I was well aware that finances generally, both Dad's and

---

> *Jesse Esdale Gray*
(1885-1946)   >   *Cecil Jesse Austen*
Gray (1908-1968)   >   *Peter Nigel Austen Gray*
(1950-present)

Mother's, would play a big part regarding progress to university and beyond. I need to pause a bit now, since I have still to update you on my 'parent' headcount at the time I am writing about. I cannot really remember much of the life Ian and I were leading prior to leaving India, and Calcutta in particular. Just snippets of things pop into my head. One such was a trip in a motor boat on the Hooghly river in Calcutta. The boat was driven by a Scotsman (a genuine one!) called Eric Butchart. He was from Dundee and was working as some kind of inspector for the jute trade that was big business in Calcutta. His job involved making checks on the docks on cargoes of jute being loaded, for which he had the use of this motor boat. I remember it being quite an exciting spin around the harbour. My brother Ian reminded me that we used to call Eric "the taxi driver", as he was giving us lifts to various places during this time in Calcutta, probably to help my mother out. I say this because things may not have been too good between my parents at the time, as Mother was preparing to return to England with us two boys, leaving our father in Calcutta, with Eric as well. Wind the clock forward about three years and the name Eric cropped up in a letter I received at St. Edmunds from Mother. She was telling me that she was going to marry again, and sure enough in May 1960 'Uncle Eric' became my stepfather! They married in Dartford, Kent and Eric joined Mother living at my Downton grandparents' house in Erith. Obviously, as a ten-year-old, one doesn't know the whole story and there are always two sides to it. My mother told me years later that she divorced my father due to his infidelity, adding she had a choice whom she could cite for the legal process! In doing research for this book, I spoke to my cousin Ann who said my father didn't want to get divorced and Mother and Eric had to involve a private investigator before obtaining the divorce. However, it panned out, this is how I came to have 4 parents by the end of 1960. It caused me a small administrative problem at school. I had to fill in a form stating how many parents would be attending on Speech Day. Thinking I was being helpful, I put a line through "1/2/none" and wrote "4" across the form; I got told off for being stupid!

That was all to explain the personnel involved in my dilemma around A level choices and whether Mother could afford to send me to university. In a similar manner to my father, Eric struggled to get jobs anything like the level he had been used to out in India, and money was always tight. At one point, Mother and Eric even tried running a newsagent's shop in Dartford but not with any great success. It was actually me who came up with the solution, no doubt partially and unknowingly influenced by both my father and Eric. You are already aware of my father's love of all things nautical and his service in the Navy. He would have loved one of his sons to have "gone to sea" and Ian actually got as far as researching into a career in the Merchant Navy. Unfortunately, he never quite got the necessary qualifications and he had

---

> *Jesse Esdale Gray (1885-1946)*   > *Cecil Jesse Austen Gray (1908-1968)*   > *Peter Nigel Austen Gray (1950-present)*

already taken matters into his own hands regarding his career. He left school after his poor O-level showing and joined the Army, as an infantryman. He actually lied about his age when enlisting, because he should have joined as a Junior soldier, being under the 17½ age restriction for being a regular soldier. I imagine this was a disappointment to our father, who never had any time for the Army! My stepfather had also served in the Royal Artillery, notably in the Burma campaign of WWII. So, a possible career in the services was obviously in my thinking and it was an advertisement in a Sunday paper that focussed my mind completely. It was inviting applications for entry into Welbeck College, the Army's 6th Form college, but essentially it was offering a total package of education, leading to an engineering degree. Successful candidates would complete two years studying science subjects at A level before obtaining entry into Sandhurst, to be trained for a commission in one of the Army's technical corps (Royal Engineers, Royal Electrical and Mechanical Engineers, Royal Army Ordinance Corps, Royal Corps of Signals, etc.). After initial service in whichever unit you were commissioned into, you then progressed to the Royal Military College of Science, Shrivenham, for university study to achieve your degree in whichever engineering discipline you had chosen. Bingo! There it was–my career path laid out for me, without any need for financial support from either 'set' of parents! I would be funding myself through 6th form and university and starting a career at the same time. Apart from compounding my father's disappointment, that neither of his sons joined the Navy, it appeared the ideal solution. From the very basic careers advice I had received at school, I had just about identified science subjects as my strongest suit and that seemed to point me towards engineering. The Welbeck–Sandhurst–Shrivenham path meant that I had time to choose which engineering discipline I would follow further down the line, as my preference would evolve through time. So, probably encouraged more by Team Mother/Eric than team Father/Phyll to be fair, I went for it.

"It" turned out to be quite a process. After an initial interview at the MOD in London, I had to attend the Regular Commissions Board establishment in Wiltshire, for a 2-day Assessment Centre–to determine if I had the necessary OQ (Officer Quality). They don't just give commissions in the Army to anyone, you know! Anyway, it turned out I had indeed got 'the right stuff' so that was me, en route to becoming an Army officer. The whole process took quite a time, such that I actually started at Welbeck College in January 1967, joining 28 Entry in Harland house. But not before I had one more term in the sixth form at Erith Grammar School. That was quite an odd term, commencing an A-level course with many of my friends of the last 4 years, knowing I would be leaving them at Christmas to go 'up north'. One bonus I had before leaving was going on a school skiing trip to Switzerland over New Year, which was great fun; the only time I have tried skiing in my life so far. My only memory of it was wondering why learning to stop didn't make it onto the syllabus until lesson 3! I had the bruises to query this fact! Whilst on the trip as a pupil of the grammar school, I had technically left at the end-of-term in December, so I felt somewhat of a free spirit in terms of being under school discipline; not

> *Jesse Esdale Gray*
> *(1885-1946)*

> *Cecil Jesse Austen*
> *Gray (1908-1968)*

> *Peter Nigel Austen Gray*
> *(1950-present)*

that I abused it in anyway.

It was an emotional 'goodbye' to my friends at the time, because I was not just changing schools. I was off to boarding school again! I know–I can hear you asking yourselves why? Given what my story so far has told you in terms of my opinion of boarding schools, why on earth was I turning my back on living at home and beginning to live a normal teenage life with my friends! With hindsight, I have asked myself that same question many times and, being honest, it was probably one of my first wrong choices in life. But back then, it seemed the right option–and an affordable one, which was the deciding factor.

Welbeck College then was actually embedded inside Welbeck Abbey, the ancestral home of the Dukes of Portland, near Worksop, Nottinghamshire. The MOD leased space in some of the less salubrious parts of this stately home, in which to operate what was effectively a boarding school. The pupils were divided into entries, with only four entries passing through the two-year cycle of A-level study at any one time. I joined 28 Entry in the January 1967 intake, with 27 Entry as the other group of 1st Years, having started in September 1966. 25 and 26 Entries made up the 2nd Years. Whilst it was a civilian

establishment, there were slight undertones of military life creeping into the disciplinary culture. These revealed itself more during the formalities of CCF (Combined Cadet Force) training, which took

---

place every Monday afternoon, and was the only time we wore army uniform.

Having said we were at school inside a stately home, the nearest we came to the "State Apartments" section of the house was using the Chapel as our place of worship, the Library as our library, one of the former servants dining quarters as our Dining Hall–oh, and the celebrated Underground Ballroom as our gym! This grand function room, complete with its' pictures and chandeliers, looked somehow odd with vaulting horses and medicine balls dotted around its' massive floor space. I believe it holds the record as the largest unsupported subterranean space in the UK. We used to get to it along Horse Corridor, an underground version of a long gallery hung with equine paintings; I am not sure if any of them was a Stubbs but we hardly gave them a second glance on our way to PE! It was a legacy of the 5th Duke of Portland, an eccentric recluse, who shunned visitors. He had fifteen miles of tunnels dug under the house which housed libraries; a billiard room large enough for twelve full size tables and an enormous subterranean ballroom large enough to take two thousand dancers– all of which remained unused. When in London, the Duke always travelled in a closed carriage; maintained a shuttered box at the Opera and kept the curtains permanently drawn at the windows of his substantial town house in Cavendish Square. I am not sure what he would have made of a bunch of teenagers playing badminton in his Underground Ballroom!

My time at Welbeck was eventful but I am going to restrict myself to telling you of one particular incident, that completely changed my career plan and hence my path on this Gray family journey. As sixth formers at Welbeck, we were all boys in the 16-18 age bracket and some of us had more of a desire to live a normal teenager's life than others. We continually sought to escape the limitations imposed by school rules, in terms of our interaction with "the world outside". We were allowed 'pass-outs', to take a bus into Worksop on a Saturday afternoon for example or go for bike rides around the local area; all carried out under strict rules and subject to curfews. Some of us in 28 Entry stretched these boundaries. We made a case for perfecting our metalwork skills on motorcycles and/or scooters that some had been allowed to bring to the college in their 2nd year. Whereas the latter spent most of the week in pieces being "worked on", they were always fully assembled by Saturday teatime–ready for a curfew-breaking night run to the pub!

It was on one such excursion that disaster struck. This particular Saturday night towards the end of the summer term in 1968 was very wet; the rain would have put sane people off from even venturing out. We, however, were not about to miss a valuable opportunity and I was a pillion passenger on my mate John Dutton's Lambretta for the trip to a pub in Mansfield. Fearing we might be late for the final college rollcall before bed, we were heading back through the driving rain along Leeming Lane South when John failed to see a small parking light hanging from the offside window of an otherwise unlit car! We crashed into the back of it and I was thrown over the car and into the path of any oncoming traffic. I did not lose consciousness but realised something was seriously wrong when I attempted to get off the road. I leopard-crawled my way to the pavement in agony, for I had suffered a compound, complicated fracture of my left tibia and fibula! Never mind about making it safely back to my bed at Welbeck; I was to spend the next month in a bed in Mansfield General Hospital! I was even stranded there when Welbeck closed for the summer holidays, as I was not able to hobble out of hospital on crutches until early August, for the trip down to Erith.

It was a very serious injury, which actually took two operations and extensive physiotherapy, spread over the following year, to rectify. More importantly, it put a very large spanner in the works in terms of my career plan. By winning my place at Welbeck, I was actually contracted to follow the 'route'–Welbeck, RMA Sandhurst, a commission into a technical Corps, a degree at RMCS, Shrivenham–subject only to passing each element of study and/or training along the way. It became clear early in my final term at Welbeck that an operation would be required. My bones had failed to knit together over the three months of being set in a full-length, non-weightbearing plaster. As I was fast approaching sitting my A levels, the necessary operation was postponed until December that year. I sat my A levels, Pure Maths, Applied Maths and Physics, with my left leg stuck out at the side of my desk in a plaster cast, in late November, 1968. Straight after the last exam, I was driven to Retford station and put on a train to London Kings Cross. An ambulance was waiting for me, actually parked up on the arrival platform, and I was stretchered off the train

---

> *Jesse Esdale Gray*
> *(1885-1946)*

> *Cecil Jesse Austen*
> *Gray (1908-1968)*

> *Peter Nigel Austen Gray*
> *(1950-present)*

and driven to the Royal Herbert Military Hospital, Woolwich. My operation was on 18th December, when it was discovered that the ends of the bones at the fracture site were dead; they would never have grown a callus to mend the break. The operation involved grafting 'fresh' bone from higher up the leg to replace the removed dead section and fixing it in place with a metal plate and screws. The end result was the leg being shortened by three-quarters of an inch. The full-length, non-weightbearing plaster cast was replaced, ready for the long process of a callus growing across the fracture site.

Apart from this whole episode being very traumatic itself, there is another reason why I remember the date so clearly–the death of my father on the day before my operation. The bearer of this shocking news was actually my aunt Marjorie, because my mother was ill with a heavy cold. She delayed travelling up to the hospital for a couple of days after my operation, hoping I would have recovered a bit from my ordeal before hearing her bombshell. It must have been horrible for her to break the news to me. I remember crying, off and on, for several days after my aunt had gone, trying to process what I had been told and feeling very, very alone. Although I was in quite a large hospital ward, surrounded by people, there was nobody to hug me, to tell me it would be alright, to help share my grief. It was the lowest I had ever been in my life to that point. When I had finally taken it all in, it turned out he had suffered a fatal heart attack. This was apparently a second attack, as he had had one earlier in the year, which I did not know about. I worked out that his visit to see me in Mansfield General Hospital in July was the last time I actually saw him alive.

I obviously missed his funeral, still being incapacitated at Woolwich. Many years later, I made a visit to the Golders Green crematorium, where there is a small memorial plaque on a wall and a record in the Book of Remembrance; it was the nearest I came to saying goodbye.

Having said that I missed his funeral, I find myself thinking that there could not have been many mourners there at all. Only when doing my family history research years later did I learn what a costly year 1968 had been, in terms of my extended family. In total, 3 members of My Magnificent 7 lost their lives that year. It perhaps sheds some light on how damaging my parents' divorce was on family matters, when I tell you that I cannot remember being told of their deaths at the time. Granny Gray died in Loughton on 1st March. Given that I was 'away' at Welbeck then, I may have been told of her passing in a letter from my mother. My father was not a great letter-writer; nor was he one for showing his feelings openly. My guess is that he never even spoke to me about losing his mother, believing the few times we were actually together should be kept light and upbeat. My father was to suffer a second loss later that year, when his younger sister Yolande died on 1st November. I cannot imagine he was in a good place emotionally at that time of his life, which was to be cut short just a few weeks later. I don't consider 60 as being particularly old, especially as he was rather late to fatherhood; 39 when Ian was born and 42 at my birth. It is sad that I only got to share eighteen years with the solitary direct male line ancestor alive when I was born. And not a lot of those eighteen years anyway, because of the life choices made around boarding schools and

---

> *Jesse Esdale Gray (1885-1946)* > *Cecil Jesse Austen Gray (1908-1968)* > *Peter Nigel Austen Gray (1950-present)*

divorce. This is why writing this book has brought me closer to my father in particular, but also to many more of my extended family. I certainly know more about them now than I did before my research!

Sorry about that detour in my story, albeit for a pivotal moment in my personal life. Back to a successful operation on my leg in December 1968 and my continuing recovery. I hobbled my way through the next few months, with my leg still in a non-weightbearing cast and using crutches. I actually gave mine names–Eddie and Wally–based on a couple of Watford footballers playing at the time. You have to know my sense of humour and love of playing with words in particular to understand why I might do such a thing. I used to listen to radio commentaries and hear mention of "Keith Eddy" or "Tom Whalley", which sounded to me like giving the commentator too many options. If he said "Eddy passes to Whalley who shoots…" followed later by "Keith and Tom have been excellent all through this game", listeners would think he was talking about different people!

Around April 1969 I was sent to RAF Chessington, home to the Joint Services Medical Rehabilitation Unit, where I was to receive intensive physiotherapy to aid my recovery. Remember that I was still on track to join RMA Sandhurst for officer training, prior to gaining my commission, even if I was just a bit delayed. Whereas every other 'patient' there was a serving member of the armed forces, 18-year-old Nigel was technically a civilian. As such, I had to be called Mr. Gray rather than Able Seaman X or Private Y or Aircraftman Z. This used to grate on the staff, especially the PTIs (Physical

Training Instructors) who couldn't quite get their heads around this long-haired, cheeky, gobby lad having to be called Mister! The other patients used to find it hilarious and goad me into answering back or questioning orders on their behalf, as I was untouchable in terms of any punishment. It was the source of much amusement but, overall, I was 'kind of' adopted by everyone there, probably because I was the youngest by quite a few years.

I was extremely lucky to benefit from this level of medical care, including physiotherapy, occupational therapy, hydrotherapy and general fitness training. Even so, it still took until the end of the summer for me to reach any reasonable level of mobility. When my plaster cast was removed soon after arriving at Chessington, it revealed a very poor specimen of a leg inside! Nine months of not being used had totally wasted my muscles away; my leg hung down at my side, virtually the same size from ankle to hip, and at the mercy of any strong gust of wind. I literally had to learn how to walk before I could run! Over the next months I had to progress through my classes, from Early Legs through the comically-named Middle Legs to arrive in Late Legs by August. By then, I could walk without crutches or sticks and even jog ever so slightly; a run around the camp perimeter was part of our training regime.

My recovery was not completed without one final twist, which involved a 'stay' in yet another hospital and a second operation. I have told you how I was adopted by my fellow patients as their 'lad' and, as I approached my birthday in the August, these mates discovered I had never been fully drunk. They took it upon themselves to rectify this omission from my life experiences with an 'excellent' night at the NAAFI. I awoke the next morning suitably hungover but there was no chance of sleeping it off, as they had planned a pleasant trip out for my birthday weekend. Four of us were going to White Hart Lane, to see my beloved Spurs play Liverpool in the opening game of the 1969/70 season. The train journey up to London was a blur, as was getting across London to start the walk up the Tottenham High Road. I was feeling like s**t (probably exactly on plan in terms of the aftermath of the previous night that my pals had arranged for me) but plodded slowly on towards Mecca and the big game! Eventually, I could not go on and a glance at my leg, which was a beetroot colour and hot to the touch, made me think there might be something else going on than just a hangover. Instead of entering the stadium, at about 2.45pm I entered the St. John's Ambulance station under it. A young cadet nearly had a heart attack on discovering I had a temperature of 104°F and they called for an ambulance. As they loaded me onto a stretcher, one of the paramedics paused, asking "you're Tottenham, ain't ya? Else you'd 'ave to walk!". I was delivered safely around to the North Middlesex Hospital, Edmonton–the third hospital to feature in Nigel's Broken Leg saga. There are not usually that many in a whole series of Casualty! After admission onto the ward, I eventually found out what I wanted to know–the score. Unfortunately, Liverpool won 2-0. Oh yes, I also found out I had osteomyelitis. A quick Google search reveals the following: Osteomyelitis is an infection of a bone. Symptoms include pain and tenderness over the affected area of bone, and feeling unwell. It is a serious infection which needs prompt treatment with antibiotic medication. Surgery is usually needed

| *William Gray* (1720-1795) | > | *John Gray* (1770-1830) | > | *James Gray* (1813-1880) | > | *Jesse William Gray* (1855-1894) | > |

if the infection becomes severe or persistent. Complications of osteomyelitis include chronic osteomyelitis, spread of infection to the blood stream (sepsis), reduced limb function and, in severe cases, amputation. Bloody hell! I am glad Google had not been invented back then; I would have been bricking it. As it was, I probably thought "Whatever" and was more worried about making yet another "Mother–I am in hospital" phone call. I would no doubt have also settled for it being an actual hangover!

It was thought that the plate and screws inserted in my first operation were the source of the infection and, as x-rays had shown them to have already done their work, they could be safely removed. But not until the infection was cleared up, which meant my buttocks became dartboards for the nurses for a good ten days before I eventually had the operation. They skilfully opened me up along the same scar line, to achieve the removal of all the redundant ironmongery in my shin, and I was discharged about the end of the month.

During my long period of rehabilitation at home and at Chessington, I had plenty of time for thinking about my future and had come to realise that an Army life was not for me. The closer I got towards actually enlisting and being a member of the armed forces, the more I knew there were too many differences between my character traits and those required to be a good fit in the military. It is probably best summarised by focussing on my central need– to know why I have to do something before I just do it. Call it too enquiring, too questioning, or just too thoughtful; I believed it to be a recipe for potential disaster within the service environment. I often joke we may have entered

WWIII, had I actually received a commission! The upshot of it was a change of mind and a desire to make a detour along my career path. Not that I knew what I wanted to do, just that I knew what I didn't want to do any more. But how best to proceed. I was technically contracted to join the Army and would have needed to 'buy' myself out of this commitment. Fortunately, my way out presented itself in the shape of my consultant at Chessington, an orthopaedic surgeon and also an RAF officer. After a series of conversations with me, he agreed to "stretch the truth" ever so slightly in terms of how long before I would attain the level of fitness and mobility required to pass the Sandhurst entry medical. He gave an assessment of approximately eighteen months, maybe a 50% mark up on the truth. Armed with this indication of the delay to continuing on my military career path, I wrote a letter to the MOD asking them to consider releasing me from my gentleman's agreement, "as disappointed as I am, etc., etc.". I must say they were most understanding, saying that they could not justifiably put my career plans on hold for so long and wishing me all the best in whatever career I chose to follow. I had done it, obtained my release from the Army without so much as a penny changing hands. The last ten months of first-class medical care and attention alone would have amounted to a tidy sum, not to mention the preceding two years of private education! One of my better economic deals on reflection–and their decision had saved the country from a possible armed conflict!

The upshot of it all was that I was home at Erith, wondering what career to pursue, having achieved presentable grades in 2 A-levels, Applied Mathematics and Physics. My Pure Mathematics A-level still remains the only examination I failed in my whole academic career. I always claim it was when I was faced with "airy fairy maths" that things started to unravel. I mean–the square root of a minus number! Really? Now give me good old-fashioned Newton's Laws of Motion or relative motion or reflection and refraction, I'm your man. There I was, pondering what career could make good use of these two subjects, when another job advert caught my eye. It was in the Erith Careers Advice office and had been posted by the South Midlands Area of the then National Coal Board. It was offering Student Apprenticeships across three engineering disciplines–mining, mechanical and electrical. There was light at the end of the tunnel after all. See what I did there? Tunnel, mining. The programme offered was a sandwich course combining a degree-level qualification in one of the 3 engineering disciplines with practical management training, leading to employment as a junior manager. As I thought I wanted to be some kind of engineer, the syllabus for a mining engineer seemed to offer me a wide enough range of subjects to find one I liked!

I had to apply to the area headquarters–Coleorton Hall, near Ashby de la Zouch, in the county of… Leicestershire! Bulls eye! The first mention of Leicestershire in this book for nearly eighty-nine years, with the death of my 2x great grandfather James Gray, who had meandered his way from said county via Nottingham, Birmingham and Camberwell out to Yokohama, where he died in 1880! I know it has taken only 234 pages and several thousands of miles travelling the globe, by sea, air and road, but we are now within touching

---

> *Jesse Esdale Gray*
(1885-1946)
> *Cecil Jesse Austen*
Gray (1908-1968)
> *Peter Nigel Austen Gray*
(1950-present)

distance of the Gray family's return to Leicestershire. Of course, it was not a 'done deal'; yours truly still had to secure my place onto the scheme. This I successfully achieved, by way of an interview held at Coleorton Hall, conducted by the Staff Manager, a jovial Welshman by the name of Evan Morgans. I shall always remember him telling me that if I had successfully proved I had enough OQ (Officer Quality) for a commission in the British army, I would be just fine as a manager within the coal industry. So, I had actually done the hard part of this interview about three years earlier, by passing the RCB's selection process in Wiltshire. I also had a glowing testimonial from my housemaster at Welbeck, about how I had endured all the trauma of my accident with admirable courage and fortitude; characteristics that equipped me well for my future working life! I hardly recognised myself in this glowing vote of confidence, but it helped launch my career as a mining engineer.

The format of the sandwich course I had embarked on was six months academic study followed by six months vocational training, each year for three years. I had come late to the recruitment process, such that I actually joined my classmates at North Staffordshire Polytechnic in Stoke-on-Trent about a week into the first term in September 1969. Evan Morgans actually drove me to Stoke, to meet David Le Jeune, the Head of Mining at the polytechnic and to settle me into my student accommodation. The latter was sharing a flat in Hanley with 3 other students. So began my Mining Engineering degree course, with six months study in Stoke. After the Easter holiday at home in Erith, I travelled by train to Nuneaton and on to my digs in Coventry, which was to be my home for six months of industry-based practical training. So, my part in the 'journey' of the Gray family direct male line had now brought me to Warwickshire, a neighbouring county to Leicestershire. I was getting nearer to closing the circle that started with my 4xgreat grandfather William Gray in Newtown Linford!

I don't intend to continue my story in any great detail here, but I do need to share enough of it for you to meet the new characters involved. This six-month period of 'practical training' was full on, in my private life much more than my career, for it saw me meet my first wife Val! She was studying at the same college that I attended as part of my apprenticeship programme. We were married in 1970.

I have actually written another book which details the first 21 years of my life, so I am not going to duplicate any more in this story. I can move the Gray family story on quite quickly now because, after completing my academic studies and receiving my mining degree, I worked my way through a graduate training programme that resulted in me obtaining my First Class Certificate of Competency, a statutory qualification required under the Mines & Quarries Act to manage a mine. I worked as both a deputy and overman (supervisory positions) at Newdigate Colliery near Bedworth, before applying for my first post as Undermanager; this is a statutory appointment also under the M&Q Act. I was appointed as Afternoon Shift Undermanager at Ellistown Colliery, Leicestershire in 1975. I finally had my foot on the bottom rung of the managerial ladder, that I hoped would lead to me managing a coalmine one

---

> *Jesse Esdale Gray*   > *Cecil Jesse Austen*   > *Peter Nigel Austen Gray*
> *(1885-1946)*   *Gray (1908-1968)*   *(1950-present)*

day. At age 25, I was in charge of a £40 million turnover business, responsible for all operations on a shift employing over 200 employees. Not bad for that 19-year-old lad who had no idea what he wanted to do! After about six months making the daily commute from a rented house in Keresley, Warwickshire, I moved my family to Markfield, Leicestershire. The family then was me, my wife Val and two daughters, Ann Cecilia born in 1971 and new baby Lorna Louise, born in 1975. I was happy that Val agreed to Cecilia as a middle name, because it is a special link to my late father who never made it to being a grandfather.

I had done it–closed the circle! A direct parental line Gray male was back living in Leicestershire. 215 years after my 4xgreat grandfather William Gray had moved his family from Colwick, Nottinghamshire to Newtown Linford for better job prospects, I had done a similar thing. I had moved from a neighbouring county into Leicestershire for a new job. For completeness of the family story, I need to guide you through the events that saw my mother join me here in Leicestershire for the last years of her life.

If you remember, Mother had become Mrs. Butchart back in page 398. Sorry, that should read "back in May 1960"! So, there was a short period when this new family unit lived together at the Erith house. Mother, stepfather Eric and I lived in a self-contained flat, upstairs in my Downton grandparents' house whilst I was at Erith Grammar School. These were probably the only four years that I lived something approaching a normal teenage life, at 'home' with two parents. Even then, my mother was the full-time carer for her elderly parents. They were both born in 1881, so they were octogenarians through this period. And, as though that wasn't enough, Grandma's sister Elizabeth Salter (known as "Aunt Bet") was also living there for a few years. She was just a year younger than Grandma, so she made it three 80-year-olds in Mother's care. This is why Mother always told my brother and me–*"I never want to be a burden on you when my time comes"*. And, bless her, she wasn't. By heading off to Welbeck in January 1967, I changed the family dynamics once more, leaving Mother at home with Eric and her two elderly parents. Mother lost them both in relatively quick succession. Gramps first in 1969, aged eighty-eight, followed by Grandma in 1972, aged ninety-one.

My stepfather Eric passed away in December 1981, leaving my widowed mother alone in the Erith house. You will probably have worked out by now that my Grandpa's house was quite a substantial property. Although a semi-detached property, it had two reception rooms and four bedrooms in the main house, along with two self-contained flats upstairs, accessed by their own entrance to the side of the building. Grandpa had built the house, as one of the very first dwellings in the road, in the early 1900s, and the flats had evolved over time, to supplement the family income. It gradually became all too much for my mother to manage on her own and she decided to look for somewhere more suited to her needs, living as a single person.

Her decision to downsize coincided with a development very close to my home called Markfield Court. It was an 'assisted-living' village of bungalows and apartments for the "over-55s" in the grounds of an old hospital. We made

---

> *Jesse Esdale Gray*
(1885-1946)

> *Cecil Jesse Austen*
Gray (1908-1968)

> *Peter Nigel Austen Gray*
(1950-present)

some enquiries into the project and shared their promotional material with Mother, who was quite taken with the idea of being near to us in Leicestershire. After viewing the site and seeing a show home of the type of accommodation available, she settled on a 2-bedroom bungalow, with lounge and bathroom, 21 Pinewood Drive, a short walk from the Community Centre. This was to be the 'hub' of the village. It was equipped with a dining hall, a large hall with a stage for shows and recreational activities such as indoor bowls and badminton, a residents' lounge, and two bedrooms for accommodating guest visitors. Her bungalow itself was linked with communications and a pull-cord alarm system to the resident warden. Exterior decoration and maintenance of the shared gardens were covered through management fees.

Mother was one of the first to take up residency at Markfield Court and always said it was the best move she ever made. She played bridge over at the centre, and actually ran classes teaching beginners. We often joked that we had to book an appointment to see her, because she played badminton, bowls and Petanque as well as bridge, attended keep-fit classes and went on outings and theatre trips. She used to make us smile when, in reply to us asking what she had done in the week, she would say "I drove some of the oldies to collect their pension". There again, she was only in her late 70s! The "us" that Mother had joined in Leicestershire was my new wife Jenny and myself. By the time Mother completed her move, I had separated from Val and had set up house in Stanton-under-Bardon with Jenny. We were married in June 1994 at the Methodist Chapel in Markfield, so Mother did not have far to travel to see me marry for the second time. In fact, I did the traditional thing and stayed the night before at her bungalow in Markfield before the big day! And she had an extended family with her in Leicestershire, as I now had two step-daughters, Sam and Charlotte, to add to my three girls. Ann, Lorna and my youngest daughter Helen (born 1981) were still in Leicestershire, living with their mother in Thornton.

My mother lived out the remainder of her days here, in her bungalow at Markfield Court. It was this period, when my mother lived in the next village to me, that meant we could have a close mother-son relationship for the first time in our lives. I have to thank my wife Jenny for this, as she was very much the catalyst for bringing us closer together. It was one of those strange coincidences in life that Jenny and I each lost one of our parents at quite a young age. You have already heard that my father died when I was eighteen; Jenny's mother Joan died when she was twenty-nine. So, we kind of made a 'whole' when we got together, as Jenny could share my mother and I could share her father. We actually found a unique way of remembering our respective departed parents some years later, when we were thinking of a name for our narrowboat. We were lucky enough to have one built, so it was an emotional day when we poured champagne on the bow of the "**Jesse Joan**", after her launch onto the Trent and Mersey canal at Stone in 2001. It was such an appropriate name, given my father's naval past and love of boats in general, coupled with Joan coming from Foxton with a canal running by the village!

A slight digression there, back to enjoying a very special time with my

---

mother nearby, playing an active part in our family life. Our children even enjoyed making memories with Grandma Katie, which I love hearing them talk about, even though it usually makes me emotional. They had the kind of relationship with a grandparent that I never really had, for all the many reasons wrapped up in this story you've been following. My mother certainly achieved her long-term wish, of never being a burden to anyone, as she lived an independent life, in her own home right up until her passing. She was even still driving at aged 87, when she had a fall in her kitchen. It was only that same morning that she had chosen to sit in a chair for the first time, to do her weekly keep-fit class! She broke her hip in the fall and was taken into Leicester Royal Hospital. It was in September 2001 and we always remember that we were visiting her in the hospital when the world experienced a tragic event. It was 11th September 2001 when terrorists flew planes into the Twin Towers in New York in the devastating '9/11' attack. September 11th is Jenny's birthday, which now always has to share the date with that tragic event. Whilst getting over her broken hip, Mother's stay in hospital unfortunately revealed a more serious problem, because cancer had returned to her liver. She had had two mastectomies to treat breast cancer through her eighties but the return of her cancer to the liver was too much for her. She never left the hospital, dying on 25th September.

My mother was the only other member of the Gray parental line, besides myself, to have brought the family back to Leicestershire. Telling the story of this amazing circular journey, across seven generations, five continents and over two centuries, was the premise of this whole book. I feel quite exhausted, as though I have led you on a climb similar to scaling Everest. I now want to draw everything together in my final chapter, by attempting to answer the question posed by the book's title–"*Too Far East?*".

WORLD HISTORICAL EVENTS	GRAY FAMILY HISTORY EVENTS
1945 VE Day (8th May) saw the end of the war in Europe; nuclear bombs dropped on Japan leading to VJ day (15th August); WWII ends	1945 All 7 Gray family members released from captivity
	1945 Yolande Gray(aunt) marries Gordon Reynolds
1946 Muslims and Hindus hold demonstrations for a separate state; thousands killed	1946 **Jesse Esdale Gray (grandfather)** dies in Shanghai; Norman Gray(uncle) marries Joyce Sexton
1947 India and Pakistan become independent countries following separation	1947 Cecil Jesse Austen Gray's 1st son Ian Robert Downton Gray born in Tsingtao, China
1948 Mahatma Gandhi shot dead in India; Britain establishes its' National Health Service	
1951 "The Archers" starts broadcasting on BBC radio; now the world's longest running drama	1950 Cecil Jesse Austen Gray's 2nd son **Peter Nigel Austen Gray(author)** born in Calcutta, India
1952 King George VI dies and is succeeded by Queen Elizabeth II	
1953 Sir Edmund Hilary and Sherpa Tenzing achieve the first ascent of Mount Everest	
1957 Asian flu starts in Guizhou, China and kills over 1 million people worldwide; Russia launches Sputnik 1, first artificial satellite to orbit Earth	1957 Kathleen Gray(mother) returns to England with her 2 sons Ian and (Peter) **Nigel** after divorce
1960 Cassius Clay(later Muhammed Ali) wins gold at the Rome Olympics; "Coronation Street" began on ITV, still running now 6 nights a week;	1960 Cecil Jesse Austen Gray returns to England
	1960 Kathleen Gray(mother) marries Eric Butchart
	1960 Cecil Jesse Austen Gray marries Phyllis Parrottt
1963 J F Kennedy assassinated in Dallas, Texas; the Great Train Robbery took place in Hertfordshire, England	
	1968 **Winifred Leila Gray(grandmother)** died in Loughton, Essex
	1968 Yolande Reynolds(aunt) died in Clavering, Essex
1968 Martin Luther King Jnr and Robert F Kennedy both shot dead in US	1968 **Cecil Jesse Austen Gray(father)** died in West Hampstead, Middlesex

The Bund area of Shanghai in 1920s

WAS IT TOO FAR EAST?

This story has covered the journey of my Gray ancestors from Newtown Linford, a small village in Leicestershire, to Markfield, a village exactly two miles away in the same county. The move began at the middle of the 18th century and finished early in the 21st century. Those simple statements don't really suggest that it needs a book to tell the story, but they might well have you questioning the efficiency of the removal firm involved! This diagram illustrates that nearly a third of my Gray family's 240-year journey time was spent in the Far East, but was it time well spent?

It is only when I explain that it was my 4x great grandfather William who began it with his move from Nottinghamshire that a spark of interest occurs. If I then add that my 3x great grandfather John moved the family into Leicester itself, looking for work, it sounds a little more interesting. When I add that my 2x great grandfather James made more moves via Nottingham, Birmingham and Clerkenwell, London in search of work, it becomes clearer that the family journey is getting longer. But three of James's children, including my great

| William Gray | > | John Gray | > | James Gray | > | Jesse William Gray | > |
| (1720-1795) | | (1770-1830) | | (1813-1880) | | (1855-1894) | |

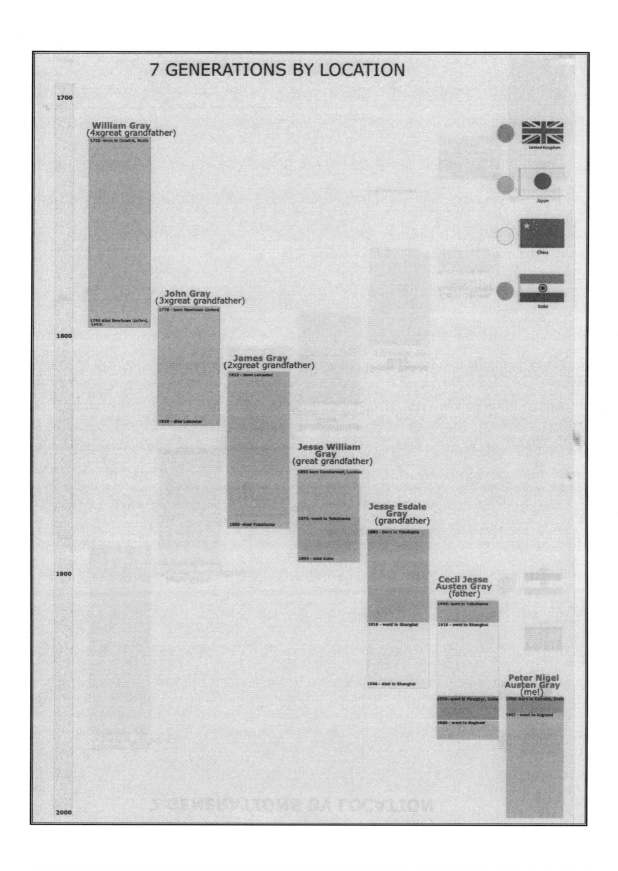

7 GENERATIONS BY LOCATION

1700

William Gray
(4xgreat grandfather)
1720 -born in Colwick, Notts

1795 died Newtown Linford,
Leics.

John Gray
(3xgreat grandfather)
1770 - born Newtown Linford

1800

James Gray
(2xgreat grandfather)
1813 - born Leicester

1830 - died Leicester

Jesse William Gray
(great grandfather)
1855 born Camberwell, London

1880 -died Yokohama

1871 -went to Yokohama

Jesse Esdale Gray
(grandfather)
1885 - born in Yokohama

1894 - died Kobe

Cecil Jesse Austen Gray
(father)
1908- born in Yokohama

1900

1918 - went to Shanghai

1918 - went to Shanghai

1946 - died in Shanghai

Peter Nigel Austen Gray
(me!)
1950- born in Calcutta, India

1950= went to Monghyr, India

1957 - went to England

1960 - went to England

2000

United Kingdom

Japan

China

India

> *Jesse Esdale Gray*
> *(1885-1946)*

> *Cecil Jesse Austen*
> *Gray (1908-1968)*

> *Peter Nigel Austen Gray*
> *(1950-present)*

grandfather Jesse William took it a step further–if you can call going to Japan a step! London to Tokyo is actually 10,746 miles and Yokohama is very close to Edo, as Tokyo was called, when Jesse William took his 'step' there in the 1870s, again looking for work. My grandfather Jesse Esdale took another 'step', to a job in Shanghai in 1917. My father Cecil took further 'steps'–to Hong Kong to serve in the Navy, to Tsingtao, China with BAT where my brother was born and to Calcutta, India where I was born. My mother took another 'step', bringing us two boys back to Erith, Kent. I took more 'steps'–to Darjeeling, Canterbury, Erith and Worksop for my education and to Warwickshire to begin my mining career. I took the final 'step' to Markfield, nearly 225 years after my 4xgreat grandfather William Gray began the journey! That is a very quick summary as to why I wanted to tell this story. I hope you are not all wishing that I had written it on page 1, to save you the job of actually reading the book!

I have used the word 'journey' to describe my ancestors' story, much like the current trend of reality shows, who use it to summarise the participants' experiences. However, I find it particularly appropriate when recounting my family's history, as travel is a consistent theme running through their adventures. Similarly, the reason they made so many moves over the years was consistent– the need to find work. One thing I have learned whilst doing genealogy is that our ancestors travelled greater distances than we might have imagined. The popular notion is that travel was minimal, restricted by slower means of transport or even the lack of it altogether. Walking to a neighbouring village, to carry out a trade or just being another "Ag. Lab."–family history shorthand for 'agricultural labourer'–seemed the norm in the countryside, whilst factory workers lived in close proximity to the industries that employed them. So, families could be centred in a particular area for generations, providing the opportunities existed to continue in their line of work.

The industrial revolution accelerated the drift from country to town. I have described how my 3xgreat grandfather John Gray moved from Newtown Linford into Leicester to run his bakery business. Several of his sons served apprenticeships, to become either a cooper, wheelwright, metalworker or even baker like him. My 2x great grandfather James then moved between Leicester, Nottingham, Birmingham and finally London, changing jobs from manual to clerical, ending up as the newsagent's clerk in Camberwell. Nothing exceptional so far then, and this book would have been totally different but for one significant world event–the Meiji Restoration. The expression 'Far East' would not have featured in the title of any book about my ancestors, had they not reacted to events in Japan the way they did. In telling the family's story, I have called Yokohama in the late 19th century "an employment Klondike", comparing the life-changing opportunities offered there, to those being sought by fortune-seekers in the goldrush to the Yukon region of north-western Canada. Incidentally I got my dates slightly wrong, because the Klondike goldrush was 1896-1899, whereas Emperor Meiji acceded to the throne in 1867. His reign spelled the beginning of the end for feudalism in Japan, and would lead to the emergence of modern Japanese culture, politics and society. Basically, Japan put an "Open for Business" notice up for the rest of the world,

> *Jesse Esdale Gray (1885-1946)*   > *Cecil Jesse Austen Gray (1908-1968)*   > *Peter Nigel Austen Gray (1950-present)*

inviting entrepreneurs to lead the westernisation of the country by setting up any businesses they wanted. Somehow, the word reached three of James Gray's sons, including my great grandfather Jesse William, and it was their migration to Yokohama in the 1870s that was the most significant factor in my family's history.

Any analysis of whether being out in the Far East was a good or bad thing for my family has to be done by examination of each generations' experiences. And that generational examination has to be set against the context of world events occurring at the time. The "Pioneer" generation–including my great grandfather Jesse William and his two elder brothers John and James Joseph–all came to Yokohama with youthful optimism, either starting businesses themselves or joining businesses started by other early settlers. The Esdales and the Vincents were two other families involved in this exciting time of growth, and joined the Gray extended family through marriage. A fourth Gray sibling, Charlotte Anne, married David Brearley, another of these pioneer businessmen, in Yokohama. For all this generation, the relationship with the host Japanese population would have been business-like and largely welcoming. The country had opened its' doors to these entrepreneurs, who were settling down into their new lives in this rapidly expanding city. This early stage of development for Yokohama saw countless opportunities for incomers, and my family members embraced them whole-heartedly. It was the start of a continuous presence of my direct parental line in Yokohama from 1875 to 1917.

My family flourished against this background of rapid growth. The city itself was in its' infancy and as it grew, these incomers grew with it. Initially, it was a pretty wild and largely lawless place, much like the frontier towns of America's Wild West. In fact, the first arrivals operated their own police force, with armed patrols each night. The Freemasonry Lodge was formed in 1870 to give some kind of structure and organisation to the burgeoning business community and membership was probably considered essential if one wanted to progress. It was a male-dominated society and an indication of the moral code prevailing at the time is given by my great grandfather Rev. William Thomas Austen's story. He was serving as a gunnery instructor in the Royal Navy and came to its' "China Station" as a young man. On seeing the temptations to which visiting seamen were exposed in foreign ports, he decided to obtain his discharge from the Navy to take up work in Yokohama for the benefit of seamen away from home. He arrived in Yokohama from Tientsin on 23rd June 1873 and became a temperance worker, initially onboard ships but later at premises in Yokohama. In 1890 he was ordained a priest in the Church of England and the following year was licensed by Bishop Bickersteth as Seamen's Chaplain for the port of Yokohama. I have reproduced an article from The Japan Gazette in an appendix to this book, which celebrates Rev. Austen's fifty years' residence in Yokohama, forty years of which he laboured in the service of visiting seamen, first as lay worker and later as Seamen's Chaplain. It describes him as *"one of the oldest British residents of the city and the senior of the missionary residents of Japan"*. I wonder if he ever felt the need

---

> *Jesse Esdale Gray (1885-1946)*   > *Cecil Jesse Austen Gray (1908-1968)*   > *Peter Nigel Austen Gray (1950-present)*

to guide my 2x great uncle James Joseph or my great grandfather Jesse William away from the city's temptations, before our two families were united by my grandfather marrying his eldest daughter! I feel tremendously proud to have his name among my forenames.

I must return to my story. In terms of housing, it was a case of new arrivals building houses as they needed them. The numbering system in the Bluff residential area reflected the order in which they were built. My 2xgreat uncle James Joseph lived in no. 46 in 1874, when he came 'ashore' after working on ships. His sister Charlotte Anne moved into no. 179 as Mrs. Brearley in 1888. Incidentally, after the Brearleys returned to England, my widowed great grandmother Sarah Anne Gray (Annie) moved her 4 young children into no. 179 in 1896, when they returned to Yokohama from Kobe. The Austens lived in no. 60, another of the earlier properties on the Bluff.

From these early days of my Gray ancestors helping to build the infrastructure of the city, the family in Japan literally 'grew' when the Pioneer generation began their families. James Joseph was the first to marry, early in 1880, followed by his sister Charlotte Anne the next year. My grandfather Jesse William was the last of the siblings to marry, in 1882; I cannot find any record that older brother John did marry. John Gray actually left Japan in 1884, after not being able to extend his government railroad contract; perhaps he didn't feel settled enough to marry and start a family. The 1st generation Grays (as in those born in Japan) arrived in fairly quick succession, in the following sequence–Ethel in 1882 to James Joseph; Vincent in 1883 to James

Joseph; Walter in 1884 to my great grandfather Jesse William; Jesse Esdale in 1885 to Jesse William; Harold in 1888 to James Joseph; Amy also in 1888 to Jesse William; William in 1889 to Jesse William. I see this pattern of births as an indication of stability and confidence, for these two brothers, in their situation in Yokohama. Maybe the first sign of things changing for them was James Joseph's decision to leave Japan around 1890. I think the city had passed through its' development stage into a more settled growth period, such that my 2xgreat uncle felt his skills were best utilised in some other location just beginning its' "boomtown" phase. Just as he had been the first Gray to arrive in Japan, he was one of the earliest to head off to 'pastures new', choosing British Columbia in north-west Canada for his next adventure. His next daughter Norah was born in Victoria, B.C. in February 1893. His leaving was one signal that the attitude of the Japanese 'hosts' towards their Westerner 'guests' was changing. From the whole-hearted welcome when they threw the country's doors wide open, it was shifting to a more cautious tolerance, as they weighed-up the overall usefulness of incomers to their change programme.

Against this background of 'a wind of change' blowing through Japan during the second half of Emperor Meiji's reign, my great grandfather Jesse William had the decision on whether to stay or leave taken away from him. I wrote earlier in my story how he continued to have a good career, first in Yokohama and then in Kobe, until tragedy struck with his sudden death in December 1894. This could so easily have been a pivotal moment in the Gray family history, taking it in a completely new direction altogether. That it didn't

| > | *Jesse Esdale Gray* | > | *Cecil Jesse Austen* | > | *Peter Nigel Austen Gray* |
| | *(1885-1946)* | | *Gray (1908-1968)* | | *(1950-present)* |

is solely down to the resilience and tenacity of yet another remarkable female Gray ancestor–my great grandmother Sarah Anne Gray, known as "Annie". When her husband died, not only was she a 36-year-old widow with four young children, she was also the 'head' of the Grays remaining in Japan at the time. This was because her brother-in-law James Joseph had taken his family to Canada in 1890, and her sister-in-law Charlotte Anne Brearley had returned to England in 1892. Undaunted at finding herself a widow alone in Kobe, Annie moved her family back to Yokohama in 1896, to live with her parents James and Hester Esdale. It seems unbelievable that she would only have this invaluable support helping to raise her young family for a relatively short time, as it was just six years before both her parents died in 1902–within eight days of each other. Now she really was alone, because her elder brother Charles had himself died in 1886, leaving a widow with four children! Despite this tragic sequence of events, Annie showed enough strength of character and optimism to carry on. She had two sons at work and a daughter and son completing their education at home, but her decision to stick it out extended the stay of my Gray parental line in Yokohama by another fifteen years, until my grandfather Jesse Esdale moved his family to Shanghai.

Given that I am meant to be making some conclusions about whether being in the Far East was good or bad, I would suggest that by the end of Emperor Meiji's reign in 1912, Westerners were beginning to believe their 'purple patch' of endless opportunity was drawing to an end, because of the changed working relationship between the native population and the incomers. One

| William Gray (1720-1795) | > | John Gray (1770-1830) | > | James Gray (1813-1880) | > | Jesse William Gray (1855-1894) | > |

of the biggest impacts on the economy that the Meiji period brought was the end of the feudal system. With a relatively loose social structure, the Japanese people were able to advance through the ranks of society more easily than before. They were able to do this by inventing and selling their own wares. More important was the fact that the Japanese people now had the ability to become more educated. With a more educated population, Japan's industrial sector grew significantly. Implementing the Western ideal of capitalism into the development of technology and applying it to their military, helped make Japan into both a militaristic and economic powerhouse by the beginning of the 20th century.

In the Meiji period, leaders inaugurated a new Western-based education system for all young people, sent thousands of students to the United States and Europe, and hired more than 3,000 Westerners to teach modern science, mathematics, technology, and foreign languages in Japan. The government also built railroads, improved roads, and inaugurated a land reform program to prepare the country for further development.

To promote industrialisation, the government decided that, while it should help private business to allocate resources and to plan, the private sector was best equipped to stimulate economic growth. The greatest role of government was to help provide the economic conditions in which business could flourish. In short, government was to be the guide, and business the producer. In the early Meiji period, the government built many factories and shipyards that were then sold to entrepreneurs at a fraction of their value. Many of these businesses grew rapidly into the larger conglomerates. Government emerged as chief promoter of private enterprise, enacting a series of pro-business policies. The development of banking and reliance on bank funding were at the centre of Japanese economic development during and after the Meiji era.

There was a gradual change in ownership and management of the country's industry, which saw a decline in opportunities for Westerners, including my Gray extended family. The drift away from Japan that had started with my 2x great uncles John and James Joseph continued with my grandfather's generation. My great uncles scattered themselves around the world–Walter Gray went to Australia, William Gray to China first and then on to Australia, Albert Austen to America, Harold Austen to Australia. My great aunt Amy, now Mrs Hawley, went to England and I believe my great grandmother Sarah Anne Gray (nee Esdale) passed away in Japan. In terms of the direct Gray male line, it was my grandfather's move to Shanghai in 1918 that finally drew the curtain down on their continuous presence in Japan, over 40 years and three generations. It is no coincidence that the dates of the family's stay in Japan match those of Emperor Meiji's reign almost exactly, because that was essentially how long Japan needed Western entrepreneurship. Having thrown out the worldwide invitation for 'change agents' to deliver their transformation, they decided when to call time on these 'interim managers'. The latter got the message that their futures lay elsewhere and gradually moved on to their next 'assignments'. As an overall assessment of my family's Japanese period, I would say it was a success. It provided stable employment for all, which allowed the

| William Gray (1720-1795) | > | John Gray (1770-1830) | > | James Gray (1813-1880) | > | Jesse William Gray (1855-1894) | > |

initial pioneer generation to raise the next generation successfully, who then started families of their own. So, Japan itself was not too far east.

For my direct Gray paternal line, their next 'assignment' was in Shanghai. In some ways, all my grandfather Jesse did was to swap one "land of opportunity" for another. The Shanghai of the early 20th century was enjoying its' own boom period, well on its' way to becoming one of the world's leading cities, alongside New York, London and Paris. Its' unique structure, of having the Shanghai International Settlement at the heart of the city, meant that it grew independently of the China all around it. Its' growth was based on mainly Western businesses and investment but also, ironically, on Japanese economic imperialism. By the 1930s the Japanese were the largest section of the International Settlement's population and also increasingly more influential within the SMC. Nevertheless, my grandfather settled well into Shanghai life. His family was completed with the birth of my aunt Yolande in the year of their arrival, and he enjoyed a steady career with the China Import and Export Lumber Company.

He gained promotion to Company Secretary, giving him a seat on the Board. He educated his children, including overseas in English private schools, and, judging by the description of my aunt Stella's wedding reception, lived in a splendid house at 104, Columbia Road. As a freemason, he rose to be Master of the Cosmopolitan Lodge. In other words, he enjoyed an elevated status in society within the International Settlement, and his children were very much part of Shanghai's 'younger set', living the good life.

> *Jesse Esdale Gray*   > *Cecil Jesse Austen*   > *Peter Nigel Austen Gray*
>   *(1885-1946)*   *Gray (1908-1968)*   *(1950-present)*

So, what went wrong? Basically, whereas he thought he had turned his back on the Japanese, they actually followed him to Shanghai! That is a rather neat summary of the pre-WWII part of the Second Sino-Japanese War, which I have covered earlier. It was one thing wanting to rule China through economics, but now it was to be ruled by the invading Imperial Japanese Army. That was when my grandfather's life changed completely, as he was to become one of My Magnificent 7. Whilst he and 3 others of his extended family were held captive in his 'home' city by invaders from the country of his birth, my parents and uncle were not even safe in Hong Kong. I have told you, or rather I have let them tell you in their own words, of the trauma these seven members of the extended Gray family suffered at the hands of the Japanese. Obviously, if I had asked my *"Too Far East?"* question of these seven ancestors right then, it would have been met with a resounding "Yes". Grandpa Jesse summarised it in his 1945 letter–*"I have good cause to hate the Japanese!"*. That was written ten months before he died, which I believe was actually caused by nearly four years of captivity seriously aggravating his existing heart condition.

So, my grandfather paid the ultimate price for being in the wrong place at the wrong time. However, his internment and subsequent death had an associated consequence on the family's circumstances, in that it left his widow homeless and virtually penniless. In his will, the estate left to his widow Winifred amounted to £164 3s 4d! Not much for the Company Secretary on the Board of a respected import/export business, with nearly 20 years' service. To put that figure in some kind of value context, the estate of a similar Shanghai-based businessman who did not lose everything, was over £30,000. Grandpa's estate meant there wasn't much to support his widow nor an inheritance to pass down to his children. Obviously, he didn't choose to be 'out East' as he was born in Japan, but he was unlucky that his voluntary move to Shanghai in 1918 to secure his family's future prosperity was undone by the Japanese capture of Shanghai–with his family in it!

Similarly, my parents had to 'start from scratch' after their captivity, since they had survived with their lives but not much else. My guess is that his job with BAT was the one stable factor in my father's life at this point; there was no 'family home' as such which he could make his base, so he resumed his career with the posting to Tsingtao. But it was to be short-lived, again due to world events. There was barely time to start his family with the arrival of my brother Ian, before Chairman Mao announced the founding of the People's Republic of China. The family were on the move again, basically with only what they could carry!

After a short period of leave in England in the autumn of 1949 (when they attended the family re-union at Erith I described in the previous chapter), they set up house again in another Eastern location, swapping China for India. The posting was to Monghyr, and family life was soon 'normal' enough for another addition–yours truly born in the summer of 1950. I have already related the events of the subsequent decade, which ended with the family all in England and my parent headcount doubled from two to four! I guess that tells you something about just how 'normal' family life actually was. I believe the failure

> *Jesse Esdale Gray*
(1885-1946)
> *Cecil Jesse Austen*
Gray (1908-1968)
> *Peter Nigel Austen Gray*
(1950-present)

of my parents' marriage was not simply as a result of living 'out East' per se, but more to do with their different backgrounds and the lifestyles of foreigners in both China and India at the time. The latter comprised an elevated status among the 'ruling' class, with native servants tending to their domestic requirements, and a social scene centred on 'the Club'–be it country, golf, tennis, swimming, dance, etc. One imagines the only time couples spent solely with each other in their own homes was when they were sleeping! I have already indicated that, from my personal memory, interaction with their children was not high up on the list for these 'colonial-style' parents. I am sure my ayah (Indian nanny) could have given you readers a far more detailed account of my childhood in India than either of my parents. To be fair to them though, I didn't spend much time with them, after taking myself off to boarding school from age 5!

Of course, one has to remember that the seven or eight years my parents lived together in India was the longest stretch in their married life that they had shared a home. They had spent approximately five of the first six years of their life together as a couple–apart! Firstly, when Dad had enlisted into the Navy before Mother travelled to Hong Kong for their wedding, and then nearly four years in different prisoner-of-war camps. They had never actually shared a prolonged period in each other's company. Even these years were hardly stable, as they involved four house moves in about seven years in a new country, with the birth of their second son thrown in for good measure. They probably started their spell in India as relative strangers, and their social life had the potential for them each to live as individuals more than as a close family unit at home. Add in my father drinking no more or no less than any other fun-loving, party-loving, dance-loving, club-loving son-of-the-Raj, and you probably have a recipe to put any marriage under threat!

Arriving as a single man in England in March 1960 aged 51, my father was hardly well equipped for 'starting again' yet again. He had nowhere to live, a CV detailing a career spent entirely overseas, was a heavy smoker and drinker, presumably with a mostly chauvinistic approach to women and definitely fully accustomed to servants meeting his domestic needs. An ideal future husband for some unsuspecting English rose? Maybe not, and yet on 23rd December, Phyllis Parrott became his third wife–and my step-mother. Maybe a bit of a hint as to his natural charisma, which thankfully I have inherited, along with his modesty! As far as I can tell, he finally met his soulmate in Phyll, and I only ever knew them as happily in love. I believe the relatively few years they had together (only 8) were good for both of them.

My father's later years in England are very reminiscent of the central character in a TV series called "*The Misfit*" which aired in 1970 -71. "Badger" had returned to England after enjoying a colonial lifestyle in Malaysia, very similar to that of my father in China and India. He is continually trying to operate in post-Swinging Sixties England with a set of values and principles more akin to an Edwardian gentleman. My father was, in most ways, a similar misfit, as this was him coming to live in England for the first time, at the very beginning of the Sixties, from a privileged, high society lifestyle. His age was against him, in terms of finding a job that might match his stature overseas,

---

>   *Jesse Esdale Gray*   >   *Cecil Jesse Austen*   >   *Peter Nigel Austen Gray*
      (1885-1946)   *Gray (1908-1968)*   *(1950-present)*

and his experience counted very little in the business and commercial sectors of a thriving, competitive London. Basically, he had changed from "a big fish in a little pond" into more of "a tiddler in a river"! I only knew of him being some kind of bookkeeper in a small advertising company based near Fleet Street. His accommodation was a rented one-bedroom flat on the top floor of a building in West Hampstead. He always seemed to be struggling to keep his head above water financially, and was always behind with alimony payments due to our mother. And yet, my memories are of him being happy, smiling mostly, living for the moment and settling for his lot, rather than hankering after the unavailable. Maybe, compared with what he had been through already, this life seemed relatively carefree, a state-of-mind that I happen to consider highly desirable. In comparing his will with my grandfather Jesse's, there was nothing to leave to Phyll. But, just like her, I would have sooner had him in my life for longer than inherit anything. I still miss him, even after fifty years.

My mother's legacy from her twenty years in the Far East was slightly different. There is no doubt she was emotionally scarred by the trauma of internment, and her health was never quite the same after captivity. My father's financial woes impacted on her, and their subsequent divorce must have taken some sort of toll. But there was one odd benefit from her time in Stanley Internment camp. She always said learning to play Bridge was a plus; she would probably have called it a "game changer" in modern parlance. It certainly gave her a vital addition to her life-skills 'toolkit'. She would play, on average, two afternoons every week, starting in the prisoner-of-war camp

| *William Gray* | > | *John Gray* | > | *James Gray* | > | *Jesse William Gray* | > |
| *(1720-1795)* | | *(1770-1830)* | | *(1813-1880)* | | *(1855-1894)* | |

and right through until her final years as a widow. It was her comfort blanket through much of her adult life. She was very good at it and my theory is that, when she was playing Bridge, she was 'living in the moment' and knew peace, regardless of what was happening around her. Not a bad game plan for life really–focus on something that allows you to just "be" rather than "do", and you will find peace where it actually lives–inside you.

In contrast to my father, and to my grandmother Winifred to some extent, she had 'a home to run to' when things went wrong with my Dad. By bringing us two boys back to her parents' house in Erith, she had family again. Whilst it meant hard work at the end, being a carer for both parents in their old age, it gave her a home and the wherewithal to make her bungalow in Markfield her final resting place. This was the move that saw two surviving members of the globe-trotting Grays both settled back in Leicestershire. I know she enjoyed this last chapter of her life, as she thanked me many times for suggesting the move. Thus, mother and son shared over fifteen years as near neighbours, a very belated 'first' in our lives, and our closeness during these years meant that I experienced genuine grief at losing someone who had been quite distant for most of my life.

It is not for me to make any overall conclusion on Mother's behalf as to whether hers was a move too far east. She was just one of the fabulous 'cast' that has played out this incredible family history drama over seven generations, set in locations across five continents, and spanning over 300 years. There is no doubt the key section of the screenplay was having one generation move from

---

> *Jesse Esdale Gray* *(1885-1946)* > *Cecil Jesse Austen Gray (1908-1968)* > *Peter Nigel Austen Gray (1950-present)*

Leicestershire to Japan. Without that, it would have been a 'short feature' rather than a full-blown Cecil B. de Mille epic! And this would have been a novelette for a short train journey rather than a blockbuster to fill a two-week holiday! It's not really my fault that this family of mine wrote their own amazing stories; all I wanted to do was share them with you.

Now for a verdict regarding my titular question. I am going to leave it to you to answer it. There is no doubt that I have shared plenty of evidence surrounding the family's circular trip, from Newtown Linford to Yokohama and eventually back to Markfield. All my extended family's individual experiences feed into the general 'melting pot' of successes and failures, highs and lows, joys and sorrows, and triumphs and defeats that characterise this entire adventure. I have actually done the job of both barristers, by presenting the cases for and against the Far East; analysing if it was beneficial or detrimental to their 'journey'. You can decide–WAS IT ACTUALLY TOO FAR EAST?

| *William Gray* | > | *John Gray* | > | *James Gray* | > | *Jesse William Gray* | > |
| *(1720-1795)* | | *(1770-1830)* | | *(1813-1880)* | | *(1855-1894)* | |

APPENDIX I
BLUFF HOUSES WHERE THE EXTENDED GRAY FAMILY LIVED

> Jesse Esdale Gray
(1885-1946)
> Cecil Jesse Austen
Gray (1908-1968)
> Peter Nigel Austen Gray
(1950-present)

Where the Grays lived - in the Bluff residential area of Yokohama (direct parental line in red)

House No. / Year	24	46	57	60	61	64	78	87	89(+89B)	119	179
1869		(James Joseph in Japan but working on ships)									
1870											
1871											
1872											
1873											
1874		James Joseph									
1875		James Joseph Jesse William									
1876		James Joseph Jesse William									
1877		James Joseph Jesse William									
1878		James Joseph Jesse William							David Brearley		
1879		James Joseph Jesse William							David Brearley		
1880		James Joseph Jesse William			James Joseph Hannah (Vincent)				David Brearley William T Austen Leila Ada (Shapcott)		
1881					James Joseph Hannah David Brearley Charlotte Anne Jesse William				William T Austen Leila Ada (Shapcott) Albert WS		
1882					James Joseph Hannah David Brearley Charlotte Anne Jesse William Sarah Ann (Esdale)				William T Austen Leila Ada (Shapcott) Albert WS Winifred L		
1883		Jesse William Sarah Anne Walter			James Joseph Hannah David Brearley Charlotte Anne				William T Austen Leila Ada (Shapcott) Albert WS Winifred L Harold C		

William Gray (1720-1795) > *John Gray (1770-1830)* > *James Gray (1813-1880)* > *Jesse William Gray (1855-1894)* >

Where the Grays lived - in the Bluff residential area of Yokohama (direct parental line in red)

	24	46	57	60	61	64	78	87	89(+89B)	119	179
1884		Jesse William Sarah Anne Walter			James Joseph Hannah Vincent Keetley David Brearley Charlotte Anne				William T Austen Leila Ada (Shapcott) Albert WS Winifred L Harold C		
House No.											
1885	James Joseph Hannah Vincent Keetley				David Brearley Charlotte Anne					Jesse William Sarah Anne Walter Jesse Esdale	
1886	James Joseph Hannah Vincent Keetley			William T Austen Leila Ada (Shapcott) Albert, Winifred L, Harold	David Brearley Charlotte Anne					Jesse William Sarah Anne Walter Jesse Esdale	
1887				William T Austen Leila Ada (Shapcott) Albert, Winifred L, Harold	David Brearley Charlotte Anne		James Joseph Hannah Vincent Keetley			Jesse William Sarah Anne Walter Jesse Esdale	
1888				William T Austen Leila Ada (Shapcott) Albert, Winifred L, Harold, Mabel			James Joseph Hannah Vincent Keetley Harold Leicester			(Jesse William & family move to Kobe)	David Brearley Charlotte Anne
1889				William T Austen Leila Ada (Shapcott) Albert, Winifred L, Harold, Mabel			James Joseph Hannah Vincent Keetley Harold Leicester				David Brearley Charlotte Anne
1890				William T Austen Leila Ada (Shapcott) Albert, Winifred L, Harold, Mabel			(James Joseph & family moved to Canada)				David Brearley Charlotte Anne
1891				William T Austen Leila Ada (Shapcott) Albert, Winifred L, Harold, Mabel, Dorothy							David Brearley Charlotte Anne
1892				William T Austen Leila Ada (Shapcott) Albert, Winifred L, Harold, Mabel, Dorothy							David Brearley Charlotte Anne
1893				William T Austen Leila Ada (Shapcott) Albert, Winifred L, Harold, Mabel, Dorothy							(this family returned to England)
1894				William T Austen Leila Ada (Shapcott)							

> *Jesse Esdale Gray (1885-1946)*   >   *Cecil Jesse Austen Gray (1908-1968)*   >   *Peter Nigel Austen Gray (1950-present)*

Where the Grays lived - in the Bluff residential area of Yokohama *(direct parental line in red)*

	24	46	57	60	61	64	78	87	89(+89B)	119	179
1895				Albert, Winifred L., Harold, Mabel, Dorothy							Sarah Anne / Walter / Jesse Esdale / Amy, William
1896				William T Austen / Leila Ada (Shapcott) / Albert, Winifred L., Harold, Mabel, Dorothy							Sarah Anne / Walter / Jesse Esdale / Amy, William
1897				William T Austen / Leila Ada (Shapcott) / Albert, Winifred L., Harold, Mabel, Dorothy							Sarah Anne / Walter / Jesse Esdale / Amy, William
1898				William T Austen / Leila Ada (Shapcott) / Albert, Winifred L., Harold, Mabel, Dorothy							Sarah Anne / Walter / Jesse Esdale / Amy, William
1899				William T Austen / Leila Ada (Shapcott) / Albert, Winifred L., Harold, Mabel, Dorothy							Sarah Anne / Walter / Jesse Esdale / Amy, William
1900				William T Austen / Leila Ada (Shapcott) / Albert, Winifred L., Harold, Mabel, Dorothy							Sarah Anne / Walter / Jesse Esdale / Amy, William
House No.	24	46	57	60	61	64	78	87	89(+89B)	119	179
1901				William T Austen / Leila Ada (Shapcott) / Albert, Winifred L., Harold, Mabel, Dorothy							Sarah Anne / Walter / Jesse Esdale / Amy, William
1902				William T Austen / Leila Ada (Shapcott) / Albert, Winifred L., Harold, Mabel, Dorothy							Sarah Anne / Walter / Jesse Esdale / Amy / William
1903				William T Austen / Leila Ada (Shapcott)							Sarah Anne / Walter / Jesse Esdale / Amy

Where the Grays lived - in the Bluff residential area of Yokohama (direct parental line in red)

Year	24	46	57	60	61	64	78	87	89(+89B)	119	179
1904				Albert, Winifred L, Harold, Mabel, Dorothy							William
1905				William T Austen, Leila Ada (Shapcott), Albert, Winifred L, Harold, Mabel, Dorothy				Sarah Anne, Walter, Jesse Esdale, Amy, William			
1906	Jesse Esdale			William T Austen, Leila Ada (Shapcott), Albert, Winifred L, Harold, Mabel, Dorothy				Sarah Anne, Walter, Jesse Esdale, Amy, William			
1907	Jesse Esdale, Winifred Leila (Austen)			William T Austen, Leila Ada (Shapcott), Albert, Winifred L, Harold, Mabel, Dorothy				Sarah Anne, Walter, Amy, William			
1908			Sarah Anne, Walter, Amy, William			Jesse Esdale, Winifred Leila, Cecil Jesse Austen		Sarah Anne, Walter, Amy, William			
1909			Sarah Anne, Walter, Mary Isabel, Amy, William			Jesse Esdale, Winifred Leila, Cecil Jesse Austen					
1910			Sarah Anne, Walter, Mary Isabel, Amy, William			Jesse Esdale, Winifred Leila, Cecil Jesse Austen, Horace Austen E					
			Sarah Anne, Walter, Mary Isabel, Amy, William			Jesse Esdale, Winifred Leila, Cecil Jesse Austen, Horace Austen E					
House no	24	46	57	60	61	64	78	87	89(+89B)	119	179
1912						Jesse Esdale, Winifred Leila, Cecil Jesse Austen, Horace Austen E, Stella W		Sarah Anne, Amy Hawley, Herbert Hawley, William			

> *Jesse Esdale Gray (1885-1946)* > *Cecil Jesse Austen Gray (1908-1968)* > *Peter Nigel Austen Gray (1950-present)*

Where the Grays lived - in the Bluff residential area of Yokohama *(direct parental line in red)*

1913		Jesse Esdale Winifred Leila Cecil Jesse Austen Horace Austen E **Stella W**	Sarah Anne Amy Hawley Herbert Hawley William		
1914		Jesse Esdale Winifred Leila Cecil Jesse Austen Horace Austen E **Stella W**	Sarah Anne Amy Hawley Herbert Hawley William		
1915		Jesse Esdale Winifred Leila Cecil Jesse Austen Horace Austen E **Stella W**	Sarah Anne Amy Hawley Herbert Hawley William Helen (Forsyth)		
1916		Jesse Esdale Winifred Leila Cecil Jesse Austen Horace Austen E Stella W Norman William H	Sarah Anne Amy Hawley Herbert Hawley William Helen		
1917		Jesse Esdale Winifred Leila Cecil Jesse Austen Horace Austen E Stella W Norman William H (Jesse Esdale takes his family to Shanghai, China)	Sarah Anne Amy Hawley Herbert Hawley William Helen		

APPENDIX 2
REV. THOMAS AUSTEN'S 50TH ANNIVERSARY TRIBUTE (The Japan Gazette, 23rd June, 1923)

FIFTY YEARS' RESIDENCE IN YOKOHAMA
JUBILEE OF WELL-KNOWN SEAMEN'S CHAPLAIN

Today, the Rev. W.T.Austen, one of the oldest British residents of this city and the senior of the missionary residents of Japan, completes fifty years' residence in Yokohama, where for forty years he laboured in the service of seamen visiting the port, first as a lay worker and later as seamen's Chaplain.

Serving in the Royal Navy as a gunnery instructor, Mr Austen came to the China Station as a young man, and seeing the temptations to which visiting seamen were exposed in foreign ports, decided to obtain his discharge to take up work in Yokohama for the benefit of seamen away from home. Arriving here on June 23rd, 1873, from Tientsin, Mr Austen was introduced to Dr. St. George Elliot, a well-known temperance worker and one of the officers of the Union Church, to whom he appealed for advice and help in securing a meeting-place for a party of temperance workers organised on one of His Majesty's warships then in port. Dr Elliot brought the matter to the attention of the missionary workers resident in in Yokohama. and an application was made to the Colonel of the Royal Marine battalion, which succeeded the old Tenth Regiment in garrison duty in Yokohama and which was quartered in the valley behind where now stands the Gaiety Theatre, resulting in permission being given to hold meetings in the military theatre.

THE EARLY WORK: With the support of the missionary residents of the port, and the co-operation of men of the regiment and of the warships, the work took shape in the formation of the Yokohama Temperance Society; the Executive of which comprised the Rev. Henry Loomis, President; Mr. John Y. Henderson (then with the firm of Lane, Crawford & Co.) Hon. Secretary; and Professor John C. Ballagh, Hon. Treasurer. Mr Austen was authorised by this meeting to appeal to the community for funds to open a Temperance Hall, and it is interesting to note that the work was endorsed by Sir Harry Parker, the first British Minister, who not only headed the list with a subscription of fifty dollars but also enlisted the sympathy of his colleagues. The appeal resulted in the raising of about fourteen hundred dollars, thus enabling the renting of a building at 114 Creekside, which was opened as the Yokohama Temperance

Hall. Concerts were given, some of the best talent in the community assisting, while Sir Harry Parker showed his personal interest by frequently presiding at the gatherings. The work prospered to such a degree that the building at Creekside was found too small. The Committee thereupon decided to borrow money, and with it, purchased Lot 86 in the Settlement, whereon was erected a two-storied building, the adjoining premises being acquired as the work developed. Here a Good Templar Lodge was established and here also was seen the formation of a branch of the Y.M.C.A., the forerunner of a work which was destined later to branch out in other directions and show such wonderful extension in this country.

In 1879 Mr Austen went home to England on a visit, and returned the following year, bringing with him as wife one who for over thirty years proved such a valuable aid in the up-building of a work which was destined to accomplish much. On his return to Yokohama Mr Austen found that the work started with such promise of success a few years earlier had during his absence been allowed to lapse, the property having been handed over to the mortgagee. With the co-operation of his wife, Mr Austen then set to work to start anew. One of the buildings hitherto in use was rented and furnished and opened as a Seamen's Mission, this being the beginning of the work in Yokohama under the direct auspices of the Missions to Seamen of England, this Society sharing with the American Seaman's Friend Society in providing the stipend. The latter society, it may be noted, had appointed Mr. Austen as their chaplain in 1874.

> *Jesse Esdale Gray* > *Cecil Jesse Austen* > *Peter Nigel Austen Gray*
(1885-1946) *Gray (1908-1968)* *(1950-present)*

With a number of sailing ships, many of them tea clippers, visiting the port and remaining for some time, and with a number of ships of the British and American navies making long visits, there was plenty of scope for the work, and its growth was so rapid that in 1884 a lease was secured on the premises at 82 Division Street, adjoining the premises now occupied by Curnow & Co., extension being made later to provide accommodation for the large numbers who visited the Mission, the new wing of which was opened by Capt. Allington, R.N., in October 1887. To facilitate the work funds were raised, and a steam launch–the *Gleaner*–was built and was in constant use in bringing men ashore to the Mission and taking them back to their ships after services and meetings.

In those days the crews of the sailing ships were all white men, and therefore the opportunities for service were considerable. That they were availed of is evident from a hurried survey of the files of this journal during the last half century and from the annual reports of the work filed with the Societies in England and America under whose auspices the work was carried on. The annual report for 1900 contains the following, and is a sample of what was done for some years preceding and following this date:

Visits to merchant vessels, 1,420; services held at the Institute, 103; at the Naval Hospitals, 58; at the Consular prisons, 39; services afloat, 10; magic lantern entertainments, 27; attendance of seamen at services, 5,812; at Gospel meetings, 641; visits of seamen to Institute, 12,768.

In 1890 Mr Austen was ordained a priest in the Church of England, and the following year was licensed by Bishop Bickersteth as Seamen's Chaplain for the port.

That the work even in those days found support and co-operation from residents is evident from the records. Among those whose names are recorded as frequently presiding at the weekly concerts and other meetings are Sir Harry Parker, Mr. Russell Robertson and Mr. J.C. Hall (both former Consuls), Mr. Robison, Bishops Bickersteth, Poole, Williams and Hamilton, and the Rev. Dr. Syle, for some years Chaplain of Christ Church, while among the visiting naval officers in the early days we observe the names (to quote a few) of Admiral the Hon. Curzon Howe, Admiral the Hon. E. Freemantle, Vice-Admiral Sir Nowell Salmon, Vice-Admiral Sir Alexander Buller, Captain (later Admiral) Winnington-Ingram (a brother-in-law of Rev. Eustace M. Strong of Yokohama), Captain Castle, R.N., Captain Allington, R.N., and Rear-Admiral Chandler, U.S.N., while the contributions to the weekly programmes included many known to the older generation. Among those still resident in Yokohama who frequently assisted we find the names of Mrs. Mollison and Mr. G.G. Brady, always ready, as now, to help forward any entertainment for the benefit or the men of the Navy or the Merchant Marine.

Any reference at this time to the work carried on by Mr Austen would be incomplete without a tribute to the effective aid rendered for many years by his wife, who has often been described by officers and men of the Navy as "a second Agnes Weston", so thoroughly did she threw her energies into all that was done for the benefit of seamen. At her home on the Bluff, Mrs. Austen, with the aid of her daughters, was constantly seeking in a quiet way to bring a little sunshine into the lives of men alone and away from home influences, and the memory of happy times spent with the Austen home circle has sent many a young officer and seaman out with a determination to "play the man" in the battle of life.

Towards the close of the first decade of the present century, a change was coming over the shipping of the port, and with the replacement of white crews with Asiatics, the demand upon the work seemed less insistent; and in consequence, in June 1913 the work was closed, having been carried on continuously for a period of thirty-nine years.

At this time the Chaplaincy of the Seamen's Mission in Hong Kong was vacant, and Mr. Austen was asked by the Committee in London to take up the work for a year. So successful were his efforts that Mr. Austen was invited by the Committee in Hong Kong to continue, but as the doctors would not consent to Mrs. Austen residing in a climate so different to Japan, the idea was abandoned. On his return to Yokohama Mr Austen, having completed forty years' service, was retired by the Seamen's Mission and the American Seamen's Friend Society, in whose behalf he had worked so strenuously and so successfully.

It should be mentioned that while the Chaplain's stipend was provided by the two Societies named, the expense for carrying out the work had to be raised locally, and the fact that this was forthcoming from the shipping and other local firms is sufficient evidence that the work was appreciated as contributing to the welfare of those for whom it was established.

During his long residence in Yokohama Mr Austen has been an interested witness of Japan's development and of the growth of Yokohama from a fishing village to the leading port of the Empire, with all that made for the religious life of the community in which he has been forever keenly interested.

Of Mr Austen's family, one daughter is in Shanghai (*Winifred*) and another in England (*Dorothy*), one son is New York (*Albert*) and the other in Australia (*Harold*), only one daughter, Miss Mabel, being in the home to share in this anniversary. From members of the family and many old friends in Japan have come good wishes on the occasion of this jubilee celebration, and no doubt these will be shared by a very large circle to whom Yokohama is now but a memory.

APPENDIX 3
MY MOTHER'S FULL DIARY FOR 1942

To set this year in context, my mother was "captured" by the Japanese when their Imperial Army seized Hong Kong in December 1941; she was working for the Commodore at the time. The diary starts when Mother is still at the Naval Hospital in Hong Kong being forced to carry out nursing duties, despite not being a trained nurse.

JANUARY 1942

Jan 1st   *So unused to late nights that I felt quite tired after seeing the New Year in. The terrific rush of casualties having eased we were able to have organised times of duty. Had the afternoon off and was glad of the rest.*

Jan 2nd   *My 'on day' duty from 8:30 to 11 and 2 till 6:30pm. The day passed as usual. A number of naval patients were brought from the Queen Mary Hospital, including Boldero, Selby and Dines*

Jan 3rd   *Worked till 1 pm and spent the afternoon on the lawn in the*

William Gray   >   John Gray   >   James Gray   >   Jesse William Gray   >
(1720-1795)   (1770-1830)   (1813-1880)   (1855-1894)

sunshine. Rollins, Tomlin, Wexie and I play Mah-jong. Miss Rollins was the winner and I was the big loser. Jean and Christine went into the Doctors House to play bridge after dinner

Jan 4th   *Long day duty, I washed my hair during my off- duty time*

Jan 5th   *Short day duty. Did a lot of washing after lunch, then sat in the sun. After tea the same four played mah-jong again and I was the winner*

Jan 6th   *Long day duty. Made the calendar on the front of this book during my short off-duty spell and brought same up-to-date. Mr Longyear & his two assistants have put up curtains in the mess and it looks quite homely now. The big dining table was also brought up for us from the Sisters' mess so we have more room for feeding. The usual four played Mah-jong and Jean and Christine went next door to play bridge. I lost at Mah-jong.*

Jan 7th   *worked till 1pm had a sleep after lunch, then after tea Wexie and I had a good walk up and down the lawn until we were tingling all over with warmth. Played Mah-jong and I won. It was a dreadfully cold night and I could not sleep for ages I was so frozen*

Jan 8th   *Long day duty did a lot of washing during my short off period. We played rummy for a short while after our evening meal.*

Jan 9th   *Miss Franklin asked me to go into Ward 6 to work instead of Miss G. because she had been upset by one of the stewards. I was so fed up because all our really bad cases are in ward 6 and I am scared to touch them. It is so depressing too and gets me down rather. Half day spent in the sunshine*

Jan 10th   Long day duty. Wrote a few lines between 11.30 & 12.30 to JJ (my father) as Gunn was hoping to go and see our people at Kowloon. Played Mah-jong in the evening

Jan 11th   Longish day duty. Having had hardly any sleep last night I tried to sleep this afternoon but there was far too much noise going on so I sat out in the sun until it was time to go on duty again

Jan 12th   Dr. Gunn tried to go to Kowloon but only got as far as the Peninsula Hotel. Half day, big wash day after lunch, spent the rest of the afternoon in the sun. Early to bed but hardly slept at all as I had such a frantic pain

Jan 13th   Susie arrived and I felt rotten so stayed in bed all day.

Jan 14th   Stayed in bed as I was still feeling awful.

Jan 15th   Got up and started work, fortunately it was my half day and so I was able to rest in the afternoon

Jan 16th   A cold which started yesterday came to a head today and so I was not feeling so good. Long day duty worse luck. How I miss and long for my darling JJ. I wonder how he is getting on. Yesterday Miss Franklin received a chit from Yvonne saying that she had been interned very soon after leaving the hospital. All her things had been looted.

Jan 17th   Long morning and evening duty otherwise the day passed as

---

usual. I had a big wash day after lunch.

Jan 18th   Most eventful day when we had to leave the R.N.H. and go to St
Albert's Convent on Stubbs Road

Jan 19th   Tried to settle down and find our way around our new premises

Jan 20th   I fainted and spent the day in bed

Jan 21st   We were told we could send a card home to England. I got up but
felt awfully dizzy, filled in my card to Mummie, poor darling I do
hope she receives it as quickly as possible as I am sure she will be
most frantically worried. Went on duty in the afternoon, felt very
weak but much better. Good concert at 7p.m.

Jan 22nd   Worked in the morning did some washing after lunch and went
for a stroll in the evening. Very little sleep during the night

Jan 23rd   Usual day

Jan 24th

Jan 25th   Went to church in the morning

Jan 26th   Christine Whyatt went to Stanley

(27th.28th, 29th, 30th and 31st–No entry)

FEBRUARY 1942

Feb 1st   Usual day but in the evening we were told to pack our luggage
ready to send to Stanley early the next morning, as we were to
follow the day after

Feb 2nd   Sent off our luggage and bedding. Mrs Greenwood went dashing

---

> *Jesse Esdale Gray*
(1885-1946)
> *Cecil Jesse Austen*
Gray (1908-1968)
> *Peter Nigel Austen Gray*
(1950-present)

off in the ambulance to Stanley and we were very glad to have a peaceful night, unfortunately we could not sleep as our mattresses having been sent away we had to sleep on the wire bed

Feb 3rd　　*Jeff managed to find enough biscuit mattresses for Mrs Tomlin, Wexie and self and so we managed to have a better night. No word about Stanley.*

Feb 4th　　*Usual day*

Feb 5th　　*very sick patients were sent to Bowen Road Hospital*

Feb 6th　　*Usual day*

Feb 7th　　*" "*

Feb 8th　　*" "*

Feb 9th　　*" "*

Feb 10th　　*Fifty odd patients who were quite fit were discharged to North Pt. We were very sorry to see them go especially young Jeff who was such a great help to us in the mess*

Feb 11th　　*Usual day*

Feb 12th　　*Usual day*

Feb 13th　　*Friday 13th passed by uneventfully*

Feb 14th　　*We had a whist drive in the afternoon which was good fun and passed the time away quite pleasantly. One of the Naval stewards won 1st prize. The Stewards who were on duty and therefore unable to attend the Whist Drive made a "Huckers" pitch. The game is exactly the same as "Ludo" with a pitch made out on the ground and a large cardboard box for a dice box and large dice made from wood. Bagges and Bond asked Wexie and me to play with them in the evening & we did; it really was a very exciting game. Wexie and Bond won.*

Feb 15th   *Usual day. No news of going to Stanley. Very damp weather*

Feb 16th, 17th,18th, 19th–no entry

Feb 20th   *As the ground was drier, played the next two legs of the Huckers game, which Bagges and I won*

Feb 21st   *Another Whist drive in the afternoon, good fun*

Feb 22nd   *I got up in the morning but had a cold so went to bed in the middle of the morning as I was feeling very shivery*

Feb 23rd   *A very good concert in the evening*

Feb 24th   *In the evening we were told we should be moving the next day, not to Stanley as we had thought but over to Kowloon, most likely to St Theresa's Hospital*

Feb 25th   *The Japanese arrived with the news that everybody but the Indians were to leave the Hospital. Cleave and the Naval Sisters were sent to Bowen Road. All our Naval stewards were sent to North Point. Drs. Page, Gunn and Jackson, Mums, Wexie, Jean and I were to go with the Army and the VADs (The Voluntary Aid Detachment was a voluntary unit of civilians providing nursing care to military personnel during both World War 1 and WW2) to Kowloon. Of course, all the upset caused Susie to come and*

> *Jesse Esdale Gray (1885-1946)*   > *Cecil Jesse Austen Gray (1908-1968)*   > *Peter Nigel Austen Gray (1950-present)*

we were waiting around for so long in the grounds of St. Albert and then on the HK side of the harbour and longer still on the Kowloon side where we had to sort out all our luggage and then we were crowded into one lorry and driven to St. Theresa's. We had been 1p.m. hanging around and moving and we arrived at St. Theresa's at about 9:30pm. I was of course soaked through and so fagged out and in such pain that I was in tears. We slept on the floor, 11 in one room.

Feb 26th   *Everyone was put straight on duty–Mums was very sick and I asked if I might stay off the wards for one day because of Susie. Matron very grudgingly allowed me to stay off but I spent most of the day looking after Mrs, T. Got a bed for her & the rest of us slept on the floor again*

Feb 27th   *Went on duty in the hospital. Very well-built hospital. Quit a lot of work to do. All had beds to sleep on thank goodness. The mosquitoes were frightful.*

Feb 28th   *Still in the bungalow. Long day duty, from 08:30 till 5:30*

MARCH 1942

Mar 1st   *Short day duty–hours 8:30 till 1 and 6 till 8*

Mar 2nd   *Long day duty*

Mar 3rd   *Short day duty*

Mar 4th   *Long day and we moved to a larger house, which indeed was a lucky thing or we would all have been mad as our rooms had been far too crowded and 30 women sharing one bathroom is no joke. We are now 7 in our room and it is a room with plenty of windows so we should be alright for coolth in the summer*

Mar 5th *Days off started. Mrs. Richards from our floor had the first day, short day duty, Susie finished.*

Mar 6th *My day off. Did a lot of washing and had a bath in the afternoon.*

Mar 7th *Short day duty, Betty Hills off*

Mar 8th *Our luggage arrived from Stanley. Long day duty, after tea I sorted my clothes. Wexie day off. Mums very sick brought to the hospital and we had a frantic day of bedpans*

Mar 9th *Short day duty, Allison Black off. It was such a joy to have a change of clothing, Mums still very ill*

Mar 26th *My day off, did a lot of washing and scrubbing, washed my hair and packed all my odds and ends and moved out of my corner so that Jean could move in as I was going on night duty. Tried to sleep in the afternoon but could not. Had tea, moved into the night staff sleeping room then Wexie and I had a quick bath each and went on duty at 8 pm. During the day 4 VADs were taken to hospital, 2 of which had dysentery and I had them all on my floor. Consequently, I had a ghastly night. Thirty bedpans between the 2 dys. patients. Another patient was vomiting and had a high temperature so she was not allowed out of bed. Day staff forgot*

> *Jesse Esdale Gray*
(1885-1946)

> *Cecil Jesse Austen*
Gray (1908-1968)

> *Peter Nigel Austen Gray*
(1950-present)

to send a relief on by 7.30am so I had to go on till 8 am and was nearly dropping with tiredness. Then, having had our breakfast and taken over breakfast to the lazy people who were about to have a day off and could not drag themselves out of bed to go to the bungalow for theirs, we staggered across for roll-call only to find the corporal had not arrived and so there would be no roll-call. That is why I cannot understand why people want to stay in bed for breakfast when they have to get up immediately afterwards for the roll-call

Mar 27th   *Slept on and off during the day–had a most frightful headache when I got up and had an even more hectic night on duty with a total of 38 bedpans to deal with*

Mar 28th   *During the day 4 more VADs went into the hospital sick. Sister Morgan took over night duty from Sister Hills. I was very nearly left with the top floor alone but for Wexie saying it was impossible for me to do it. We had a total of 46 B.P.s*

Mar 29th   *Did not have nearly enough sleep during the day and awoke with a splitting headache and aching all over. Wexie was the same. We decided that we would get up for tea. Before tea Wexie had a jolly good cry because she was feeling so rotten and after tea, which consisted of plain rice and hot water, I also had a good cry. Fortunately, the B.P.s slackened slightly during the night so we did not have quite so much to do. Day staff played tennis*

William Gray		John Gray		James Gray		Jesse William Gray	
(1720-1795)	>	*(1770-1830)*	>	*(1813-1880)*	>	*(1855-1894)*	>

Mar 30th   *I slept a bit more but Wexie felt very rotten. She came on duty but felt too rotten to do anything, had a temperature of 100 and a very troublesome tummy. At 5.30 she went back to the house and went to bed and was brought to the hospital as a patient at about 10am on 31st Mar*

Mar 31st   *I had a much better sleep. Mrs Simpson came on duty to help me in Wexie's place but was only with me during the quietest parts of the night as Sister took her onto the 2nd Floor at 5:30 am when all the washings, temperatures and beds had to be done, so I had a lot to do. Major Officer was demoted and sent to Sham-po and Dr. Jackson was made Commanding Officer of the hospital. So, we now have a Military hospital run by 3 Naval Doctors entirely*

APRIL 1942

Apr 1st   *Got to sleep at 11am. Had to get up at 10 to 1 for an inspection by the Japanese Governor of Internment Camps who was due at 1:30 pm–having dressed ready we were told it would not be until 2:30 and when I first got up I had a frantic pain in my tummy and consequently could not sleep when I eventually got back to bed–the result being a total of 3.5 hours sleep. Mrs Mills and Dr Jackson admitted to hospital on day floor. At 8:20 Betty M. staged a faint in the bathroom and was sick afterwards–good beginning to my night's work. Dr Page came up and chatted for a short while* *and offered to loan me $10 so that I could buy some sugar to share between Mums and Wexie and self–our finances having been nil for so long I must say I felt extremely thankful and grateful for the offer. Slightly easier night.*

Apr 2nd   *We ordered 5 lbs. of sugar, a tin of cocoa and a tin of jam after Parade. I do hope they will arrive quickly as we are feeling so dreadfully weak from lack of sugar. This rice and water diet is certainly awful when you have to work so hard. It was such a glorious day it seemed a pity to go to sleep but I had 4.5 hours and then got up for a bath and tea. Did some scrubbing after breakfast and some washing in my bath. Had an operation case during the night, apart from which everything was as usual, Mrs Rudolf left hospital*

Apr 3rd   *Had about 5 hours sleep and then got up about 4:30 in time for a bath before tea. Betty Longbottom left hospital. Generally, a quieter night with fewer bedpans. The only troublesome patient was Betty Mills suffering from illusions and I had a most unpleasant 10 minutes with her. Good Friday.*

Apr 4th   *Hardly had any sleep during the day, got up at 4:30 for a bath and tea. Went on duty at 8 pm and received profound apologies from Betty who was much better and slept all night thank goodness. Everyone was greatly improved but my hopes of getting a sleep were spoiled because the mosquitoes were so bad.*

Apr 5th	*Easter Sunday which I could hardly believe. I slept better and had the quietest night on duty since I started nights and managed to rest quite a bit.*
Apr 6th	*Had a fair day and a peaceful night. Page loaned me Yen 10*
Apr 7th	*Had another fair day and peaceful night, finished my sponge bag which I started a couple of nights before.*
Apr 8th	*Slept fairly well and my last night duty night passed by peacefully. Jean came out of hospital.*
Apr 9th	*Moved Wexie's and my belongings to our new quarters which was pretty hot work as everything had to come downstairs from the Night staff sleeping room. Then I made up our beds and arranged all our goods and it was 12 o'clock. After lunch I tried to have a sleep but could not as people kept coming in and out of the room, being the main entrance to the house. Wexie came out of hospital about 3 pm. Felt dreadfully tired and went to bed early but in our room it was impossible to sleep until 10:30 or 11 because of disturbances. People coming in and out and the Burnie crowd having their nightly feast and laughing and screaming in the next room*
Apr 10th	*My day off. Did lots of heavy washing and ironing, washed my hair. We had a Whist Drive in the afternoon, quite pleasant. Did some more ironing and sewing after tea. A terrific rumpus about screens, Wexie came out of hospital*

Apr 11th   *Started work on the 1st Floor of the hospital–all new patients to me having been on the 3rd for 6 weeks. Long day duty. I asked Matron if we might have the red screen from the ward as we were going to be left with one only to screen us from the eyes of all and sundry walking through the room but of course because we are just Naval people and not Brigadiers' and Colonels' wives we cannot have it. All we want is a screen frame as we have a cover and she has a frame which she hangs her washing on–but still one cannot expect anything else from the Army*

Apr 12th   *Short day duty. Had a church service in the morning. Rested and had a bath in the afternoon and made covers for my locker and cushion in the evening and so to bed. Mums taken to hospital pm. Mrs Rudolf very kindly took pity on us and said we might have a screen frame from the laundry if Sgt, Roberts fixes some lines for hanging clothes.*

Apr 13th   *Long day duty, did a lot of washing during my off time in the morning. Betty Long's day off before going on night duty. Saw Mums and the other VAD patients before retiring*

Apr 14th   *Short day duty. Rested in the afternoon having scrubbed and cleaned frantically at the hospital all morning. We got our screen from the laundry and returned the Ellis' to them. Visited Mums after tea.*

Apr 15th   *My day off. Did some washing in the morning, rested after lunch*

| *William Gray* | | *John Gray* | | *James Gray* | | *Jesse William Gray* | |
| *(1720-1795)* | > | *(1770-1830)* | > | *(1813-1880)* | > | *(1855-1894)* | > |

and saw Mums after tea. Four R.A.F. officers amongst whom were Sullivan the C.O., Bennett and Gray, were brought in by the Japanese but locked in a room and nobody was allowed to see them or speak to them. Jean started duty 3rd Floor

Apr 16th   *Long day duty–Sgt. Roberts and Morgan fixed up a very snappy light for me in my corner so that I can read in bed, I was very thrilled with the result. Saw Mums morning during my off time and after 8 pm when I came off duty. Wexie started duty but on the dining room staff while Mrs. Burnie has a week's leave. Alison Black's 21st birthday–she did not do at all badly in the way of presents and a cake was made for her & decorated with flowers by the Matron. Most people gave what little things they could find amongst their few possessions*

Apr 17th   *Short day duty–rested in the afternoon and had a bath after which I watched a bridge lesson until tea time. Saw Mums afterwards. A terribly sick patient was brought from Argyle Street.*

Apr 18th   *Long day–rather a long afternoon with the new patient who is very likely to die. The Army officers arrived at Argyle Street Camp from Sham-shui-Po in the afternoon and then, to our great joy, the Navy arrived in the evening but we did not see them at all as it was dark before we heard they had arrived.*

Apr 19th   *Whoopee! I saw J.J. before breakfast which was a wonderful start to the day. Saw him also when I went across to the house during the morning and after lunch. Rested in the afternoon, Saw him in the evening. Very sick patient died and we nurses had to form a guard of honour for the funeral.*

Apr 20th   *Mummie's Birthday. Saw J.J. before breakfast. Long day duty. I saw him while I was off in the morning also from the verandah in the afternoon and evening. Mrs Tebbutt gave me a dress length. Saw Mums in the evening after duty at 8pm*

Apr 21st   *My day off. Saw quite a lot of J.J. It really is most dreadfully tantalising being able to see him & not be able to rush over and hug him and kiss him as I should so love to do–but still it is grand seeing him and knowing that he looks so fit and well. Did some washing and sewing, rested in the afternoon. Saw Mrs Tomlin in the evening * Mrs Macleod*

Apr 22nd   *Long day duty. Did not see J.J. before breakfast but after I came off in the morning. Missed him at lunchtime but saw him at 4:30pm and 6:15pm * Mrs Simpson*

Apr 23rd   *Short day duty. Saw quite a lot of J.J., Mums came out of hospital.*

Apr 24th   *Long day duty. 4 very sick patients were brought in from Argyle St. Camp hospital one of which came to our floor–he had a wee note for me also Mrs. Newnham. Very busy time, saw little of J.J.*

Apr 25th   *Leo Ellis' birthday–we had a piece of cake and a lovely cup of coffee with milk and sugar in it. Saw quite a lot of my darling as it was my half day*

Apr 26th   *Long day duty. Morning uneventful but the afternoon was hectic with one mental patient and McGill the new patient delirious. I spent most of the time with McGill–the Matron who has a wounded hand asked me to give him an injection and showed me how to do it.–I was afraid I might make a mess of it but managed very well and she told me I had, so I was quite pleased with myself. She knew that it was too late to save his life but it was all we could do for him & then I stayed with him for the rest of the afternoon. Matron relieved me whilst I dished out the other patients' teas and then Cpl. Elliott took over whilst I had my tea and then I took over again. He eventually died at 7:30 and I helped to wash and dress and lay him out. So, after that & dealing with the mental patient who wanted to commit suicide all afternoon, I felt absolutely done in. Found notes in a pocket of McGill's for Betty Long & Muriel McCaw also Y10 for Muriel. I wish J.J. could send me some money.*

Apr 27th   *Short day duty, did a spot of washing after forming a guard for McGill's funeral then rested a wee while & had a bath and spent the evening looking at J.J. till 7:30 then went to see Mrs Gubbey & Rosie in hospital. Saw Gorman for a few minutes–he came in last Friday with pneumonia*

Apr 28th   *Long day–Alison started night duty so I had the whole floor to myself–Moore the mental patient was extremely trying and nearly drove me mad but still we got through all right. Only saw J.J. in the morning whilst ironing and once walking round from the verandah as I was so busy.*

Apr 29th   *My day off–washed my hair, brought this diary up to date and did some sewing. Saw a lot of J.J.*

Apr 30th   *Long day–Moore was terribly ill, in fact dying all afternoon and evening and we had to sit with him all the time as he was trying to get out of bed. He eventually died at 10.10pm * Mrs Richardson*

MAY 1942

May 1st   *Lt. McGee's 21st birthday–he was made a small cake–a hot roll with butter and marmalade, and also a boiled egg that was produced by one of our 13 chickens that were bought a week ago. Moore was buried and we had to form a guard again. My half day–I did a spot of washing in the afternoon and saw a quite a lot of my darling. Rations came in at last including bread, also in the evening our stuff came from the Comprador. Matron says I may start my weeks' leave on Monday if no V.A.D.s go sick before then. Saw my darling.*

May 2nd   *Long day duty, not so busy without Moore to look after. Saw J.J. quite often*

May 3rd   *Half-day, did some ironing and sewing in the afternoon and evening * Anne Muir*

May 4th	*Started my week's leave–Whoopee. Did some sewing, rested in the afternoon. Saw J.J. in the evening. Went visiting patients in hospital. Margie's birthday (her sister Marjorie, in America)*
May 5th	*Did some washing & ironing, also sewing and ironing. Rested after lunch*
May 6th	*Betty Tebbutt started cutting out my white dress of the material she very kindly gave me. Did some sewing and saw plenty of my darling one.*
May 7th	*More sewing, washing and ironing as per usual*
May 8th	*" "*
May 9th	*Mrs. McLeod went to hospital as she was very worn out and needs a good rest. Today is the second anniversary of my arrival in Hong Kong to be married*
May 10th	*My last day on holiday. The week has gone far too quickly and my dress is not yet finished*
May 11th	*Started work again on the 1st Floor–17 new patients in so I felt quite a stranger amongst them. Had a short day duty*
May 12th	*Found out that my poor darling has an abscess in his ear, and I know what agony he suffers. I love him so dearly and hate to think of him suffering and me not being able to comfort him. I wish they would send him to the hospital. Long day duty, saw Ovans after 8 pm, don't much like him. Mrs Richards had an operation*
May 13th	*Poor darling J.J. has both ears bad now. Oh, how I wish they*

---

would let him come over here. Short day duty

May 14th   *Long day duty. Saw J.J. in the morning but not in the evening. Poor darling, I feel for him so much, I know how he must be suffering.*

May 15th   *J.J. spent the day in bed so I did not see him. I did miss the sight of his darling face, I love him so. Short day duty*

May 16th   *Did not see my darling before breakfast but, to my joy, he appeared at 10:15 am. Long day duty, saw him from the verandah*

May 17th   *My day off–washed my hair and clothes, towels, pillow cases etc. Saw my darling one. Mums read my cup and said the gates will be opening on July 28th & my darling Jimmy James will be outside waiting for me. Mrs Gubbay died*

May 18th   *Long day duty, very busy. We have 22 patients, some of whom are very ill indeed. Saw my darling J.J. Wexie started on the 1st Floor so as to get to know the patients before starting night duty. Mum*

May 19th   *Busy morning, half day off, it was cold so had a hot bath and slept. Saw lots of my precious. Wexie started night duty. Canteen arrived but bread stopped*

May 20th   *Long day duty. Saw my darling one, I wonder how much longer we will have to endure this strain when we long for each other so much. Very busy afternoon and evening*

May 21st   *My day off, Had a sore throat and cough just before tea. I lost my voice after tea. Matron told me to get the inhaler from the hospital and inhale before retiring and stay in bed the next day, which I did*

May 22nd   *In bed all day, Saw J.J. at 10:15 and pointed to throat,*

May 23rd   *Stayed in bed until 4pm, got up for tea, saw my darling after tea.*

May 24th   *I was given a day's convalescence–lovely weather*

May 25th   *Started work on the 2nd floor–very nice and peaceful after the hectic work on the 1st Floor. Long day duty*

May 26th   *Short day duty. Milk was brought in for the patients. Bread came in.*

May 27th   *Long day. Everybody received a present from the Japs consisting of a towel, toilet paper, a toothbrush, some foul-smelling tooth powder and 3 cards for writing home. We were allowed to write a letter or card home which had to be printed on one side of the paper only. No bread or rations came in so we were down to starvation diet again. I received 100 yen from my darling J.J., what a thrill it was to see the writing of his signature too, sweet thing. I shall now be able to settle my debts and buy some more necessaries.*

May 28th   *My day off–washed my hair, saw J.J., helped Jean with her diary and the morning was almost over*

May 29th   *Short day, was on alone all afternoon and evening which was very hectic as we have many more operations now*

May 30th   *Long day–nothing unusual*

May 31st   *Short day–Barbara Hills birthday–news came then that V.A.D.s*

> *Jesse Esdale Gray*
>   *(1885-1946)*

> *Cecil Jesse Austen*
>   *Gray (1908-1968)*

> *Peter Nigel Austen Gray*
>   *(1950-present)*

with relations at Stanley who wanted to go and join them could do so

JUNE 1942

Jun 1st   *Short day duty–we were given permission to open the windows facing the Camp in the Mess. There was a terrific hullabaloo with the sentries who came around in the evening as they had not been told about it.*

Jun 2nd   *Still a certain amount of trouble re windows. Long day duty*

Jun 3rd   *Short day duty–2 patients came in, one died and the other was Peggy Scotcher's father*

Jun 4th   *Long day duty. 16 patients left hospital including Ovans. 14 new ones arrived. J.J.s ears are bad again*

Jun 5th   *My day off–did odd jobs of sewing. Saw plenty of J.J. Poor darling seems to be suffering with his ears. More canteen arrived thank goodness. Expected excitement did not occur*

Jun 6th   *Long day duty–same as ever*

Jun 7th   *Short day*

Jun 8th   *Long day duty–no rations in, consequently meals absolutely punk*

Jun 9th   *My day off–Betty Mills 1st wedding anniversary. Started new meal hours–which meant we had to get up earlier as breakfast is now 7:30 instead of 8 am*

Jun 10th   *Started working on the 1st Floor again (Bed Pan Alley as we call it), not so nice. Long day duty, my darling J.J. came out at 7.25 thanks to Jock calling him*

Jun 11th	*Short day duty, Jock called J.J. again at 7.25 am. Saw plenty of him during the evening*
Jun 12th	*Long day duty–pretty hectic all day with B.P.s*
Jun 13th	*Susie arrived as soon as I got up. Felt pretty lousy. Sister Buckle very kindly sent me off at 12:20 instead of 1 pm. As I was looking wretched. Rested a lot*
Jun 14th	*Got off at 9,30. Started night duty at 8 pm*
Jun 15th	*Fairly hectic night, I was very tired*
Jun 16th	*Fairly hectic night, again I was very tired. It is grand being able to sit on my bed in the night duty sleeping quarters and see my darling. Very little sleep during the day, 11 new patients in*
Jun 17th	*Sleep was impossible as all the Stanley people left and volunteer replacements arrived. Amongst the new arrivals were 5 trained sisters making us 4 short on the nursing staff and more people to give orders which I feel is going to be a very bad thing. I was alone on Bed Pan Alley the whole night which kept me very busy.*
Jun 18th	*Having only had ¾ of an hours' sleep yesterday, I managed to sleep from 10 until 4 without waking–what a day to spend one's wedding anniversary–but still it was grand being able to see each other. Mums put flowers on the table for me by way of a celebration. Mrs. Crabbe joined me on night duty and we had a*

> *Jesse Esdale Gray*   > *Cecil Jesse Austen*   > *Peter Nigel Austen Gray*
>   *(1885-1946)*   *Gray (1908-1968)*   *(1950-present)*

reasonable night.

Jun 19th   *Did not sleep so well–6 new patients in and we broke all records,*
                having 126 BPs in 11;5 hours. It really was a ghastly night and we
                were thoroughly exhausted at the end of it

Jun 20th   *Fairly good sleep. We had a pretty hectic night but not at as bad*
                as last night

Jun 21st   *Fairly good sleep, not too hectic during the night*

Jun 22nd   *Slept badly as the wind was too strong and blinds flapped*
                terrifically. Not a bad night, one patient rather troublesome,
                being mentally deficient

Jun 23rd   *Slightly better sleep–fair night*

Jun 24th   *" "*

Jun 25th   *Wexie's 15th wedding anniversary–Ellis's baked her a currant*
                loaf which was very nice

Jun 26th   *Rather a bad night with mental patient*

Jun 27th   *Had a better sleep–some new patients have come in & I hope I*
                shall not have too bad a night, being my last–Had a very bad
                night as I was greeted with a death immediately I got on duty.
                It was one of the new patients and another one was very ill with
                diphtheria and the mental patient was worse. Also, to crown
                everything I had awful pains

Jun 28th   *Slept most of the morning and had some lunch at about 2:30–*
                moved my mattress and bedding after tea and thoroughly enjoyed

---

William Gray   >   *John Gray*   >   *James Gray*   >   *Jesse William Gray*   >
(1720-1795)   *(1770-1830)*   *(1813-1880)*   *(1855-1894)*

my evening knowing that I had not to go on duty. Slept like a top

Jun 29th   *Had a day off,–Westwood, the mental patient, died and one patient came in with typhoid and died during the night*

Jun 30th   *Went back to duty on Bed Pan Alley again, not so much to do though. W.O. Mitchell arrived in hospital*

JULY 1942

Jul 1st   *Long day duty–Busy afternoon as five new patients came in, three were diphtheria cases and were transferred to the top floor so as to keep all diphs. together*

Jul 2nd   *Damp weather caused me to suffer very badly with rheumatics. Half day thank goodness*

Jul 3rd   *Long day duty–Bosco's birthday, was sorry I could not wish him many happy returns. Big inspection by Japanese "Big Noises" and Swiss representatives of the Red Cross. Things must have been going against them outside because they were particularly B-minded. The affair finished up by us having to bow by way of showing our respect and we are going to be starved for 10 days*

Jul 4th   *Sisters and nurses are to be trained to parade properly. Amusing joke by Sister Morgan re dressing*

Jul 5th   *Mitchell was brought down to our floor–he is dreadful ill with dysentery, jaundice and a very infectious skin disease. I doubt very much if he will live through the day–Long day duty, two new patients in, one Cripps very ill*

Jul 6th   *Short day duty–Canteen arrived thank goodness. Mitchell slightly improved, but I don't think he will live. Funeral for two diphtheria patients, I had to stay on the ward as Mitchell and Cripps could not be left.*

Jul 7th   *Long day duty–We had a dreadful afternoon with Mitchell and Cripps who were both incontinent the whole time. At 8pm we had a diversion by way of a "Quiz and Spelling Bee" which was good fun and just what I needed to make me forget BPs etc. for a while. I did very well and answered most of mine correctly*

Jul 8th   *My day off, for which I was truly thankful as both Mitchell and Cripps died. Went to see Muriel in the evening. 6 more patients came to our floor*

Jul 9th   *My darling J. J's birthday–he got his fags alright I am pleased to say. It looks as though I am in for a bad afternoon on the wards… Yes I was very busy. We had a cup of coffee in the morning and a spot of lunch left over with one Oxo between the three of us to give it flavour by way of celebrating*

Jul 10th   *Half day,–was very worn out with rheumatics and hard work, lugging heavy screens around the ward every two minutes of the day. Had a very sleepless night with a fever feeling hot and cold and aching badly*

Jul 11th   *Got up but felt like death with a raging headache & aches all over*

---

and went over to breakfast but just could not make it and somebody told Matron who came to see me and took my temperature and pulse. After she had seen Dr, Gunn she came back and told me I was to go into hospital and the stretcher would be sent for me in 15 minutes. Well, knowing that J.J, would be expecting to see me at that time I decided to get over before the stretcher so as not to scare him too much. Poor darling, he looked so staggered as it was and here I am with acute rheumatism and have to lie still & flat all the time or I might get a weak heart. My "sweet adorable Beast" sent me more money. Oh my darling one, if only I could thank you properly

Jul 12th	*Having been dosed with Sodii Sal 2 hourly I felt horribly sick and dizzy*
Jul 13th	*The medicine has been cut down to 4-hourly, still feel wretched. 8 more diphtheria cases came in, and 2 previous diphs died during the night*
Jul 14th	*Muriel and I are now surrounded by diph cases and there is talk we will have to be moved to the house to be nursed which will be dreadful as we won't be able to see Henry and J.J.*
Jul 15th	*Still feeling wretched*
Jul 16th	*Still feeling wretched*
Jul 17th	*We were shifted down to the 2nd Floor which we don't like so much as the screen has to be in front of the window. I am next to*

it though so can peep round the corner. My poor darling did not know where I had got to and it was heartrending to watch him walking up and down looking so depressed.

Jul 18th   *Thank goodness J.J. has found me and so he looks happier*

Jul 19th   *Feeling a wee bit better*

Jul 20th   *Allowed to sit up for a short time & the most important thing, allowed to use the commode*

Jul 21st   *Wexie's Birthday–Mums and I gave her 3 pkts of cigarettes, Miss Ellis made her a small cake*

Jul 22nd   *Gradually improving, was able to get up to wash myself and potter around the room*

Jul 23rd   *Same sort of day*

Jul 24th   *I went to the staff bathroom and had a bath in one bucket of hot water which was a terrific event. 15 new patients came in–9 dysentry, 1 septic sores and 5 diphtherias; one diph and one dysentery died during the night*

Jul 25th   *Dr Gunn tested my heart and seemed quite satisfied with it and says I may leave hospital tomorrow morning. Mrs T. is coming at 4 o'clock to read Muriel's and my tea cups*

Jul 26th   *Came out of hospital at 4:30 pm, had tea at the house, saw J.J. before parade*

Jul 27th   *I managed to go on parade but was feeling very week and was excused drill. Had an excellent show in the evening consisting of*

4 sketches which were very well done indeed

Jul 28th   *Nothing startling occurred–I washed my hair and had a pulse*
               rate of 108 after doing it which was not so good

Jul 29th   *Rested a lot, saw J.J.*

Jul 30th   *ditto, did some sewing*

Jul 31st   *Rested a lot, saw J.J.*

AUGUST 1942

Aug 1st   *Did sewing and rested. Mums and I went to see Muriel in the*
               afternoon to tell her fortune

Aug 2nd   *Spent quiet day*

Aug 3rd   *Started nursing again. Felt very weak, my pulse is 106 and I really*
               should not be working. Heard the news that we are all to be sent
               to Stanley (the Civilian Internment Camp at Hong Kong) on
               Monday 10th August. Long day shift, Morgan tried to commit
               suicide

Aug 4th   *Usual working day, Half day, Morgan as a patient a definite strain*

Aug 5th   *Long day*

Aug 6th   *A buzz that we might be leaving for Stanley within 48 hrs so I*
               spent the afternoon packing

Aug 7th   *J.J. the pet sent me Y30 but unfortunately the canteen did not*
               come

Aug 8th   *Saw as much as possible of my darling when I was off duty*

Aug 9th   *Long day which was my last day of duty; finished nursing for good*
              I hope at 8pm when we were told we would not be allowed to take
              beds or even mattresses with us only clothes

Aug 10th   *The awful day for parting from my precious has arrived again*
              and how I hated waving goodbye but it is better for me at Stanley
              and I don't think it will be for too long. The trip out to Stanley was
              not bad and the arrangements for our arrival and billeting were
              extremely well done. Had a few callers & was grand seeing new &
              familiar faces. Tommy, Wexie and I together in one room, grand

Aug 11th   *Busy settling in. Went to tea with Sheila down in the slums*

Aug 12th   *More settling in. Went for a walk with Sheila around Stanley after*
              tea

Aug 13th   *Getting more homelike after having a few odd jobs done. Having*
              discovered a worm, I went to the doctor & got a prescription and
              set to de-worming. Did a spot of typing for Mr. Webb, the Block
              Representative, who looks after me and is snowed under with lists
              he has to complete

Aug 14th   *Stayed in after all my dosing. Did some more typing. Went down*
              to the slums to watch a very amusing soft ball match with the men
              dressed up as girls

Aug 15th   *Ray Mabb and I went to tea with John Stenker and he stuffed us*
              up with waffles & sandwiches & coffee, it really was a wonderful
              feed and then Tommy, Wexie and I went to see Mrs. Dawes and

---

she also fed us up with cocoa & jam tart and currant pasties

Aug 16th   *Bunty Green had Wexie and I down for cocoa & bread & jam and we met her Mother and Father. Went to church in the morning.*

Aug 17th   *Made more improvements to our home. Got camp beds for Tommy and me*

Aug 18th   *A marvellous Tea Party was given by the Women of Stanley as a welcome to all the nurses and sisters who arrived on the 10th August. There were turns from a concert which had taken place before we arrived which were excellent*

Aug 19th   *Had to stay indoors all day as we had a typhoon which blew all the rain into our window which was most trying. I did a lot of typing*

Aug 20th   *Rained most of the day. Did sewing and went for a walk after our evening meal.*

Aug 21st   *Pottered around. Yvonne and Christine came to see me in the morning. Weighed ourselves–my weight 117 lbs. Went walking in the evening*

Aug 22nd   *Went swimming in the afternoon, it was grand. Went to a Minstrel Concert in the evening which was jolly good*

Aug 23rd   *Swam in the morning and then went to church. Had Mrs. Dawes and Mrs. Greenwood to tea. Went for a walk in the evening*

Aug 24th   *Spent a quiet day as Susie arrived. Did some typing and checking cigarette money. Had 2 shares in the canteen*

Aug 25th   My name was officially sent in as Secretary for Block 10. Did some work, had a good rest in the afternoon. Went out for a spot of air in the evening.

Aug 26th   Did plenty of work and did not travel far from home because of Susie but went to see Sheila

Aug 27th   Went to see Mrs. Dawes who gave me a beautiful pair of Gordons shoes. Tommy and Wexie went swimming with Mrs. Dawes and Smalley. I could not go of course so I rested

Aug 28th   Did some work and sewing, Watched a soft ball match in the evening.

Aug 29th   Concert in the evening which was very good

Aug 30th   Went to church, Cyril Brown preaching, very good indeed. Was frightfully windy again so we did not bathe as we had intended

Aug 31st   Very busy arranging the Welfare draw, also did a lot of machining

SEPTEMBER 1942

Sept 1st   Did a lot of work and went to a piano concert in the evening

Sept 2nd   Carried out the Welfare draw and filled in all the Welfare chits

Sept 3rd   Cholera inoculations

Sept 4th   My birthday started off wonderfully with grapefruit for breakfast, also toast with marge and jam on it. Tommy gave me a cute green buckle and Wexie gave me 2 diamante slips and Webb flowers, a hankie and toilet soap. We received $5 from the Pope. Had Sheila *to tea and Tommy told our cups. Some of the musicians in the Block played "A Happy Birthday to you Mrs Gray" and other tunes outside my window which was very pleasant indeed. We played the "Spooks" game which was really uncanny;*

Sept 5th   *An excellent "Pierrot" concert in the evening which we thoroughly enjoyed. Had a lovely bath in the afternoon. List of money sent from Argyle Street; none for me, very worried*

Sept 6th   *Went to church in morning and when I got back to the Mess received a message to go to "The House on the Hill" and collect some money. Whoopee so my darling had not forgotten me after all. T, Wexie and I went out to tea and so much to eat we could hardly eat our 5 o'clock meal*

Sept 7th   *Went to the beach for a bathe which was grand. Tommy, Wexie and I went to see Mrs. G and Mrs. Dawes. It was Mrs D's Birthday and we had a pasty and a piece of cake each. Walked back through the cemetery.*

Sept 8th   *Spent all afternoon on the beach, Tommy, Wexie and I, it was grand*

Sept 9th   *Had Mrs. Dawes and Godfrey to tea, played "Spooks"*

Sept 10th *Went swimming in the afternoon, took our tea with us, it was lovely*

Sept 11th *Beryl Farrar came to tea–very busy evening, collecting names of people who wanted to write cards to the Camps etc.*

Sept 12th	*Spent all afternoon on the beach again, with tea and sandwiches. Concert of "Request Items" which was quite good*
Sept 13th	*Had a morning bathe which was grand. Slept a wee while and did a spot of issuing of cards–wrote mine to my darling J.J. and went for a stroll in the evening.*
Sept 14th	*Spent a quiet day and worked in the office. Went to listen to Elizabeth Brown and Heath playing on two pianos, it was really wonderful, it makes me feel very sentimental and long for my darling more than ever. Inoculated cholera and typhoid*
Sept 15th	*Went down to Mrs. Dawes for "Chow fan" which was super. We were supposed to have picnic with Jean but it was wet so she brought her tea up to our room. Canteen in the morning*
Sept 16th	*Went picnicking on the beach with Mrs. Godfrey. It rained but we were wet already so it did not matter*
Sept 17th	*Tommy went out to tea and Wexie had Mary Wilson to tea. Had a walk in the evening*
Sept 18th	*Did a lot of sewing, completely made a swimsuit and cap. Went for a walk after tea, looked in on Sheila who could not walk with us as she was typing Norwegian verbs.*
Sept 19th	*Swimming Gala on the beach which went off very well. We took our tea with us and had a good time. Evelyn Kilber, Dorothy and Sheila joined us on the beach. Concert in the evening.*
Sept 20th	*Was going to church but my ear went deaf so I went to the doctor*

and had it syringed. Went to the beach in the afternoon. Did some office work in the evening.

Sept 21st   *Collected sandals from the Welfare and went to the library. Went to St. Stephens to hear Mrs Brown's and Heath playing which was wonderful.*

Sept 22nd   *Spent most of the day at home. Did some washing and ironing. Went for a walk in the evening and called on Mrs Dawes who had a bad throat.*

Sept 23rd   *Spent the afternoon on the beach. Lots of Jelly bugs in the water.*

Sept 24th   *Played Bridge in the afternoon and went for a walk after tea.*

Sept 25th   *Did some washing and ironing and walked after tea.*

Sept 26th   *Spent afternoon on beach–swarms of Jelly fish and Jelly bugs so we did not stay in the water long. Sunbathing was super. Usual concert was cancelled because of the 'V' signs made whilst being filmed last Saturday. Had a lovely message from J.J. thro' Spooks.*

Sept 27th   *Went to church–MacKenzie Dow was preaching, a very good sermon. Mrs Dawes came to tea and we spent a lazy evening reading. Played Spooks after supper.*

Sept 28th   *A very sudden meeting was called at HQ at 9 am which lasted until 11.45 am. We thought it must be some terrific changes but it was just a general meeting. Usual lovely piano concert.*

Sept 29th   *Wexie and I took a flask of tea and our books and sat on the rocks which was rather lovely. Worked during evening.*

Sept 30th   *Collected from canteen and saw about passports–only Wexie's ready. Went to HQ to do some typing. Played Bridge after our evening meal.*

OCTOBER 1942

Oct 1st   *Very windy day so we stayed in. Payed Bridge in the evening. Had a bad typhoon consequently did not sleep all night.*

Oct 2nd   *Typhoon still continuing. Received a certificate of nursing duty period from Miss Franklin. Played Bridge in the afternoon. Betty Long's 21st birthday.*

Oct 3rd   *Typhoon abated. Walked to the hill overlooking the beach and watched the lifesaving class. Played Bridge in the evening.*

Oct 4th   *Went to the beach in the afternoon. Had a good long swim out to where the 'lifesavers' were rescuing their subjects , was amusing to watch.*

Oct 5th   *Susie turned up so spent a quiet day and went to hear the Monday Piano concert in the evening.*

Oct 6th   *Ann's birthday. Felt rotten and spent all day lying down was stung by a beastly centipede–gosh how they sting.*

Oct 7th   *Still suffering agonies, played Bridge during the afternoon. Very windy blowing up for another typhoon, curse it.*

Oct 8th   *Having gone to bed prepared for rain it did not–thank goodness. Still windy but sunny. Still feeling lousy so did not do much apart from sewing and reading. Played Bridge in the evening.*

Oct 9th   *Quiet day–Susie still troublesome–did a little work. Mums and Wexie went to the beach. Played Bridge in the evening.*

Oct 10th   *The wind was worse than ever and it rained all day. Played Bridge all afternoon. Tommy and I played 'Casino' for a while p.m. Slept with a blanket for the first time.*

Oct 11th   *Still frightfully windy and quite chilly. Rained all day.*

Oct 12th   *Went for a walk after 10 o'clock meal and heard the awful news that the "Lisbon Marn" had been torpedoed and that 900 out of 1,800 of our 'prisoners of war' from H.K. had been lost. We suffered a dreadful shock and felt thoroughly sick. Could get no definite news as to who had left HK. Went for a picnic which was already arranged as we felt the need for fresh air having been in the house for so much thro' bad weather and Susie. Listened to Mrs Brown and Heath in the evening and took ages to get to sleep.*

Oct 13th   *Wrote my postcard to J.J. and read. Weather foul again, rainy and windy all day. Heard that at present there is no hope of getting postcards delivered to camps.*

Oct 14th   *Still windy and raining all day–did some washing. Played Bridge.*

Oct 15th   *Still windy and raining–did some sewing–showed Tommy a few hands of Bridge for 'calling' which she has difficulty with. Did some ironing. Tommy and I went for a walk after tea as it had cleared up.*

Oct 16th   *Weather improved–did some washing. Tried to wash my hair but the water supply ran out. Mary Wilson to tea & Bridge. Also played Bridge p.m.*

Oct 17th   *Weather good. We took our tea and books out to the rocks and enjoyed the air. Played one rubber of Bridge evening time.*

Oct 18th   *Went to church a.m. Walked in the afternoon.*

Oct 19th   *Went to the doctor as my mouth was full of ulcers and hurt badly; been bad for about 5 days. Went to music evening.*

Oct 20th   *Doctor's afternoon–walked evening.*

Oct 21st   *Doctor's afternoon–walked round the camp–went into St. Stephens and listened to Hyde-Lay paying the piano.*

Oct 22nd   *Doctors p.m.–had tea with the Ritchies, heard about Ban. Very kind they were–listened to Betty Brown and another lady playing–jolly good. Sent R. Cross letter forms, M and Margie.*

Oct 23rd   *Took a walk. Doctor visit. Red Cross letter message to Margie.*

Oct 24th   *St. Stephens do in the evening. Doctor's visit.*

Oct 25th   *Went to doctor–mouth much improved–picnic afternoon, Beryl swam–C.R.H. evening listening to music. 1st Allied raid over H.K. Great excitement in the camp.*

Oct 26th   *Went out on the rocks reading in the sunshine, very hot in the sunshine. Could hear planes all the time. Evening music.*

Oct 27th   *Sewing and work–visited the doctor and went for a walk evening.*

Oct 28th   *Went to the Canteen–sewing–had some birthday cake given us*

---

by Miss S Ellis. Another raid which made us all very excited. Listened to Hyde-Lay not so good as last week.

Oct 29th   *Money from Jimmy & Bosco = Y30. Grand and I hope it means they are both still at Argyle Street or I should say H.K. Went to the doctors in the afternoon and walked back through the cemetery. Two Piano concert evening. (Y10 was not from Bosco, not for me. I had to return it to a Mrs Cath Gray).*

Oct 30th   *Went out for some air during the afternoon and went to see Mrs Dawes p.m.*

Oct 31st   *Last day at the beach–closing for the winter. Took our tea and books with us. Very amusing and enjoyable evening at St. Stephens.*

NOVEMBER 1942

Nov 1st   *Took the air during afternoon. Listened to Heath and Betty Brown in the C.R. hall–jolly good. Had a meeting re "parcels" which are due tomorrow.*

Nov 2nd   *Oddment canteen–I drew a ticket but most unlucky as the only things I wanted sold out before my turn and so I spent the whole morning buying for other people. Usual Monday piano concert. Parcels arrived.*

Nov 3rd   *Our Red Cross parcels were supposed to be given to us today having arrived yesterday but of course that was too much to expect and there is a hitch. Whoopee I received a letter from Yolande–what a relief to know the family are O.K.–today is definitely my lucky day because I managed to get a pair of slacks sent in from town through a friend of Bill's.*

Nov 4th
Beryl Farrah came to tea and we played Bridge. Canteen draw– we were not very lucky as far as sugar was concerned but O.K. on dates and nuts. Walk p.m.

Nov 5th
Went out for air in the morning, took our books. Tommy and I went to hear the music p.m. and took a brisk walk round.

Nov 6th
Went for a picnic in the afternoon–men between the ages of 21 and 40 of Police and 21 and 35 other civilians had to spend the night in the gaol–this practice is to continue for 3 weeks. Poor devils lights out at 8 p.m. and stone floors to sleep on.

Nov 7th
The lads came out of gaol at 7 a.m. apparently they did have lights until 10 p.m. which was not so bad. Worked in the morning. Went to the canteen in the afternoon. Went to listen to a 'Quiz'–"Church v Lawyers and Medical v School Teachers"–very amusing.

Nov 8th
Went to church–good service. Parcels due tomorrow at 10 a.m. Listened to Heath playing in the evening.

Nov 9th
"Parcels" arrived safely–grand excitement–mine contained–1 tin 10oz tomatoes, 2 pkts sugar, ½ lb bacon, 1 lb curried beef and rice, ½ lb Peek Freans biscuits, 2 oz cheese, ½ lb Golden Syrup, 1 lb Creamed Rice, 2 oz Maypole Tea, ¼ lb Margarine, large tin

Nestles Condensed Milk, 1 Apple Pudding, 1 tin Lusty's Galantine, ¼ lb Vitamanized Chocolate. Wexie swallowed a tooth eating her biscuits. Sheila came along full of beans having received a message that her fiancé wishes to know if she is willing to marry him if her release can be obtained–thrilling. Played 4 sets Deck Tennis.

Nov 10th   *Felt very stiff after my game–went out for an airing.*

Nov 11th   *Susie arrived, felt rotten took things quietly. Beryl came to tea and Bridge. Mouth very sore again with ulcers.*

Nov 12th   *Took plenty of rest–Marjorie Buckle asked us in to tea and Bridge.*

Nov 13th   *Rested–did a spot of sewing and ironing. Few people in from town.*

Nov 14th   *Did nothing all day except lie with my feet higher than the rest of my body and managed to get across to the "Gilbert and Sullivan" show which was grand. (note at top of page–Sat Nov 14th at 10.55 a.m. dentist)*

Nov 15th   *Mouth still terribly painful but unable to visit the doctor–rested all day.*

Nov 16th   *Weather terrible so unable to see the Doc. Rested morning and played Bridge in the afternoon.*

Nov 17th   *All the bulk goods were taken from the Go Down and we received dried fruit, raisins, cocoa, corned beef and meat and veg.*

Nov 18th   *Weather still foul–went to see Dr. Dean-Smith who was not in.*

Beryl came to tea and Bridge. Started fruit juice. 1st mail arrived from England–none for me worst luck.

Nov 19th   *Raining and windy still–went to Dr. who was again out. Went to the dentist. Told that my gums were badly infected starting p. Tommy received a Welfare Parcel, she and I went to collect in the rain–great excitement. Played Bridge p.m.*

Nov 20th   *At last Dr. Dean-Smith was in, so I was able to get my prescription for medicine. Went to Dr. Hackett who advises that I have my crowned tooth extracted. Went to tea with Greenwood. Played Poker at St, Stephens. (note at top of page–Thurs Nov 20th 11 a.m.)*

Nov 21st   *The best show yet at St. Stephens–had tea and played Bridge with Mary Wilson.*

Nov 22nd   *Spent all day out in the sun and fresh air after church. Mackenzie-Dow preached a very good sermon. Listened to the 2 pianos in the evening.*

Nov 23rd   *Spent most of the morning out on the hill had Vera Murrell to tea and Bridge in the afternoon and went to Piano Recital p.m.*

Nov 24th   *Spent most of the day out on the hills in the sun.*

Nov 25th   *Spent most of the day out on the hills in the sun.*

Nov 26th   *All day in the sun. Had a Welfare Parcel–whoopee contained Pineapple, Bloater Paste, Tomatoes and Mixed Ginger. A show given by Blocks 8,9 10 and 11–quite good.*

| *William Gray* | > | *John Gray* | > | *James Gray* | > | *Jesse William Gray* | > |
| *(1720-1795)* | | *(1770-1830)* | | *(1813-1880)* | | *(1855-1894)* | |

Nov 27th   *Went out in the sun during morning–Sheila gave a tea party in celebration of 1 year being engaged. Jolly good party, grand eats, 11 of us all together.*

Nov 28th   *Sunning a.m. Tea party at P.W.D. mess and an excellent St. Andrews Show in the evening.*

Nov 29th   *Went to church–Mackenzie-Dow preaching excellent service.*

Nov 30th   *Had a foul cold so stayed in all day.*

DECEMBER 1942

Dec 1st   *Went out in the sun during the morning saw the Doc. Afternoon and stayed at home. Tommy and I played "Huff Patience".*

Dec 2nd   *Had a spot of sun a.m. Beryl came to Bridge afternoon. Tommy and I went for a stroll. Jail cancelled.*

Dec 3rd   *I had to go to a "Clothes" meeting re I.R.C. clothing at 12 o'clock. Block concert at 6.30 p.m.*

Dec 4th   *Tommy in bed with a bad cold.*

Dec 5th   *Tommy still in bed–concert evening quite good.*

Dec 6th   *Tommy's birthday–Beryl came to tea after which Wexie and self went out into the sunshine for a while then went to usual Sunday music.*

Dec 7th   *Nothing much doing. Went to music evening. Spent most of day in sun. Played Deck Tennis.*

Dec 8th   *Nothing unusual doing.*

>   *Jesse Esdale Gray*
        (1885-1946)   >   *Cecil Jesse Austen*
         Gray (1908-1968)   >   *Peter Nigel Austen Gray*
         (1950-present)

Dec 9th   Nothing unusual doing. Beryl to tea and Bridge

Dec 10th   Very busy day, went to the Go Down checking clothes a.m. and
               collected and distributed same during afternoon, being slightly
               late for evening entertainment at St. Stephens.

Dec 11th   Nothing special.

Dec 12th   Susie arrived and Sheila came to tea. Did not go to concert.

Dec 13th   Tommy's postponed Birthday Party at Mess 9–Block 9. She had a
               very lovely souvenir given her.

Dec 14th   Clothing meeting. Bridge with Simmie and Marjorie Buckle.

Dec 15th   Tommy went to play Bridge with S.M. and Rosie Judah and as I
               was alone, they asked me in.

Dec 16th   Beryl to tea and Bridge.

Dec 17th   Busy writing Christmas card and making up a parcel to send to
               Jimmy. I sincerely hope he receives same.

Dec 18th   Went to canteen for flask a.m. Saw Doctor and went to library.
               Afternoon played Bridge with Goley next door–had a lovely tea.
               Went for a walk afterwards Susie having gone.

Dec 19th   We had to have our Xmas Parcels ready for despatch. Jolly good
               show given by Police.

Dec 20th   Went to church. Was going to play Deck Tennis but one of 4 had
               bad cold so we played Bridge instead. Listened to music. I went to
               see Nellie and Sheila.

Dec 21st   Tommy and I managed to get a seat at St. Stephens but to our

---

great disappointment they cancelled the show because of a case of diphtheria in the camp. Spent all morning drawing and dishing out clothing.

Dec 22nd *Grand news, to go to the house on the hill for money from my darling J.J. so feel a wonderful relief knowing that he is in the Colony still. It was Nov. & Dec. allotment in one amounting to Y45. He also sent Nellie Y5.*

Dec 23rd *Lots of Xmas Cakes arrived in Camp but I did not get one from J.J.–Marjorie Buckle had one from Vernall, Muriel had one from Henry and heaps of other people received them. Lots of people came from Town and people were collecting from the Hill after 10 p.m. Tommy and I went for a walk called in on Nellie.*

Dec 24th *People took all day leaving for S'hai. Carols evening on the bowling green. Did up parcels–I did not go to the Carols on the Green as I had to help Bill arrange the Block Party and dress him up as Father Christmas with a cotton wool beard etc. The Party was a success songs and carols.*

Dec 25th *Paid a call to Block 9 with small gifts of sweets and cigarettes. Had people dropping in on us all morning. Had a wonderful Xmas dinner at 1 p.m. consisting of:–mince, Corned Beef Pasties and fried veg, fruit tarts and Xmas Pudding with custard. Our capacity for eating large meals having decreased we could not go farther than the Pasties on the menu, leaving the tarts for evening*

---

and pudding for next day. Tommy, Simmie and I went for a walk but halfway we met a friend of Simmie's who took us back to C. Bungalow for a drink. Had Sheila and Simmie to tea also Bill came in. Wexie brought Jimmie Bendall in to play cards.

Dec 26th   *We heard that our presents and cards had arrived at the camps and lots of lucky people received cards from their husbands etc. Tommy had 6, I had one from an ex patient & 1 from a Corporal in R.A.M.C, Wexie did not get one at all unfortunately. There were a few in from Argyle St. but I did not. Oh, how I would love just 10 words from my darling.*

Dec 27th   *Went to church–MacKenzie-Dow preaching grand. Played Deck Tennis p.m. with Wexie and her friends from over across. They stayed to tea.*

Dec 28th   *My first effort with the P.T. class was good fun. Went to pay Bridge with Mary Stirling. Muriel McCaw's birthday party after 8 grand fun.*

Dec 29th   *Jimmie's birthday–he gave a tea party for which Tommy made a cake and we supplied lots of food stuff.*

Dec 30th   *Did a lot of work arranging New Year's Eve party. Got our costumes ready. Nativity Concert very good.*

Dec 31st   *Had a very good party in the evening. Betty Brown's concert beforehand which was excellent. Tommy, Wexie, Simmie, Marjorie and I went as the "Quins".*

| William Gray | > | John Gray | > | James Gray | > | Jesse William Gray | > |
| *(1720-1795)* | | *(1770-1830)* | | *(1813-1880)* | | *(1855-1894)* | |